By the Medway Marsh

Published by Pre-Construct Archaeology Limited 2022

Copyright © Pre-Construct Archaeology Limited

Typesetting and layout by Cate Davies
Printed by Henry Ling Limited, The Dorset Press

ISBN: 978-1-9996155-6-7

Front cover: The mausoleum and coffin under excavation.

Back cover: Silver-gilt Anglo-Saxon brooch; gold and variscite necklace or bracelet; lifting the lead coffin.

By the Medway Marsh

Excavations at Grange Farm, Gillingham, Kent 2003–2006

James Gerrard and Guy Seddon

With contributions by: Jon Allison, Murray Andrews, Philip Armitage, Rob Batchelor, Barry Bishop, Nick Branch, David Dungworth, Jane Evans, Märit Gaimster, Rebecca Haslam, Kevin Hayward, K. Le Hégarat, Richard Hobbs, Eniko Hudak, Lynne Keys, Christopher Jarrett, James Langthorne, D.E. Mooney, Kevin Rielly, Berni Sudds, John Shepherd, Gemma Swindle, Victoria Ridgeway, Marina Vaggi and Andrew Welton

Pre-Construct Archaeology Limited, Monograph No. 24

PCA Monograph Series

Contributors

Principal authors	James Gerrard and Guy Seddon
Volume editor	Victoria Ridgeway
Academic adviser	Simon Esmonde Cleary
Project manager	Peter Moore
Post-excavation managers	Victoria Ridgeway, Jon Butler
Graphics	Mark Roughley
Finds illustrations	Cate Davies, Helen Davies
Photography	Strephon Duckering
Struck flint	Barry Bishop
Roman coins	James Gerrard
Roman small finds	James Gerrard
Romano-British pottery	James Gerrard and Eniko Hudak
Roman glass	John Shepherd
Lead coffin lining	Victoria Ridgeway
Anglo-Saxon, medieval and post-medieval small finds	Märit Gaimster
The Anglo-Saxon spearheads	Jon Allison, James Gerrard and Andrew Welton
Medieval coins and jetons	Murray Andrews
Roman necklaces	Richard Hobbs
Post-Roman pottery	Chris Jarrett
Iron slag	Lynne Keys
Silver working residues	David Dungworth, Marina Vaggi and Lynne Keys
Stone	Kevin Hayward
Ceramic building materials	Berni Sudds
Animal bone	Kevin Rielly and Philip Armitage
Human bone	James Langthorne
Oyster and marine shell	Rebecca Haslam
Archaeobotanical remains and charcoal	K. Le Hégarat and D. E. Mooney
Pollen	Nick Branch, Rob Batchelor and Gemma Swindle
Stable isotope analysis	Jane Evans

Foreword

This volume is the culmination of archaeological research that began in 2002 at Grange Farm, Gillingham, Kent. As with many archaeological projects the process of excavation, research and publication has been long and painstaking. The results which form this volume shed new light on how the region now occupied by Gillingham and the Medway Towns was used in the ancient and not so ancient past. It is a long story, starting in the Mesolithic/Neolithic with the subtle and transitory activities of our hunter-gatherer ancestors and the earliest farmers. By the end of the Iron Age Rome's Mediterranean Empire reached out and seized Britain. Consequently, much of our tale is concerned with the changes wrought by the coming of the Roman Empire on people's lives and the landscape. Those changes unfolded over nearly four centuries and by the fifth century AD the waning of Roman power in Northern Europe gave rise to a complex and difficult transition from Roman Britain to Anglo-Saxon England. The site revealed tantalising, if subtle, traces of that process, which will be of interest to students of the 'end of Roman Britain' and the 'Early Anglo-Saxon' period. In the aftermath of the Norman Conquest a manorial centre emerged, which would dominate the locality well into the post-medieval period. The story ends with nineteenth-century farming and Second World War bombing.

The excavations were supervised by Guy Seddon, who also produced a substantial unpublished post-excavation assessment (Seddon *et al.* 2008). That work, available from the Archaeology Data Service, forms the foundation of this report and also contains considerable detail about individual features that could not be included here. This volume has been produced by James Gerrard (based at Newcastle University), who not only worked for many months on the excavations as a site assistant, but also undertook much of the post-excavation analysis of the Romano-British finds. The consequence is that the volume is something of a rarity, in that the primary author has been involved at of every stage of the project in different capacities. Along the way many other specialists and students have been involved and their work, as a glance at the contributors page demonstrates, is an integral part of the volume. The end result is a rich and detailed narrative of the archaeological discoveries made on land at Grange Farm, Gillingham, Kent. The contributors to this volume hope that it will be of interest and use to other archaeologists, specialists and the people of Gillingham.

Dr James Gerrard, Newcastle University, 2022

Contents

Figures

Tables

xii

Appendices

Summary

The site at Grange Farm lies to the north-east of the modern town of Gillingham, on a slightly elevated terrace at the edge of the North Downs, overlooking Gillingham Reach and the River Medway. Medieval activity was anticipated here, where the ruins of the fourteenth-century chapel and refectory of the manorial centre of Grace (formerly Grench) Manor still survive. The excavation revealed evidence of this complex and these results are published elsewhere (Meddens and Draper 2014). Open area excavations also revealed limited prehistoric evidence, and extensive Romano-British features, which form the focus of this publication.

Watling Street, the Roman road which ran from *Durovernum Cantiacorum* (Canterbury) to *Londinium* (London), lies around 2km to the south of Grange Farm. The region, and in particular the marshlands to the north, was especially significant between the first and third centuries, with industries involved in the production and distribution of ceramics and salt. But it is arguably the evidence for Late Roman occupation that is particularly notable at Grange Farm.

The earliest indications of activity suggest sporadic visitation of the area from the Mesolithic through to the Bronze Age. Activity increased in the Late Iron Age and early post-conquest periods, with the establishment of agricultural enclosures. The latter half of the first century AD saw activity increase, as exemplified by the construction of further enclosures and associated buildings, pits and hearths.

A significant development occurred in the early second century with the construction of a routeway running on a sinuous, but roughly north–south-aligned, trajectory. This route may have had an earlier precursor and was certainly modified, enhanced and further formalised with the addition of a cobbled surface through the succeeding centuries. The origin and trajectory of this route was not established; however, it is tempting to see it as linking the main route of Watling Street to the south, with the Medway marshes and associated river system to the north.

The general layout of enclosures and routeway established by the mid-second century continued into the Late Roman period, when a fundamental change came about in the way the site was being used. The enclosures remained, but many of the ditches which defined these were replaced by upstanding masonry walls.

Significantly, at some point probably in the fourth century, a square, stone-built mausoleum with tessellated floor was constructed; occupying a slight elevation in the land, this would presumably have been visible for some distance from the Medway to the north. This mausoleum contained the burial of a woman in a lead-lined coffin, which had apparently been disturbed in antiquity; despite this, fragments of gold and jewelled necklaces were recovered from demolition deposits. Other burials in the vicinity were indicated by the recovery of disarticulated bone.

Other major changes in the site's use occurred. An aisled building was constructed to the east of this mausoleum and the routeway, which apparently still continued to the north, was apparently cut-off in its southern trajectory by the construction of masonry walls, defining an area of intensive hearth use, indicative of blacksmithing.

The later fourth and early fifth centuries saw the continuation of use of much of the enclosure system. Hearths demonstrate that the aisled building continued to be occupied and the road running northwards was maintained suggesting continued importance of links with the river, whilst to the south there was little evidence for any activity. The recovery of quantities of litharge point to silver working during this period. The mausoleum may have begun to fall into disrepair, and it is perhaps during this Late Roman period that the central grave was disturbed. The structure, however, remained standing into the twelfth century and, at some point before its final demise a tawny owl appears to have chosen the abandoned mausoleum as a place to roost.

The site saw little archaeologically visible activity between the fifth and eleventh centuries; the land may well have been grazed or farmed from the sixth century onwards. The boundary walls collapsed, or were demolished, and a 'dark earth'-type deposit accumulated. This deposit, disturbed by later ploughing, nevertheless contained a large and significant very late Roman finds assemblage, probably indicative of reworked midden and occupation material.

A settlement at Grange is documented from the eleventh century and, although no structural evidence of this was identified, a cross staff terminal and lead cross point to religious activities nearby in the eleventh or twelfth centuries. Intriguingly it appears that the mausoleum may have remained standing until this time, albeit in a ruinous state. The manorial estate survived to the south and remained a focus of activity into the post-medieval period. The final episode in the story of the site is represented by a large, irregular feature interpreted as a Second World War bomb crater, due to the recovery in nearby topsoil of thirty incendiary bombs. Initially found through metal detecting, these were ultimately disposed of by a professional ordnance removal company.

Acknowledgements

Pre-Construct Archaeology Limited would like to thank Duncan Hawkins of CgMs Consulting Ltd for commissioning the work that led to production of this monograph on behalf of Taylor Woodrow and Persimmon Homes, who generously funded the archaeological investigations. Thanks also to Simon Mason and David Britchfield, Kent County Council's Officers, for monitoring the archaeological works.

The fieldwork was managed by Peter Moore. The excavations were supervised by Guy Seddon, who produced the unpublished post-excavation assessment under the management of Jonathan Butler. Thanks are also due to Pete Boyer for his preliminary work on the stratigraphic analysis. Part of this report was written by James Gerrard during a period of research leave funded by the School of History, Classics and Archaeology at Newcastle University. The 'Empires and After Research Strand' in History, Classics and Archaeology was also kind enough to provide a small grant to fund radiocarbon dating and isotopic analysis of the human remains from the mausoleum. Work on finalising the graphics for the publication was undertaken with the assistance of a grant from 'MATCH' (Materiality, Artefacts & Technologies in Culture & History Research Group at Newcastle University). Jon Allison, James Gerrard and Andrew Welton would like to thank Drs. Tania Dickinson and Andreas Rau for their kind help and assistance with the spearheads. James Gerrard would like to thank various students at Newcastle University and especially Emma Gooch and James Hopper who assisted with the publication analysis of the small finds. James Gerrard would also like to thank Professor Bill Manning for his assistance with the identification of the iron tools and Malcolm Lyne for his assistance with pottery identifications. Victoria Ridgeway managed the production of this volume and would like to thank Mark Roughley for assistance with the graphics, Amparo Valcarcel for checking bibliographic referencing throughout, Cate Davies for final graphics work and typesetting, and Frank Meddens for compiling the index.

We are indebted to Professor Simon Esmonde Cleary for reading and commenting on an earlier version of this text.

Chapter 1

Introduction

Following a proposal to develop agricultural land at Grange Farm, Gillingham, Kent (Fig. 1.1) for residential purposes an archaeological desk-based assessment was commissioned as part of the planning process, which determined that there was moderate to high potential for prehistoric and Roman activity at the site. Medieval occupation was thought likely to exist in the immediate environs of Grace (formerly Grench) Manor (Hawkins 2002), where surviving parts of the manorial centre include a ruined fourteenth-century chapel and refectory (Meddens & Draper 2014). Given this, and in accordance with planning policies, the area was archaeologically evaluated using trial trenches between 2nd February and 28th March 2003 (Haslam 2003). These revealed some prehistoric features and far more extensive traces of Romano-British activity.

The findings of the evaluation were sufficient to require open area excavation in the north and west, where archaeological potential was highest and also in smaller areas around Grace Manor. This work was undertaken between 26 September 2005 and 2 May 2006 and revealed a long and complex sequence of archaeological activity focussed on the Roman period (Seddon *et al.* 2008). After the completion of these excavations further archaeological monitoring and recording took place between August and September 2006 (Pooley 2007). It is the main phase of open area excavation that forms the focus of this report, but reference is made where relevant to the other interventions (Fig. 1.2).

The site is located at Grange Farm, on the eastern side of Gillingham and is within the Medway Towns Conurbation, centred on NGR TQ 7930 6850. At the time

Fig. 1.1   The site location (scale 1:400,000)

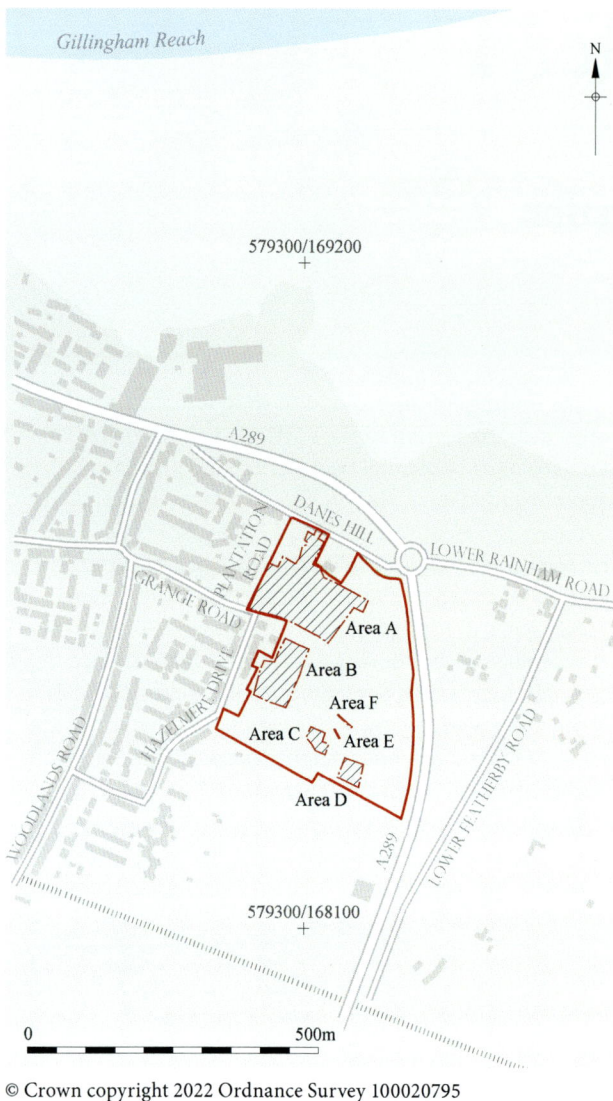

Gillingham Reach

579300/169200

Area A

Area B

Area F

Area C   Area E

Area D

579300/168100

0   500m

© Crown copyright 2022 Ordnance Survey 100020795

Fig. 1.2   Detailed trench location (scale 1:12,500)

During the course of the archaeological investigations, compact, natural brickearth of variable colour was recorded across much of the site (Phase 1), from a high point of 18.27m OD to the south, sloping down to 5.83m OD to the north-west, where the site forms part of the edge of the Medway valley (Fig. 1.4). Underlying Pleistocene gravels were also exposed in the lowest elevated areas towards the north-west corner of the site.

Archaeological and historical background

The desk-based assessment carried out a detailed review of previous finds, sites and archaeological interventions within the immediate vicinity of the study area (Hawkins 2002). Scattered finds and discoveries in the marshes to the north and similar evidence, along with aerial photographs, from the dryland to the south, point to prehistoric exploitation of the wider landscape. Little evidence of Iron Age activity has been identified from the immediate vicinity of the site.

The early years of the Roman Conquest saw the establishment of a fort and then town at *Durobrivae* (Rochester) 5.3km west, where a bridge carried Watling Street (now the A2), a major Roman arterial route (Margary 1955, route 1), on its way from *Durovernum Cantiacorum* (Canterbury) to *Londinium* (London) (Fig. 1.3). This road passes Grange Farm some 2km to the south. Significant Roman period settlement existed in the Medway Valley and along the North Downs (Millett 2007, 152: fig 5.9). The region (and especially the marshes to the north), was also a significant industrial zone from the first to the third centuries. There is considerable evidence for the production of *mortaria* at Rochester, flagons at Hoo and coarse wares (North Kent Shell Tempered wares, BB2 and Thameside Kent grey wares) with wide distributions to London, the Northern Frontier and elsewhere (Pollard 1988). Salt production in the same marshes (Hathaway 2013) hints at the production and movement of other, less archaeologically visible commodities, such as salted meat, leather, grain, and the like.

Roman material from the immediate vicinity of the site includes fragments of Roman tile and pottery from archaeological excavations at Grace Manor by the Kent Archaeological Rescue Unit (Keller and Chenery 1992). Roman burials have also been identified to the north-east at the junction of Featherby Road and Lower Rainham Road and a large first-century cremation urn found in 1927 to the west probably indicates an early Roman cremation cemetery. For the late Roman period a large hoard of 722 *nummi* (deposited in or after the reign of Honorius 393–423), was found *c.* 1906 by a 'workman engaged in grubbing up an old tree on the outskirts of the village of Gillingham'. The location is further defined as 'along the Lower Road to Rainham' (Payne 1909, xcii; Robertson 2000, no. 1542), which places the discovery in close proximity to Area A.

During the fifth century the Greater Thames Estuary was a major conduit for early Anglo-Saxon settlement. Mucking (Essex) (Clark 1993, Hamerow 1993), separated

of the excavations the site was bordered to the east by the A289, to the north by Lower Rainham Road, to the west by Plantation Road and Hazelmere Drive and to the south by a sports complex. The site was bisected east–west by Grange Road and covered some nine hectares of which more than 2.5 hectares were investigated archaeologically.

1.1 Geology and topography

The site is located on the south bank of the River Medway, overlying bedrock geology of Cretaceous Chalk covered by sand, silt and clay deposits of the Thanet Sand Formation. These deposits are overlain by Pleistocene Terrace Gravels, which are capped by Late Glacial brickearth on which present day soils have formed. To the north of the site and south of the current course of the Medway, much of the floodplain is dominated by areas of marshland, comprising Gillingham Marshes to the north-west, Cinque Port Marshes to the north and Copperhouse Marshes to the north-east (Fig. 1.3).

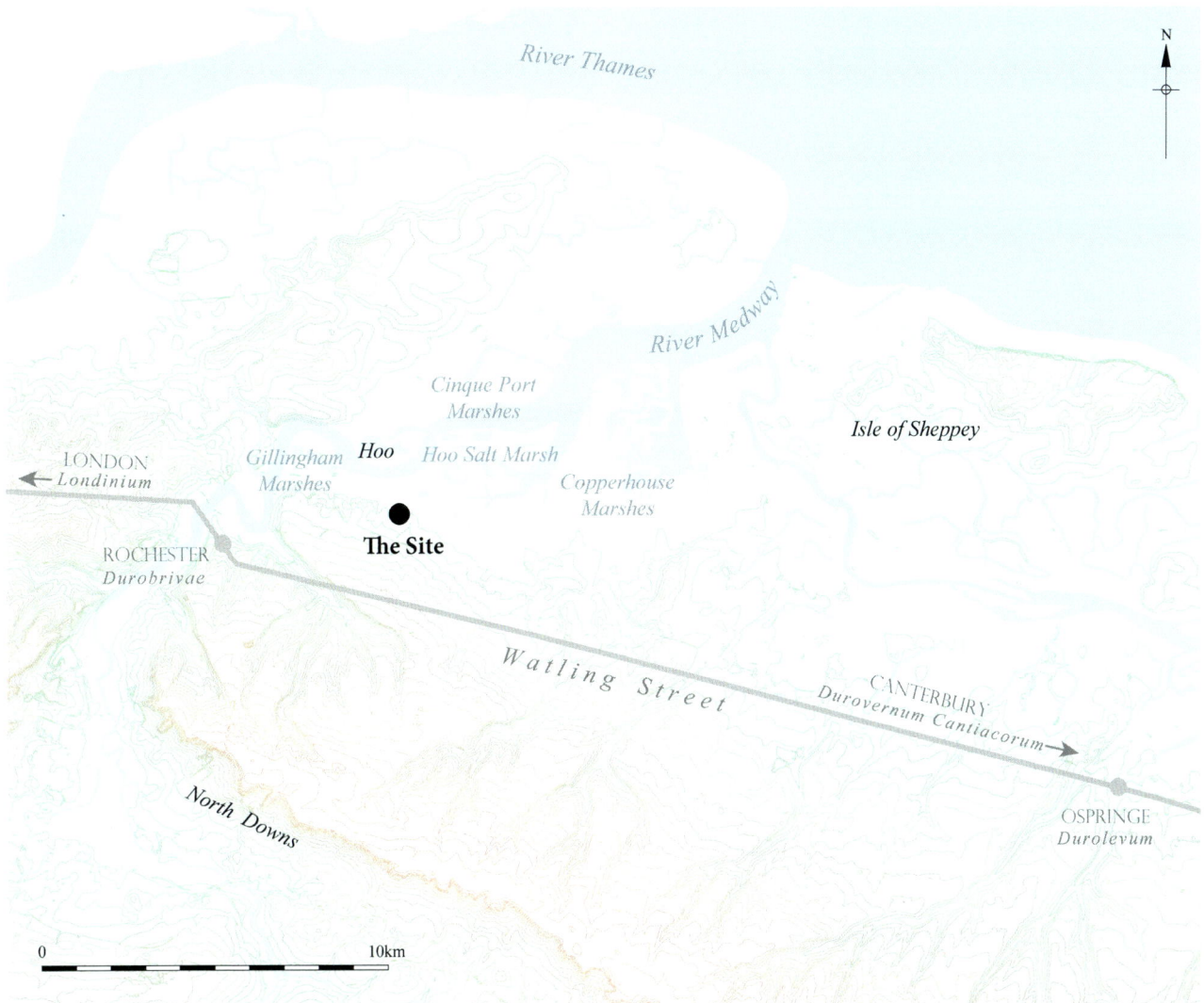

Fig. 1.3   The topographic setting of Grange Farm and relevant sites in the vicinity in relation to Roman Watling Street (scale 1:200,000)

Fig. 1.4   Excavations at Grange Farm looking north across site towards the Medway

from North Kent by not many miles of easily traversable open water, is, perhaps, the type-site for fifth-century Anglo-Saxon settlement and extensive traces of early Anglo-Saxon activity have been identified in Kent (Welch 2007). How this related to the preceding late Roman activity in the county is a matter for discussion (for instance Welch 2007, Gerrard 2013), but the transformation of the placename *Durobrivae* ('Bridge-fort': Rivet and Smith 1979, 346–348) to Rochester indicates, at the very least, that speakers of the West German dialects that would become Old English, had contact with speakers of Brythonic (Gelling 1984, 56). Archaeological evidence from the vicinity of the site includes a fifth- to sixth-century burial 450m to the west and further Anglo-Saxon inhumations were disturbed in 1934 during the building of Gillingham's Central Hotel (Meaney 1964, 121). We may also note in passing a recent metal-detector find of a late-fourth to early fifth-century supporting arm brooch with a trapezoidal foot (*Stützarmfibel mit Trapezfuß*) from just east of Cliffe about 10km north-west of the site (Dr Stuart Laycock pers. comm.). This is probably a variant of Böhme's (1974, 11) 'Gallic Type B' and seemingly the only example of its kind from Britain.

There is little evidence of Middle or Late Saxon activity but by the time of the Domesday Survey in AD 1086 two estates existed at Gillingham. One of these, held by the Archbishop of Canterbury, developed into the later medieval town. The other, valued at £3 in AD 1086, comprised ploughlands, meadows and a (tidal?) mill, held by Odo, Bishop of Bayeux, Earl of Kent and half-brother of William the Conqueror, developed into the Manor of Grange. The early twelfth-century *Textus Roffensis* records a chapel in the Rochester diocese at a place called *Grenic* (Grange) (Meddens & Draper 2014, 11–12). The subsequent history of this manor is described in detail by Meddens & Draper (2014) and does not need to be repeated here. The key point is that by AD 1285 (if not in the late eleventh century) the manor had become a 'limb' or detached portion of Hastings and thus a Liberty of the *Cinque Ports*. This area can be mapped as a rectangle of land stretching from Watling Street northwards to the marshes, where the absence of saltings and mudflats and a series of small embayments enabled the development of a small landing area or hythe (Meddens & Draper 2014, 4). This little haven in the estuary enabled Grange Manor to function for most of its life as an interface between the land and sea. By the late thirteenth century, the manor was required to provide men, perhaps local pilots, for the ships the *Cinque Ports* were required to render in service to the king. Other surviving documents hint at the smuggling of wool and other commodities during the medieval period (Meddens & Draper 2014, 4).

In the late fourteenth century the Philipot family acquired Grange Manor. Their business interests included the wool trade, but also pirate hunting in the Thames Estuary and backing the Earl of Buckingham's expedition to Brittany in AD 1380. The wealth and power of the Philipots allowed the manor to be refurbished and the chantry chapel to be rebuilt (Meddens & Draper 2014, 8). The descent of the land can be traced through the Bammes and the Hawards. The latter of whom lived in the manor during the seventeenth century. Eventually the manor was let to tenants and then sold in 1796.

The manor underwent further rebuilding and alterations during the eighteenth and nineteenth centuries. By 1867, as the 1st Edition Ordnance Survey map shows, a substantial part of the north-eastern quarter of the site was occupied by the 'Cinque Port Brickfield' and the remainder of the site was being used for agricultural purposes with orchards of fruit trees predominating.

During the Second World War the Medway Towns were heavily bombed due to the presence of important rail and road infrastructure, alongside the naval docks at Chatham and other military facilities and strategically important industries such as the Shorts aircraft works in Rochester. In the decades after the Second World War the towns of Rochester, Chatham and Gillingham underwent industrial decline and have since re-emerged as developing commuter communities for London as part of the so-called 'Thames Gateway'. The A289 Medway Towns Northern Link road was constructed to the east of the site as part of urban regeneration and opened in 1999.

1.2 Textual and graphical conventions used in this report

The basic unit of cross-reference throughout the archive that supports this project is the context number: a unique number given to each archaeological 'event' within a particular site (such as a layer, wall, grave cut, pit cut or fill, road surface and so forth). These are contained within square brackets (e.g. [123]) and are only cited in this publication text where a specific reference is required. Group numbers and landuses (e.g. pit group 4, Building 5) are used in preference, or in addition. Context numbers not included on phase plans within this report are contained within circular brackets and referenced to group or landuse. Indices linking contexts to groups and landuses are held within the archive, which will be deposited with Sittingbourne Museum under the unique site code KKGF03.

Registered finds, or 'small finds' are individually identified using a unique small find number, within angular brackets, e.g. <36>, whilst environmental samples are individually identified a unique environmental sample number within curving brackets, e.g. {94}.

Graphical conventions used are indicated within the keys to individual figures.

Chapter 2

The stratigraphic sequence

2.1 Phase 2: Prehistoric

The excavations produced very little evidence for any activity pre-dating the Late Iron Age. The presence of a largely residual lithics assemblages suggests activity from the Mesolithic to the Bronze Age and a handful of features containing struck flint may be of Neolithic date (Bishop 2008). Gully [380], posthole [389] and pits [428] and [638] may be remnants of Neolithic activity. Pit

[638] contained 5.6kg of burnt stone, perhaps indicative of large-scale cooking, but defining the nature and scale of the prehistoric activity otherwise remains elusive.

Late prehistoric activity appears equally ephemeral. A large, oval pit [708] contained a small assemblage of Late Bronze Age to Middle Iron Age pottery and was cut by a smaller feature [712], containing a single struck flint flake. An isolated posthole [558] contained a small quantity of Middle Iron Age pottery.

Fig. 2.1   Phase 2 and 3: late Iron Age to the middle of the first century AD, with insert to show contemporary features in Area D (scale 1:1250)

2.2 Phase 3: Late Iron Age to the middle of the first century AD

The Late Iron Age saw the beginnings of a more intense mode of land use (Fig. 2.1). Ditched boundaries were dug in Areas A, B and D. In the south-eastern corner of Area A a curvilinear ditch [526] and lengths of other ditches such as [1245] and [1247] (Ditch group 1) may have defined elements of enclosures [Enclosure 1], which might be associated with a length of ditch identified in the north of Area B [1001]. Other landscape divisions were identified in Area D where two ditches at right angles to each other were investigated [1012], [1121] (Ditch group 2). The fills of these features contained pottery assemblages dating to the Late Iron Age or immediately post-conquest decades. Presumably these features functioned at least in part to divide the landscape in the Late Iron Age and they may have formed elements of a system of agricultural enclosures.

Little evidence for other forms of Late Iron Age activity was forthcoming. In Area A there were a small number of stakeholes, postholes, pits and a hearth which are likely to have been contemporary with the ditches and, together with the associated finds assemblages, may be the last vestiges of settlement activity which has otherwise been removed by truncation.

2.3 Phase 4: Earliest Roman *c.* AD 43 to *c.* AD 100/120

The decades following the Roman Conquest saw activity at the site develop along new trajectories (Fig. 2.2). Elements of the Late Iron Age ditch systems in Area A seem to have largely fallen from use with the exception of ditch [1245], which was retained and incorporated into a new enclosure system. The main component of this system was a long ditch [860] aligned almost east–west with a north–south return at its western end [Group 3] [864]. A small but significant group of pottery was recovered from the fills of [860] (Gerrard & Hudak, this volume Key Group 1). In the south-eastern corner of Area A elements of the Phase 3 ditch system seem to have been modified. Ditch [1245] was retained and extended to the south-east as ditch [684] (Group 4). The alignment and character of these ditches was different from those to the west. Together these features either define one large enclosure or, more probably, two enclosures: a large rectilinear enclosure in the west (Enclosure 2) and a smaller enclosure in the east demarcated by slight ditches (Enclosure 3). There was, however, no sign of a boundary separating the two putative enclosures. Perhaps it was a slight feature truncated by later activity or demarcated in an archaeologically invisible fashion with a hedgeline. The boundary may even have been a precursor of the later Phase 5 later road/holloway (below). Activity in later phases seems to have been of a different character east of the end of this holloway and this

may support the identification of two enclosures in the southern part of Area A.

One further ditched enclosure can be defined in this phase. Two parallel ditches originated under a later recut of [1405] and ran north-north-eastwards until they were truncated by the erosion of the holloway in Phase 5. Together with east–west aligned ditches to the north-east these features defined a trapezoidal area north of ditch [1245] (Enclosure 4; Group 5).

The difficulties of dating the digging of ditches are well known and it is must be said that the small quantities of pottery and, in places, recutting in later phases means that the chronology of these enclosures is not as firm as one might ideally wish for. Nevertheless, the small pottery assemblages from the fills of these features, along with their stratigraphic positions is strongly indicative of the late first century. A zoomorphic mount, possibly the terminal from a fire-dog <896> was recovered from ditch [645] and is probably of Late Iron Age or Early Roman date.

Traces of activity within the enclosures also points to a fundamental change in the way the site was being exploited. Enclosure 2 appears to have been largely empty but ephemeral traces of activity may have been truncated in this area. Enclosure 3 contained a metalled surface [598] cut by a group (Group 6) of five postholes or pits. If these features were postholes, then their arrangement north-east–south-west in two parallel lines is suggestive of a structure aligned on ditch [1245]. To the south of this possible structure was a patch of metalled surface and hearth [533], filled with two deposits of burnt material, the lowest of which contained ten sherds of transitional Late Iron Age/Early Roman pottery of pre-Flavian date. To the west of this hearth were three further pits on a similar alignment (Group 7). Very few finds were recovered from these features.

In Enclosure 4 a rather more coherent and convincing pattern is evident. Structure [871] was a timber building measuring 16.8m by 8.8m and constructed from earthfast posts set in substantial postholes (Group 8, Building 1). No internal features were identified but such single-roomed buildings are very common on Romano-British rural settlements (Smith *et al.* 2016, 64–65 and fig 3.16). There is no evidence for the function of the structure and its interpretation in the assessment as a possible granary is without warrant (Seddon *et al.* 2008, 39).

A number of probably contemporary features existed around Building 1. To the north-west rectangular pit [633] contained fragments of a Gallo-Belgic White Ware flagon, early North Kent shell-tempered wares and pottery in a Late Iron Age tradition, which together are indicative of a pre-Flavian date. To the east of the building was a posthole and square pit [432] containing a large and fresh assemblage of early Roman pottery including South Gaulish samian, Hoo ware (including, unusually a *mortarium* sherd), North Kent Fine Ware, some unidentified amphora and other late first-century fabrics and forms (Gerrard & Hudak, this volume, Key Group 2) (Fig. 2.3). There was also another pit [1090] containing late-first-century pottery. The function of these pits

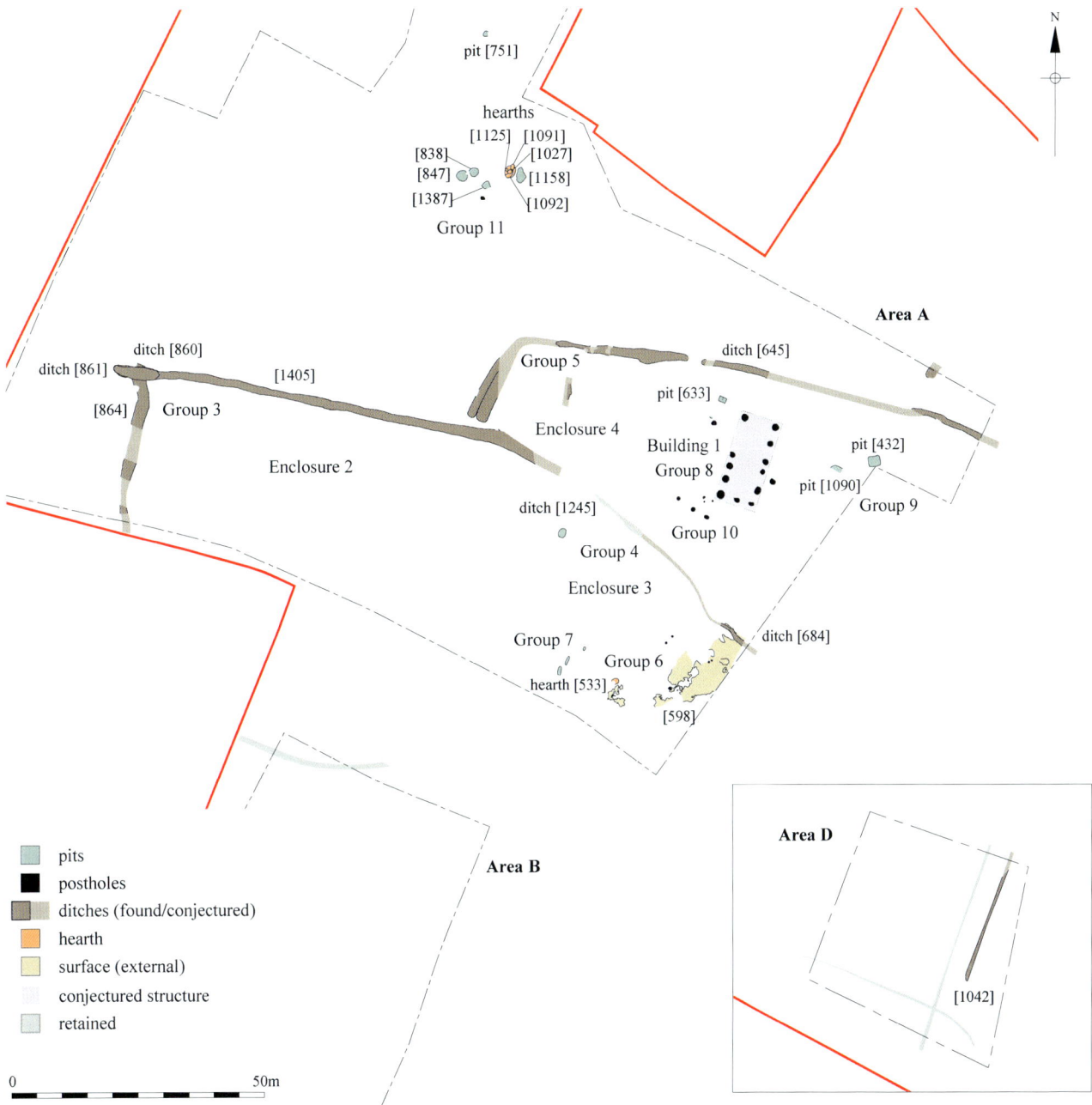

Fig. 2.2   Phase 4: earliest Roman features (*c.* AD 43 to *c.* AD 100/120), with insert to show contemporary features in Area D (scale 1:1250)

(Group 9) is obscure. To the south-west of Building 1 was a group of post- and stakeholes (Group 10). These may be remnants of fencelines and other ancillary structures.

Elsewhere a cluster of large pits was identified north of Enclosure 2 (Group 11) [838], [847], [1092], [1158], [1387]. The fills of these features produced a small quantity of ceramic building material (CBM), animal bone and a mere eight sherds of early Roman pottery. The fill of [1158] also yielded a fragment of stone quern <1236>. Four small hearths [1125], [1097], [1091] and [1027] formed of burnt flints overlain by burnt debris were located just to the west of [1158] and may be associated with the pitting. Small quantities of charred organic material from these features yielded evidence of seeds, chaff, wheat, common spikerush and legumes (Hégarat & Mooney, this volume) {248} and

Fig. 2.3   Complete handmade pottery vessel (fabric TSK) in the base of square pit [432] (scale 0.5m)

{268}. Finally, one further feature, pit [751], located a little to the north, may be included in this group; unfortunately it produced only scraps of CBM. These pits and hearths can be assigned to this phase on the basis of the limited finds evidence and also stratigraphic grounds. The features are suggestive of a focus of activity and occupation but its purpose is difficult to reconstruct.

Little evidence of activity dateable to this phase was forthcoming from the other excavation areas. In Area D the Late Iron Age boundary ditches appear to have continued in use with some modification. A new ditch [1042] was dug to augment these boundaries.

2.4 Phase 5: Early to mid-second century *c.* AD 100/120–*c.* AD 150

Phase 5 represents both continuity and change in relation to the preceding Phase 4 activity (Fig. 2.4). In Area A alterations to the western end of ditch [1405] are apparent, probably occurring early in this phase. Phase 4 ditch [864] appears to have been filled in or silted up and was cut by a pit containing residual Iron Age pottery [842] (Group 23). Recutting of the western end of [1405] manifested itself as a new western boundary to Enclosure 2 (Group 12). Both this ditch and at least the western half of [1405] must have gone out of use by at least the middle of the second century when a large oval pit [801] was cut into the line of the enclosure (Group 13). The fills (and thus disuse) of this pit contained significant quantities of domestic waste that were clearly tipped into the cut from the east. Pottery, animal bones (including parts of a piglet), small finds (including five hairpins, e.g. <986> Fig. 3.10.3) and considerable quantities of marine shell were present; oysters were most common, with the twenty percent sample size suggesting that nearly 500 oysters were represented, along with much smaller numbers of whelks, cockles and mussels (Haslam, this volume). Other links to the littoral zone are suggested by fragments of briquetage (Sudds, this volume). The pottery assemblage is discussed in more detail below (Gerrard & Hudak, this volume: Key Group 5), but numbered 1442 fresh sherds dating from the first half of the second century. It was probably deposited towards the end of this phase *c.* AD 150.

The evidence of pit [801] demonstrates that Enclosure 2 had fallen out of use. Its replacement was a more ambitious enclosure system covering much of the western end of Area A. Ditch [1404] seems to have been a replacement for ditch [1405]. Its western end was located just to the west of [1405] and it turned through a right angle to run eastwards in parallel with the line of [1405] (Group 14). At the north-west corner of ditch [1404] was a short gap, serving as an entrance, and then another ditch [1403] ran northwards and returned eastwards paralleling [1404] (Group 15). The fills of these ditches contained small quantities of early Roman pottery. The two large enclosures formed by these ditched boundaries have been termed Enclosure 5 (south) and Enclosure 6 (north).

There was some evidence for activity in the areas bounded by these ditches. In Enclosure 5 an arc of plough-truncated postholes was identified towards its western end (Group 16). One of these postholes contained a well-defined postpipe and its upper fill contained a significant assemblage of burnt daub and an iron nail. The diameter of the arc of postholes is approximately 7m and it seems reasonable to interpret these features as the vestiges of a timber roundhouse (Building 2) along the lines of the structure reconstructed by University College Dublin (O'Sullivan & O'Neill 2019). Timber roundhouses are being increasingly recognised as a component of Roman period rural settlement (Smith *et al.* 2016: fig 3.6) and the slight traces here perhaps hint at what may have been lost to plough truncation elsewhere on the site.

Enclosure 6 was almost devoid of evidence for activity, but in the south-east corner a square pit [276] (Group 17) contained a large part of a North Kent Fine Ware bowl (Gerrard & Hudak, this volume Key Group 3) and a small group of charcoal (Hégarat & Mooney, this volume). In Phase 7 this area was occupied by a high-status late Roman mausoleum and it is tempting to think that this pit and its contents were an early Roman indication of the 'specialness' of this area.

The eastern sides of Enclosures 5 and 6 were probably defined by what is the other major development during this phase. A routeway [1329] (not planned) seems to have developed running southwards from the northern limit of excavation in Area A, which in later phases was manifested as a metalled road at the bottom of a significant holloway and flanked, at least in places, by ditches (Group 18). The southern end of this holloway was identified in Area B [966]. Probably in Phase 5, if not earlier, this route existed and began the process of downcutting. If so, it will have formed the eastern boundary of Enclosure 6. Enclosure 5's ditch [1404] turns south-eastwards at its eastern end, which suggests that it was following the line of the holloway. In the middle of Area A the road doglegged in later phases and it seems likely that ditch [1404] was turning to reflect this change of direction in the road's earlier incarnation. An iron linch-pin <417> from ditch [223], the eastern end of [1404] is probably related to the passage of vehicles on the road.

To the east of this routeway ditch [259] was identified cutting Phase 4 and earlier features in the south-east corner of Area A and, along with ditch [289] to the north, may represents parts of further enclosures, although their form is not recoverable. Loosely associated with these enclosures are two groups of pits. The first (Group 21) comprised a posthole [531] and a pit [686] to the west of ditch [259]. Somewhat further north, in the vicinity of Phase 4 Building 1, a group of two pits (Group 22) contained small assemblages of second-century pottery.

Elsewhere the only features of note lay north of Enclosure 6 and to the west of the line of the roadway. Pits and hearths (Group 20) appear to represent a continuation of the activity in this area in Phase 4. Another pit [1065] to the east of the roadway should

Fig. 2.4   Phase 5: early to mid-second century features (*c.* AD 100/120–*c.* AD 150) (scale 1:1250)

also be noted. Small quantities of second-century pottery and CBM from these features date them to this phase. A little further north two other pits also contained small quantities of pottery and CBM and can be assigned to this phase (Group 19). Together these pits and hearths indicate activity and occupation in this part of the site.

Some evidence for activity in this phase was also forthcoming from the other excavation areas. In Area B ditch [1001] continued in use and perhaps formed an enclosure (Enclosure 7) with ditch [1085]. This ditch is aligned with the roadway and the cut for the holloway and may represent a roadside ditch. Elsewhere a single pit encountered in Area C may date to this phase.

2.5 Phase 6: Mid-second to mid-third century (*c.* AD 150–*c.* 250)

Enclosures 5 and 6 continued in use during this phase. Some evidence of land management north of Enclosure 6 was evident in a shallow terrace cut into the slope and lined with a flint revetment wall [822] (Fig. 2.5). This presumably demarcated the western edge of a land unit (Enclosure 8) bounded to the east by the roadway. A

number of pits were identified in Enclosures 5, 6 and 8 and can be assigned to this phase on the basis of their small pottery assemblages (Group 28). Pits [1273], [1196] and [1197] are notable for containing fragments of *opus signinum*, charcoal and a walnut shell respectively (Hégarat & Mooney, this volume) {270}.

The road continued to be defined by the ditches of Group 18 to a point east of Enclosure 6. It may be during this phase that cambered road surface [1068], formed of medium to large flint nodules and identified in a sondage,

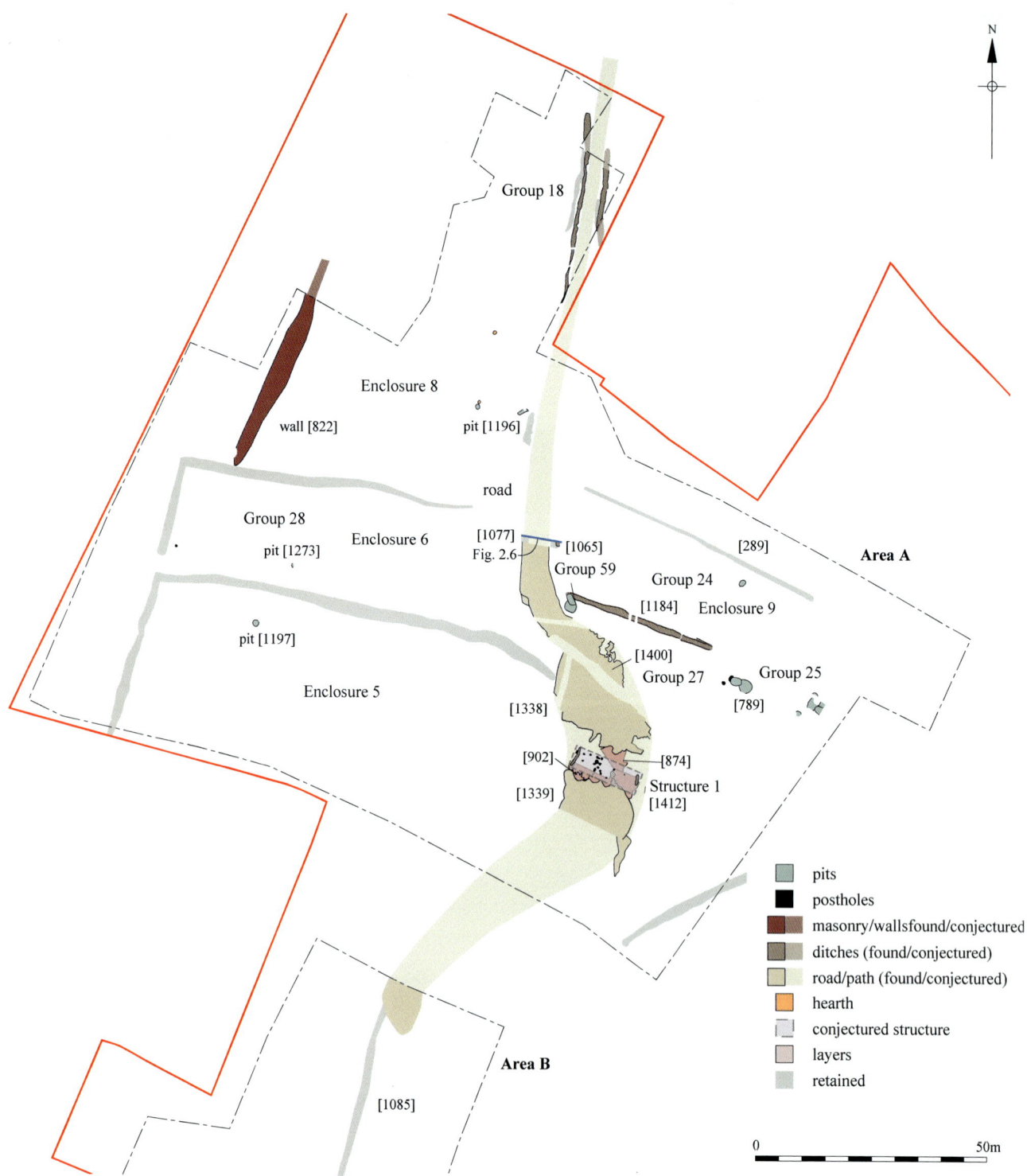

Fig. 2.5   Phase 6: mid-second to mid-third century features (*c.* AD 150–*c.* 250) (scale 1:1250)

W
E

9.50m OD

(201)   (463)   (456)

(464)   (462)

(1069)
[1071]

(1070)

(1072)

surface (1068)

(1066)

(1061) (1064)

(1074)

(1073)

(1075)

(1062)

[1065]

(1077)   (1076)

(1067)

[1063]

9.50m OD

■ Phase 5
■ Phase 6
□ Phase 7
□ Phase 9

0   2.5m

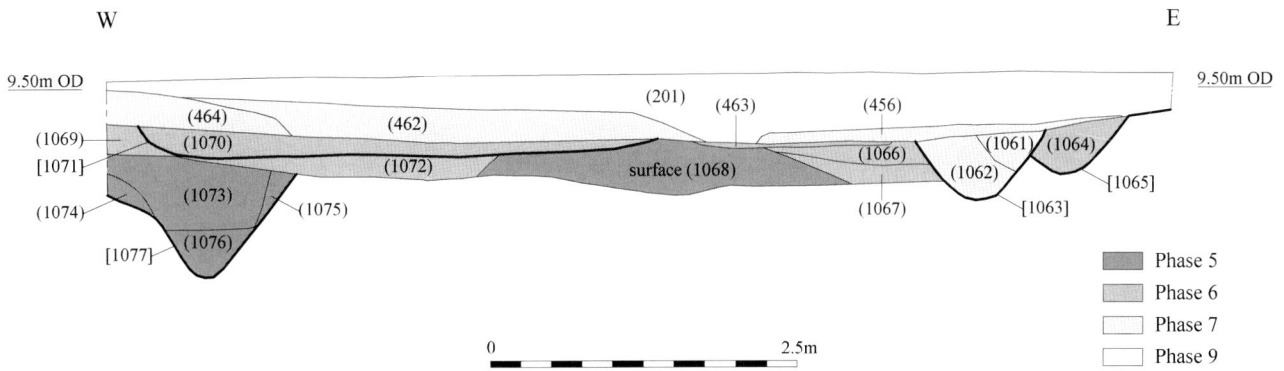

Fig. 2.6   Section through the road and associated roadside ditches (scale 1:60)

Fig. 2.7   Ditch [1184], which defines the northern side of Enclosure 9 during excavation (scale 1m)

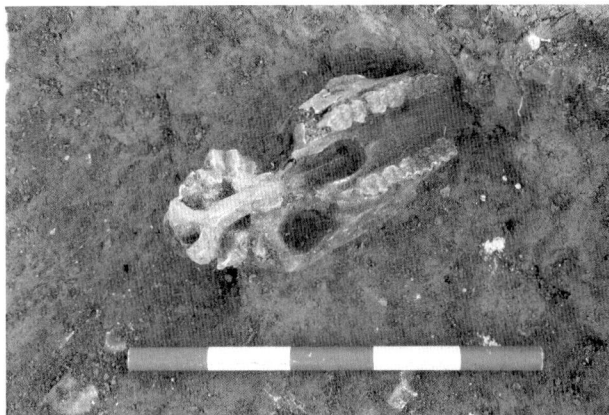

Fig. 2.8   Cow skull in the base of pit [789] (scale 0.5m)

was constructed (Fig. 2.6). Two pits contained few finds but appear to have demarcated the eastern edge of the road (Group 59). Further to the south the road turned eastwards as [1400] (the surface of which contained an early Roman brooch <1263>) and then seems to have turned southwards again (Group 27). In this part of the site, south of evaluation Trench 40 (Haslam 2003, 29), the road surface (here numbered [1338]) produced an iron pick-head <544> and an illegible first- or second-century coin <1253>. There was then an apparent gap (with a few patches of metalling) before the road continued on as [1339] to terminate in Area B.

In the 'gap' between [1338] and [1339] a number of postholes and narrow linear features were identified as Structure 1 ([1412]). These postholes do not make a coherent plan and the linear features are unconvincing as structural beamslots. Furthermore, there is depth to this sequence with some of the postholes intercutting and a layer [902] stratigraphically dividing these features. Layer [902] contained a number of iron objects, including nails, a knife <1072> and a ferrule <1064>, fragments of Roman glass, 512 sherds (3.8kg) of pottery dated *c.* AD 150–250 and faunal remains. Sealing Structure 1 was layer [874], which also sealed the southern end of [1338] and contained 1736 sherds (17.7kg) of pottery dated AD 170–250 and an assemblage of animal bones that included elements from a pig foetus and a bone from a tawny owl (Rielly & Armitage, this volume). Other finds included a bone hinge <1226>, two iron knives <1057> and <1234>, an iron double-spiked loop <1058>, an iron pruning-hook <1059>, a melon bead <1062>, as well as two bone needles <1056> and <1214>, a hairpin (Crummy 1983, Type 1) (Gerrard, small finds, below) and fragments of lava quern (Hayward, this volume). There was also an *as* of Antoninus Pius <1230> from this deposit.

Interpreting Structure 1 presents some difficulties. What survives is far too narrow to be a building and its position in the road is problematic. One possible explanation is that the arrangement of posts and other features represents a series of temporary, perhaps seasonal, gates or barriers erected across the line of the road. These might have served to restrict access to the north in combination with hedgerows or fencelines (traces of which did not survive). In favour of this interpretation is the alignment of Structure 1 ([1412]), which follows that of Enclosure 9 to the north (below). Small patches of metalling between [1338] and [1339] would then represent the eroded remnants of the road surface. Erosion would be more prominent at an ingress point where people and animals are concentrated. The dumped material in layers [902] and [874] would thus represent the residues of an attempt at consolidating an area which would have been poached by frequent traffic, especially of large domesticates. Against this interpretation is the absence of any surviving evidence for associated boundaries and the seemingly unsuitable nature of [874] and [902] as hardcore.

North of the road's eastwards dogleg, Phase 5 ditch [289] seems to have been retained in this phase. It presumably formed the northern side of an enclosure (Enclosure 9) with ditch [1184] (Group 24) (Fig. 2.7). To the east of the surviving termini of these ditches a number of pits were dug (Group 25). They contained small quantities of domestic rubbish, including animal bones (Fig. 2.8), second- to third-century pottery and small groups of charcoal in [276] and [789] (Hégarat & Mooney, this volume).

In Area B ditch [1085] continued to mark the line of the road and the holloway was surfaced with a layer of flints analogous to those to the north. Elsewhere all of the ditches in Area D appear to have been abandoned and the area to the south may have reverted to an open landscape or been divided using archaeologically invisible boundaries like hedgerows.

2.6 Phase 7: Late third century to early to mid-fourth century *c.* AD 250–325/350

The general form of the site established in Phases 5 and 6 continued into the Late Roman period. Enclosures 5, 6 and 8 at the western end of Area A had been defined by ditches. However, by Phase 7 these had either silted up or been deliberately filled in. The lines of both [1403] and [1404] were maintained in this phase by the creation of boundary walls (Groups 29 and 30) and Enclosure 8 acquired a surviving limit to the north in the form of wall [681] (Fig. 2.9). The surviving remnants of these features were rather scrappy mortary deposits with flint and it may be that these features should be visualised as the foundations of cob walls (Fig. 2.10, Fig. 2.11). If so, then a large brickearth quarry pit in the north-eastern corner of Area A [344] (Group 26) may have provided the raw materials for these walls, as well as daub for construction purposes elsewhere.

The features dividing Enclosure 5 from 6 were formed of two walls with irregular edges ([1152] and [1160]) offset from one another and the line of the earlier ditch. In the west ditch [1404] was certainly silted up by the end of

the third century, as its line was cut by a rubble-filled pit containing late third-century pottery from its lower fills and two coins of AD 318–324 and AD 324–330 from its upper fill (which may in fact be a remnant of a slumped overlying layer). A new length of ditch [294] was dug, recutting the eastern end of the silted Phase 4 ditch [1405]; one of its fills produced 88 sherds (1.7kg) of late third-century pottery.

The creation of ditch [294] in this phase may be significant because in the south-east corner of Enclosure 6 a stone-built mausoleum, Building 3, was constructed. The ditch [294] and wall [1152] and [1160] would thus form either side of a route approaching the mausoleum from the west. This putative route approached a stone built mausoleum that had been heavily robbed, but a construction cut [226] defined a square building measuring 6.42m x 6.27m and internally the walls projected at the angles giving a cruciform plan (Fig. 2.12). Presumably, each corner held a pillar supporting an arch, which would provide four arched niches and a cross-vault. Tufa from Phase 9 deposits nearby (Hayward, this volume) would have been suitable for constructing this vault. The surviving fragments of walling were flint and mortar footings that survived only in patches (Group 42). The structure may thus be envisaged as a tall, towerlike building and its landscape position and probable height may mean that the structure served as a navigational marker for vessels sailing the Gillingham Reach. There were no finds from these features and thus the date of the construction of the mausoleum cannot be fixed with any certainty. A late Roman date seems most likely on the basis of the burial (below) and Roman pottery from the robbing deposits is of fourth-century date.

Within the mausoleum a patch of *opus signinum* lay roughly in the middle of the southern niche. This has been interpreted as a postpad (Seddon *et al.* 2008, 67) but it may be that this feature marked the entrance to the structure. The creation of ditch [294] in this phase would thus be explained as it would provide a vista of the tomb and its entrance which a boundary wall would obscure. In the northern niche a rectangular and shallow (0.15m deep) robber cut was interpreted in the field as the location of an internal feature [208]. It may be, given the level of truncation, that this feature actually represents a robbed grave.

Immediately to the south of [208] was grave cut [206] within which was a lidless lead-lined wooden coffin [221]. The wooden coffin survived as traces of a nailed wooden container (the nails do not survive in the archive) and there was evidence that the lid had been removed in antiquity. The coffin contained the bones of middle-aged or elderly female laid in a supine position [231] (Fig. 2.13). Evidence of textiles preserved on the back of the skull indicate that the corpse was probably shrouded, or perhaps wore a head covering (Fig. 2.14). The woman suffered from osteoarthritis in her right hand and spine (Langthorne, this volume). Pollen analysis may suggest that she had consumed a cereal-based meal before death (Branch *et al.*, this volume). There were no surviving grave-goods, but it is tempting to interpret pine pollen from the feet as indicative of the inclusion of a pine cone in the coffin (Branch *et al.*, this volume). Pinecones, as the reproductive elements of an evergreen tree, are well-established funerary and religious symbols in Roman art (Lodwick 2017).

The burial was subjected to radiocarbon dating, with two determinations from separate institutions, of samples taken from rib bones. These returned dates of 140–390AD (95.4% probability: SUERC 84364; 1841±21) and 122–340AD (95.4% probability; BRAMS-2809; 1868±25) respectively (see Appendix 10; Fig. A10.2; Fig. A10.3).

Over the wooden coffin [327] was a deposit ([237] Phase 9; Group 53) containing faunal remains typical of species preyed upon by tawny owls (Rielly & Armitage, this volume). This was sealed by a deposit of brickearth

([220]/[320]) containing a single piece of medieval pottery dated AD 1100–1250 and 46 CBM tesserae. Above this was a mortary layer 'abundant with tesserae' (Seddon *et al.* 2008, 67), of which only seven exist in the archive. This in turn was sealed by a demolition deposit containing 687 CBM tesserae, fragments of CBM, mortar and *opus signinum* (Group 54). There were also two, probably third-century, gold and jewelled necklaces <233> and <234> from this demolition deposit (Hobbs, this volume). The fact that half of the tesserae from the site come from these deposits and further tesserae were recovered from the fills of the robbing of this structure must be a strong indication that the mausoleum had a tessellated floor. Such an embellishment would be unusual, but the mausoleum at Bancroft (Bucks.) with its mosaic floor offers a parallel (Williams & Zeepvat 1994, 259).

Fig. 2.9   Phase 7: late third century to early to mid-fourth century features (*c.* AD 250–325/350) (scale 1:1250)

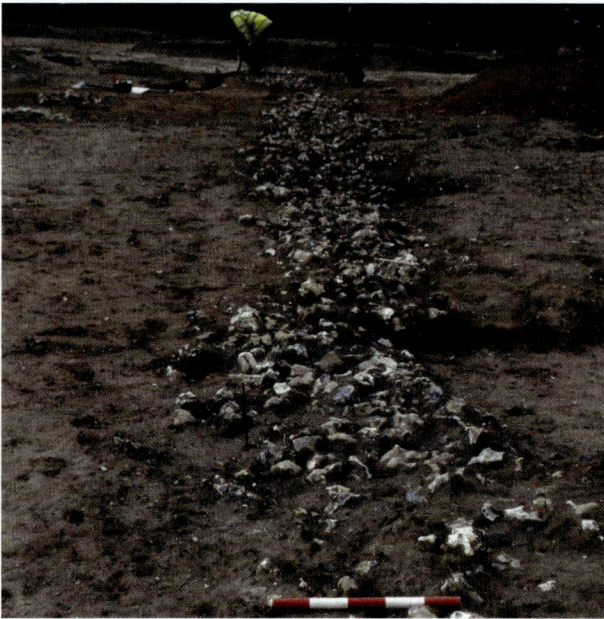

Fig. 2.10   Phase 7 boundary wall [1050] during excavation looking north (scale 0.5m)

Fig. 2.11   Phase 7 boundary wall [717] looking south (scale 2m)

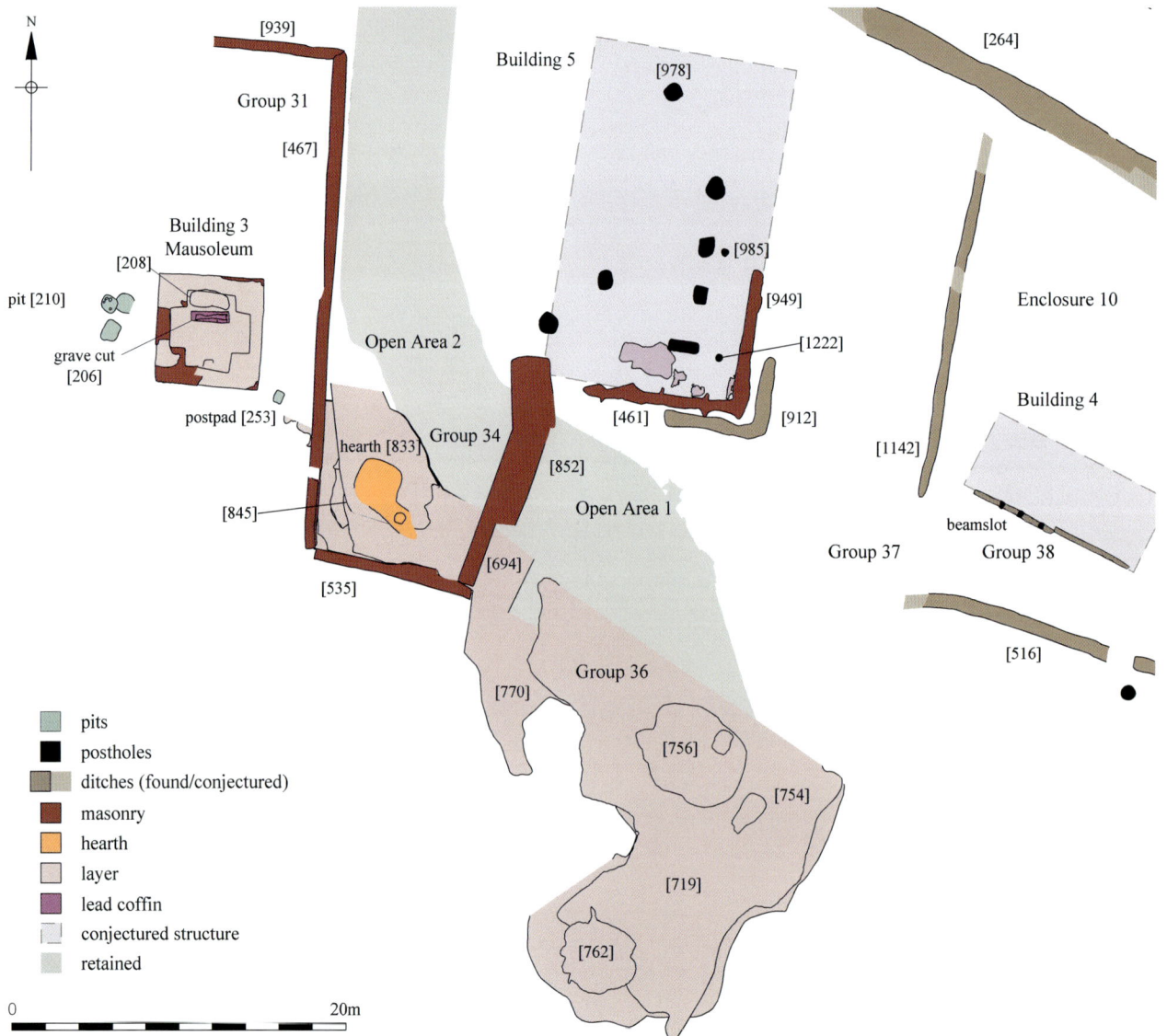

Fig. 2.12   Detail of mausoleum, Building 3 (scale 1:400)

Fig. 2.13   Skeleton of a female adult [231] supine within lead coffin [221]

0   5cm

Fig. 2.14   Evidence for textiles on the base of skull [231]

The original interpretation of this sequence was that the lead coffin lining [221] was sealed, lidless within a timber coffin [327]. The grave was then backfilled [237] and overlain by a brickearth formation layer ([220/320]) for a tessellated floor [211] (Seddon *et al.* 2008, 66–67). There are clear difficulties with this interpretation. First, examples of lidless lead linings for wooden coffins are almost unknown in Roman Britain and beyond (Ridgeway, this volume). Second, grave backfill [237] contains the remnants of what are plausibly interpreted as owl pellets. This suggests an owl roosting in the structure and it seems implausible to suggest that this would occur between placing a coffin in a grave and its subsequent backfilling. Thirdly, there is medieval pottery from the brickearth deposit ([220]/[320]).

A more plausible interpretation is that the grave was disturbed. Such disturbance might explain the absence of a lid to the lead coffin liner and would allow time for owl pellets to accumulate. Overlying layers ([220]/[320], [237], [211] and [205]) may all represent deposits disturbed during the robbing of the structure. Examination of the primary archive supports this interpretation. In particular it makes it clear that the timber coffin lacked a lid and that there were signs of disturbance or robbing of the grave. Some traces of what were thought to be timber planks were interpreted as the remnants of the coffin lid thrown back into the grave.

Other deposits associated with the robbing of the mausoleum contained fragments of human bone from at least a man, a woman and a child (Langthorne, this volume). These suggest that other humans were interred in the mausoleum, although no traces of further grave cuts either within or around the structure were discernible, except for [208] (above). Possibly human remains were stored above ground in some fashion, perhaps in sarcophagi within the niches.

In the immediate environs of the mausoleum a postpad [253] was identified to the south-east of the structure. A group of three shallow pits to the west of the mausoleum contained very little, the only finds of note coming from pit [210] which contained some fourth-century pottery, burnt brickearth and oak charcoal (Hégarat & Mooney, this volume) (Group 41).

Elsewhere within Enclosures 5 and 6 small lengths of flint-and-mortar walls may be the only evidence for structures. In Enclosure 5 three walls possibly defined a rectangular structure (Structure 2). In Enclosure 6 traces of walls and may have defined a structure along with boundary wall [1160]. On the northern side of the enclosure, further wall elements may have defined another structure (Structure 3). In the south-west corner, a further wall element wall may have been part of another structure with [1050], Structure 4. The only feature possibly associated with these walls was pit [1036]. Any other features or floor surfaces associated with these walls (assuming they existed) must have been ploughed away. Another pit [783] within Enclosure 5 contained late third to fourth-century pottery, animal bone and a coin dated to AD 317 (<937>).

Fig. 2.15   The mausoleum and coffin under excavation

Fig. 2.16   The coffin [231] during excavation

Fig. 2.17   Detail of substantial posthole forming part of aisled Building 5 (scale 0.5m)

The eastern boundary of Enclosure 6 was defined with considerable clarity in this phase by the construction of walls [467], [535] and [939] (Group 31). These were built from well-mortared flint nodules and performed the dual function of both enclosing land and revetting the western slope of the holloway (below).

To the east of the road a new enclosure was dug (Enclosure 10) and demarcated by [264] on the north, with a return to the south and a southern boundary [516]. Interestingly, the lower fills of [264] produced the skeleton of a skinned otter and parts of two badgers (Rielly & Armitage, this volume) and [516] contained a hobnailed shoe <1287>. This enclosure seems to have been divided in eastern and western halves by a narrow ditch [1142] (Group 37). Within the eastern half of this enclosure a beamslot with three postholes (Group 38) probably represents the last vestiges of an otherwise completely truncated timber building, Building 4. Within the western half a large aisled building (Building 5) was built. This building had been truncated by ploughing, but its south-eastern corner survived to show its construction. The external wall was formed of unworked flint nodules bonded with a clayey sandy-silt matrix, probably forming masonry footings for timber framing. Following this wall externally was an eavesdrip gully [912] and internally two rows of substantial posts were identified (Fig. 2.17). Posthole [978] to the north may also be a structural element. Postholes [985] and [1222] may represent internal divisions and traces of tile floor surfaces survived in the south-east corner next to the wall (Group 34).

The surviving elements of Building 5 measure 12m east–west by 13m north–south but it must have been considerably longer than this. It cannot, however, have extended further than wall [852] to the west (below) and fourth-century ditch [264] to the north (Phase 8, below). This would suggest maximum possible dimensions of *c.* 25m x *c.* 13m. It is now well-established that aisled buildings were an alternative form of multi-purpose, including residential, architecture in Roman Britain (Taylor 2001, 2013; Smith *et al.* 2016, 66–69). Some aisled buildings contained elaborate decoration and evidence for complex internal activities. Evidence for these is lacking in Building 5 due to truncation but there seems no reason to presuppose anything other than a residential or mixed use function for this building. Rural aisled halls are often smaller than examples from villa sites with figures of 230m^2 versus 380m^2 being quoted (Smith *et al.* 2016, 69). Building 5 with a maximum area of 325m^2 falls neatly between these figures but towards the 'non-villa' end of the range.

The construction of Building 5 appears to have brought with it a fundamental change in the way the site was being used. The road, established in Phase 5, no longer seems to have turned east in the middle of the site. Instead it ran south from the northern limit of excavation in Area A, alongside the aisled building and terminated at wall [535]. It could no longer turn to the east because a new and substantial wall [852] constructed of flint nodules ran north between [535] and Building 5, thus blocking access eastwards. This turned the road surfaces to the east of this north–south return into what was essentially a cobbled yard south of [461] (Open Area 1). This process may have begun with the posthole arrangements of Structure 1 across the road line in Phase 6 (above).

The construction of revetment walls [467] and [535] probably involved truncating existing deposits and created a roughly rectangular space. This area was defined by the right-angle of walls [467] and [535] and was enclosed to the east by [852]. Its northern extent was limited by the still extant road surface. Within this space a complex sequence of interleaving deposits and surfaces were excavated (Open Area 2) along with a circular feature [833] which was some form of hearth (Group 34). The recovery of ferrous slags, including hammerscale from these deposits (Keys, this volume), strongly suggests that [833] may have been used for blacksmithing. Small finds from these deposits include an iron yoke ring <1046>, a copper-alloy toilet spoon <1067> and a third-century military belt-mount <1047>. Parts of a dog skeleton were found in [845], Open Area 2. The pottery from these deposits totals 281 sherds weighing 3.2kg and contains a strong residual component: the two large flint-tempered prehistoric sherds from one context are a particularly obvious example of this phenomenon. Nevertheless, the assemblage (dominated as it is with BB2 and TSK) would indicate a date closer to the middle of the third century than the end.

All of the activity bounded by walls [467], [535] and [852] came to an end with the demolition of wall [852] and the deposition of a layer [694] (Phase 7, Open Area 1), Group 35). This deposit contained 1060 sherds of pottery weighing 12.6kg, the majority of which could be dated to the mid-to late third century. The layer contained: an iron knife <985>; three late Roman bone hairpins <984>, <1036> and <1037> (Crummy 1983, Type 3) and a coin of Julia Paula (AD 219–220) <900>, along with two fourth-century coins of AD 335–341 <943> and AD 353–361 <944>, which must be intrusive or indicate activity on the surface of this deposit into the fourth century. The latter may be more likely as [694] was recorded as overlying part of road surface [463].

To the east of wall [852] a large layer [770] was identified running over the old road surface to overlie the area occupied by Phase 6 Structure 1. Layer [770] was similar in nature and stratigraphically equivalent to [694]. It contained large quantities of occupation debris (Open Area 1) including: 3318 sherds of pottery, weighing 32.2kg; substantial quantities of animal bones as well as late Roman bone hairpins <995> and <1210> (Crummy 1983, Type 3), a bone needle <1013>; an iron key <961> and a latch-lifter <1212>; an iron cleaver <990> and an iron knife <1211>; a green-glass bead <963; an iron pruning-hook <1012> and an iron bucket-mount <979>, an iron loop-hinge <989>, two early Roman brooches <1024> and <1061> and a number of other objects, including a clenched boat-nail <1001>. Dating evidence includes two late-third-century coins <977> and <981>, a late Roman bead <963> and the

large pottery assemblage is essentially of late third-century date, perhaps running into the very early fourth century.

Over the top of layer [770] a number of smaller deposits with similar characteristics seem to have been deposited or accumulated [719], [755], [756], [762] (Group 36) (Fig. 2.18). There was also a small patch of metalling [754], which might indicate attempts at consolidating this area. The finds from these deposits were similar in nature to those recovered from [770]; [719] contained an illegible late Roman coin <908> and a late Roman hairpin <915>. The only unusual aspect of these deposits is the concentration of litharge within them (Dungworth, this volume).

The interpretation of these deposits in Open Area 1 presents some difficulties. The large finds assemblages suggest the dumping of material and waste that was being used on site. It seems likely that some of this material may have been generated by the inhabitants of the buildings in Enclosure 10. The other possibility is that some of the material in these deposits was ultimately derived from activity focussed on [833], because both [694] and [770] contained considerable quantities of ferrous slags. Once wall [852] was demolished it may be that accumulated occupation debris was redeposited into these layers. Alternatively, it is possible that these deposits have been biologically reworked and that traces of clay-and-timber sill-built structures may have been lost in this area. Any of these explanations, or combinations of these explanations are likely but little of the material seems to extend far into the fourth century: a point discussed further below.

South and east of Open Area 1 and south of Enclosure 10 the only evidence for activity during this phase comprises two clusters of features. The first consists of two pits and a hearth [669] that produced some late Roman pottery and a piece of Roman glass (Group 39). The other group comprised a large pit [517] containing 596 sherds (10.8kgs) of late Roman pottery as well as a number of small finds, including a hairpin <902> and an iron ring <871>. Just to the east of this pit were a number of intercutting features. In stratigraphic order they comprise a hearth [621], which contained an iron knife <1278>, a posthole, a hearth and a pit (Group 40).

Fig. 2.18　Metalled surfaces overlying layers [694] and [770] associated with demolition of wall [852] (scale 2m)

2.7 Phase 8: Late fourth to early fifth century *c.* AD 325/350–AD 420/450

Phase 8 embodies many of the difficulties inherent in studying the end of the Roman period in Britain. When does the Roman period end and how can the decades of the fifth century be characterised? The approach taken here is that the demolition of the enclosure boundary walls, visible as large spreads of rubble in the holloway, is an event of the 'early medieval' Phase 9. The final phase of occupation below these deposits is classed as Phase 8, which runs from some time in from the second quarter of the fourth century until perhaps as late as the mid-fifth century (Fig. 2.19).

The general arrangements of the land created in Phase 5 and modified during Phases 6 and 7 continued into Phase 8. Enclosure 5 seems to have been maintained, although no internal features could be assigned to this phase. Enclosure 6 also continued. The mausoleum was standing but ditch [294] had probably silted up or been backfilled by the middle of the fourth century at the latest. In the south-west corner of the enclosure three postholes (Group 43), one of which contained a small number of fourth-century sherds, may represent the last vestiges of some kind of structure. Enclosure 8 also continued to be used with further features dug along the roadside. These include three postholes or small pits cutting a series of layers containing a small quantity of late fourth century pottery, elements of a

Fig. 2.19   Phase 8: late fourth to early fifth century features (*c.* AD 325/50–AD 420/450) (scale 1:1250; inset 1:625)

chip-carved belt-set <1093> and <1094>, a late Roman bracelet fragment <1095> and a coin <1083> of AD 318–324 (layer [867]). West of the road a group of intercutting pits (Group 44), contained groups of mid to late fourth century pottery and animal bones with pit [1231] containing articulated bone groups representing elements from two horses, three cows and a dog. A further pit in this group ([1236] – not seen in plan) also producing a charcoal assemblage dominated by oak (Hégarat & Mooney, this volume).

The road appears to have been maintained into this phase. Roadside ditches from the northern part of Area A produced fourth-century pottery and in the holloway a well-made road surface of small, closely set roughly broken flints and rounded stones was laid [463]. This road surface produced coins of AD 335–341 <868> and 354–361 <867>. As it approached the northern end of wall [467], road [463] was flanked to the west by a gravelled surface [1070], which was only seen in section (see Fig. 2.6).

In area of land between the road and walls [467] and [535] layer [694] may have functioned as a land surface in the early fourth century (above), although little deposition of diagnostic material culture occurred.

Fig. 2.20 A slot excavated through pit [1231] showing elements of articulated bone groups representing elements from two horses, three cows and a dog (scale 0.5m)

Over [694] another layer [537] was deposited early in Phase 9 and contained 27kgs of slag, including eighteen smithing-hearth bottoms and hammerscale (another seven smithing hearth bottoms were found in stratigraphically related Phase 9 demolition deposits in this part of the site: Keys, this volume). Other finds from the deposit include bones from a human foot (Langthorne, this volume) and 83 tesserae, suggesting that the nearby mausoleum was in a state of disrepair, as well as a riveted piece of copper alloy <880>, an iron L-shaped box-fitting <884>, fragments of vessel and window glass and a pottery assemblage of 114 sherds (1.2kg). This group includes a convex-sided dish in AHFA (Lyne & Jefferies 1979, Type 6A9, AD 330–420), fresh sherds of PORD and CALC, fabrics typical of the late fourth and early fifth century in Kent. There is also a fragment of a vessel in an unusual GROG fabric that Dr Malcolm Lyne considers to be from East Sussex. This fabric has been previously identified in a very late-fourth- or early-fifth-century group at Burgess Hill (Lyne 1999). Given that the deposit also contains a single sherd (one of only 25 sherds from the site) from an early 'Anglo-Saxon' vessel in EMS1D (Jarrett, this volume) there seems to be a *prima facie* case for suggesting that [537] is an early-fifth-century deposit.

To the east of the road Enclosure 10 seems to have undergone some modification. The northern ditch [264] stayed open and produced a small quantity of fourth-century pottery along with coins of AD 354–361 <7> and AD 388–394 <1934>. In contrast the eastern and southern ditches of the enclosure seem to have silted up by this date as both were cut by features assigned to this phase, as was the ditch [1142] that divided Enclosure 10 during Phase 7. The major thread of continuity in this enclosure was Building 5. Within the footprint of the building five hearths were identified (Group 45). Only [1155] can be assigned to the fourth century with certainty along with some charcoal (Hégarat & Mooney, this volume); [1136] contained a broken iron knife <1238>; [1046] held parts of two sheep; [982] and [1136] contained charcoal (Hégarat & Mooney, this volume). The remaining hearths contained only residual pottery and small charred archaeobotanical assemblages of limited significance (Seddon *et al.* 2008, 242).

To the west of Building 5 a number of pits lined road [463] and paralleled the alignment of the aisled building. In the south these pits began with [979], then there was a gap, broken only by posthole [1087] before further pits [909], [1060], [1081] and [1205] were dug (Group 47). Pit [979] contained only a sherd of fourth-century pottery, but the other pits contained a coherent assemblage of late-fourth- or early-fifth-century pottery (Gerrard & Hudak, this volume Key Group 6) dominated by AHFA, CALC, PORD and white painted OXRC. Pit [909] contained elements of a late Roman (Hawkes & Dunning 1961) Type IIA belt-set (ring <1073>) and buckle <1075>) (Gerrard, small finds, this volume), a melon bead <1082> and fragments of two bracelets <1208> and <1217>. Pit [1081] contained a coin of AD 335–341 <1220>.

Probably this material represents waste generated by the inhabitants of Building 5.

At some point later than the infilling of [979] a layer of trample [616] accumulated over road surface [463]. This deposit ran along the road in parallel to the aisled building and contained: 53 sherds (643g) of late fourth- or early fifth-century pottery; 32 tesserae; a fragment of a late Roman bracelet <947> and a deposit of slag (Keys, this volume) concentrated in the south-west corner. Stratigraphically this deposit seems best positioned towards the end of Phase 8 or during Phase 9.

In the eastern part of Area A a number of pits and postholes were dispersed across what had been the eastern part of Enclosure 10. Some of these pits cut the ditches of that enclosure (Group 46). Of these features [411] produced an iron bolt-head <449>, [420] an iron joiner's dog <1334> and [671] a copper-alloy hairpin <902> and a copper-alloy stud <903>. The small pottery assemblage (Gerrard & Hudak, this volume Key Group 7) contained residual material but also fresh sherds of mid-fourth-century and later fabrics.

There is little evidence for activity in Phase 8 Enclosure 10 during the later fourth century. Possibly any evidence had been truncated, but a few cut features (Group 47), to the south can be assigned to this phase. They make no discernible plan and cannot be meaningfully interpreted.

It is necessary to finish this discussion of Phase 8 with a consideration of the finds recovered from Phase 9 'dark earth' layer [201] (for which see below). Much of the material culture from this deposit comprised an assemblage of objects that together point towards what would now be interpreted as fifth-century activity. The 170 coins from this deposit included twenty-one coins of the House of Valentinian (AD 364–378), two coins of AD 378–388 and five coins of the House of Theodosius (AD 388–402). The deposit also contained a large number of mid-fourth-century *nummi*. Small finds included fragments of sixteen late Roman bracelets, two of which had been cut down and modified into finger-rings <137> and <530>. This phenomenon is characteristic of the end of the Roman period (Swift 2012). There were also other finds, including a fragment of another Hawkes and Dunning (1961) Type IIA belt buckle, which are typical of end of the fourth- and early fifth-century deposits. There are also two 'early Anglo-Saxon' spears from this layer (Gerrard & Allison, this volume). The other remaining objects from this deposit are discussed further below. The pottery assemblage, which is large (3611 sherds, 58.1kg, 61.24 EVE), contains a significant early Roman residual component. Nevertheless, there is also a very important late-fourth- to early-fifth-century aspect to this group (Gerrard & Hudak, this volume Key Group 9). There were also 190 CBM tesserae. All of this material was deposited in the fill of the holloway in Phase 9 but must be the product of Phase 8 occupation. It provides some insights into the connections and character of the site at the very end of the Roman period in Britain.

2.8 Phase 9: Early medieval *c.* AD 400/450–1000/1066

Phase 9 encompasses the six or so centuries that span, in historical terms, the period of time from the 'fall' of the Western Roman Empire to the final decades of Late Saxon England. We have deliberately chosen to term this period 'early medieval', a fairly uncontroversial choice of nomenclature, but one which deliberately avoids ethnic connotations implicit in labels like 'Early Anglo-Saxon'. However, using the term early medieval does enshrine and maintain the break between the ancient, Classical world and Medieval Europe.

At Grange Farm Phase 9 is defined in stratigraphic terms as beginning with the collapse or demolition of the enclosure walls into the holloway (Fig. 2.21). This was marked by extensive spreads of flint rubble, CBM and tesserae (Group 49) (this included [456] coin <1330> AD 270–90; [464] coin <942> AD 364–378; [468] coin <890> AD 354–361; [619] coin <899> AD 270–290). Pottery from these deposits dated almost exclusively from the end of the fourth and into the fifth century and the coins tell a similar story.

It is difficult to define in absolute terms when the collapse of demolition of these walls occurred. The layer [537] (Group 49), stratified below the collapse deposits, contained a small but probably early-fifth-century group of pottery, as well as a pottery sherd manufactured in a handmade technological tradition that has its origins in the barbarian lands in the north of what is now Germany: in culture-historical terms this sherd is 'Anglo-Saxon'. Stratigraphically below this was a layer ([694]) which contained coins, the latest of which dated to AD 354–361 (<944>). The earlier (Phase 8) road surface [463] also produced a coin <867> of AD 354–361. In terms of a *terminus post quem*, the group (from [537]), which can be dated to the early fifth century, holds sway. Of course, a *terminus post quem* is exactly that, there is no reason why the walls could not have collapsed in, say, AD 470 or later.

By the same token it is impossible to determine precisely when Building 5 was abandoned. It seems to have existed at the very end of Phase 8 and thus probably still existed at the beginning of Phase 9. A layer [449]/[900] sealed the Phase 8 hearths within the building and contained 136 sherds (1.9kg) of fourth-century pottery, along with a pruning-hook <565> and two mid-fourth-century coins <15> and <16>. There was also a fragment of post-medieval glass, which was probably introduced into the deposit through a plough strike. The mausoleum appears to have continued to stand and it may be in this phase that coffin [221] was disturbed [237], following which the structure became a roost for a tawny owl (for a detailed discussion of this sequence see Phase 7 above). It may have continued to function, in its ruinous form as a navigational marker for vessels sailing the Gillingham Reach.

To the north of the mausoleum and beyond the line of collapsed wall [939] within Enclosure 8, a Nydam-style silver-gilt brooch <917> (Gaimster, this volume)

Fig. 2.21 Phase 9: early medieval features (*c.* AD 400/450–1000/1066) (scale 1:1250)

was found by metal-detecting early in the course of the excavations. Some time later its findspot was investigated and proved to be a spread of flint nodules and stones apparently 'levelling' an undulation in the natural brickearth [1134] (Seddon *et al.* 2008, 85). Other than the brooch the context contained three sherds of early Roman pottery. The feature was interpreted, somewhat unsatisfactorily, as a plough damaged platform (Seddon *et al.* 2008, 85). What seems more likely (and is suggested in the primary record) is that this deposit of rubble with irregular edges, is actually a spread of demolition rubble from the truncated westwards extension of [939]. It survived because the undulation in the brickearth protected the deposit from ploughing.

Further to the north a layer ([937]) accumulated over the fills of various Phase 8 features, the only find of note from these deposits was a residual coin of Salonina <1085> AD 260–268 and a fragment of litharge (Dungworth, this volume). On stratigraphic grounds it

can be assigned to Phase 9. Further to the north again, pit [732] can definitely be assigned to Phase 9 because its fill contained sherds 'Anglo-Saxon' pottery from at least three vessels dated AD 450–700. The function of this pit is unknown and it was partially truncated by Phase 10 well [563].

One major element of this phase is layer [201] (Fig. 2.22; Fig. 2.23). This deposit was found overlying the demolition rubble in the holloway and proved to be a homogenous dark brown humic soil containing large quantities of finds (summarised below). As the layer was immediately below the ploughsoil ([200]), it had been subjected to some disturbance by ploughing and the deep roots of crops such as horseradish. Due to this, there were small quantities of intrusive material ranging from medieval and post-medieval ceramics to modern plastic.

Layer [201] is more or less analogous to the kinds of deposits labelled as 'dark earth' in urban environments. Current consensus would see these

Fig. 2.22   Section through layer [201] (scale 1m)

Fig. 2.23   Working shot showing detail of a temporary section through layer [201], looking north-east; the extensive rubble and road metalling sealed by this later are visible under [201]

Fig. 2.24   The holloway under excavation, looking north. The boundary wall to the west is visible along with extensive flint rubble deposits filling the trackway. Layer [201] has largely been removed but it remains *in situ* north of the temporary section

deposits as the product of the biological reworking of existing stratigraphy (for instance Macphail *et al.* 2003). In the absence of detailed analysis, such as soil micromorphology, it is impossible to tell how this deposit formed or what processes of biological transformation it had undergone. Nevertheless, the quantities of material from this deposit need to be considered.

The finds include residual material but also a significant very late Roman assemblage. Much of this survived in a reasonable state of preservation. The average sherd weight, which can be used as a crude proxy for abrasion, is 15.8g, which is reasonably high. Interestingly, the late Roman fabrics seem to have consistently higher average fabric weights than early Roman fabrics (Table 3.14; Fig. 3.46; Fig. 3.47). This suggests that different parts of the assemblage have been subjected to different post-breakage processes (for further discussion see Gerrard & Lyne 2008, 172–176).

The Roman small finds assemblage from this deposit includes as complete or incomplete objects:

Personal adornments
- four early Roman brooches
- two hairpins
- six late Roman bracelets
- two bracelets cut into finger-rings
- elements from at least one late Roman 'military-style' belt

Structural fittings
- five hinges
- a wall-hook
- two double-spiked loops

Transport and horses
- a hipposandal
- a curb-bit cheek-piece

Household and domestic
- a needle
- a stylus
- two weights
- two furniture studs
- a box fitting

Tools and weapons
- one axe and one paring-chisel blade
- six knives

The assemblage also included a number of other objects of indeterminate function. In addition to the 61 Roman small finds recovered, layer [201] also produced the following:

- 22 pieces of struck flint
- 3251 sherds of Roman pottery
- 177 Roman coins
- Two Anglo-Saxon spearheads
- One sherd of Anglo-Saxon pottery
- 3893 animal bone fragments
- Five sherds of post-Roman pottery
- Nine fragments of glass
- One fragment of clay tobacco pipe
- 21 smithing hearth bottoms

Amongst the small assemblage of unusual 'Anglo-Saxon' objects recovered from layer [201], the two complete spearheads (Allison *et al.* this volume), which are in an excellent state of preservation and so unlikely to be redeposited from graves, hold pride of place, but a single sherd of pottery is also of interest. The vessel from which this came was probably from a burnished biconical jar or carinated bowl with a faceted rib above vertical evenly spaced ribs (Fig. 3.69.2) (Jarrett, this volume). This type of decoration has not been previously reported from Kent.

How these assemblages came to be deposited over the demolition rubble is a question of considerable interpretative importance. The simplest explanation, the implications of which are explored more fully below (Gerrard, Chapter 4), is that during Phase 8 household waste and the like accumulated as surface midden heaps, a phenomenon that may be related to changes in the way waste was treated during the fourth century (for a useful discussion of this phenomenon see Evans *et al.* 2013). During Phase 9 the contents of those heaps were redeposited either by a natural process or human agency into the rubble-choked holloway. Biological reworking of the redeposited waste then produced the homogenous 'dark earth' deposit [201].

A possible analogy for [201] was encountered at Bloodmoor Hill, Suffolk (Lucy *et al.* 2009, 22–37, 116–120, 340–357). Here long stretches of Roman-period trackways, defined by ditches, were sealed by what were termed 'surface deposits' in the excavation report. These extensive deposits were dark layers containing large quantities of Roman material and also significant quantities of sixth- and seventh-century Anglo-Saxon finds. Detailed analysis of the finds assemblages at Bloodmoor Hill suggested that these deposits were the product of *in-situ* middening, the redeposition of midden material and possibly the dumping of topsoil stripped from elsewhere on the site, prior to the construction of Anglo-Saxon timber buildings. A close association between the Anglo-Saxon settlement features (timber buildings and sunken-featured buildings) and the surface deposits was noted. We lack any evidence at Grange Farm for Anglo-Saxon buildings but processes similar to those suggested at Bloodmoor Hill seem likely.

The final feature that can be assigned to Phase 9 is a small length of ditch [497]. This ditch, which was cut through [201], ran in a roughly east–west direction and also cut across the line of demolished Phase 7 and 8 wall [467]. It contained only three sherds of late-fourth-century pottery and thus is assigned to this phase and not Phase 10.

2.9 Phase 10: Medieval AD 1000–1550

From *c.* AD 600 onwards there is a hiatus in visible activity across all of the excavated areas. By the eleventh century documentary sources record a settlement at Grange but no traces of this were found in the excavations. Instead there is intriguing evidence that the mausoleum still survived, albeit in a presumably ruinous state (Fig. 2.25). On the basis of pottery from robber trenches it seems to have been systematically robbed in the twelfth century (Group 57). An eleventh- or twelfth-century cross-staff terminal <321> indicates religious activity nearby, as does a twelfth-century lead cross <355>. Both of these objects were recovered from the ploughsoil.

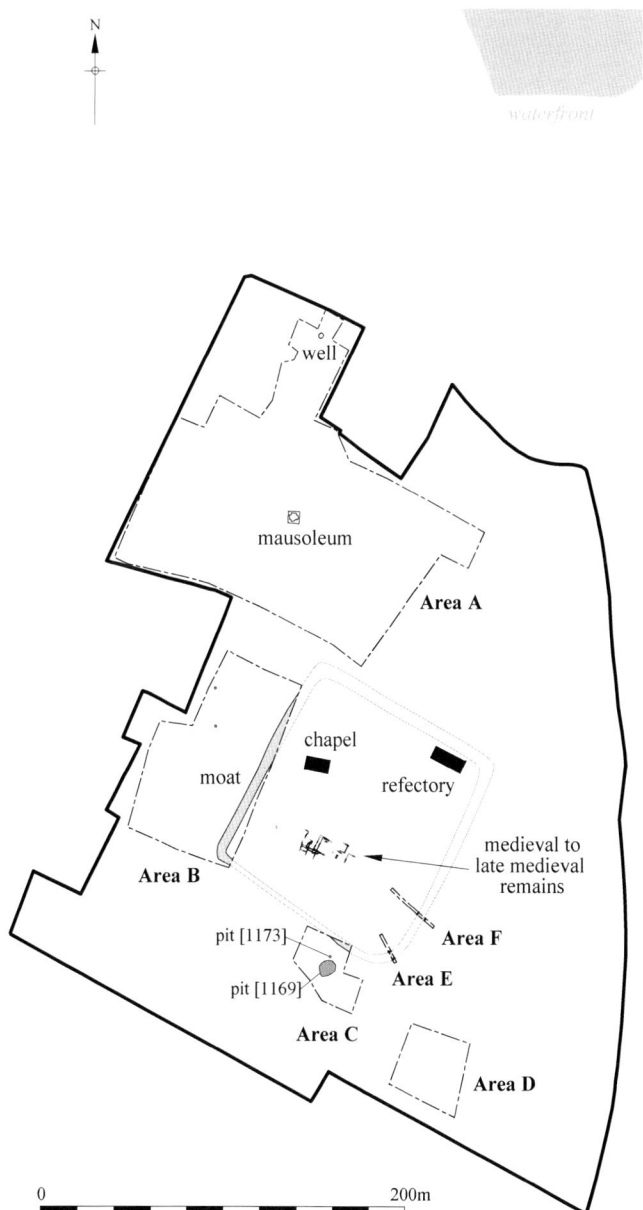

Fig. 2.25   Phase 10: medieval features (AD 1000–1550) (scale 1:4000)

Somewhat later activity is indicated by a well in the northern part of Area A [563] (Fig. 2.26). The fills of this feature contained pottery dated AD 1250–1350 and an iron knife <904> (Gaimster, this volume). The large assemblage of local and imported pottery from this well is clear evidence of nearby domestic occupation (Jarrett, this volume) but any traces of the buildings that generated this waste have either been truncated or lie beyond the limits of excavation. There were also traces of ridge-and-furrow visible in the northern part of Area A [634] and a posthole [407] in the eastern end (Group 50).

The manorial site to the south of Area A, of which extant remains still survive, was clearly a major focus of activity in the medieval period (Meddens & Draper 2014). In the current excavations the manorial site was not investigated, but in Areas B, C, D, E and F a very large ditch [473]/[1366] was identified running southwards down the eastern side of Area B, turning eastwards across the northern part of Area C, and then returning northwards in Areas E and F (Group 51). A section across this ditch showed it cutting pit [475] and filled with a complex sequence of deposits, but only produced a small group of pottery dated AD 1525–1550 from its uppermost fill (Jarrett, this volume) (Fig. 2.27). Other medieval features include pits in Area C. Of these pit [1173] produced pottery dated AD 1100–1150 and pit [1169] pottery dated AD 1150–1225 (Jarrett, this volume) (Group 52).

Fig. 2.26   Medieval well [563] during excavation

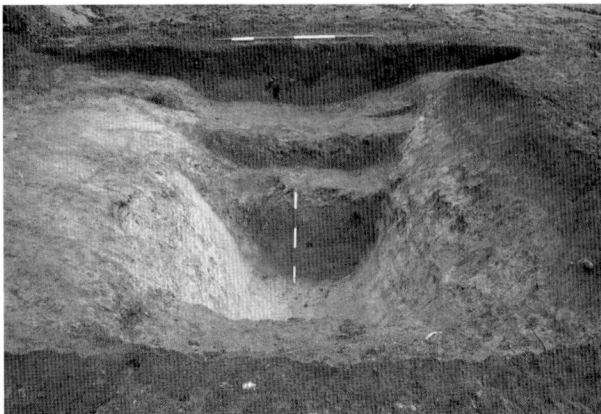

Fig. 2.27   Section through the moat [473] (scales 2m, 1m)

2.10 Phase 11: Post-medieval

The manor continued to exist as a primary focus of activity into the post-medieval period. In the middle of the sixteenth century the ditched enclosure around the manor seems to have been infilled and there is also evidence of some pit-digging in the sixteenth and seventeenth centuries (not illustrated here). Other activity in Area A included a small brick-built structure of nineteenth-century or later date but of unknown function in the south-east corner, a number of postholes and a Victorian boundary ditch along the northern edge of the excavated area. Two French drains are evidence of agricultural improvements.

In Area B regular rows of circular features spaced 8m apart were clearly planting pits for trees. The fills contained some medieval objects, but cartographic evidence links these planters to the orchards that covered the area in the nineteenth century. Finally, Area C contained a number of ditches, two of which perhaps defined a trackway and Area D contained a single pit of post-medieval date

The last archaeologically identifiable sub-period of Phase 11 concerns a feature in Area A and a number of finds from Areas B, C and D, which can be associated with the Second World War. During the 1939–1945 conflict the Medway Towns become a target for the Luftwaffe because of the presence of strategic industries and military facilities. Gillingham was targeted on a number of occasions and was heavily bombed in the summer of 1940, with considerable loss of life and damage to the town. A number of anti-aircraft guns were positioned around the town as a defence, one of which lay to the south east of the site.

In Area A a large and irregularly shaped feature, truncating archaeological deposits in the north east of the trench, was interpreted as a bomb crater. In Areas B, C and D metal-detecting during topsoil removal led to the discovery of thirty German incendiary bombs. These were removed and disposed of by Babtec, an ordnance removal company. For obvious reasons these bombs were treated as a hazard rather than 'finds' but they represent an important phase in the site's history. Probably they were B1E 1kg incendiary bombs (IWM 2018), which could be dropped by a German bomber such as the Heinkel 111 in their hundreds; over 24,000 incendiary bombs were dropped on the Medway region during the war (Smith 2011, 185). The land at Grange Farm would not have been a 'target' but simply hit as part of the indiscriminate and inaccurate nature of area bombing.

Chapter 3

The Specialist Reports

3.1 The struck flint

Barry Bishop

The excavations at Grange Farm resulted in the recovery of 180 pieces of struck flint. Each piece has been catalogued and a report on the material was compiled as part of the Post-Excavation Assessment (Bishop 2008a).

The raw materials used comprise a good knapping quality mottled translucent black and opaque grey fine-grained flint with a thick but weathered cortex. This is typical of flint from the chalk of the North Downs and the presence of both recorticated thermal (frost fractured) surfaces and thermal flaws within the flint indicate that it had been gathered locally, most probably from colluvial (Head) deposits that are present to the east of the site or from mass-weathered deposits found on the surface of the Chalk which outcrops to the south (Gibbard 1986). There are also a few pieces made from 'bullhead bed' flint which can be found at the junction of the Upper Chalk and overlying Thanet Sands (Shepherd 1972), such as occurs immediately to the south of the site.

Technology and typology

Despite the reasonable size of the assemblage there were no truly typologically diagnostic pieces present, the assemblage consisting predominantly of knapping waste. Only three possible retouched pieces were identified; a cortical flake from Phase 6 pit [994] (pit group 47) that has been blunted along one edge and has traces of use-wear on the opposite margin suggesting it had been used as a cutting implement akin to a blunt backed knife, a cortical convex end-scraper came from Phase 2 gully [380] and a small angular fragment that had been blunted, possibly to form a piercer, was found in Phase 7 pit [783]. The proportion of retouched pieces, at 1.7%, is low but a number of flakes do exhibit edge chipping and notching that may be deliberate, although this cannot convincingly be distinguished from post-depositional damage. Also rather under-represented are cores, of which only two were recovered. One of these, from Phase 6 pit [994], has a single platform that has produced a series of short, narrow flakes and blades. The other, from Phase 2 pit [638], consisted of an angular chunk with a simple flaked striking platform from which only a few small and short flakes had been removed but which also exhibited several incipient Hertzian cones from failed attempts at removing further flakes. A high proportion of the overall assemblage consisted of decortication flakes which probably reflects the short nature of knapping sequences as well as the possibility of decorticating raw materials found at the site, prior to them being removed for further working elsewhere.

The technological attributes of the assemblage would suggest that it might have been manufactured over a long period of time. The core from pit [994] along with a number of blades and flakes with blade characteristics, such as parallel margins and dorsal scars (blade-like flakes), would be most characteristic of Mesolithic or Early Neolithic industries. Some of the other features may be later in date however; the flint core from pit [638] is perhaps more reminiscent of later Bronze Age or Iron Age examples, although it is not closely dateable.

The majority of the assemblage, perhaps as much as three-quarters, comprises more-crudely and opportunistically produced flakes. These vary considerably in size and shape although they tend to be thick and broad, and they frequently have wide striking platform and a notably obtuse striking platform/core-face angles, being comparable to Martingell's 'squat' flakes (Martingell 1990, 2003). Many had very prominent points of percussion and some flakes exhibited incipient Hertzian cones from failed earlier attempts at detaching the flake. Bulbs of percussion tend to be pronounced and several flakes have ventral surfaces that partially follow thermal flaws. Such reduction strategies and technological attributes are most commonly seen within later second and first millennium BC industries (Herne 1991; Young & Humphrey 1999; Humphrey 2003).

Distribution

The struck flint was found across the site although the largest quantities occurred in its central and eastern parts. It was mostly recovered from Roman or later features and these pieces can be regarded as residually deposited. The largest quantity came from layers in Open Area 1, particularly Phase 7 [770], a late Roman occupation accumulation, which contained 29 struck pieces, with a further three struck flints coming from comparable deposit [719], with the overlying late/post

Roman 'dark earth' soil deposit [201] producing a further 22 struck pieces. The presence of struck flint suggests that these layers are at least partially formed from soils containing an abundance of prehistoric material. The only contexts that may have contained *in situ* assemblages consisted of a number of Phase 2 features, notably a posthole and gully [380], which contained 20 and 12, struck pieces respectively, and smaller quantities of flintwork were recovered from pits [428], [542] and [638]. None of these assemblages is particularly diagnostic; those from posthole [389] and gully [380] were both dominated by knapping waste although a scraper (see above) came from gully [380]. However, none of the pieces from these features refitted and they are in a variable but often chipped and abraded condition. Whilst residual deposition remains likely, it is possible that these features contain deliberately deposited assemblages. The mixed condition and range of raw materials present would indicate that if deliberately deposited, the material must have been selected from a larger accumulation of knapping debris. The lack of diagnostic pieces means dating the assemblages is difficult although the presence of some blades and numerous blade-like flakes would be most characteristic of Neolithic industries, with the deliberate deposition of midden material within pits being a noted feature of the Neolithic period (e.g. Thomas 1999; Garrow 2006; Anderson-Whymark & Thomas 2012).

Discussion

Prehistoric occupation is well-attested in Kent and not least on the northern edge of the North Downs and from along the Thames' estuary margins. In many cases the evidence takes a similar form, comprising substantial spreads of multi-period prehistoric flintwork, which testify to the easy availability of lithic raw materials as well as the persistent and often dense levels of occupation witnessed in these localities (e.g. Philp 1973; Mudd 1994; Bishop & Bagwell 2005; James 2006; Bishop 2014). Grange Farm produced small quantities of Early Neolithic material, some of which may have been associated with pits and other features. Flintwork of this date has been recovered from numerous excavations conducted in the area and it is normally regarded as the remains of temporary campsites of largely mobile communities, which are only otherwise represented by occasional pits or other, often rather ephemeral, features (e.g. Dunning 1966; Bishop & Bagwell 2005). The bulk of the flintwork from Grange Farm belongs to the later prehistoric period, from the later second or first millennia BC. By the later Bronze Age and throughout the Iron Age the archaeological record in north Kent takes on a different character and it is becoming clear that extensive and intensified agricultural landscapes were being established from the North Downs to the coast (e.g. Mudd 1994; Yates 2001, 2006; Bishop & Bagwell 2005; Bishop 2008b). The flintwork produced by these communities can only be described as casually produced with little investment of skill and no complex knapping strategies. It reflects an expedient approach to obtain serviceable edges and much of it appears to arise from little more than randomly hitting pieces of raw material until sufficient flakes had been procured. Flint use is usually regarded as being largely confined to the domestic sphere and mostly associated with the realms of food production, craft and industrial activities (Ford *et al.* 1984; Herne 1991; Edmonds 1995; Young & Humphrey 1999). At Grange Farm there are few other traces of settlement at the site although further evidence for such may exist in the vicinity. Alternatively, it is possible that the lithic assemblage derives from repeated but perhaps relatively temporary

Table 3.1: Quantification of struck flint by archaeological phase

Context	Decortication Flake	Rejuvenation Flake	Unclassifiable Flake Fragment	Chip	Flake	Blade	Blade-like flake	Core	Minimal Core	Retouched	Conchoidal Chunk
Phase 2 features	7	1	3	2	9	2	12		1	1	2
Phase 3 features				5	5	2					
Unstratified and Roman or later features	45	1	2	8	47	11	5	1		2	6

occupation, associated with the seasonal movement of stock from the lowlands bordering the Thames Estuary to the higher ground of the North Downs, a form of transhumance argued to be as important in north Kent during the later Bronze and Iron Ages as it was during the historic period (Mudd 1994; Bishop & Bagwell 2005; Yates 2006).

Burnt flint

Just over 10kg of burnt stone, comprising mostly flint but with occasional siliceous sandstone fragments present, were recovered during the excavations at Grange Farm. These had been modified by being burnt but exhibited no other evidence of previous or subsequent working, although it is always possible that some had been struck prior to heating but are now no longer identifiable as such.

Over half of the burnt stone, 5,635g, was recovered from a single feature, Phase 2 pit [638], along with an unburnt flint core of probable later prehistoric date. This material was thoroughly and uniformly burnt, the flint having turned a consistent light grey in colour and it had severely shattered, although individual fragments weighed up to 150g. It would appear that large nodules had been collected and deliberately burnt, in a manner characteristic of 'potboilers'.

The material from the pit appeared to originate from the extensive and systematic production of burnt flint, such as identified at 'burnt mound' sites and usually interpreted as representing industrial activities or large-scale cooking, although many other activities that may produce such material have been proposed (e.g. Barfield & Hodder 1987; Barfield 1991). Roman layers [770] and [719] (Phase 7, Open Area 1) as well as containing high numbers of struck flints also produced relatively large quantities of unworked burnt flint, amounting to 1,580g in total, although this is inherently undateable and may derive from the prehistoric occupation or the more contemporary Roman activity, possibly being associated with the metalworking that has been identified here.

The remainder of the stone was burnt to varying degrees and it was mostly recovered in small quantities and from a variety of features. This would be more suggestive of general 'background' residual waste, most probably from activities involving hearth-use. A few contexts produced slightly larger quantities, such as some of the Phase 3 ditches, which may suggest either the presence of close-by hearths or that the features were used to dump the refuse from such hearths.

3.2 The Roman coins

James Gerrard

The excavations produced 453 Roman coins. The high number is a direct consequence of the large area excavated and the use of metal detectors on site. Almost half (230) of the Roman coins were either unstratified or came from the ploughsoil and a further 170 coins were recovered from Phase 9 layer [201]. This means that only 53 came from discrete contexts and the use of the coins to date stratigraphic events is thus limited. Nevertheless, the coins do have an important story to tell.

The coins are presented in this report in a summary form using Reece's (1991) chronological periods and a more detailed catalogue is available from the site archive. As is typical of many Romano-British sites the state of preservation is variable. Some coins are crisp, as if newly struck, others heavily worn and more still badly corroded. All of the coins were examined shortly after excavation and a sample of coins were x-rayed but none have been cleaned. The coins were re-examined before this report was written and 372 could be assigned to a date of minting or Reece Period.

Table 3.2   Summary table of all Roman coins by Reece (1991) period

Reece Period	Date	No. of coins	Per mills
1	to AD 41	0	0.00
2	AD 41–54	0	0.00
3	AD 54–69	0	0.00
4	AD 69–96	1	2.70
5	AD 96–117		0.00
6	AD 117–138	1	2.70
7	AD 138–161	2	5.41
8	AD 161–180	0	0.00
9	AD 180–193	0	0.00
10	AD 193–222	1	2.70
11	AD 222–238	1	2.70
12	AD 238–259	2	5.41
13	AD 259–275	2	5.41
14	AD 275–294	35	94.59
15	AD 294–317	8	21.62
16	AD 317–330	14	37.84
17	330–348	112	302.70
18	348–364	121	327.03
19	364–378	52	140.54
20	378–388	5	13.51
21	388–402	13	35.14
Illegible		83	-
Total		453	1000

Even the most cursory examination of Table 3.2 or Fig. 3.1 demonstrates that the majority of the coins from the site were struck in the late Roman period. Only eight coins were struck before AD 222 and this total includes four illegible first- or second-century bronzes. This broad pattern of coin loss is reflected in the wider history of the site, but features, pottery and small finds show that there is far more evidence for early Roman activity than the coins might suggest.

The fourth-century pattern is of some interest. The late third-century radiate peak in Periods 13 and 14 is subdued. Periods 15 and 16, the Tetrarchic and early Constantinian coin reforms, are usually poorly represented but the low numbers are reasonably significant: many sites produce no coins in Periods 15 and 16. Two great peaks of coin loss (Constantinian *nummi* and their copies) in Periods 17 and 18 are quite striking and are followed by a reasonable peak in Period 19 (House of Valentinian). Period 20 is always a low point but the six coins, including a *nummus* of Magnus Maximus, represent above-average loss. Period 21 has a small peak, but this indicates that the site was still receiving and losing coins during the final phase of Roman coin use in Britain. Current thinking might put this as late as the AD 430s (Moorhead & Walton 2014) and the discovery nearby in *c.* 1906 of a hoard of bronze coins of AD 388+ is relevant too (Robinson 2000, no. 1542). These fourth-century coins represent an important insight into the late Roman activity at the site and demonstrate that occupation continued into the early years of the fifth century.

Comparison of the site finds with Walton's (2011, table 7) British Mean values is enlightening. Reece (1995) first developed the idea of a 'British mean' based on the values for the 140 sites he had gathered together (Reece 1991). Walton (2011) has argued that Reece's values were biased towards urban and military centres and were also skewed by the inclusion of Richborough, with its anomalously high number of Theodosian coins. Her mean, based on Portable Antiquities Scheme (PAS) finds, is likely to be more representative of the rural situation and is used in

Fig. 3.2. This emphasises the above-average coin loss at the site from AD 330 onwards.

Comparing the coins from the site with the groups recovered (either unstratified, or from the ploughsoil and those from layer [201]) shows that there are few differences (Fig. 3.3). Layer [201] has more coins of AD 348–364 but otherwise the two groups are broadly comparable. If the coins in [201] or the ploughsoil were derived from individual dispersed hoards, for instance, then significant differences might be expected. It remains possible that many of the coins in Periods 17 and 18 could be derived from a dispersed hoard (for instance Brickstock 1987) but a mechanism that would disperse these coins across the large excavated area is difficult to imagine. Ploughing would be unlikely to achieve such a distribution.

There were few coins of individual note. Three were, however, pierced for suspension: <704> a denarius of Alexander Severus; <800> a *follis* of Licinius and <977> a third-century radiate. Piercing Roman coins for suspension is often associated with early medieval grave finds (White 1988; Moorhead 2006) but such coins do appear in Roman period burials as well (Philpott 1991; Puttock 2002, 97–98).

A small 'hoard' or 'purse group' of third-century radiates <483> (201)

A group of coins <483> nos. 1–11 were found fused together as a small lump (PAS-383B92). X-rays of this corroded mass demonstrated that it was formed of some small stacks of coins and in 2015 the coins were separated, cleaned and conserved by Karen Barker.

The separated lump was found to contain eleven individual coins. They are all extremely poorly preserved but their size, shape and details (where they survive), indicate that this is a small hoard or purse group of late third-century radiates. No. <483.9> would suggest a date that the coins were assembled no earlier than AD 286.

Table 3.3 The coins from the purse group: references are to the Cunetio and Normanby hoards (Bland et al. 2009)

SF <483>	Obverse	Reverse	Diameter (mm)	Reference
1	Illegible	Illegible	13	
2	Illegible (Tetricus I?)	Spes	14	Normanby 1948/3
3	Illegible radiate	Possibly altar, Consecratio	14	
4	Illegible	Illegible	12	
5	Illegible	Illegible	19	
6	Illegible	Illegible standing fig	16	
7	Illegible radiate	Illegible	15	
8	Illegible	Pietas Augustorum, implements	13	Cunetio 3036.1
9	Illegible (Carausius?)	Pax, II to L.	18	Normanby 1593
10	Illegible	Illegible	16	
11	Irregular radiate	Illegible	14	

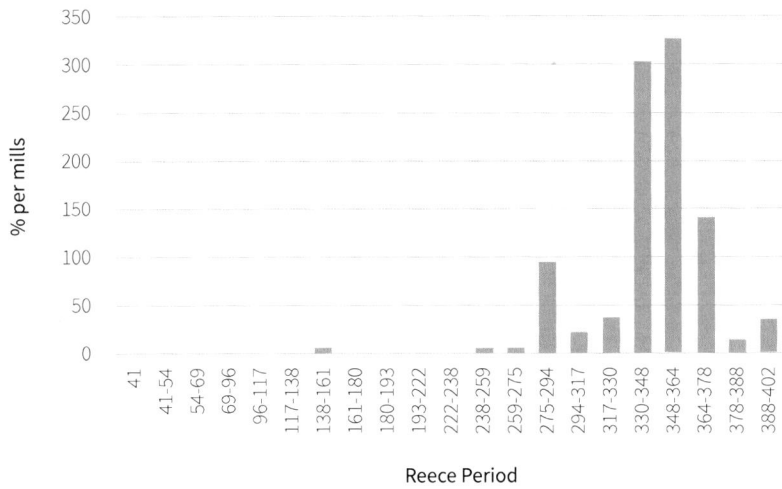

Fig. 3.1 The coins (% per mills) by Reece (1991) period.

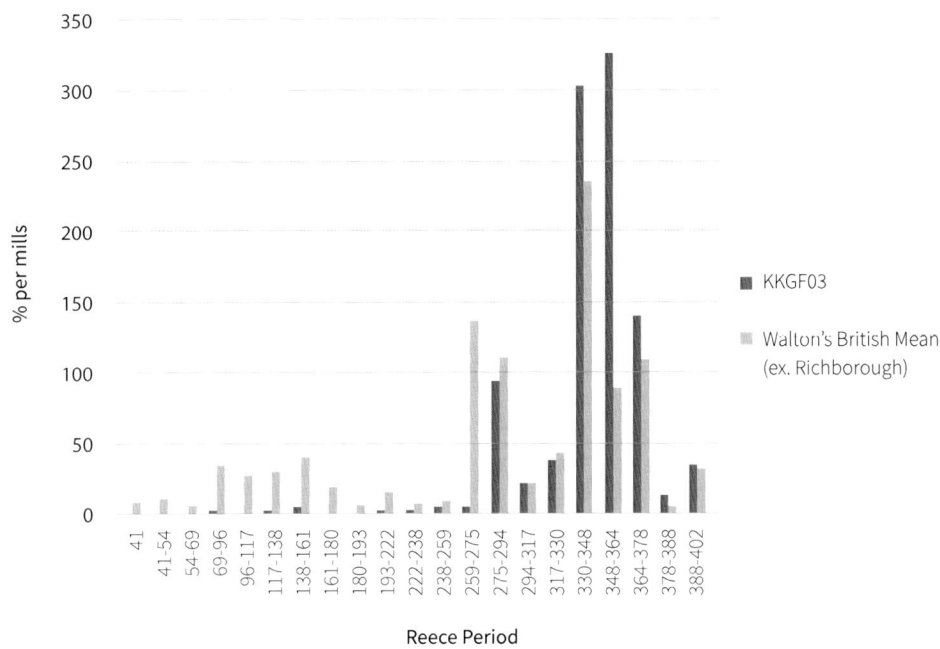

Fig. 3.2 The site finds compared with Walton's (2011, table 7) British Mean (excluding the Richborough finds).

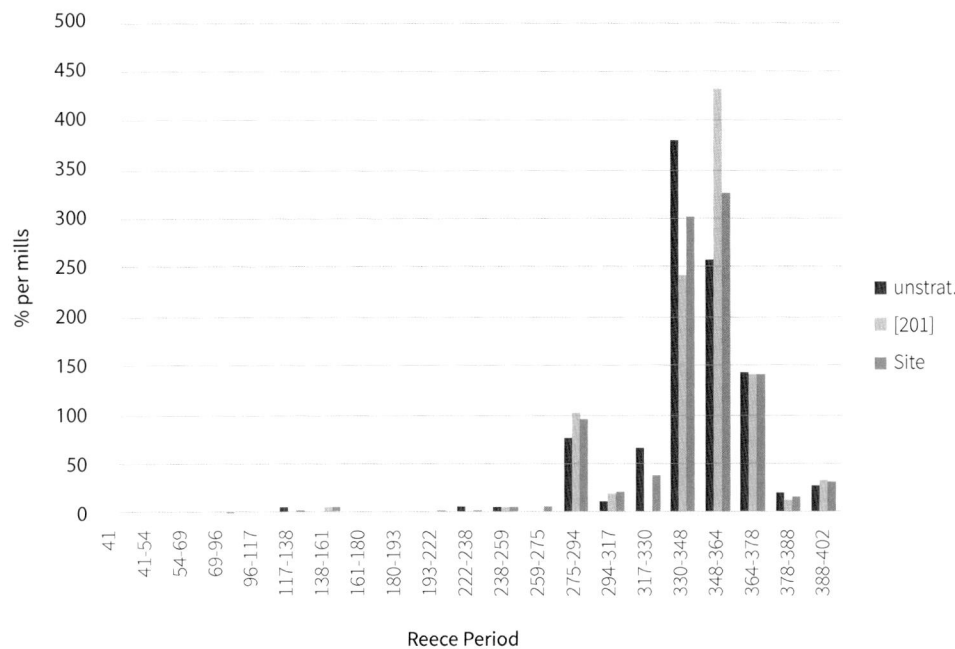

Fig. 3.3 The unstratified coins and coins from the ploughsoil (unstrat); coins from layer [201] and all the coins from the site by Reece (1991) period.

3.3 The Roman small finds

James Gerrard with contributions by Emma Gooch, Ben Howson, James Hopper, Brian McConnell and Kristine Whaley

The excavations produced a large number of small finds (281). Many of these were either unstratified or from Phase 9 layer [201] and recovered with the aid of on-site metal detectorists. The remaining finds from archaeological features and deposits are too few in number to allow a meaningful discussion by phase.

This report presents a selection of identifiable finds according to the system of functional categories first used at Colchester (Crummy 1983). This system is not without its problems, but it remains a useful way of discussing small finds assemblages. Where appropriate, reference is made to standard typologies, the Portable Antiquities Scheme (PAS) and the UK Detector Finds Database that provide useful comparanda or parallels. Nails and lead waste are excluded from this discussion but further information on these objects can be found in the site archive.

Personal adornments and dress accessories

As is typical of Romano-British sites many small finds related to personal adornment and dress were recovered.

Brooches

The excavations produced seventeen examples of complete and fragmentary copper-alloy brooches. All of them were of early Roman date and more than a third were unstratified. Four of the most complete are illustrated here (Fig. 3.4).

Necklaces (Richard Hobbs)

Fig. 3.5 <233> [205] (Phase 10 deposit within mausoleum, Building 3) Fragment of a bracelet or necklace (3.37g).

The surviving section of bracelet or necklace <233> is composed of a series of gold filigree double-loop links, the bars of which were threaded with polyhedral faceted

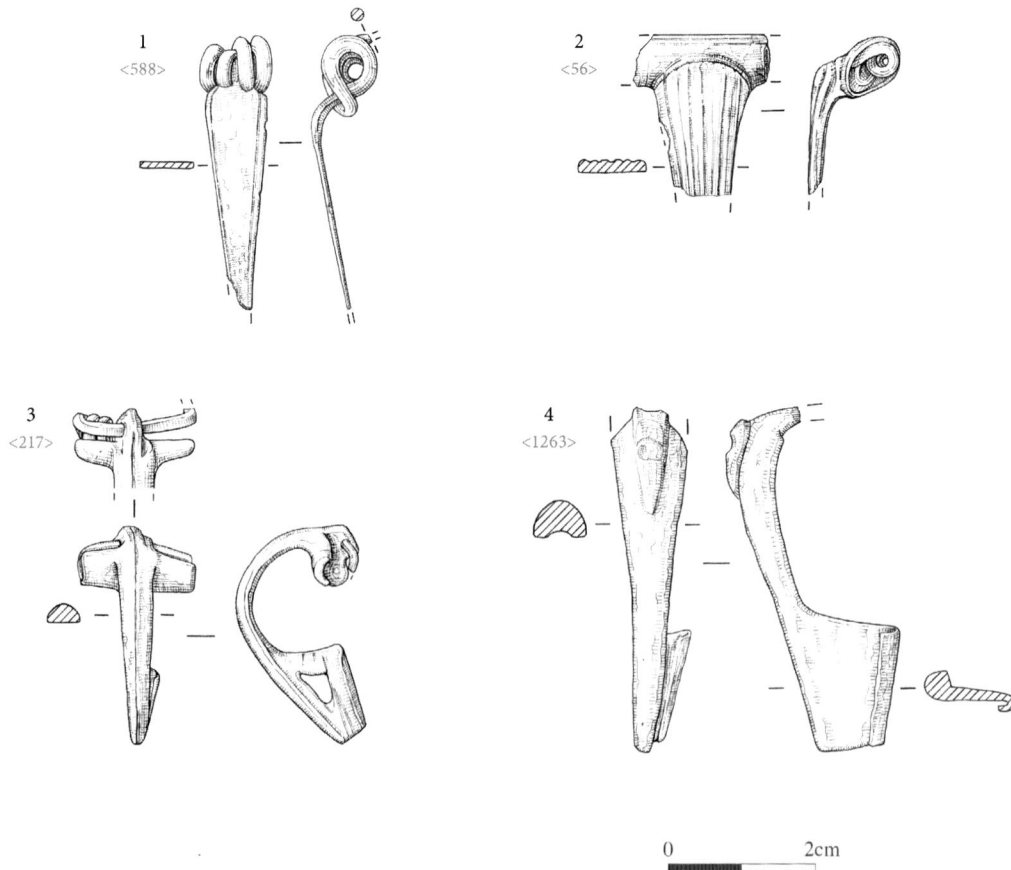

Fig. 3.4   Roman small finds: brooches (scale 1:1)
Fig. 3.4.1   <588> [201] (Phase 9) A copper-alloy Nauheim style brooch (Mackreth 2011, 14, Pl. 4 no. 3946). Late Iron Age.
Fig. 3.4.2   <56> [+] A copper-alloy Aucissa style brooch (Mackreth 2011, 132–133, Pl. 89–90). First century AD.
Fig. 3.4.3   <217> [+] A copper-alloy Colchester style brooch (Mackreth 2011, 77–78, Pl. 50). First century AD.
Fig. 3.4.4   <1263> ([1400]) (Phase 6, road deposit) A copper-alloy Colchester derivative style brooch (Mackreth 2011, Pl. 60). First to second century AD.

Fig. 3.5 Gold and variscite necklace or bracelet <233>

Fig. 3.6 Gold, garnet and emerald necklace <234>

beads of the green stone variscite (Middleton *et al.* 2007). Seven beads survive. The terminals consist of a hook and eye attachment, each of which were soldered onto the last link chain by means of a triangular plate. Both terminals survive attached to each other; one part of the chain is missing, and it is unclear exactly how long the chain was originally, although it has been suggested that this item of jewellery was a necklace turned into a bracelet for a child, other examples of which are known.

Fig. 3.6 <234> [205] (Phase 10 deposit within mausoleum, Building 3) Incomplete necklace (4.32g).

The gold, garnet and emerald necklace <234> is constructed in the same manner as <233>, although the terminal, of which only the hook part survives, has a rectangular sheet metal cover plate wrapped around it. The chain is irregularly interspersed with a series of cut stones: there are ten reddish-brown facetted garnets, two disc-shaped garnets, and three cylindrical emeralds of different

sizes. It is possible that some of the beads were added to substitute for missing originals, with the ten facetted garnets perhaps representing original stones and the other, cruder stones later replacements. There are a number of links which do not have a stone, and this would imply that the necklace had been in use for some time.

Both <233> and <234> can be paralleled with an example in a child's grave from Bonn (Sas & Thoen 2002, no. 99e) and a more elaborate necklace, nevertheless employing the same construction technique, from Pouilly-sur-Saône (Sas & Thoen 2002, no. 111). The triangular terminals on <233> are paralleled in items from Archar, Bulgaria and a find in a third-century tomb from Lyon; these have been described as stylised palmette endings (Ruxer & Kubczak 1972, 212–230: fig 30j; terminal Type E). An early to mid-third century AD date seems likely and the use of variscite perhaps suggests the necklaces were made on the continent and travelled to Britain with their owners.

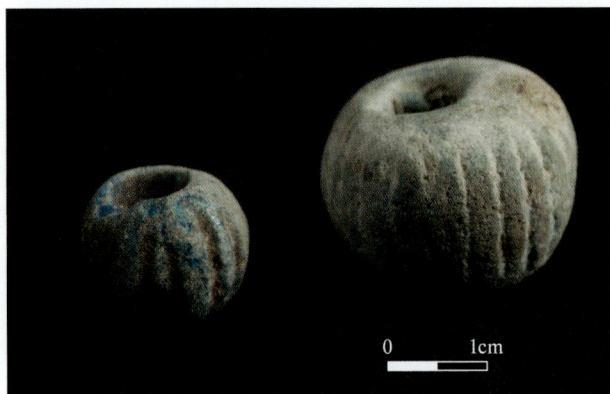

Fig. 3.7   Melon beads <1062> (left) and <1082> (right)

Fig. 3.8   Green glass bead <963>

Beads

Three glass beads were recovered: a blue frit melon bead; a green frit melon bead and a hexagonal green glass bead (Fig 3.7; Fig. 3.8). The melon beads <1062> [874] (Phase 6, Structure 1) and <1082> [908] (Phase 8, pit group 48) are typical early Roman artefacts (Guido 1978, 100) and the hexagonal glass bead <963> [770] (Phase 7, Open Area 1) is a late Roman form (Swift 2003) imitating beads manufactured from precious and semi-precious stones as seen in necklaces <233> and <234>.

Bracelets

Eighteen bracelet and bracelet fragments were recovered which include strip, cable and penannular examples (Fig. 3.9.1–Fig. 3.9.18). Interestingly, the assemblage lacks any 'toothed' or 'cogwheel' bracelets and this is somewhat unusual as the form is a relatively common one (Swift 2010). Bracelets were used as personal adornments throughout the Roman period, but they only became prevalent in the late Roman period. The earliest examples in this assemblage might be the cable twist bracelets <1217> and <545>. The remaining bracelets are all of typical late Roman form. These heavily decorated strip bracelets are known from a large number of sites and have been discussed in detail by Crummy (1983, 38–46) and Swift (2000). They are generally considered to be a female dress accessory of the second half of the fourth century and some women in Roman Britain were buried with several examples on their arms.

Fig. 3.9.1   <100> [201] (Phase 9) Fragment of strip bracelet. Rectangular section. Intricately decorated with multiple motifs: with large circles-within-circles spanning the width of the bracelet at the centre and both ends, separated from smaller circles contained within rectangular box by transverse lines (Crummy 1983, no. 1728).

Fig. 3.9.2   <228> [201] (Phase 9) Fragment of strip bracelet. Squashed cylindrical section with crudely-made eyelet. The eyelet appears to have been flattened, which has resulted in an irregular-shaped and off-centre hole.

Fig. 3.9.3   <643> [+] Fragment of strip bracelet. D-shaped and tapering section with block and hook at end. Decorated with transverse lines running the length of the bracelet until they reach the block (Allason-Jones & Miket 1984, no. 3.225; Bayley 1993, no. 4026).

Fig. 3.9.4   <738> [201] (Phase 9) Fragment of strip bracelet. Thin rectangular section. The 'head' of the bracelet is flattened and widens slightly, with an off-square eye punched through. Decoration: five bands of transverse lines, each separated by plain segments of decoration. Scratch marks are noticeable running along the length of the bracelet (Brodribb *et al.* 1968, 192).

Fig. 3.9.5   <835> [201] (Phase 9) Fragment of strip bracelet. Thin rectangular section. The 'head' widens slightly and has circular eye punched through. Multiple motif decoration: two strips of three large punched circles, separated by a diagonal strip of four smaller stamped circles. The diagonal stamp may have been aligned as such because there was no room for horizontal alignment. Following this are transverse lines, a horizontal section of nine smaller stamped circles, transverse lines and a large 'X' marked across the 'head' and eye.

Fig. 3.9.6   <947> [616] (Phase 8, trample over road) Fragment of strip bracelet. Thin rectangular section. Singular motif decoration: transverse lines set within marginal lines running along the entire length of the bracelet. (Crummy 1983, no. 1679; Bayley 1993, no. 3741).

Fig. 3.9.7   <1065> [+] Fragment of strip bracelet. D-shaped section. Decorated with bands of transverse lines separated by chevrons and plain decoration. Well-worn with evidence of cuts or nicks (Blockley *et al.* 1995, 367).

Fig. 3.9.8   <1095> [867] (Phase 8) Fragment of strip bracelet. Rectangular section. The 'head' widens and has an ovular eye punched through the centre. Decorated with faint transverse lines running along the length of the bracelet until they reach the 'head' (Allason-Jones & Miket, 1984, no. 3.225; Bayley 1993, no. 4026).

Fig. 3.9.9   <1208> ([945]) (Phase 8, fill of pit [909], Group 48) Fragment of strip bracelet. D-shaped section. Appears to be plain, although decoration, may be obscured by extensive corrosion.

Fig. 3.9.10 <58> [+] Fragment of strip bracelet. D-shaped and tapering section with hook at end. Decorated with bands of transverse lines and sections of ring and dot decoration (Brodribb *et al.*, 1968, 192).

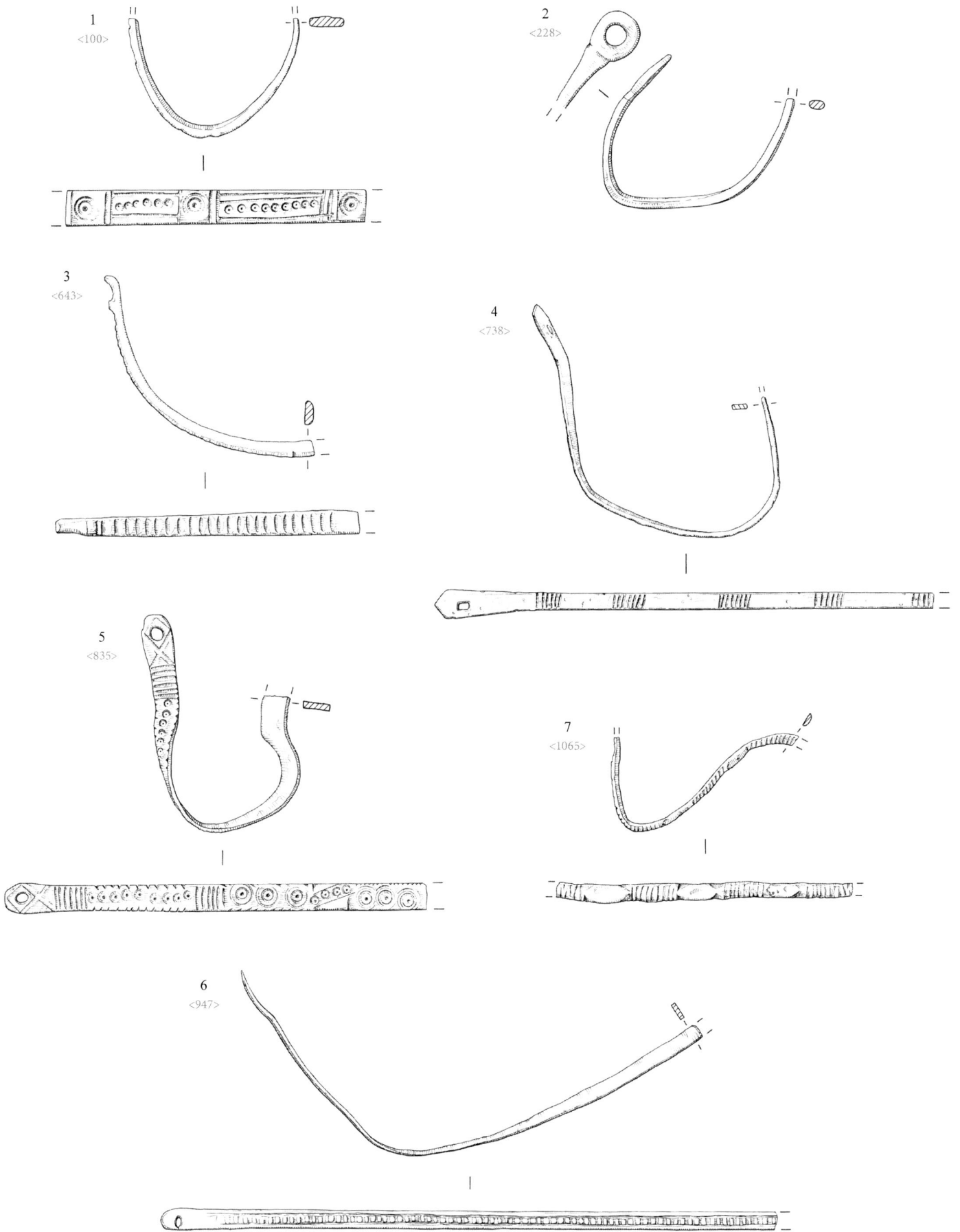

Fig. 3.9   Roman small finds: bracelets (scale 1:1)

8
<1095>

9
<1208>

10
<58>

11
<615>

12
<431>

13
<545>

14
<1217>

15
<746>

16
<1221>

17
<137>

18
<530>

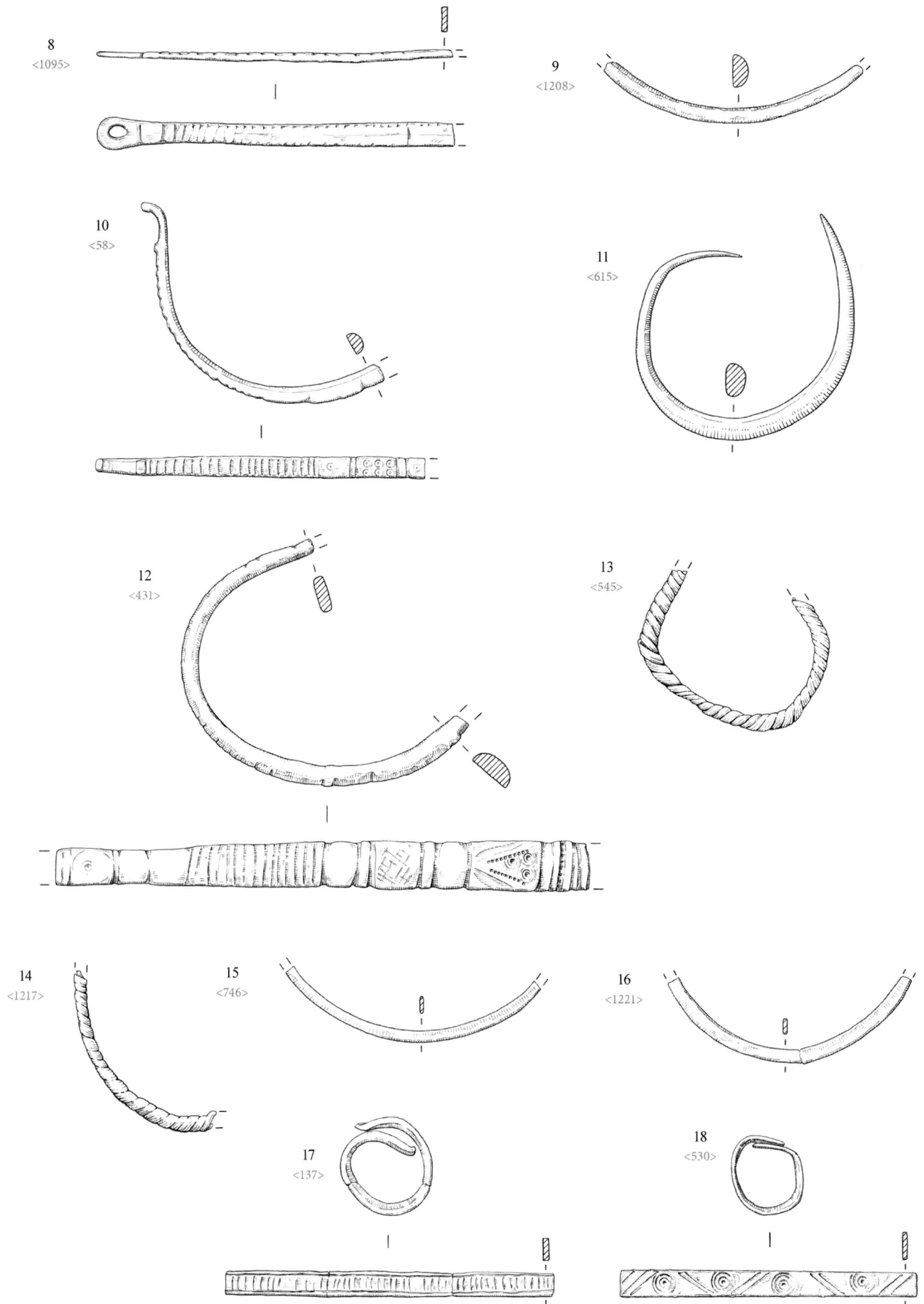

Fig. 3.9   Roman small finds: bracelets and bracelets modified as finger rings (scale 1:1)

0   2cm

Fig. 3.9.11 <615> [+] Solid cast bracelet. D-shaped section, penannular style with central swelling and tapering ends. Plain decoration (Crummy 1983, no. <1710>).

Fig. 3.9.12 <431> [201] (Phase 9) Fragment of solid cast bracelet. D-shaped and gradually tapering section, before section widens at the end quarter. Intricately decorated with multiple motifs: transverse cuts followed by three small circles contained within a triangle, followed subsequently by area of cross-hatching and transverse lines, interspersed by plain segments.

Fig. 3.9.13 <545> [201] (Phase 9) Fragment of cable bracelet. Contains three strands of copper-alloy wire twisted clockwise. Heavily corroded, though with exposed sections of cable at various angles and damaged section just above lower half (Crummy 1983, no. 1628; Bayley 1993, no. 2062).

Fig. 3.9.14 <1217> ([1016]) (Phase 8, fill of pit [909], Group 48) Fragment of cable bracelet. Contains two strands of copper-alloy wire twisted clockwise. (Crummy 1983, no. 1628; Bayley 1993, no. 2062).

Fig. 3.9.15 <746> [201] (Phase 9) Fragment of wire bracelet. Thin rectangular section. Plain decoration with slight corrosion. (Brodribb *et al.* 1968, 73; undecorated).

Fig. 3.9.16 <1221> ([1058]) (Phase 8, fill of pit [1060], Group 47) Larger fragment of wire bracelet. Thin rectangular section. Plain decoration with areas of extensive corrosion (Brodribb *et al.* 1968, 73, undecorated).

Bracelet fragments modified as finger-rings

Two of the eighteen bracelets discussed above were fragments that were modified to make finger-rings (Fig. 3.9.17–18). This is a phenomenon that has been recently studied by Swift (2012). She has argued that this modification only occurs very late in the Roman period (after AD 370) and these 'finger-rings' were found in fifth-century contexts and early Anglo-Saxon graves. Therefore, these two objects must be set alongside the late Roman belt-fittings (below), the early Anglo-Saxon spears (Allison *et al.* this volume) and the early Anglo-Saxon brooch (Gaimster, this volume) as evidence of fifth-century activity.

Fig. 3.9.17 <137> [201] (Phase 9) Two fragments of a finger-ring produced from a recycled strip-bracelet. Rectangular section. Decorated with transverse lines set within marginal lines (Crummy 1983, no. 1679; Bayley 1993, no. 3741).

Fig. 3.9.18 <530> [201] (Phase 9) Finger-ring, likely to have been produced from a recycled strip bracelet. Rectangular section. B15 decoration: large stamped circles interspersed by diagonal transverse lines.

A shoe

Fifty-nine iron hobnails <1287> [866] (Phase 7, Fill of ditch [516], Enclosure 10) were found in close association and are clearly the remnants of a leather shoe.

Hairpins

There were sixteen bone hairpins, or fragments of bone hairpins, and two fragments of copper-alloy hairpin present in the assemblage. All of them are typical Roman forms well-paralleled in existing typological schemes (Crummy 1979, 1983, 20–25; Greep 1995).

Fig. 3.10.1 <1056> [874] (Phase 6, Structure 1) Bone hairpin of Crummy's (1983) Type 1.

Fig. 3.10.2 <915> [719] (Phase 7, road) Bone hairpin of Crummy's (1983) Type 3.

Fig. 3.10.3 <986> ([800]) (Phase 5, fill of pit [801], Group 13) Bone hairpin of Crummy's (1983) Type 2. Stained green.

Fig. 3.10.4 <995> [770] (Phase 7, Open Area 1) Bone hairpin of Crummy's (1983) Type 3.

Fig. 3.10.5 <1210> [770] (Phase 7, Open Area 1) Bone hairpin of Crummy's (1983) Type 3.

Fig. 3.10.6 <902> ([670]) (Phase 8, fill of pit [671], group 46) Copper-alloy hairpin with a decorated knob head. A good match for Cool's (1990) Group 12 (although the incised decoration is a little different), which have a North Kent distribution (Cool 1990: fig 16).

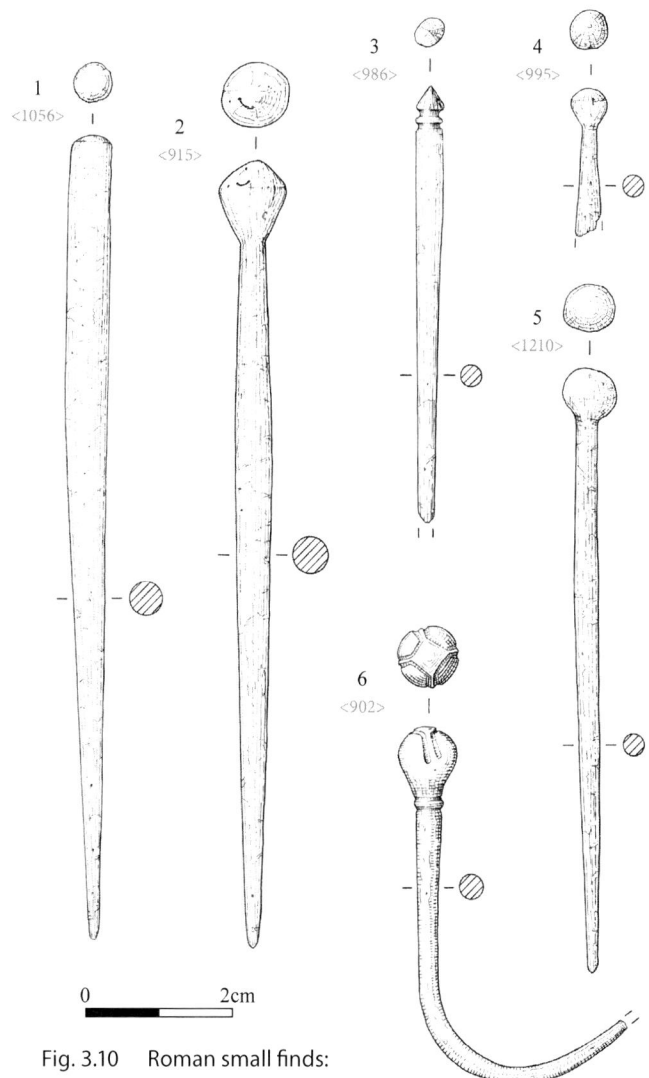

Fig. 3.10   Roman small finds: hairpins (scale 1:1)

Toilet instruments

Toilet instruments were poorly represented with only a single copper-alloy toilet spoon recovered (Crummy 1983, no. 1897); <1067> [845] (Phase 7, Open Area 2) (not illustrated).

Textile working equipment

Very little textile working equipment was recovered. The absence of spindle whorls is particularly noticeable.

Fig. 3.11.1   <1013> [770] (Phase 7, Open Area 1)   Bone needle of Crummy's (1983) Type 1.

Fig. 3.11.2   <1214> [874] (Phase 6, Structure 1) Bone needle of Crummy's (1983) Type 1. Stained green.

Fig. 3.11.3   <592> [201] (Phase 9) Copper-alloy needle (Crummy 1983, no. 1991).

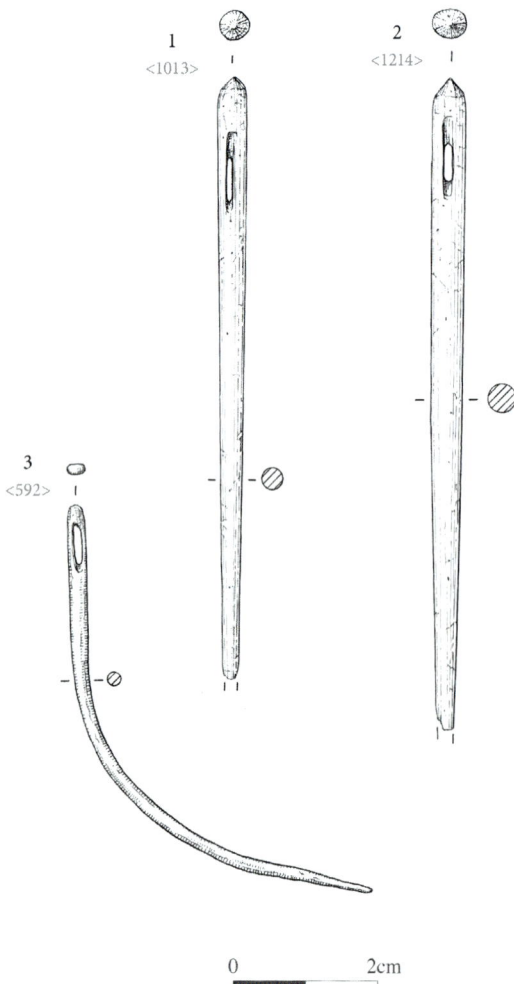

Fig. 3.11   Roman small finds: textile working equipment (scale 1:1)

Household utensils and furniture

Fig. 3.12   <896> [643] (Phase 4, fill of [645], Enclosure 4)   A copper-alloy cast bull's-head finial.

The bucranium <896>, modelled in the round, is strikingly naturalistic. The horns are crescentic and clearly intended to be phallic. The ears are forward-facing, the eyes bulbous and the muzzle and nose are indicated by a horizontal and vertical line. The reverse of the head has a small, round socket clearly intended to take a fitting. At the base of the head is a 'skirt'. The bottom of the finial is obscured by iron corrosion, which seemingly obscures an iron rod or bar that fits into the base of the bull's head.

The function of this object is something of a mystery. It is possible that it served as a terret. There are some skirted terrets that might at a stretch be considered zoomorphic and bovine (eg PAS: SUSS-924F27 and WMID-68FFB4) but out of the 800 terrets on the PAS database none are modelled naturalistically like the present example, which in any case lacks a lower loop. The next obvious interpretation is that the object was an escutcheon or bucket-mount. The hole on the reverse might support such an interpretation and bovid bucket-mounts are relatively common (PAS: GLO-63AEF2) (Hawkes 1951, 177–178; Megaw & Megaw 1989, 220). Nevertheless, the apparent need for an iron fitting in the base of the item and the 'skirt', appear to preclude this function. The best suggestion for this bovid mount's function is that it served as a finial at the top of a firedog. Firedogs were often decorated with bovid imagery (Piggott 1971, 245) and there is a broad parallel offered by a bovid Iron Age firedog from North Yorkshire (NCL-51AB07).

Whatever the true function of this object it is an impressive piece of early Romano-British workmanship and the bull with its phallic horns was a potent symbol (for instance Jackson 2010; Worrell & Pearce 2014, 408).

Fig. 3.12   Cast copper-alloy bull's head finial <896>

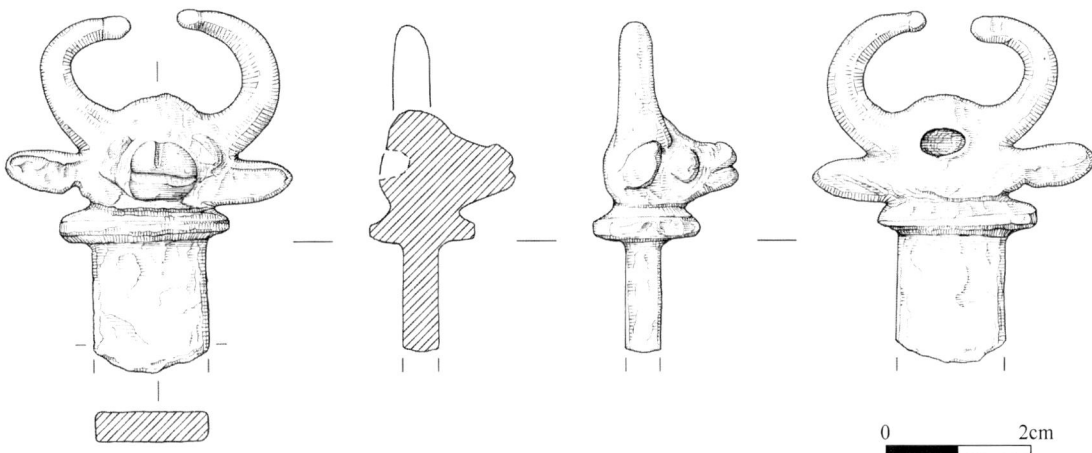

Fig. 3.13   Cast copper-alloy bull's head finial <896> (scale 1:1)

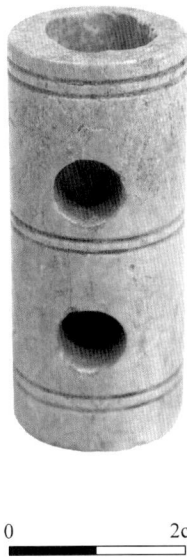

Fig. 3.14   Roman small finds: household utensils and furniture; bone hinge <1226>

Fig. 3.14 <1226> [874] (Phase 6, Structure 1) Bone hinge (Friendship Taylor & Greep 2012) Two holes 7mm in diameter have been drilled through one wall. Six transverse grooves have been incised, grouped in pairs, on either side and in between the drilled holes.

Fig. 3.15.1 <1045> ([827]) (Phase 8, fill of [828], pit group 46) An iron box-fitting (Crummy 1983, no. 2202).

Fig. 3.15.2 <979> [770] (Phase 7, Open Area 1) Iron bucket-mount (Wilmott 1991: fig 85.392).

Fig. 3.15.3 <237> [201] (Phase 9) Possibly part of an iron flesh-hook. The teeth, which should be longer and hooked, are damaged (Manning 1985, 105).

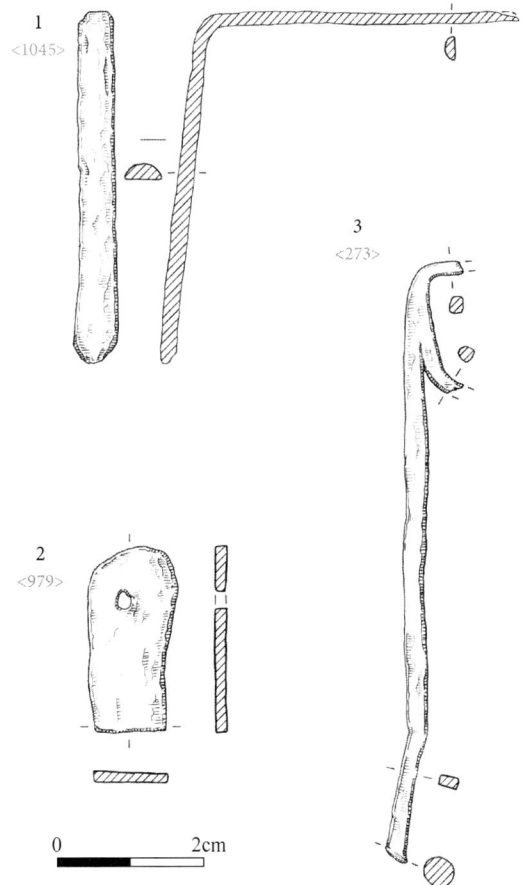

Fig. 3.15   Roman small finds: household utensils and furniture (scale 1:1)

Recreational items

Fig. 3.16   <247> [200] (Phase 11, ploughsoil) A fragment of a copper-alloy dodecahedron (Allason-Jones & Miket 1984, 218).

Rather surprisingly the only recreational object was a fragment from a copper-alloy dodecahedron. These items are sometimes considered to be gaming pieces, but their real function is unknown. The absence of counters (made from bone or pottery) is noticeable.

The function of dodecahedrons such as <247> is a mystery, with candle holders, surveying instruments and gaming pieces all being suggested at one time or another (Allason-Jones 2002, 215; 2011, 241). Compare Fig. 3.17 (Hinds 2018).

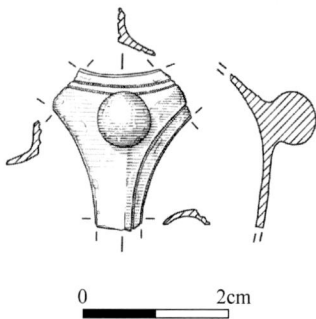

Fig. 3.16   Roman small finds: recreational items; <247> (scale 1:1)

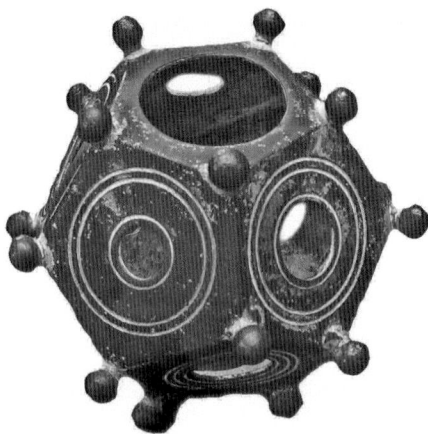

Fig. 3.17   Complete cast copper-alloy dodecahedron (Wikimedia commons: https://commons.wikimedia.org/w/index.php?curid=11691999)

Weights and measures

Four lead weights were recovered. A biconical example with iron suspension loop <27> [+] weighed 132g (Fig. 3.18); a globular example <105> [201] (Phase 9) weighed 63g (Fig. 3.19); a pear-shaped weight <245> [200] (Phase 11, ploughsoil) weighed 22g (Fig. 3.20) and a ball-shaped weight with iron suspension loop <260> [201] (Phase 9) weighed 82g (Fig. 3.21). These are all common Roman forms (Greep 1987, 188–189) but do not easily fit divisions of the standard Roman pound (usually argued to be 327g) (Maher & Makowski 2001).

Fig. 3.18   Biconical lead weight with iron suspension loop <27>

Fig. 3.19   Globular lead weight <105>

Fig. 3.20   Pear-shaped lead weight <245>

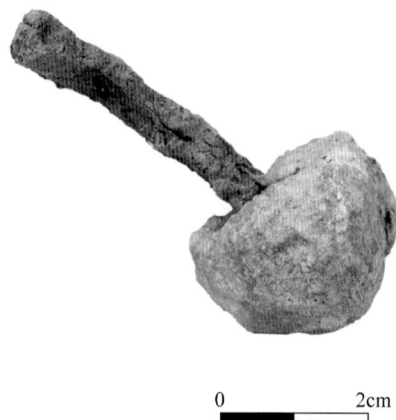

Fig. 3.21   Ball shaped weight with iron suspension loop <260>

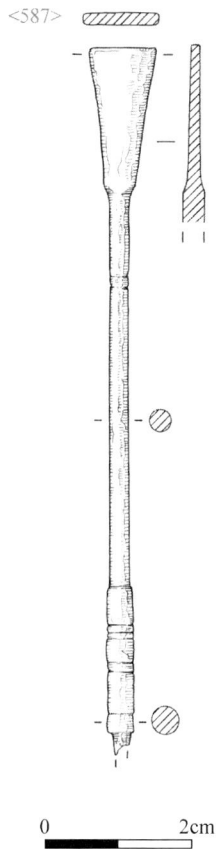

Fig. 3.22   Roman small finds: evidence for literacy (scale 1:1)

Evidence for literacy

Fig. 3.22   <587> [201] (Phase 9) Probably a corroded iron stylus.

The only evidence in the small finds assemblage for literacy was a single iron stylus, <587> [201] (Phase 11) (Manning 1985: fig 24). Graffiti on the pottery provide firmer evidence of the use of writing by the site's inhabitants (Gerrard & Hudak this volume).

Transportation

Transportation is represented by four objects. The iron linch-pin, fragment of iron hipposandal (unillustrated) and cheekpiece from a curb-bit are all definitely associated with carts and horses. The final object is a yoke ring and thus associated with the harnessing needed to pull a cart.

Fig. 3.23.1 <417> [296] (Phase 5, fill of ditch [223], Enclosure 5) Iron linch-pin with spatulate head (Manning 1985, Type 2b).

Fig. 3.23.2 <433> [201] (Phase 9) Iron trilobate cheekpiece from a curb-bit (Manning 1985, 68 and H18).

Fig. 3.23.3 <1046> [845] (Phase 7, Open Area 2) An iron yoke ring or skirted terret (Benes 2018, Obr. 11). These fittings are more commonly manufactured from copper alloy.

Fig. 3.23.4 <1001> [770] (Phase 7, Open Area 1) An iron nail, missing its head. The shaft of the nail has been driven over at a right angle and the tip driven back to 'clench' a plank. The nail is approximately 140mm long. The form of clenching and length makes this object comparable with the clenched boat-nails from the Barlands Farm vessel (Nayling & McGrail 2004, 154–155).

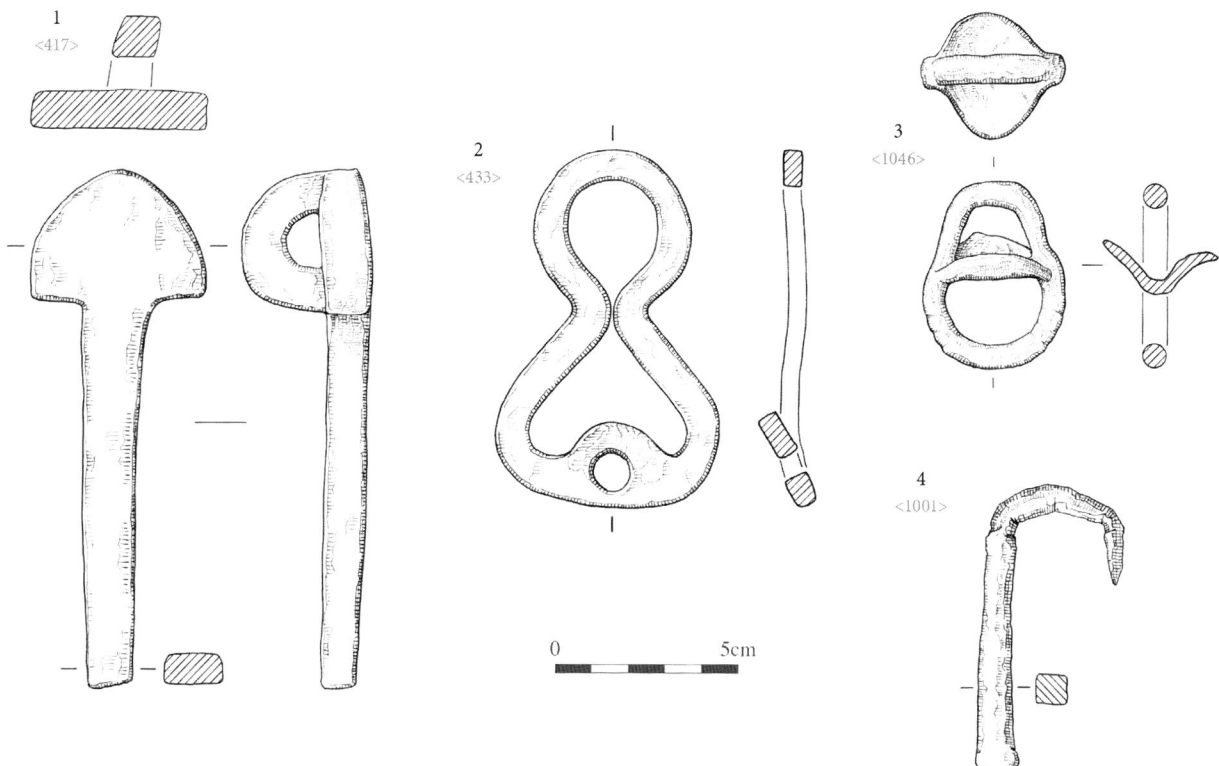

Fig. 3.23   Roman small finds: transportation (scale 1:2)

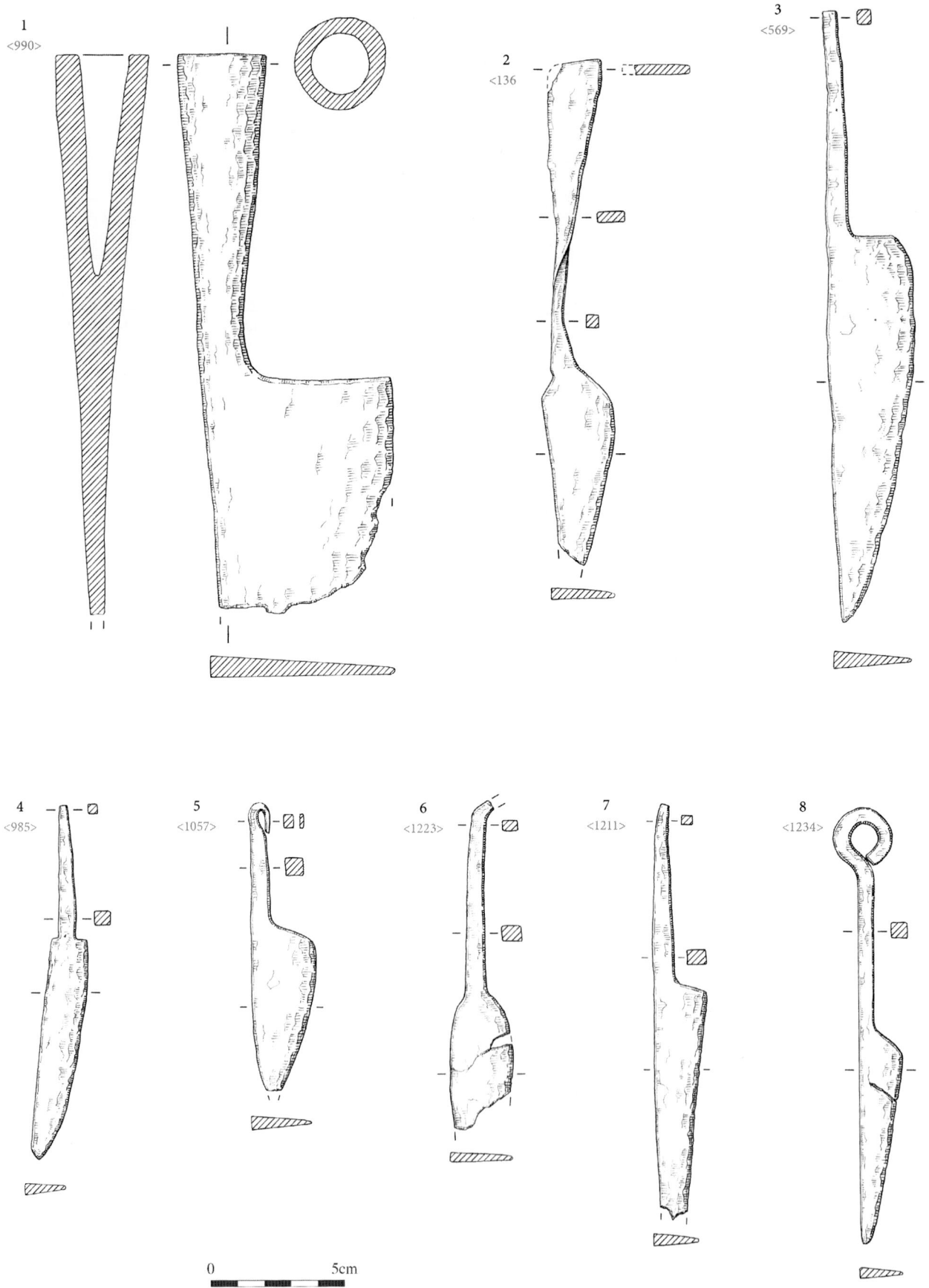

Fig. 3.24   Roman small finds: tools; knives and cleavers (scale 1:2)

Tools

The excavations produced a surprisingly large number of tools. The majority of these items were iron knives, cleavers and fragmentary blades. Knives and their ilk are not uncommon on Romano-British rural sites but the sheer number (22) is of interest. Unfortunately, knives are such a generic object that it is impossible to determine what activity or activities these cutting implements relate to.

There were also five ferrules, which are pointed iron sheaths used to protect the bottom of staffs. These are everyday objects and might have been applied to any number of tools.

An axe and a paring-chisel blade are suggestive of woodworking. The tool assemblage also includes an out of the ordinary object: a pick of unusual form. Picks are occasional finds in Roman Britain, especially in ironwork hoards and special deposits. Nevertheless, this pick is of unusual form. Its recovery from road surface [1338] suggests that it might have been used to mine flint nodules and become incorporated into the raw material for the road metalling.

Knives and Cleavers

The iron objects included two cleavers, nine knives and eleven fragments of blade.

Fig. 3.24.1 <990> [770] (Phase 7, Open Area 1) A heavy iron cleaver of Manning's (1985) Type 2. Incomplete.

Fig. 3.24.2 <136> [201] (Phase 9) Unusual knife or razor not easily paralleled in Manning's (1985) typology.

Fig. 3.24.3 <569> [201] (Phase 9) Iron knife of Manning's (1985) Type 11.

Fig. 3.24.4 <985> [694] (Phase 7, Open Area 1) Small iron knife of Manning's (1985) Type 16.

Fig. 3.24.5 <1057> [874] (Phase 6, Structure 1) Small iron knife of Manning's (1985) Type 11

Fig. 3.24.6 <1223> ([1058]) (Phase 8, fill of [1060], Group 47) Iron knife of Manning's (1985) Type 16.

Fig. 3.24.7 <1211> [770] (Phase 7, Open Area 1) Iron knife of Manning's (1985) Type 11.

Fig. 3.24.8 <1234> [874] (Phase 6, Structure 1) Iron knife of Manning's Type 11, with a suspension loop at the end of the tang.

Ferrules

Fig. 3.25.1 <1064> [902] (Phase 6, Structure 1) Iron ferrule (Manning 1985, 140–141).

Fig. 3.25.2 <1244> ([1218]) (Phase 7, Open Area 2) Iron ferrule (Manning 1985, 140–141).

The pick

Fig. 3.25.3 <544> [1338] (Phase 6, Road) Iron pick. This form is not paralleled in Manning's catalogues (1976; 1985) but implements approaching this form are known from mines in Baetica (Shepherd 1993, fig 3) and quarries in Dacia (Wollman 1996, Pl. LXXI and CIV).

Paring chisel

Fig. 3.25.4 <869> [462] Phase 9 A small iron paring-chisel blade (Frere 1972, 164: fig 62.11). The blade is strongly splayed with a slightly curved edge. The object appears to be complete with a damaged butt end with corrosion obscuring some detail.

Axe

Fig. 3.25.5 <480> [201] (Phase 9) A small iron axe-head of Manning's (1985) Type 3. Small axes of late Roman date have recently been discussed by Booth (2014, 261–262) in the context of late-fourth- and fifth-century weapon graves.

Fasteners and fittings

As is typical of Romano-British sites the assemblage includes a large number of fasteners and fittings. There are considerable numbers of nails (Manning 1985, 134–137) and a wide variety of typical structural ironwork, which might have a variety of uses. Wallhooks, rings, chain links and double-spiked loops are all well-represented and a selection are illustrated here. Of greater interest is a small group of security fittings: two latch-lifters and a lift-key. They are joined by a number of hinges suitable for hanging doors. This indication of structures is, of course, confirmed by the stratigraphic evidence. However, the finds provide evidence of access to some structures being restricted and controlled.

Fig. 3.26 <432> [201] (Phase 9) Copper-alloy stud with enamel inlay. A seven pointed 'star' divides the surface into a central roundel of white inlay and seven triangles of white and blue enamel (Crummy 1983, nos. 3217–3221).

Fig. 3.27 <945> [694] (Phase 7, Open Area 1) Copper-alloy stud with a convex head (Crummy 1983, no. 3173).

Fig. 3.28 <962> [770] (Phase 7, Open Area 1) Copper-alloy nail with a flat head (Crummy 1983, nos. 3057–3073).

Fig. 3.29.1 <1058> [874] (Phase 6, Structure 1) Iron double-spiked loop (Manning 1985, 130–131).

Fig. 3.29.2 <1334> [419] (Phase 8, fill of pit [420], Group 46) An iron joiner's dog (Mannning 1985, 131).

Fig. 3.29.3 <591> [201] (Phase 9) Iron double-spiked loop and ring.

Fig. 3.29.4 <1043> ([802]) (Phase 5, fill of pit [801], Group 23) An iron ring. Items such as these performed a variety of functions.

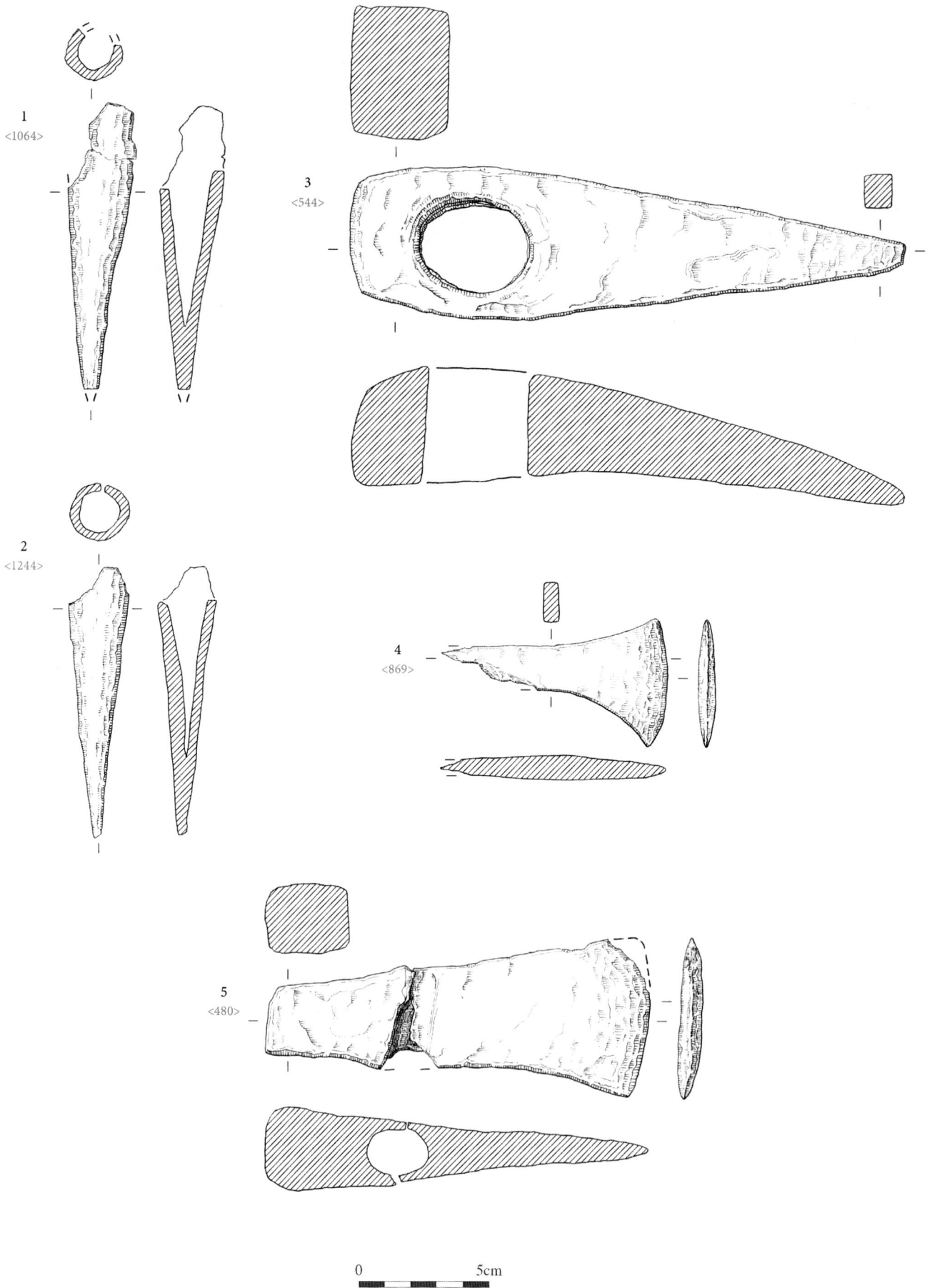

Fig. 3.25   Roman small finds: ferrules, pick, paring chisel and axe (scale 1:2)

Fig. 3.26   Copper-alloy stud <432> with enamel inlay

Fig. 3.27   Copper-alloy stud with a convex head <945>

Fig. 3.28   Copper-alloy nail with a flat head <962>

Security fittings and door furniture

Fig. 3.29.5 <528> [+] Iron loop-hinge (Manning 1985, 126).

Fig. 3.29.6 <533> [201] (Phase 9) Iron loop-hinge (Manning 1985, 126).

Fig. 3.29.7 <567> [201] (Phase 9) Iron loop-hinge (Manning 1985, 126).

Fig. 3.29.8 <989> [770] (Phase 7, Open Area 1) Iron loop-hinge (Manning 1985, 126).

Fig. 3.29.9 <1233> ([1130]) (Phase 6, Fill of pit [1131], Group 59) Iron drop-hinge (Manning 1985, 126).

Fig. 3.29.10 <1007> ([800]) (Phase 5, fill of pit [1131], Group 13) Iron latch-lifter (Manning 1985, 88–89).

Fig. 3.29.11 <1212> [770] (Phase 7, Open Area 1) Iron binding (Manning 1985, 88–89).

Fig. 3.29.12 <961> [770] (Phase 7, Open Area 1) Iron L-shaped lift-key with a suspension loop (Manning 1985, 90–92).

Agriculture, horticulture and animal husbandry

The small finds assemblage includes four so-called 'pruning-hooks'. The name suggests that these tools were used primarily for pruning, but Manning (1985, 56–57) suggests that they were probably a multipurpose tool. They are not uncommon, but it is a little unusual to identify four of these artefacts.

Fig. 3.30.1 <1059> [874] (Phase 6, Structure 1) Small iron pruning-hook (Manning 1985, 56–57).

Fig. 3.30.2 <565> [449] (Phase 9 layer) Small iron pruning-hook (Manning 1985, 56–57).

Fig. 3.30.3 <726> [201] (Phase 9) Small iron pruning-hook (Manning 1985, 56–57).

Fig. 3.30.4 <1012> [770] (Phase 7, Open Area 1) Small iron pruning-hook (Manning 1985, 56–57).

Military equipment

The assemblage contains a small number of items that might be considered 'military equipment'. These objects are not unequivocal evidence of a military presence at the site. Military items could enter civilian life through a number of different mechanisms; the bolt/arrowhead could have been used for hunting and the belt-fittings might be indicators of status and position as much as membership of a late Roman military unit (Gerrard 2013, 152–153).

Belt-plates such as <1094> were important symbols of 'military' or 'official' status in the late fourth-century West. Distributional studies have shown that the majority of these belt-sets come from sites along the Rhine-Danube frontier. They are relatively rare in Britain with most finds coming from the South-East and are probably of continental manufacture.

There are a number of parallels for the particular decorative arrangement exhibited on this fragment. A find from Alfriston in Sussex (Böhme 1986, fig 2) bears some similarities but a grave-good from Guer (Morbihan), France (Böhme 1974, 317–318 and Taf. 124.12) is probably closest. This grave also contained a coin of Valens dated AD 364–378. Böhme (1986) dates this type of belt-plate to the second half of the fourth century but there seems no compelling reason to think that it must have been lost before AD 400. The general form went on to influence the fifth-century Quoit Brooch Style belt set from Mucking (Gerrard 2013, 199–200) and this particular fragment was found in association with coins of the House of Valentinian and Theodosius and related stratigraphically to a number of contexts containing very late Roman pottery.

1
<1058>

2
<1334>

3
<591>

4
<1043>

5
<528>

6
<533>

7
<567>

8
<989>

9
<123>

10
<1007>

11
<1212>

12
<961>

0   5cm

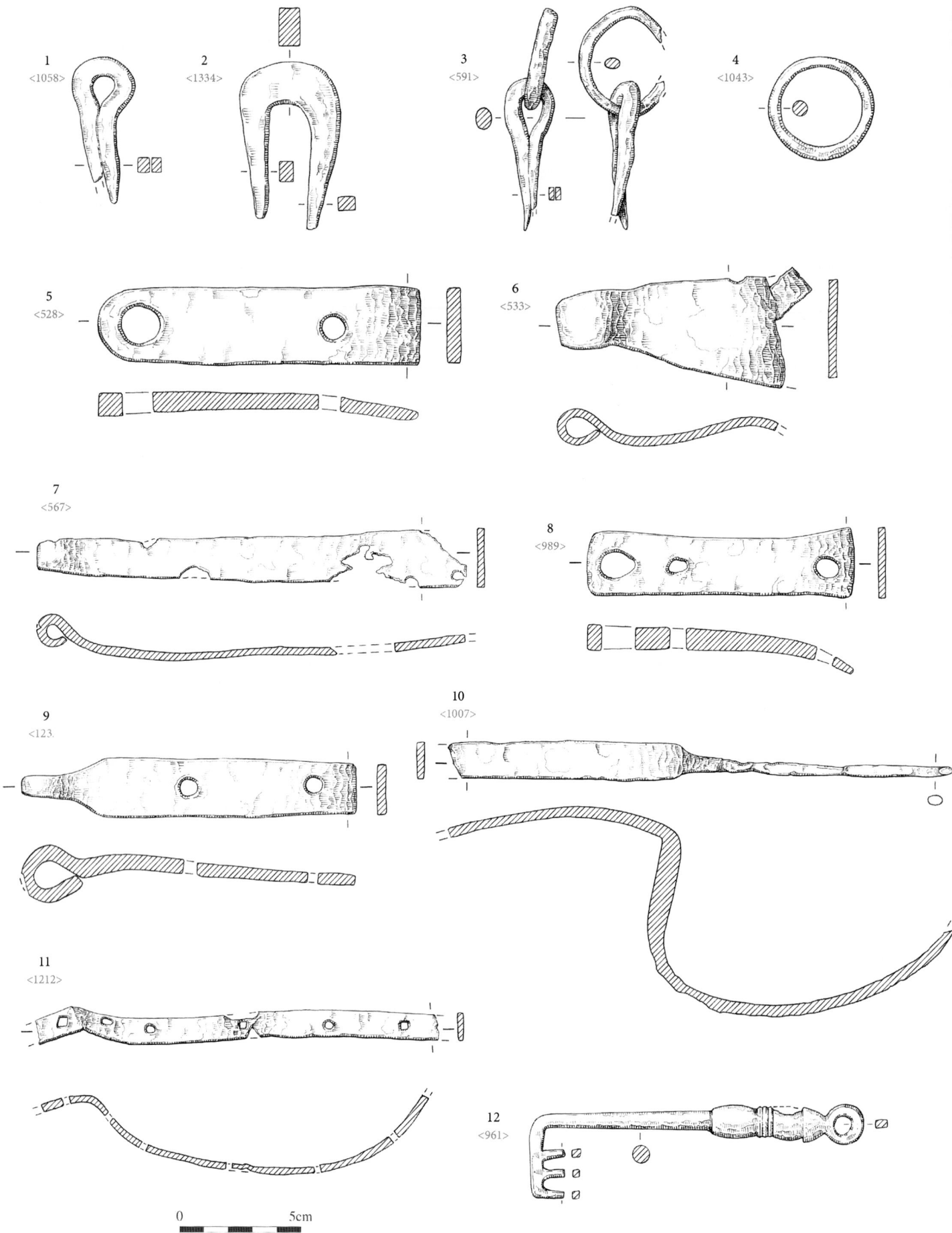

Fig. 3.29   Roman small finds: fasteners and fittings, security fittings and door furniture (scale 1:2)

Both fragments of copper alloy buckle <1075> and <532> can be classed as elements of Hawkes and Dunning (1961) Type IIA buckles, which are usually dated to the second half of the fourth century and there is clear evidence for their manufacture in Britain (Paddock 1998). Much like the chip-carved example discussed above this type of buckle is one that could quite easily have been in use during the decades either side of AD 400.

Fig. 3.31.1 <449> [410] (Phase 8, fill of pit [411], Group 46) A small leaf-shaped and socketed bolt- or arrowhead. Manning (1985, 177) illustrates a number of tanged arrowheads. The socketed examples (Manning 1985, v254) he classifies as small bolt-heads.

Fig. 3.31.2 <1047> [845] (Phase 7, Open Area 2) A copper-alloy belt-mount or stiffener in the form of two peltae joined by an openwork rectangle. There are two integral rivets on the reverse at either end. Similar objects are discussed by Mills (2000, 74 and fig: RB214) and considered to be of third-century date and military issue.

Fig. 3.31.3 <1094> [867] (Phase 8, layer associated with pit group 44 in Enclosure 8) A fragment from a copper-alloy 'chip-carved' belt-plate decorated with a central rosette of four peltae (or double spirals) set within a circle.

Fig. 3.31.4–Fig. 3.27.5 <1075> [908] (Phase 8, fill of pit [909], Group 48) and <532> [201] (Phase 9) Two fragments of openwork copper-alloy belt-buckles.

Fig. 3.31.6 <1073> [908] (Phase 8, fill of pit [909], Group 48) Copper-alloy ring. Rings such as these occasionally formed parts of late Roman belt-sets (Hawkes & Dunning 1968, fig 24). Two further examples <1093> [867] (Phase 8, layer associated with pit group 44) and <229> [201] (Phase 9) were identified.

Religious beliefs

No items with demonstrable religious or cult functions were identified.

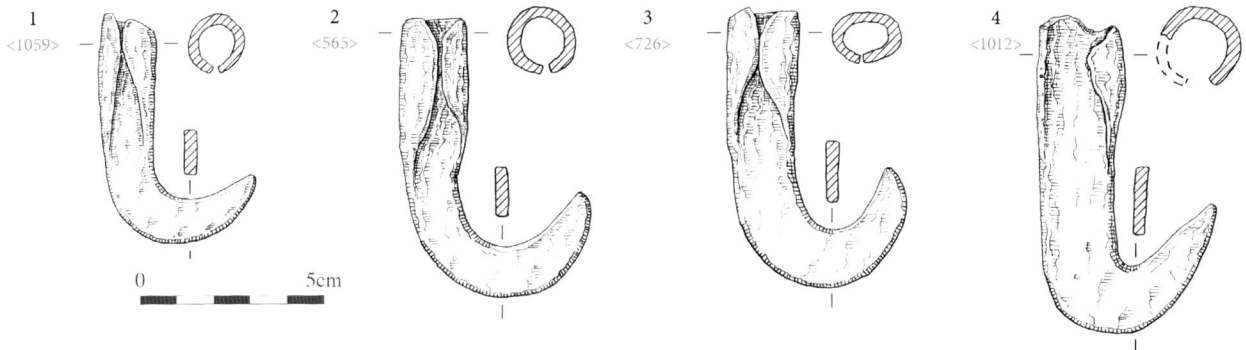

Fig. 3.30   Roman small finds: agriculture, horticulture and animal husbandry; 'pruning hooks' (scale 1:2)

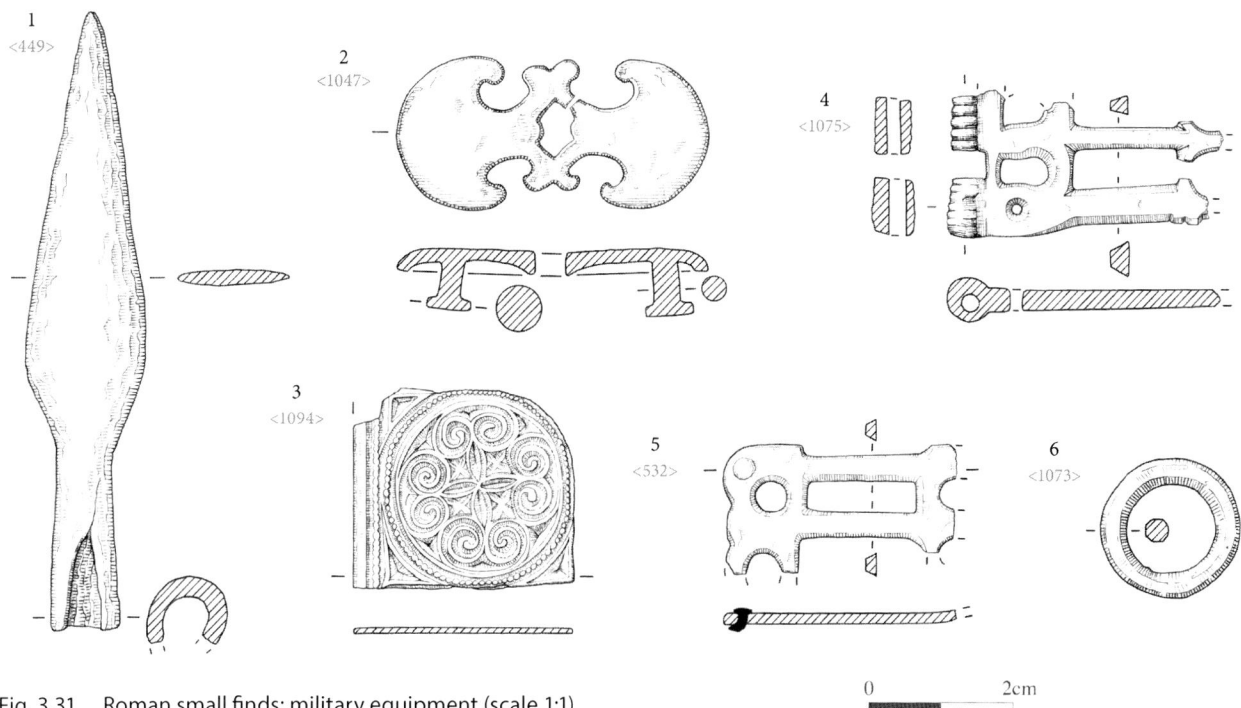

Fig. 3.31   Roman small finds: military equipment (scale 1:1)

Metalworking waste

The slag and litharge assemblages provide important evidence of metalworking and are considered by other specialists below (Keys, this volume; Dungworth, this volume). Evidence from the small finds for metalworking is equivocal. For non-ferrous metalworking there is the usual lead waste typical of any Romano-British site and points to the low-temperature working of lead. There are also two copper-alloy objects – a small bar <648> [+] and a beaten piece of copper-alloy with a central groove and bevelled edges as if strips had been cut from each side <662> [201] which may suggest that bronze was also worked at the site.

Evidence for ferrous metalworking is more difficult. Keys (this volume) identified many small fragments of iron (quantified apart from the main assemblage in Table 3.4) from deposits containing slag as potentially 'blanks used by smiths to make objects [or] wasters from the smithing process'. This is possible, although it has to be said that the material is poorly preserved, amorphous and lacking in form. Much of it can be described as thin fragments of sheet but the material does include two nails, a broken piece of an iron link from a chain and a swivel-hook. In general terms the assemblage looks like scrap and there are no obvious blanks for the manufacture of objects (Fig. 3.32).

Table 3.4   *Quantification of amorphous iron sheet and other objects from contexts containing large quantities of ferrous slag.*

Context	SF	Phase		No. of Fe objects
[770]	<1323>	7	Open Area 1	32
[770]	<1324>	7	Open Area 1	5
[770]	<1325>	7	Open Area 1	8
[770]	<1322>	7	Open Area 1	68
[770]	<1321>	7	Open Area 1	22
[770]	<1326>	7	Open Area 1	1
[616]	<1317>	8	Trample over road	4
[694]	<1319>	7	Open Area 1	16
[694]	<1280>	7	Open Area 1	5
[537]	<1315>	9	Group 49	43

Evidence of horn and boneworking

Three fragments of worked antler were recovered. Two pieces were recovered from Phase 9 [201] and one fragment from Phase 8 [1019], fill of pit [1020] in Group 44.

Objects of unknown function

A large number of objects of unknown function were identified. Many of these were too poorly preserved for any reasonable attempt at identification to be made. With others it is simply impossible to determine what their function may have been.

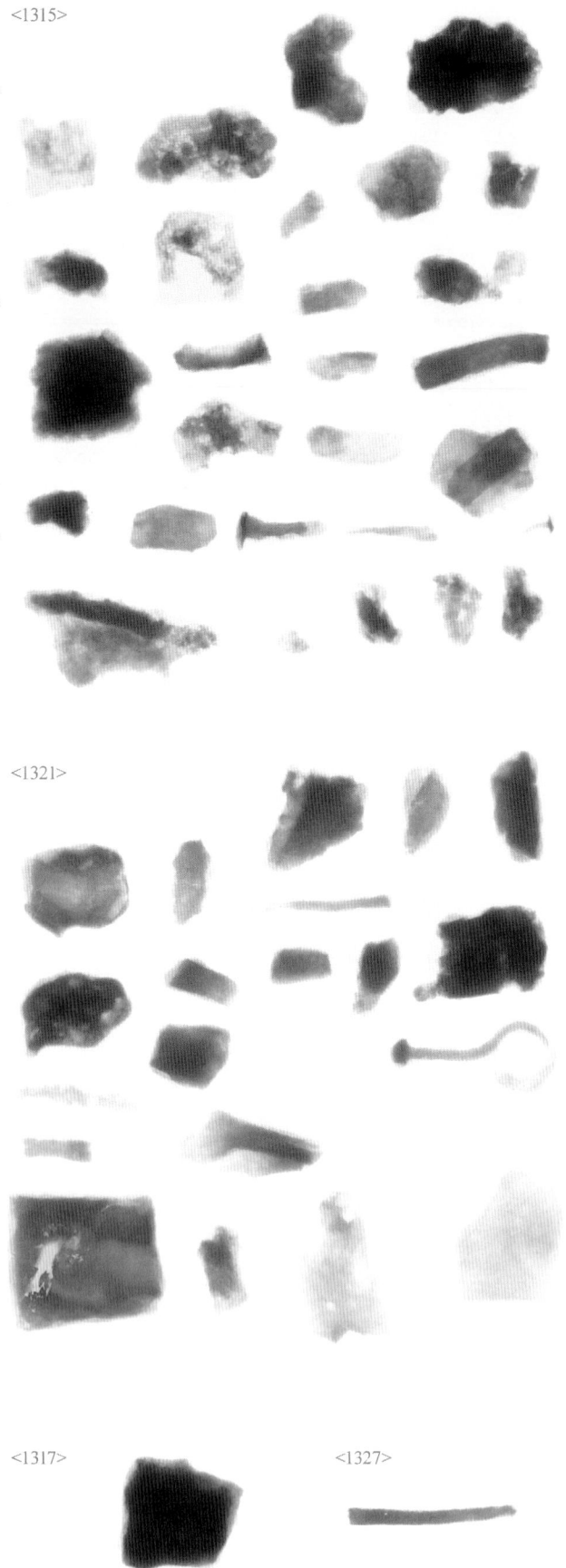

<1315>

<1321>

<1317>   <1327>

Fig. 3.32   Inverted x-rays of a selection of items of metalworking waste

<1022>

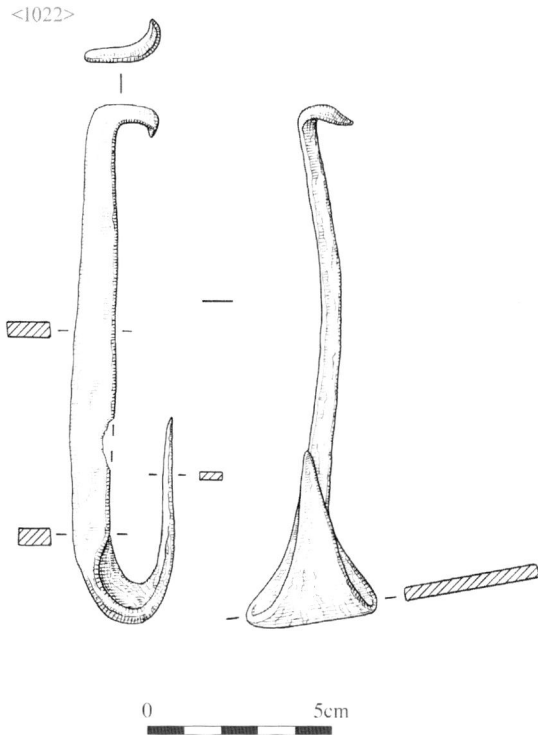

Fig. 3.33   Roman small finds: objects of unknown function (scale 1:2)

Fig. 3.33 <1022> [770] (Phase 7, Open Area 1) A rectangular-sectioned iron bar. One end has been beaten flat to form a leaf-shaped point. This has been bent up and over, so it lies parallel to the bar. The other end has been bent upwards and the tip turned over. This end is incomplete.

A fragment of fluted copper-alloy sheet, <946> [694] (Phase 7, Open Area 1), possibly a patera handle (Lundock 2014), was also recovered (not illustrated).

Discussion

At first sight this assemblage appears typical of many groups of small finds recovered from Romano-British rural sites. There is an abundance of personal adornments, a large number of fixtures and fittings, a significant number of unidentifiable objects and smattering of other items. However, the real story here lies in the detail of the finds, rather than the broad overview.

The personal adornments include many typical objects. The ratios of these objects to one another are of interest though. The hairpins are dominated by bone examples (there are only two copper-alloy hairpins), which is interesting, and one might expect, in an assemblage of this size, to see rather more hairpins of both materials present. The large number of bracelet fragments is also intriguing, as is the absence of cogwheel examples. Finger-rings are also under-represented in the assemblage (Table 8.6), although two bracelet fragments were modified into such items.

Toilet and textile equipment are under-represented. Toilet instruments usually form a noticeable component of most Romano-British assemblages and the absence of nail-cleaners, tweezers, toilet-spoons and probes (with one exception) is striking. One might also expect, given the evidence for late activity, bone combs to be present, although their fragility might explain their absence. The textile weaving equipment is also poorly represented. The lack of spindle-whorls and the small numbers of needles would seem to indicate that spinning did not take place and that any textile working was limited, perhaps to the maintenance rather than the manufacture of clothes and the like.

The household items are a rather mixed group of objects. Many of them (and some of the fixtures and fittings) are probably derived from furniture. Attention may be drawn to the bone hinge, which is likely to be from a cabinet or the like. The excavation of Hayton (East Yorkshire) demonstrated that rural settlements could be associated with quite elaborate and sophisticated items of furniture (Gerrard 2013, fig 4.15).

The only recreational object – the dodecahedron fragment - is perhaps more reasonably described as an object of unknown function. It is an unusual find and less than a dozen are known from Britain. Interpretations range from gaming pieces, to candle-holders, surveying instruments and sceptre-heads. As its function is uncertain its interpretive significance is limited but it is certainly an oddity. Even stranger is the absence of any pottery, bone or glass counters/gaming pieces. These are well known from Romano-British sites and might have been expected in an assemblage of this size.

Weighing of commodities is indicated by a small number of weights. The absence of writing equipment (except for a single potential stylus) could suggest that this interest in weighing was not accompanied by a similar interest in keeping written records. Some late Roman rural sites do produce numbers of styli, but they are difficult to identify (even with the assistance of x-rays) in poorly preserved iron assemblages and this might explain the lone example here. The graffiti in the pottery assemblage are possibly a better indicator of the spread of literacy.

The objects associated with transportation provide a small but intriguing group. The linch-pin is a reasonably common type of object, as is the fragment of hipposandal. The yoke ring is a form of terret more normally encountered in copper alloy. The cheekpiece from a curb-bit bridle is an unusual item that Manning (1985, 67) argues was used to provide rapid control of a mount. He tentatively suggests an association with cavalry units but presumably any rider wanting a rapid response from his steed would need this sort of equestrian equipment. There is also the clenched nail, which might point to the reuse of boat timbers at the site.

The tools present a fascinating group of items. The large number of knives and cleavers suggests a significant interest in cutting, slicing and chopping. The preparation of foodstuffs, as well as other activities, might account for this number of bladed instruments and is reflected in the animal bone assemblage where the distribution pattern shown by the cattle bones reflects waste from all stages of slaughter and carcass preparation (Rielly & Armitage, this volume). Knives were also seemingly important personal possessions in the late Roman period and could also serve as a weapon on occasion.

The size of the axe and the paring-chisel suggests woodworking rather than forestry and like the knives these objects could have served as weapons. Axes are not particularly common finds on Romano-British sites, but they would surely have been in everyday use. They also serve as symbols of power in late prehistory, the Roman period and the early middle ages (Theuws 2009, 301–303). The pick is an unusual object and a normal connection might be made with mining or quarrying. However, picks were presumably useful items and the recovery of this one from road surface [1338] might indicate that it had been either used in the construction of the surface or was transported to the site in a cart-load of aggregate from a nearby quarry.

The fixtures and fittings include a large number of objects. Some of these can probably be associated with furniture, others are more likely to be associated with structures. Double-spiked loops, joiner's dogs and iron rings are typical objects found on Romano-British sites and must have been commonplace. More interesting are the hinges, latch-lifters and keys. These suggest structures with substantial doors and an interest in controlling private space. Locking devices in particular are perhaps suggestive of a settlement where structures were left empty or contained items of value and are perhaps more common in urban contexts where there was less community cohesion. The security fittings from this assemblage are not abnormal for a late Roman rural site but are perhaps an insight into the way individuals perceived space, property and the trustworthiness of their neighbours.

The only agricultural and horticultural implements are the so-called 'pruning-hooks'. These were probably multipurpose tools but Manning (1985, 56–57) hypothesises a connection between the objects and the preparation and movement of animal fodder. They might have served in this capacity, or to prune branches and bushes. Certainly, the presence of four in the assemblage is of note and their presence could be linked to the growing of trees within the walled enclosures of Phases 7 and 8 or the provision of fodder for animals.

The military equipment assemblage is mainly a small number of fragments derived from late Roman belt-sets. These belts do not necessarily indicate the presence of soldiers. Instead, we are probably looking at the accoutrements of officials (who were '*milites*' in the late Roman world) and members of the elite aspiring to military or para-military identities (Gerrard 2013). Perhaps the exception to this is the fragment of chip-carved belt-set, which is likely to be an import from the Rhineland. The small socketed arrow/bolt-head might perform a military function, or be an object associated with hunting.

The assemblage contains little evidence for metal- or bone-working, but evidence from the former activity is far more visible in the assemblages of slag and other metalworking residues (Keys, this volume; Dungworth, this volume).

Characterising the activity

It is difficult to characterise activity on the site with any certainty, but this brief summary provides some tentative interpretations of the significance of the small-finds assemblage. A brief comparison of selected elements of the Grange Farm assemblage with other sites that might be considered comparable is made for illustrative purposes only (Table 3.46).

The finds assemblage gives some indications of gender. The bracelets and hairpins are likely to be female personal adornments (although not exclusively so) and indicate the presence of women on site. The belt-fittings are usually seen as male and 'martial' accoutrements and probably indicate the presence of men. Many of the other objects carry no connotations of gender; a knife or an axe, for instance, could have been used by either sex.

Many of the objects one might anticipate from 'domestic' contexts are not present. The complete absence of spindle-whorls and the near absence of needles is in sharp contrast to many comparable sites (Table 3.46). If textile working was a household activity customarily carried out by women (Eckardt 2014, 143–144) then the absence of its equipment suggests that the activity may not have been 'domestic'.

The large number of knives might indicate the processing of meat, skins and furs (Rielly & Armitage, this volume), as well as more mundane activities such as the preparation and serving of food. Comparison with other sites suggests that the bladed instruments are over-represented in the assemblage. The same can be said of so-called pruning-hooks. These might have been used for reaping cereals (perhaps unlikely given their small size), or for cutting leafy-fodder, or for tending to fruit trees and bushes.

Maritime activities may be indicated by the axes and the clenched nail. The Gillingham Reach is just north of the site and the presence of imported ceramics as well as a sherd bearing a graffito of a boat (Gerrard & Hudak, this volume) suggests a strong connection between the site and maritime movement through the Greater Thames Estuary area. Similar connections are suggested by the evidence for marine foodstuffs (Rielly & Armitage, this volume). Boat repairs and the like are also activities that are likely to have taken place nearby and the waste timbers and salvage from these activities may have been recycled at the site.

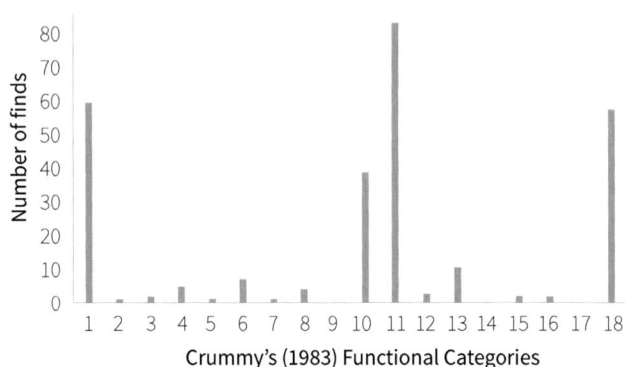

Fig. 3.34   The number of Romano-British finds from the site according to Crummy's (1983) functional categories (see Table 3.4)

Table 3.5 Crummy's (1983, v) functional categories for the analysis of small finds.

Category No.	Description
1	Objects of personal adornment or dress
2	Toilet, surgical or pharmaceutical instruments
3	Objects used in the manufacture or working of textiles
4	Household utensils and furniture
5	Objects used for recreational purposes
6	Objects employed in weighing and measuring
7	Objects used for or associated with written communications
8	Objects associated with transport
9	Buildings and services
10	Tools
11	Fasteners and Fittings
12	Objects associated with agriculture, horticulture and animal husbandry
13	Military equipment
14	Objects associated with religious beliefs and practices
15	Objects and waste material associated with metalworking
16	Objects and waste material associated with horn and boneworking
17	Objects and waste material associated with pottery working
18	Objects of unknown function

Considering transportation more generally brings us to the small number of objects associated with horses and carts. Such items are not uncommon on rural settlements (for instance Booth *et al.* 2008, 175) but it is rare to have the range of items represented here. They certainly indicate the presence of carts as well as horses, which are also attested by the faunal remains (Rielly & Armitage, this volume).

The weights represent an interesting group of objects. They are all of a kind suitable for use with a steelyard. At Westhawk Farm (Booth *et al.* 2008, table 5.13) a large number of weights and fragmentary steelyards were discovered. In the discussion they were expressed as a percentage of the number of brooches at the site and compared with seventeen comparable assemblages. Grange Farm would come third in this analysis with 29% and shows that the number of weights is above normal.

It is tempting to associate the weights with the extraction of silver that is indicated by the metalworking residues (Dungworth, this volume). Silver routinely circulated by weight in the late Roman world and late Roman silver ingots (for instance Painter 1972) and contemporary imitations of silver *siliqua* were also being produced in the late fourth and early fifth century (Guest 2005, 102–117). These were used alongside regular coinage to pay taxes, tributes and make high-value transactions.

Presumably the extraction of silver would have then required the refined product to be weighed, recorded (the stylus and graffiti) and stored securely. This might be indicated by the door-fittings, latch-lifters and key. The silver might also go some way to explaining the presence of soldiers or members of the late Roman elite, who are indicated by the belt fittings.

Overall, the impression is of a site that has a number of activities that places it outside the normal parameters of rural settlement. It is a pity that there is not more unambiguous structural evidence but activities associated with the movement of goods to and from the estuary, commercial transactions, taxation and the processing of agricultural surpluses all seem to be represented in the finds.

Table 3.6 Comparison of selected object types from Grange Farm compared with potentially comparable sites, by number (note that poor bone preservation has depressed the number of hairpins at Westhawk Farm).

Site Name	Hairpins	Finger-rings	Toilet instruments	Needles & spindle whorls	Knives & cleavers	Axes	Pruning Hooks	References
Grange Farm	18	2	1+2	3	22	1	4	This volume
Westhawk Farm	1	0	6	2	0	0	0	Booth *et al.* 2008
Higham Ferrers	59	108	21	10	22	0	0	Scott 2009
Catsgore	19	7	5	17	13	2		Leech 1982
Shepton Mallet	39	5	8	7	12	0	1	Leach 2001
Shiptonthorpe	6	0	1	2	2	0	1	Allason-Jones 2006

3.4 The Romano-British pottery

James Gerrard and Eniko Hudak

The excavations produced a large quantity of pottery totalling 20,077 sherds of Late Iron Age and Romano-British ceramics weighing 263.363kg. The assemblage was originally quantified by James Gerrard with the assistance of Malcolm Lyne using standard and widely accepted ceramic methodologies (Orton *et al.* 1993; Gerrard & Lyne 2008). The assessment report contains considerable detail, including spot-dates for each individual context and will be of assistance to any researcher examining the archive. Unfortunately, resources did not permit full analysis of the ceramics for publication and this report focuses on a broad overview of the assemblage and the presentation of quantified data from a small number of key groups which were revisited by the authors.

The individual fabrics have been identified using three mutually supporting systems. Most of the Romano-British pottery has been assigned fabric codes using the Museum of London system. London received much of its pottery from Kent during the Roman period and these codes can be easily correlated with the national codes (Tomber & Dore 1998). The ceramic codes used by the Canterbury Archaeological Trust have also been used for Late Iron Age/Early Roman fabrics not represented in the London system. Expansions for the London and Canterbury codes are presented in Appendix 2. Finally, unsourced 'coarse' fabrics were given full fabric descriptions prefixed by 'C' (see Appendix 1). Vessel forms are usually related to industry specific typologies and are referenced where appropriate in the text.

Assemblage overview

The large pottery assemblage is dominated by groups of material of varying sizes and condition deriving from ditch fills and layers. Often these groups have a high degree of residuality and as such discussing the pottery by phase is unhelpful. Instead the decision was made to provide an overview of the entire quantified assemblage (Appendix 2) and to this end the pottery has been divided into three 'broad' Ceramic Phases: LIA-AD 120, AD 120–250 and AD 250–400/550.

Ceramic Phase 1: LIA–AD 120

The Late Iron Age/Earliest Roman pottery can be divided into that which was made in an indigenous style, using indigenous techniques until sometime roughly in the Flavian period and so-called 'Romanised' fabrics. Of the indigenous style ceramics two broad groups can be discerned: the first is so-called 'Belgic' material manufactured in a variety of fabrics defined by the Canterbury Archaeological Trust. In total these fabrics

amount to 796 sherds weighing 7.152kg, or 2% and 2.7% of the site assemblage by count and weight. The second group includes a diverse range of coarse fabrics tempered with sand, flint, silt and glauconite. These are described in Appendix 1 and total 565 sherds weighing 10.198kg, or 2.8% and 3.9% of the site assemblage respectively.

The 'Romanised' fabrics include small quantities of imported material. Most notable here are a chip of what may be Arretine ware (1 sherd, 1g) and tiny quantities of Gallo-Belgic white ware, Terra Nigra and Terra Rubra. The South Gaulish samian should also be included here too. Production at Hoo (3.4% count and 3.3% weight) and elsewhere in the North Kent Marshes (NKFW: 11.8% count and 6.8% weight NKSH: 5.6% count, 10.6% weight) represents the establishment of potteries using 'Roman' techniques in the Lower Medway region. Romano-British imports could feasibly include tiny quantities of Alice Holt Surrey Ware and Verulamium Region wares (VRW and VCWS).

Ceramic Phase 2: AD 120–250

The second ceramic phase is marked by the continuation of some of the earliest Roman fabrics (NKFW, NKSH) and the introduction of Dorset Black-Burnished Wares and their imitation by the Thameside BB2 producers *c.* AD 120 (Monaghan 1987). Alongside the locally wheel-thrown Black-Burnished wares was a significant greyware industry producing what were essentially BB2 vessels but in an unburnished fabric. In London these are known as Thameside Kent Greywares (TSK) and dated AD 180–300, but it seems clear that in Kent this fabric began earlier than this and probably lasted a little longer too. Together BB2 and TSK account 53% of the assemblage by count and 43% by weight and are testimony to the dominance of these very local pottery producers during the second and third centuries.

Imported fabrics include Central, East Gaulish and probably most of the unsourced samian (1.6% by count and weight), Baetican oil and Gaulish wine amphora (0.5% count, 3% weight). Other imports include small quantities of Gaulish finewares. Romano-British wares include some of the earlier Nene Valley Colour Coated wares, finewares, coarsewares and *mortaria* from Colchester and elsewhere across the Thames Estuary.

Ceramic Phase 3: AD 250–400/450

The production of BB2 and TSK continued to the end of the third century and perhaps just into the fourth century. Nevertheless, the Late Roman pattern of ceramic supply is one which reflects significant structural changes in the nature of the North Kent pottery industry and arguably the wider Romano-British economy. With the virtual disappearance of local production on the marshes, pottery in the fourth century was drawn from geographically distant sources. Dorset BB1 and Alice Holt Farnham ware become major suppliers of coarse wares (0.21% and 4.3% by count and 0.33% and 7% by weight respectively) along with the Kentish Late Roman grog-tempered wares. Finewares include red- and white-slipped wares from Oxfordshire, other colour-coated wares from the Nene Valley and vessels from the Hadham kilns (0.26% by count and 0.38% by weight). Oxfordshire and the Nene Valley also supplied white-ware *mortaria*. Towards the later fourth century, late Roman shell tempered wares, probably from Harrold in Bedfordshire and Overwey/Portchester D ware become important if minor elements in the assemblage. Imported material includes very small quantities of Late Roman German Marbled fine wares, red slipped roller-stamped Argonne ware and coarse lid-seated jars from the Mayen region of Germany.

Unusual aspects of the assemblage include hard-fired blue-grey sand-tempered jars, seemingly imitating late Alice Holt forms that Dr Malcolm Lyne (pers. comm.) considers to be products of the kilns identified in the late nineteenth century at Preston, near Wingham, Kent (Dowker & Roach Smith 1878). There are also three unusual grog-tempered sherds. One of these appears to be so-called 'Thundersbarrow ware' (Oakley 1933) and the other sherds are similar to material excavated at Burgess Hill (both sites in Sussex) (Lyne 1999). The movement of vessels in these fabrics with very restricted 'normal' distributions may indicate either the movement of people with their goods and chattels in the fourth century, or possibly demonstrate demand for pottery in the fifth century when traditional 'late Roman' suppliers were difficult to access.

Discussion

In general terms the assemblage confirms the broad outlines of the patterning of ceramic supply during the Roman period discerned by Pollard (1988) and confirms the importance of the pottery producers on the North Kent marshes (Monaghan 1987). For the interpretation of the site the assemblage offers a number of useful insights.

The complete dominance of local suppliers during the Ceramic Phases 1 and 2 (equivalent to Site Phases 3–6) is unsurprising but really does underline the intimate economic connections between the site and the marshes to the north. A corollary of this is limited evidence for connections further afield. It was noted during the assessment, but unfortunately resources were too limited to follow this up for publication, that some of the NKFW, BB2 and TSK were clearly 'seconds'. These vessels were the result of imperfect firings and thus destined for local consumption, rather than export. The importation of ceramics from Gaul and further afield would suggest that this estuarine community also had access to elements of the extra-provincial trade network.

It would be easy to paint a picture of late Roman decline from the ceramics (Ceramic Phase 3, Site Phases 7–9). The end, for reasons that are currently unknown and may be unknowable, of the Thameside producers in the fourth century would seem to represent a major economic dislocation. This left the inhabitants of the site reliant on the kinds of pottery that were still being produced in Kent, but also on ceramics manufactured further afield in Surrey/Hampshire, Oxfordshire, Dorset and the Nene Valley (Fig. 3.35). This would suggest that provincial exchange networks were still robust during the fourth century and is in keeping with the pattern elsewhere in Kent, London and Essex. There was also the importation of small quantities of pottery from the Rhineland is indicative of continuing trade across the North Sea with the Continental *limes*. The conclusions is, perhaps, that the inhabitants were now reliant on pottery along the Thames and throught the Thames Estuary, rather than produced locally on its shores.

Key groups

Nine groups of ditch and pit fills were selected as representative of the changing ceramic supply to the site between the Early and Late Roman periods.

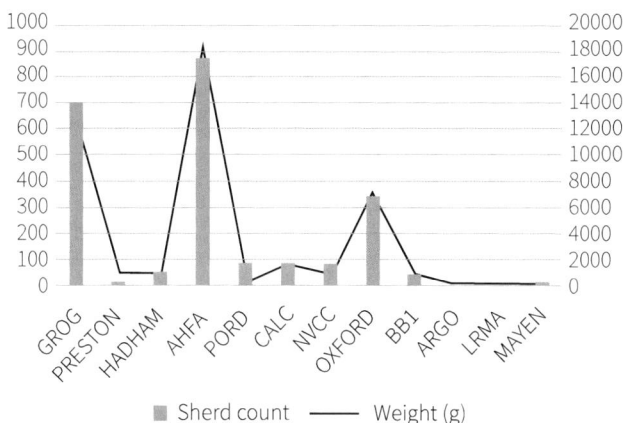

Fig. 3.35 Quantification of selected Late Roman pottery fabrics by sherd count (left) and weight (g) (right) by distance from the site. HADHAM, NVCC and OXFORD refer to all fabrics from those sources

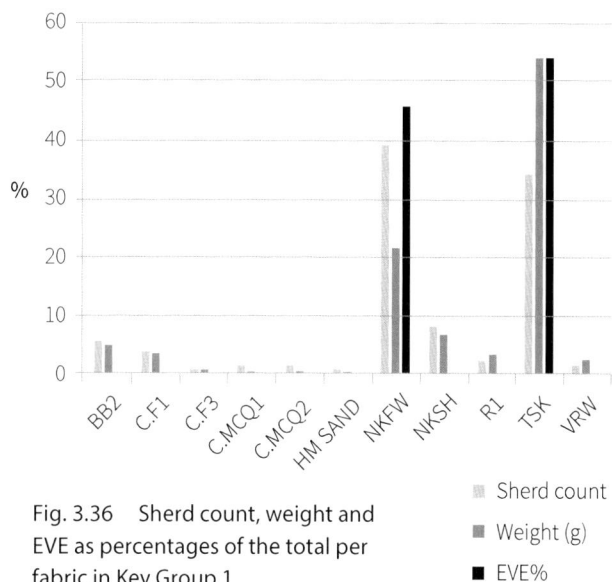

Fig. 3.36 Sherd count, weight and EVE as percentages of the total per fabric in Key Group 1

Key Group 1 Ditch [860], (Phase 4, Enclosure 2)

Key Group 1 (Table 3.7; Fig. 3.36) consists of the pottery recovered from the fills of a ditch dug into the backfill of an earlier boundary ditch. The ditch contained a moderate amount of pottery: 127 sherds weighing 1.614kg (1.09 EVE). The earliest fills yielded 14 sherds only (0.123kg, 0.13 EVE): 10 sherds were in handmade flint-, quartz-, and sand-tempered fabrics and NKSH; the other four sherds were in VRW and NKFW. The latter included carinated bowls of Monaghan's (1987, 130–131) Form 4H. Handmade fabrics were also present in the rest of the assemblage from the upper fills, but those were dominated by NKFW and early sand tempered Thameside products in forms of carinated bowls and everted rim jars, and BB2 also appears (AD 120).

Key group 1 illustrations

Fig. 3.37.1   NKFW 4H bowl 70–130 [936] (Monaghan 1987, 130–131).

Fig. 3.37.2   NKFW 4H1 bowl 70–130 [804] (Monaghan 1987, 130–131).

Fig. 3.37.3   TSK 12B1 lid 50–100 [806] (Monaghan 1987, 166–167).

Fig. 3.37.4   TSK 3H1.5 jar 100–200 [806] (Monaghan 1987, 94–95).

Fig. 3.37.5   TSK 3G3.3 jar 50–70 [806] (Monaghan 1987, 91–92).

Fig. 3.37.6   TSK 5C bowl 100–150 [804] (Monaghan 1987, 140).

Key Group 2 Pit [432] (Phase 4)

The pottery in this group (232 sherds, 3.301kg, 0.46 EVE; Table 3.8; Fig. 3.38) was recovered from the fills of a square pit. Almost half of the pottery from the second fill of the pit was in a handmade quartz-tempered fabric (50 sherds, 0.926 kg); the rest consisted of TSK products and a few sherds of NKFW. Notable is the presence of a complete, but smashed pot (26 sherds) in an early, handmade TSK fabric, which might have been a deliberate, structured deposit. The upper fill contained seven sherds only: six from a NKFW jar and one in NKSH tempered fabric.

The upper fill contained the most pottery by sherd count (122 sherds 0.956 kg 0.27 EVE). The fill assemblage is dominated by NKFW, followed by TSK. HOO ware is also present in considerable quantities and includes a sherd of a *mortarium*. This is an unusual vessel because there is, as yet, no evidence of *mortarium* production in the north Kent marshes (Monaghan 1987, 160). Imported pottery also appears in this fill: six amphora sherds and a single sherd of South Gaulish Samian.

Key Group 2 illustrations:

Fig. 3.37.7   TSK complete handmade pot [448].

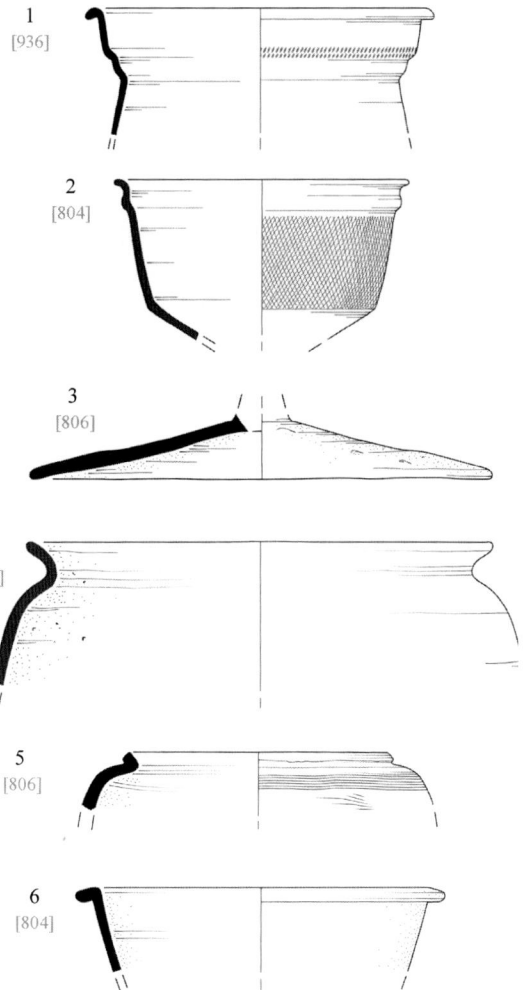
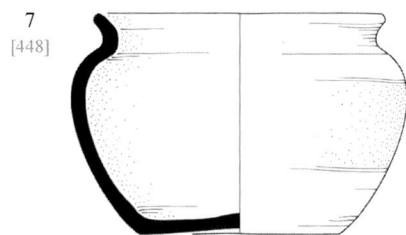
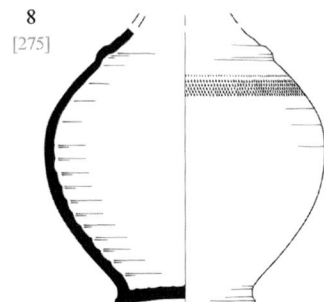

Fig. 3.37   Key group 1, Key Group 2 and Key Group 3 pottery (scale 1:4)

Table 3.7 *Total quantification of Key Group 1 pottery*

Fabric	Sherd Count	Sherd Count %	Weight (g)	Weight %	EVE	EVE%
BB2	7	5.60%	78	4.83%	0	0.00%
C.F1	5	4.00%	58	3.59%	0	0.00%
C.F3	1	0.80%	11	0.68%	0	0.00%
C.MCQ1	2	1.60%	10	0.62%	0	0.00%
C.MCQ2	2	1.60%	10	0.62%	0	0.00%
HM SAND	1	0.80%	7	0.43%	0	0.00%
NKFW	49	39.20%	351	21.75%	50	45.87%
NKSH	10	8.00%	112	6.94%	0	0.00%
R1	3	2.40%	59	3.66%	0	0.00%
TSK	43	34.40%	875	54.21%	59	54.13%
VRW	2	1.60%	43	2.66%	0	0.00%
TOTAL	125	100%	1614	100%	109	100%

Table 3.8 *Total quantification of Key Group 2 pottery*

Fabric	Sherd Count	Sherd Count%	Weight (g)	Weight%	EVE	EVE%
AMPH	6	2.59%	106	3.21%	0	0.00%
B2/R1	1	0.43%	20	0.61%	0	0.00%
C.Q1	50	21.55%	926	28.05%	0	0.00%
HOO	15	6.47%	75	2.27%	0	0.00%
HOO MORT	1	0.43%	12	0.36%	0	0.00%
NKFW	81	34.91%	564	17.09%	12	26.09%
NKSH	5	2.16%	130	3.94%	15	32.61%
OTHER	3	1.29%	48	1.45%	0	0.00%
OXID	1	0.43%	3	0.09%	0	0.00%
PATCH	4	1.72%	51	1.54%	0	0.00%
SAMSG	1	0.43%	2	0.06%	0	0.00%
SAND	2	0.86%	3	0.09%	0	0.00%
TSK	36	15.52%	520	15.75%	19	41.30%
TSK HM	26	11.21%	841	25.48%	0	0.00%
TOTAL	232	100%	3301	100%	46	100%

Key Group 3 Pit [276] (Phase 5)

Key Group 3 is a very small group of pottery included here for its intrinsic interest as it may have been a deliberate deposit. It consists of only ten fresh sherds of NKFW nine of which belong to the same vessel, an S-profile bowl with grooved and cordoned neck (Monaghan 1987, 112–113). There is also a single sherd of an early fine ware with smooth black surface. The bowl was found in the centre of the pit and no other finds were associated with this feature, suggesting that this, like Key Group 2, might have been a structured deposit.

Key Group 3 illustrations:

Fig. 3.37.8 NKFW 4A1 bowl 70–150 [275] (Monaghan 1987, 112–113).

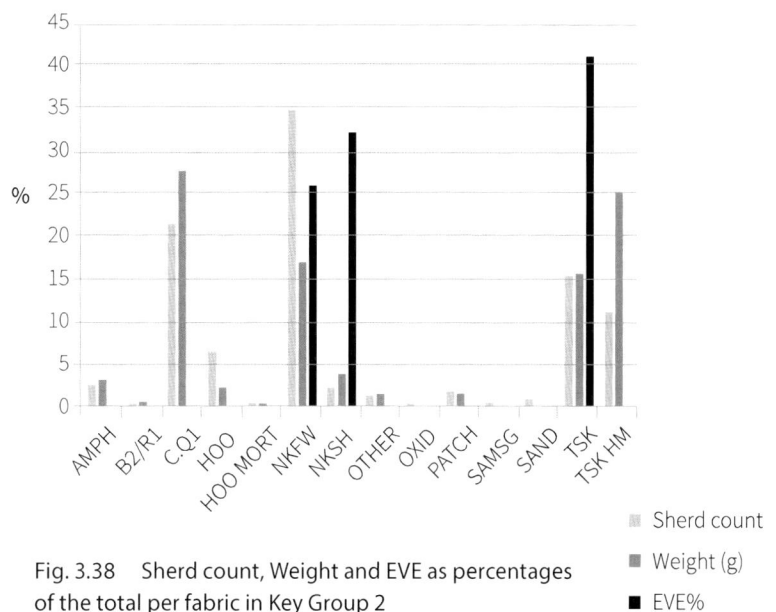

Fig. 3.38 Sherd count, Weight and EVE as percentages of the total per fabric in Key Group 2

Sherd count
Weight (g)
EVE%

Key Group 4 Pit [801] (Phase 5, pit group 13)

A total of 1442 sherds weighing 25.992 kg (26.12 EVE) were recovered from the fills of a large oval pit form Key Group 4 (Table 3.9; Fig. 3.39). This pottery forms a very coherent early-second-century assemblage, which is dominated by coarse wares, especially TSK and BB2 pottery. Fine wares are mainly NKFW, but HOO and Samian are also present. Notable is a large HOO ware jar/amphora, a form that is otherwise unattested in this industry's repertoire (Davies *et al.* 1994, 38–40).

It was possible to date this group very closely to the middle decades of the second century through the forms represented in the assemblage. The early BB2 forms suggest that the group was deposited between AD 120–150 and this date is confirmed by the presence of NKFW poppyhead beakers (form 2A3 – Monaghan 1987, 55) dated to AD 100–150 and NKSH jars dated to 50–150 (Davies *et al.* 1994, 101–102).

There is a small quantity of earlier material, such as bead-rim jars dated to the end of the first century, which may represent old vessels still in use. The upper fills yielded a Samian sherd stamped by Lillutius dated to AD 160–260 (die 3b, Hartley & Dickinson 2010, 81); and two sherds of a Colchester *mortarium* with a retrograde stamp. Stamped *mortaria* in Colchester fabric are generally dated to AD 140–170/80 (Tyers 1996, 120).

Key Group 4 illustrations:

Fig. 3.40.1 TSK 12F lid 70–140 [802] (Monaghan 1987, 166–167).

Fig. 3.40.2 PTSK 12C lid 50–300 [802] (Monaghan 1987, 166–167).

Fig. 3.40.3 BB2 3J1 jar 120–150 [802] (Monaghan 1987, 103–104).

Fig. 3.40.4 TSK 3J1 jar 120–150 [800] (Monaghan 1987, 103–104).

Fig. 3.40.5 TSK 3H jar 100–300 [802] (Monaghan 1987, 94).

Fig. 3.40.6 TSK 3H jar 100–300 [800] (Monaghan 1987, 94).

Fig. 3.40.7 TSK 3H jar 100–300 [800] (Monaghan 1987, 94).

Fig. 3.40.8 TSK 3F1 jar 40–150 [802] (Monaghan 1987, 88–89).

Fig. 3.40.9 TSK 3G3.3 jar 50–70 [802] (Monaghan 1987, 91–92).

Fig. 3.40.10 BB2 3F4 jar 70–150 [800] (Monaghan 1987, 88–89).

Fig. 3.40.11 TSK 5C1 bowl 120–250 [802] (Monaghan 1987, 140–141).

Fig. 3.40.12 BB2 5D1.2 bowl 120–180 [802] (Monaghan 1987, 144–146).

Fig. 3.40.13 BB2 5D1.1 bowl 120–180 [800] (Monaghan 1987, 144–146).

Fig. 3.40.14 BB2 5D5 bowl 110/120–150/170 [800] (Monaghan 1987, 144–146).

Fig. 3.40.15 BB2 5D7 bowl 110–180 [800] (Monaghan 1987, 144–146).

Fig. 3.40.16 BB2 5E1 dish with wavy line 130–300 [800] (Monaghan 1987, 147–148).

Fig. 3.40.17 BB2 5F3.5 dish with wavy line 130–300 [800] (Monaghan 1987, 152–153).

Fig. 3.40.18 NKSH 3D5 jar 50–100 [802] (Monaghan 1987, 79–84).

Fig. 3.40.19 NKSH 3D3 jar 50–150 [799] (Monaghan 1987, 79–84).

Fig. 3.40.20 COL MORT 7BEF *mortarium* with stamp 140–180 [800].

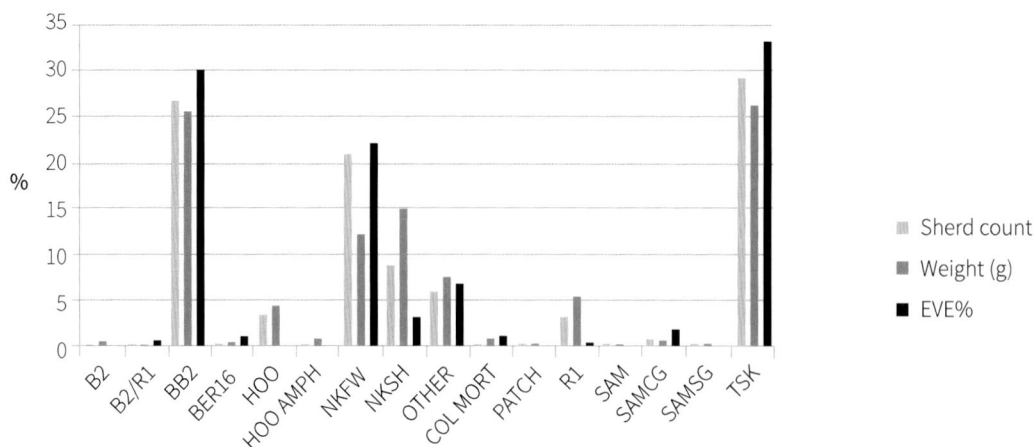

Fig. 3.39   Sherd count, weight and EVE as percentages of the total per fabric in Key Group 4

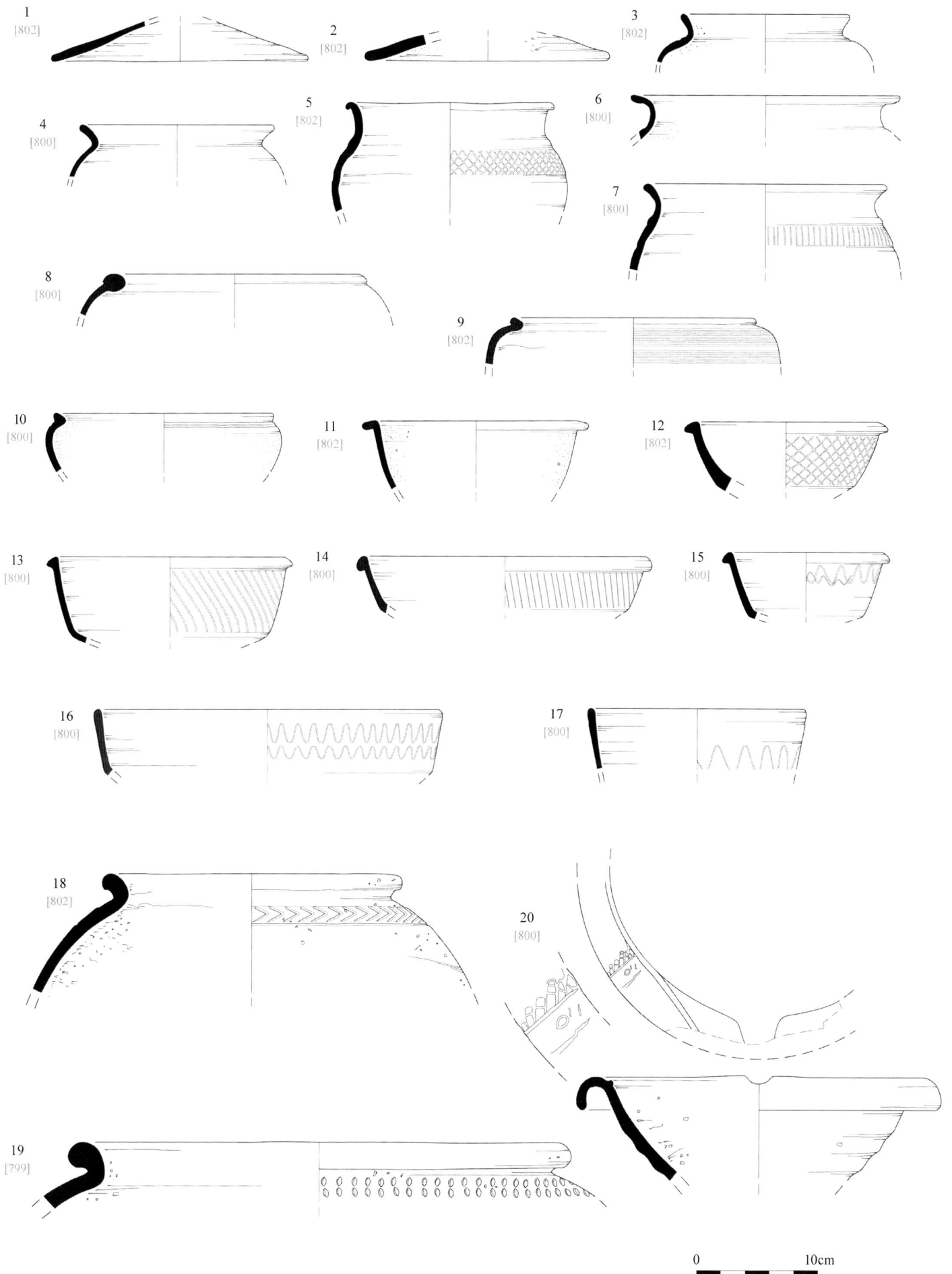

Fig. 3.40   Key Group 4 illustrated pottery (scale 1:4)

Table 3.9   Total quantification of Key Group 4 pottery

Fabric	Sherd Count	Sherd Count%	Weight (g)	Weight%	EVE	EVE%
B2	2	0.14%	127	0.49%	0	0.00%
B2/R1	1	0.07%	30	0.12%	0.16	0.61%
BB2	386	26.77%	6666	25.65%	7.84	30.02%
BER16	4	0.28%	99	0.38%	0.28	1.07%
HOO	47	3.26%	1121	4.31%	0	0.00%
HOO Amph	2	0.14%	231	0.89%	0	0.00%
NKFW	301	20.87%	3177	12.22%	5.74	21.98%
NKSH	128	8.88%	3884	14.94%	0.81	3.10%
OTHER	85	5.89%	1932	7.43%	1.8	6.89%
COL MORT	2	0.14%	248	0.95%	0.3	1.15%
PATCH	2	0.14%	30	0.12%	0	0.00%
R1	45	3.12%	1400	5.39%	0.09	0.34%
SAM	2	0.14%	26	0.10%	0	0.00%
SAMCG	11	0.76%	166	0.64%	0.44	1.68%
SAMSG	2	0.14%	40	0.15%	0	0.00%
TSK	422	29.26%	6815	26.22%	8.66	33.15%
TOTAL	1442	100%	25,992	100%	26.12	100%

Table 3.10   Total quantification of Key Group 5 pottery

Fabric	Sherd Count	Sherd Count%	Weight (g)	Weight%	EVE	EVE%
AHFA	11	7.19%	419	12.19%	0.79	30.74%
BB1	1	0.65%	53	1.54%		0.00%
BB2	9	5.88%	193	5.62%	0.78	30.35%
GROG	3	1.96%	68	1.98%		0.00%
HADG	1	0.65%	14	0.41%		0.00%
NKFW	9	5.88%	148	4.31%		0.00%
NVCC	6	3.92%	67	1.95%	0.08	3.11%
OXMO	1	0.65%	16	0.47%		0.00%
PATCH	3	1.96%	25	0.73%	0.1	3.89%
TSK	109	71.24%	2433	70.81%	0.82	31.91%
TOTAL	153	100%	3436	100%	2.57	100%

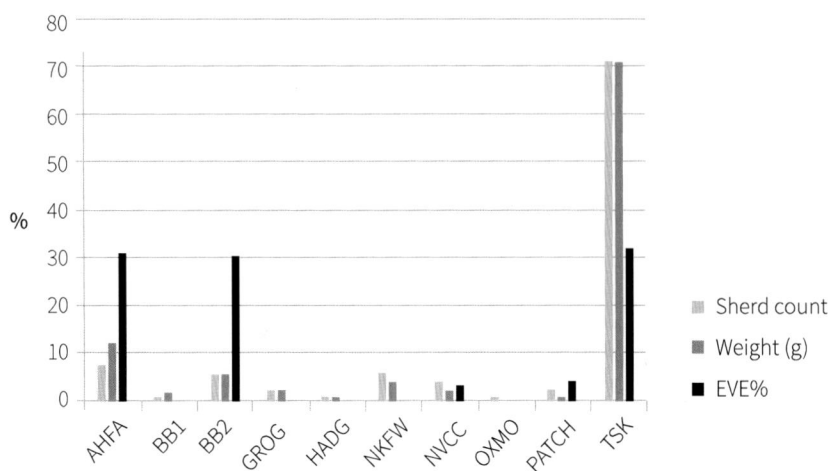

Fig. 3.41   Sherd count, weight and EVE as percentages of the total per fabric in Key Group 5

Key Group 5 Pit [783] (Phase 7, Structure 3)

The pottery in Key Group 5 (Table 3.10; Fig. 3.41) was recovered from a shallow oval pit: 153 sherds weighing 3.436 kg (2.57 EVE). The assemblage is dominated by TSK (more than 70%), but products of the Alice Holt and Oxfordshire potteries, and BB1 also appear in small quantities, which suggest a late-third-century date and herald the beginning of the 'late Roman' period. This date is further reinforced by the presence of 'swan's neck' pendant rim jars (type 3H5, Monaghan 1987, 96), a Nene Valley colour-coated sherd, with overslip white-painted decoration (fourth century), and a pentice-moulded beaker (late third to fourth century) (Perrin 1999, 96).

Key Group 5 Illustrations:

Fig. 3.42.1 NVCC beaker sherd with painted 'B' fourth century [769] (Perrin 1999, 96).

Fig. 3.42.2 NVCC beaker sherd with white painted decoration fourth century [769] (Perrin 1999, 96).

Fig. 3.42.3 AHFA 5B4 bowl 270–350 [768] (Lyne & Jefferies 1979: fig 32).

Fig. 3.42.4 TSK 3H5 jar 150–300 [768] (Monaghan 1987, 94–97).

Fig. 3.42.5 BB2 5A5 flanged bowl 180–350 [768] (Monaghan 1987, 136–137).

Key Group 5

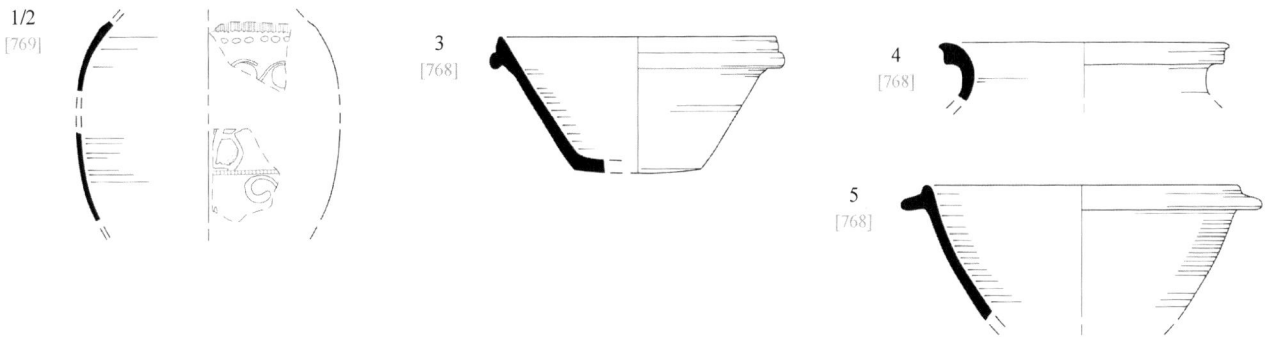

Key Group 6

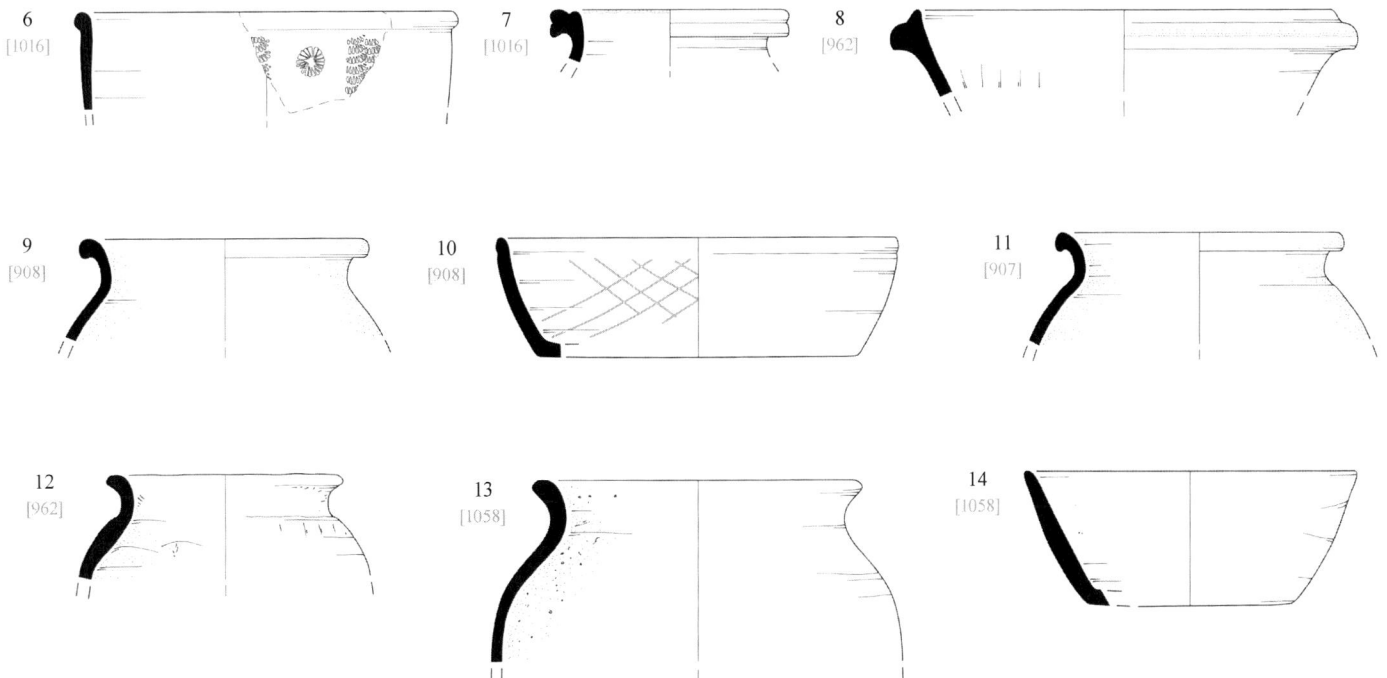

Fig. 3.42   Key Group 5 and Key Group 6 illustrated pottery (scale 1:4)

0   10cm

Table 3.11 Total quantification of Key Group 6 pottery

Fabric	Sherd Count	Sherd Count%	Weight (g)	Weight%	EVE	EVE%
AHFA	210	39.11%	7150	52.58%	6.16	50.62%
AHSU	4	0.74%	15	0.11%	0	0.00%
AMPH	2	0.37%	36	0.26%	0	0.00%
B1.1	2	0.37%	19	0.14%	0	0.00%
B2/R1	4	0.74%	104	0.76%	0	0.00%
BAETL	1	0.19%	231	1.70%	0	0.00%
BB2	22	4.10%	432	3.18%	0.52	4.27%
CALC	33	6.15%	911	6.70%	0.13	1.07%
CGWH	1	0.19%	2	0.01%	0.09	0.74%
COLCC	1	0.19%	12	0.09%	0	0.00%
FINE	2	0.37%	7	0.05%	0	0.00%
GROG	99	18.44%	2277	16.74%	2.42	19.88%
HADBS	2	0.37%	18	0.13%	0	0.00%
HADG	4	0.74%	101	0.74%	0	0.00%
HADOX	6	1.12%	115	0.85%	0.39	3.20%
HOO	1	0.19%	8	0.06%	0	0.00%
LIA-ER	2	0.37%	54	0.40%	0	0.00%
LR14	5	0.93%	33	0.24%	0	0.00%
MISC	13	2.42%	119	0.88%	0	0.00%
NKFW	13	2.42%	108	0.79%	0.43	3.53%
NKSH	14	2.61%	610	4.49%	0.08	0.66%
NVCC	3	0.56%	102	0.75%	0.27	2.22%
OXMO	2	0.37%	104	0.76%	0	0.00%
OXRC	22	4.10%	276	2.03%	1.54	12.65%
PATCH	3	0.56%	25	0.18%	0	0.00%
PORD	2	0.37%	8	0.06%	0	0.00%
PRESTON	3	0.56%	36	0.26%	0	0.00%
R1	3	0.56%	18	0.13%	0	0.00%
SAMCG	1	0.19%	5	0.04%	0	0.00%
SAND	22	4.10%	200	1.47%	0	0.00%
TSK	35	6.52%	463	3.40%	0.14	1.15%
TOTAL	537	100%	13,599	100%	12.17	100%

Key Group 6 Pits [909], [1020], [1060] and [1205] (Phase 8, pit groups 47 and 48)

Key Group 6 consists of pottery recovered from a series of inter-cutting pits (Table 3.11; Fig. 3.43). They are considered together here because the pottery from these pits is very similar in composition and the features comprise a discrete stratigraphic sequence.

The pottery in Key Group 6 comprises 537 sherds weighing 13.599kg (12.17 EVE). The group is dominated by AHFA and GROG and includes PORD, CALC and OXRC. The latter fabric includes forms C83, C84 and C70 (Young 1977, 170) decorated with demi-rosettes and white paint. This combination of fabrics is typical of very late fourth-century and early-fifth-century ceramic groups in London and the South East (Pollard 1988, Symonds & Tomber 1991, Gerrard 2011). The very small quantities of TSK and BB2, which are likely to have ceased production *c.* AD 350–370, confirms a very late fourth- or early-fifth-century date for this assemblage (Pollard 1988, 143–145).

Key Group 6 illustrations:

Fig. 3.42.6 OXRC C83 bowl 300–400+ [1016] (Young 1977, 170).

Fig. 3.42.7 AHFA 1A16 jar 300–420 [1016] (Lyne & Jefferies 1979: fig 23).

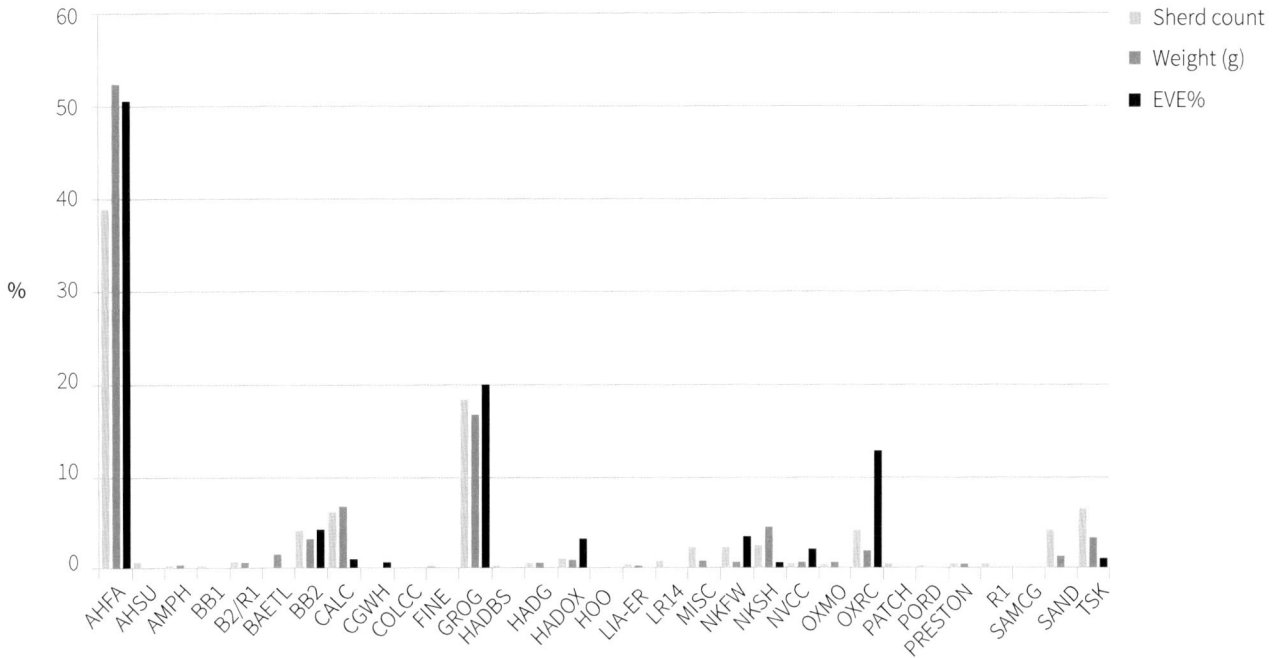

Fig. 3.43   Sherd count, weight and EVE as percentages of the total per fabric in Key

Table 3.12   Total quantification of Key Group 7 pottery

Fabric	Sherd Count	Sherd Count%	Weight (g)	Weight%	EVE	EVE%
AHFA	6	16.22%	77	13.34%	0.29	42.65%
BB2	2	5.41%	13	2.25%	0	0.00%
GROG	3	8.11%	26	4.51%	0	0.00%
GROG LR1	6	16.22%	97	16.81%	0.05	7.35%
NKFW	1	2.70%	7	1.21%	0.08	11.76%
OXRC	1	2.70%	43	7.45%	0	0.00%
PATCH	4	10.81%	118	20.45%	0	0.00%
PORD	11	29.73%	135	23.40%	0.13	19.12%
PRESTON	1	2.70%	11	1.91%	0	0.00%
TSK	2	5.41%	50	8.67%	0.13	19.12%
TOTAL	37	100%	577	100%	0.68	100%

Fig. 3.42.8 AHFA 5B6 bowl 270–400+ [962] (Lyne & Jefferies 1979, fig 32).

Fig. 3.42.9 AHFA coarse 3C9 jar 300–420 [908] (Lyne & Jefferies 1979, fig 29).

Fig. 3.42.10 AHFA type 6A10 dish 370–420 [908] (Lyne & Jefferies 1979: fig 36).

Fig. 3.42.11 AHFA 6A10 jar 270–420 [907] (Lyne & Jefferies 1979: fig 36).

Fig. 3.42.12 GROG LR 1 jar [962] (Pollard 1988, fig 53.209–211).

Fig. 3.42.13 GROG LR 1 jar 300–400 [1058] (Pollard 1988, fig 53.209–211).

Fig. 3.42.14 GROG LR 1 dish 370–420 [1058] (Pollard 1988, fig 53.204).

Key Group 7 Pits [371], [384], [403], [411] and [420] (Phase 8, pit group 46)

Key Group 7 includes the pottery from five small inter-cutting pits in the north-western part of the excavated area. The individual assemblages from the fills of the pits were very small (1–13 sherds), however, they seem to form an unusual mixture of sherds (Table 3.12; Table 3.13). There is no clear pattern in the deposition: typically-late Roman pottery, such as PORD and AHFA, or early pottery, such as PATCH (Pollard 1987), are present both in the stratigraphically earliest and latest pits. In terms of forms jars are dominant, but a platter in NKFW (Type 7A2, Monaghan 1987, 158), and very abraded sherds of AHFA beaded and flanged bowls (Type 5B, Lyne &

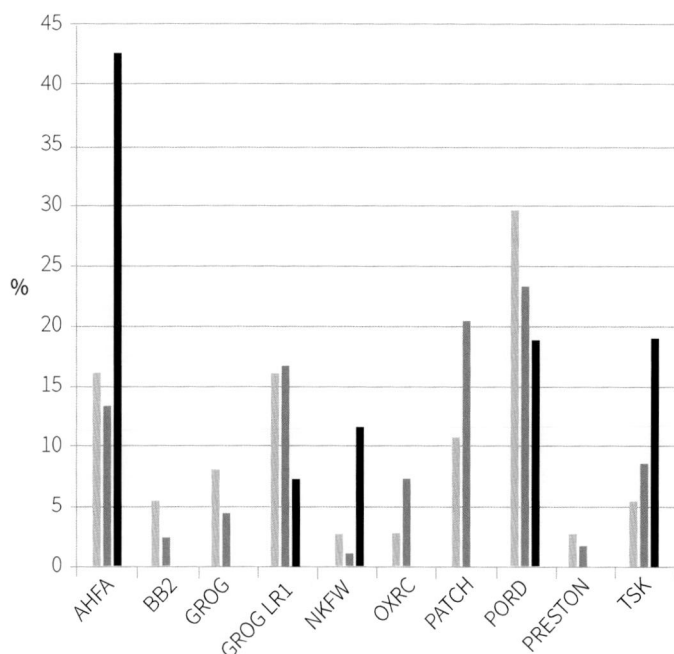

Fig. 3.44   Sherd count, weight and EVE as percentages of the total per fabric in Key Group 7

- Sherd count
- Weight (g)
- EVE%

Jefferies 1979, 46) are also present. Notable is the quantity of PORD, a total of eleven fresh and unabraded sherds (0.135kg, 0.13 EVE). The unusual composition of this small assemblage might suggest an early-fifth-century date by analogy with sites in Essex (Lucy 2016).

Key Group 8 Layer [537] (Phase 9, Group 49)

Key Group 8 is small (113 sherds, 1.14kg; Table 3.13) but is nonetheless significant because of its composition and stratigraphic position immediately below the Phase 9 demolition deposits. Much of the pottery is small and a minority of sherds are heavily abraded. By sherd count and weight AHFA, GROG and OXRC are the dominant fabrics. These fabrics, along with the PORD and CALC appear fresher than the clearly residual earlier Roman fabrics like BB2 and TSK.

The OXRC includes two C51 bowls (Young 1977, 160): one with the flange removed and the other heavily burnt. There is also a white-painted flange from a C48 bowl (Young 1977, 158). The grog-tempered wares include a narrow-necked everted-rim jar and two beaded and flanged bowls. Both forms are typical of late Roman Kentish grog-tempered pottery (Pollard 1988, fig 53). There are also two body sherds in an unusual GROG fabric originating in East Sussex (Dr Malcolm Lyne pers. comm.). The Alice Holt/Farnham ware includes two coarse, high-fired jars (Lyne & Jefferies 1979, Type 3C) as well as a small convex-sided dish (Lyne & Jefferies 1979, Type 6A11). The CALC includes a single abraded jar rim (Brown 1991, fig 29).

The poor showing of BB2 and TSK, coupled with the dominance of AHFA, GROG and OXRC alongside the presence of PORD and CALC suggest that this group should be dated late in the fourth century at the earliest. The convex-sided dish in AHFA is one of the latest products of that industry and along with the East Sussex GROG sherds, previously identified in very late-fourth- or fifth-century deposits at Burgess Hill (East Sussex) (Lyne 1999) would indicate a date at the very end of the fourth or early into the fifth century. The presence of a sherd in a fifth-century handmade fabric of non-indigenous inspiration (ie 'Early Anglo-Saxon') (Jarrett, this volume) is further evidence that this may be a small group of early-fifth-century pottery and invites comparison with the pottery assemblages in some of the 'early' phases of the Anglo-Saxon site at Mucking (Lucy 2016).

Table 3.13   Total quantification for Key Group 8 pottery (percentages for EVEs not provided because of the small assemblage size)

Fabric	Sherd Count	Sherd Count%	Weight (g)	Weight%	EVE
AHFA	37	32.7	398	32.8	0.29
BB2	11	9.7	117	9.6	0.17
CALC	3	2.7	28	2.3	0.05
GROG	28	24.8	337	27.8	0.45
GROG Burgess Hill	2	1.8	15	1.2	
HADBS	4	3.5	43	3.5	0
HOO	1	0.9	7	0.6	0
NKFW	2	1.8	14	1.2	0
NVCC	1	0.9	7	0.6	0
OXRC	6	5.3	86	7.1	0.08
PORD	4	3.5	52	4.3	0
R5	2	1.8	8	0.7	0
SAND	4	3.5	33	2.7	0
TSK	8	7.1	69	5.7	0
TOTAL	113	100.0	1214	100.0	1.04

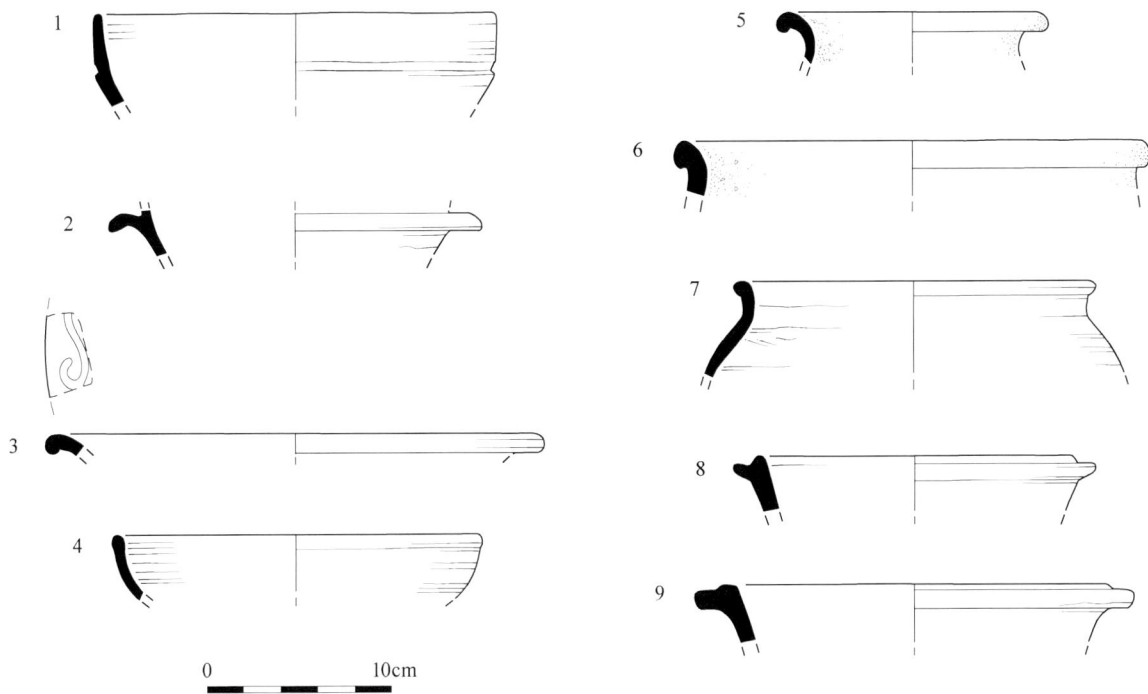

Fig. 3.45   Key Group 8 illustrated pottery (scale 1:4)

Key Group 8 illustrations

Fig. 3.45.1 OXRC C51 bowl with flange removed 240–400+ [537] (Young 1977, 160).

Fig. 3.45.2 OXRC C51 bowl, burnt and abraded 240–400+ [537] (Young 1977, 160).

Fig. 3.45.3 OXRC white painted C48 bowl 300–400+ [537] (Young 1977, 158).

Fig. 3.45.4 AHFA fresh 6A11 convex-sided dish 370/370–420 [537] (Lyne & Jefferies 1979, 48).

Fig. 3.45.5 AHFA fresh, coarse 3C jar 300–420 [537] (Lyne & Jefferies 1979, 43).

Fig. 3.45.6 CALC abraded jar 300–400+ (Brown 1994, 64).

Fig. 3.45.7 GROG fresh everted rim jar (Pollard 1988, fig 53.212).

Fig. 3.45.8 GROG fresh beaded and flanged bowl (Pollard 1988, fig 53.205–207).

Fig. 3.45.9 GROG fresh beaded and flanged bowl (Pollard 1988, fig 53.205–207).

Key Group 9 Layer [201] (Phase 9)

Key Group 9 deserves attention due to the nature of the deposit from which it was recovered. This deposit was reminiscent of so-called 'dark earth' layers typically encountered in urban contexts and was dated to the late fourth to early fifth century AD based on the stratigraphic and numismatic evidence. It contained an extensive assemblage of pottery, a total of 3611 sherds weighing 58.140 kg (61.24 EVE), which forms about a fifth of the total site assemblage.

Approximately 40% of the group by EVE is composed of local coarsewares, such as TSK and BB2. The importance of this is discussed below. The next most substantial group in the assemblage is Alice Holt/Farnham ware and the allied PORD fabric (16% of total by EVE), followed by local GROG wares. Other pottery fabrics traded over relatively long distances included red-slipped tableware and *mortaria* from the Oxfordshire kilns (8%). Other fine wares include MHAD and NVCC products, but in very small quantities. Long-distance trading connections are suggested by the presence of small quantities of fabrics imported from the Rhineland. These include MARB, roller stamped ARGO and MAYEN ware indicating links with the Continent during the late fourth and very early fifth century (Gerrard & Lyne 2008).

Table 3.14 Average sherd weights for selected pottery fabrics from layer [201]

Fabric	Sherd Count	Weight	Average weight (g)
AHFA	428	7454	17.41589
CALC	21	495	23.57143
GROG	360	6842	19.00556
MAYEN	2	106	53
OXMO	39	2227	57.10256
PORD	62	1012	16.32258
OXRC	182	2470	13.57143
OXWS	12	307	25.58333
LRMA (GERM)	4	103	25.75
ARGO	4	100	25
BB2	589	8023	13.62139
TSK	996	11,789	11.83635
NKFW	105	977	9.304762
SAM	29	664	22.89655

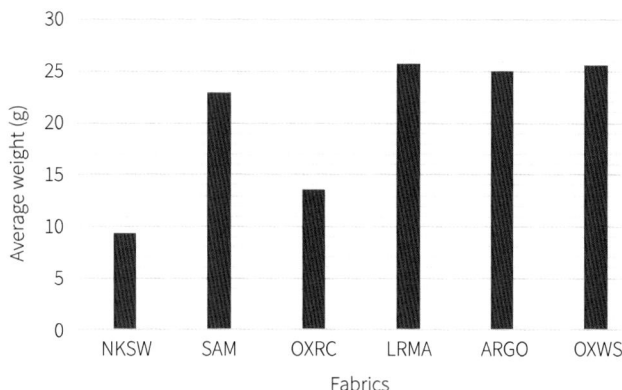

Fig. 3.46   Average sherd weights for early Roman fineware fabrics SAM and NKFW with late Roman average fineware sherd weights (for data see Table 3.13)

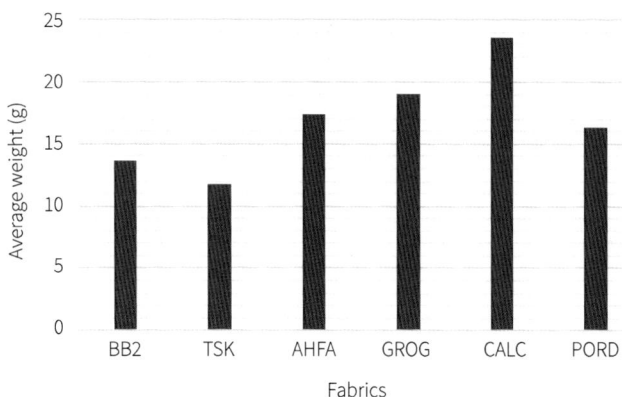

Fig. 3.47   Average sherd weights for early Roman coarseware fabrics BB2 and TSK compared with late Roman average coarseware sherd weights (for data see Table 3.13)

Sherds with graffito and an unusual rim

Two sherds exhibit partial, post-firing graffiti. The first is a small TSK jar base incised externally with the letters AMR (Fig. 3.48.1). The second, a BB2 jar base, is incised with a number of letters and/or numerals (Fig. 3.48.2). These appear to read IIIRII or IIIRVI. A number of other sherds have incised graffiti depicting a variety of subjects. Of these the most notable and intrinsically interesting is an example depicting a ship (Fig. 3.48.3) (Gerrard & Ridgeway 2018).

A fourth sherd may be particularly significant. It is a small, simple rim in a first-century, handmade, grog- and flint-tempered fabric (Canterbury B3) that has been stamped repeatedly with the letters VICCF (Fig. 3.48.4). The letters are thin, good quality and impressed pre-firing. They are stamped both on the top and the bottom of the sherd but seem to be smoothed off on the bottom. They might have been impressed using a metal brand for marking leather and their occurrence on an early sherd is noteworthy and may suggest the production of hides and leather at the site in the post-conquest period.

Illustrated sherds with graffiti

Fig. 3.48.1 <1305> TSK base sherd with letters [770] (Phase 7, Open Area 1).

Fig. 3.48.2 <1302> BB2 base sherd with letters [201].

Fig. 3.48.3 <1304> BB2 5E1 dish sherd with ship [293].

Fig. 3.48.4 <1303> B3 handmade grog tempered rim with stamp [844].

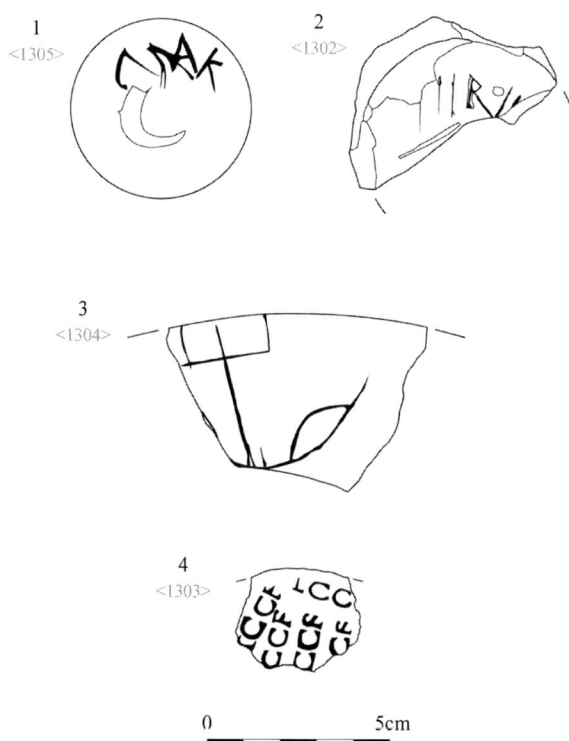

Fig. 3.48   Pottery sherds with graffiti (scale 1:2)

Discussion

Key Groups 1 and 2 embrace the Late Iron Age and Early Roman periods up to the mid-second century AD. When compared to early Roman pottery assemblages in west Kent (Pollard 1988), Key Group 1 shares the characteristics of immediately post-conquest and early-second-century assemblages. The dominance of handmade vessels in Late Iron Age tradition in the lowest fills is replaced by the dominance of post-conquest wares and early TSK products. The absence of imported wares and PATCH is notable, but might be due to the small size of the assemblage. Key Group 2 is very similar to Key Group 1 in terms of the transition from handmade to wheel-thrown pottery, but a greater range of fabrics is represented. There are more types of fine wares, and PATCH and imported pottery are also represented, even if in very small quantities only. The absence of BB2 and the less prominent presence of TSK products might indicate a shorter usage period than that of Key Group 1.

The beginning of the next ceramic phase of the site is marked by the appearance of Central Gaulish Samian, BB2 and the allied TSK fabric. The latest fills of Key Groups 1 and 2 have already shown signs of this phase, but Key Group 4 is the most important assemblage of the period. Although there are some sherds dated to the second half of the second century in the upper fills of the Key Group 4 pit, the pottery recovered is a coherent early-second-century group, which represents the development of forms of the emergent BB2 and TSK producers, and compares well to second- and early-third-century pottery assemblages in Kent (Pollard 1988, 87).

The end of this ceramic phase is heralded by the appearance of typical late Roman pottery and the demise of local products, as we can see in Key Group 5. Although the assemblage is dominated by TSK products, AHFA and OXRC and NVCC products and late third century forms, such as 'swan's neck' pendant-rim jars and pentice-moulded beakers are also present. The composition of this assemblage compares very well to third century assemblages in west Kent. According to Pollard (1988, 123) the most prominent fabrics of the period are TSK and BB2, with AHFA and BB1 appearing in the final quarter of the third century. Similar is the case of Late Roman pottery assemblages in London, where the most significant change in the mid-third century is thought to be the changing relationship of BB1 and BB2 with the former increasing and the latter decreasing (Symonds & Tomber 1991, 71).

Key Group 6 represents the Late Roman pottery assemblages from the site. Both London and west Kent pottery assemblages of the fourth century are characterised by the dominance of AHFA pottery following the decline of BB2 production (Symonds & Tomber 1991, 73, Pollard 1988, 143). The production of handmade grog-tempered wares also re-emerged and they form the next most important group. The predominant fine wares are from the Oxfordshire and Nene Valley potteries, but there is an increase in Continental imports, such as ARGO, MARB and MAYEN, which are present in Key Group 8. Pottery appropriate to the stratigraphic and numismatic date of Key Group 8 compares very well to Late Roman assemblages. The ARGO roller stamped products (produced up to AD 420) and MAYEN ware strongly suggest that this group also may have an important early-fifth-century component. However, the high percentage of TSK and BB2 in Key Group 8 is in sharp contrast to the composition of Key Group 6 assemblages. While some of the BB2 and TSK forms in Key Group 8 are of late-third- and fourth-century date, notably beaded and flanged bowls and so-called 'swan's neck pendant rim' jars of Monaghan's (1987, 136 and 96) classes 5A4 and 3H5 (Pollard 1988, 136), much of the TSK/BB2 assemblage is characterised by earlier forms, like the so-called pie-dish (classes 5C and 5D, Monaghan 1987, 140–147) of second- and earlier-third-century date. This suggests that a considerable component of the Thameside/BB2 products represent redeposited material, which can probably be linked to the formation processes of 'dark earth' type deposits (Yule 1990).

Functional analysis of the Key Group assemblages shows a general predominance of jar forms in all periods despite the proliferation of form types through time. Next in importance are bowls and beakers. This suggests a rural or villa type site (Evans 2001). Following Evans' analysis the low proportions of fine wares and amphorae also suggest the same. On the other hand the number of sherds per graffito in the total site assemblage (7000 sherds/graffito) is too low for rural type sites, and places Gillingham into the rural/sub-urban category (Evans 2001; fig 12).

Conclusions

The pottery assemblage described above has shed some light on the changing nature of the pottery supply to Gillingham spanning from the Late Iron Age to the early fifth century AD. The appearance and disappearance of certain types of pottery mark distinctive phases of ceramic supply and are well represented in selected groups.

The assemblage and the archive offer further opportunities to explore ceramic supply and use in northern Kent during the Roman period. In particular the ceramics from the site allows us to examine the changing use of pottery by a community living in relatively close proximity to the kilns located on the North Kent coast.

3.5 The Roman glass

John Shepherd

A total of fifty-three fragments of Roman glass came from the site (see catalogue, 1–53). The following report briefly examines this material.

Of the fifty-three fragments of Roman glass, twenty-one are body fragments from unidentifiable forms. There are five fragments of window glass (49–53) of which three fragments (49–51) are of the cast matt/glossy type that appears to have been made from at least the first century AD onwards, but two (52 and 53) are of the cylinder-blown variety. This type of window glass is later, first appearing during the late second or early third centuries. There are also three glass beads, reported on elsewhere in this volume (see Gerrard, Chapter 3.3).

The identifiable vessel fragments assemblage is dominated by the well-known and ubiquitous prismatic, square-sectioned bottle (Isings 1957, form 50). These bottles, designed as in-transit packages for all manner of liquid foodstuffs and cosmetics, were first made during the first century and continued in use into the third century. The decorations on the bases are a common feature of these bottles. Their function is varied, but it might be that the more elaborate designs were intended to allow bottles to be identified in some way, so that they could be returned for reuse by the purveyor of their original contents. The designs here (4 and 5; Fig. 3.49.3 and 3.49.4) have just parts of circles on them. Bases with concentric circles make up the largest number of base design types.

The colourless foot fragment (1, Fig. 3.49.1), from a dish or bowl, belongs to a distinctive group of late-first-century bowls and beakers. These were made of a good-quality colourless glass and finished off by wheel-cutting. Many have facet-cut decoration on their bodies and, in the case of many bowls, on their outsplayed rims too. Although small, this fragment represents what may have bene a very high-quality vessel. Pliny the Elder describes a type of glass that so valued that '…the highest value is set upon glass that is entirely colourless and transparent, as nearly as is possible resembling crystal in fact' (Pliny *Naturalis Historia* 36, 198–9). He adds that such vessels had replaced the use of silver and gold as drinking vessels. Many examples are known from London, both north and south of the river (Shepherd 2008, 247, no. 25; Shepherd 2008, 21; Shepherd 2008, no. 31; Shepherd 2008, 17–19, 22–24, 28), and these primarily derive from late-first- or early-second-century dated contexts. Further afield in Britain examples are known from Caerleon (Boon 1972–3, 116), Caerwent (Boon 1972–3, fig 2, no. 19), Fishbourne (Harden & Price 1971, fig 138, no. 26), Gloucester (Charlesworth 1974, fig 29, no. 4) and Lullingstone (Cool & Price 1987, 111, nos. 325 and 326), as well as more widely across the Empire (Harden 1936, Class IB I, 49–50, plxii, no. 166; Clairmont 1963, 18f, no. 90; Alarcão 1965, 76; Isings 1971, 77–8, nos. 136–139).

In summary, the presence of the colourless bowl fragment and the square bottles shows that glass from the two ends of the glass use spectrum were being supplied and used on this site. Of interest, however, is that there are not many fragments at all from between these two extremes. Only two jug or bottle handle fragments survive (20, Fig. 3.49.5 and 21). Both are probably tableware items and one (21), is likely to be late Roman in date and so not contemporary with the colourless dish or the square bottles.

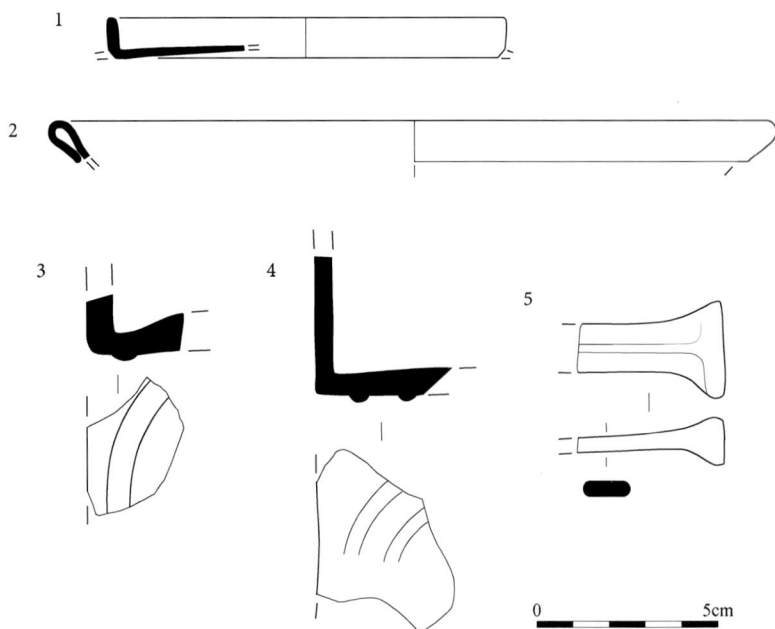

Fig. 3.49   Roman glass (scale 1:2)

Illustrated glass

Fig. 3.49.1 [800] <992> Fragment from the base of a large dish. Late first century (Cat no. 1).

Fig. 3.49.2. [874] Fragment from the vertical rim of a bowl. Late first to third century (Cat no. 2).

Fig. 3.49.3 [537] <881> Fragment from the base of a square-sectioned prismatic bottle. Late first or second century (Cat no. 4).

Fig. 3.49.4 [907] <716> Fragment from the base of a square-sectioned prismatic bottle. Late first or second century (Cat no. 5).

Fig. 3.49.5 [800] <1008> Part of the handle from a small jug or bottle. Applied; thick colourless glass with a green tint. Roman (Cat no. 20).

Catalogue

1. [800] <992> (Phase 5, [801], pit group 13). Fragment from the base of a large dish. Cast and polished; colourless glass. Flat base with a vertical, tall base ring. Late first century (Fig. 3.49.1).

2. [874] (Phase 6, Structure 1) Fragment from the vertical rim of a bowl. Free-blown; natural green blue glass. Rim folded out and down to form a collar. Late first to third century (Fig. 3.49.2).

3. [770] (Phase 7, Open Area 1) Fragment from the rim of a bottle. Free-blown; natural green blue glass. Rim folded inwards and flattened down. Late first or second century.

4. [537] <881> (Phase 9, layer group 49)
Fragment from the base of a square-sectioned prismatic bottle (Isings form 50). Mould-blown; thick natural green blue glass. Base decorated with design, of which just part of one circle survives. Late first or second century (Fig. 3.49.3).

5. [907] <716> (Phase 8, pit group 47) Fragment from the base of a square-sectioned prismatic bottle (Isings form 50). Mould-blown; thick natural green blue glass. Base decorated with design, of which parts of two circles survive. Late first or second century (Fig. 3.49.4).

6. [874] <1240> (Phase 6, Structure 1) Numerous, shattered fragments from the handle and neck of a square-sectioned prismatic bottle (Isings form 50). Mould-blown; natural green blue glass. Reeded handle. Late first or second century.

7. [731] (Phase 9, Pit [732]) Small fragment from the handle of a bottle. Applied; natural green blue glass. Late first or second century.

8–19. [549]; [694] (Phase 7, Open Area 1) x2; [770] (Phase 7, Open Area 1) x2; [874] (Phase 6, Structure 1) x5; [902] (Phase 6, Structure 1); ([937]) Twelve fragments from the bodies of a square-sectioned prismatic vessels. Natural green blue glass.

20. [800] <1008> (Phase 5, [801] pit group 13) Part of the handle from a small jug or bottle. Applied; thick colourless glass with a green tint. Roman. (Fig. 3.49.5).

21. [769] <938> (Phase 7, Structure 3) Fragment from the neck of a handle jug or bottle. Free-blown; thick natural green glass. Part of upper sticking art of handle survives. Probably third or fourth century.

22–24. [201] (Phase 9 layer); [530] (Phase 5, pit [570]); [949] (Phase 7, Building 5) Three fragments of natural (i.e. uncoloured) green glass from free-blown vessels of indeterminate form. Roman.

25–45. A further twenty-one fragments of natural green-blue glass from free-blown vessels of indeterminate form were recovered from a range of contexts. Roman.

46–48. Three fragments of free-blown colourless glass from vessels of indeterminate form were also recovered. Roman.

Window glass

49–51. [200] <1044> (Phase 11 ploughsoil); [201] (Phase 9, layer); [756] (Phase 7, Road)
Three fragments from the edges of cast matt/glossy window panes. Natural green glass. Roman.

52. [537] <923> (Phase 9, layer group 49) Fragment of double glossy, cylinder-blown window glass with a grozed edge. Natural green glass. Roman.

53. [619] <920> (Phase 9, layer group 49) Fragment of double glossy, cylinder-blown window glass. Natural green glass with surface decomposition. Roman.

3.6 The lead-lined wooden coffin

Victoria Ridgeway

A single, lidless, lead coffin-lining [212] originally contained within a wooden outer coffin was recovered from the mausoleum, block lifted and excavated off site and conserved by Dana Goodburn-Brown. Frequently referred to simply as 'lead coffins' (Toller 1977; Taylor 1993) this example, in common with many others, might be better described as a lead-lined coffin, given the presence of a timber outer coffin (Toller 1977, 1; and see Mills 1993). The coffin and lining were aligned east–west within and towards the northern end of a square mausoleum; the head of the skeleton lay to the east. An east–west orientation is the most common observed for lead-lined coffins both in Britain and Gaul (Toller 1977, 9; Gillet & Bechennec 2017, 75) reflecting the most commonly observed orientation of burials of the period generally.

The mausoleum had been extensively plough-truncated and the excavators considered that this had caused damage to the upper edges of the coffin (although other explanations are considered more probable, see below). In Roman Britain the archaeological evidence suggests that burial in a lead-lined coffin was unusual. A rapid assessment of the published literature suggests fewer than 300 have been reported on in any detail from the country as a whole, around 30 of which come from from the Kent region (see below), indicating that only *c.* 2% of the buried population were treated in this way, based on a figure of *c.* 13,000 excavated Roman burials in Britain (Pearce 2013). Lead-lined coffins contained within mausolea are rarer still (six examples, see below). Furthermore, the coffin displays some unusual characteristics, particularly relating to its internal decoration. The following report describes the coffin-lining, comments on its condition and places it within the broader context of similar items found locally, as well as within Britain and Gaul.

Methodology

The coffin-lining was block-lifted on site with contents intact and excavated under laboratory conditions. Following excavation, the coffin-lining was consolidated and provided with a steel framework which provides support and assists with moving the object (Goodburn-Brown in Seddon 2008). The coffin is stored upside down, packed internally with supporting foam. It was recorded by the present author in August 2018 and drawn at a scale of 1:5; it was not possible to record internal details at this time due to the position of the steel framework and presence of packing materials and such details are based on records made during excavation. The coffin is recorded according to Toller's (1977) typologies. The sides, end and base of the coffin have been labelled to assist description (Fig. 3.50).

Description

Lead coffin-lining

The lead coffin-lining is of Toller Type 2 (1977, 11: fig 2), constructed from a single sheet of lead, cut away at the corners, with the ends and sides folded up (Fig. 3.50). The sides and ends generally abut, although there were indications that the edge of side D had been folded over end A. During conservation it was noted that the inside vertical seams appeared to have been smeared with molten lead or tin. This simple form of construction appears to be common in both Britain and Gaul (Toller 1977; Mills 1993; Gillet 2000, 80–82, Type A).

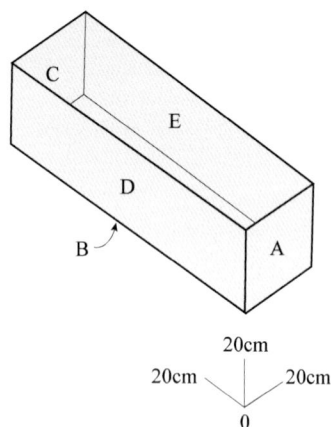

The lead coffin-lining is rectangular in plan, non-tapering, with square ends and measures 1.82m by 0.35m x 0.35m. No trace of a lid survived. Where visible in cross section the lead sheet from which the coffin was constructed varied in thickness from 2.5mm to 4mm. Whilst this variation might be due in part to post-depositional conditions, the method of manufacture might tend to result in a slightly uneven thickness of lead sheet. It is considered most likely that the lead sheets which were used to construct coffin-linings would have been formed by pouring molten lead onto a casting bed of damp sand or alternatively clay (Mills 1993, 127).

The lead coffin-lining displays some unusual attributes. It appears particularly long and narrow, slightly shorter but significantly narrower and shallower than the mean recorded by Toller for non-tapering adult-sized coffins (at 1.83m x 0.57m x 0.43m; see Toller 1977, 5, table 1). Using Toller's evidence for breadth and length of 68 'adult sized' coffins, gives ratios which range from 1:2.16 to 1:5.40. With a ratio of 1:5.20 the Grange Farm lead coffin lies very much towards the upper end of this range and is only exceeded by three examples in terms of overall breadth to length ratios.

There is no evidence for any external decoration or graffiti. The coffin-lining is simply decorated internally with a 'bead and reel' border around the base (Fig. 3.52). This closely respects Toller's 'double reel' form of 'bead and reel decoration', falling close to his B3o category (Toller

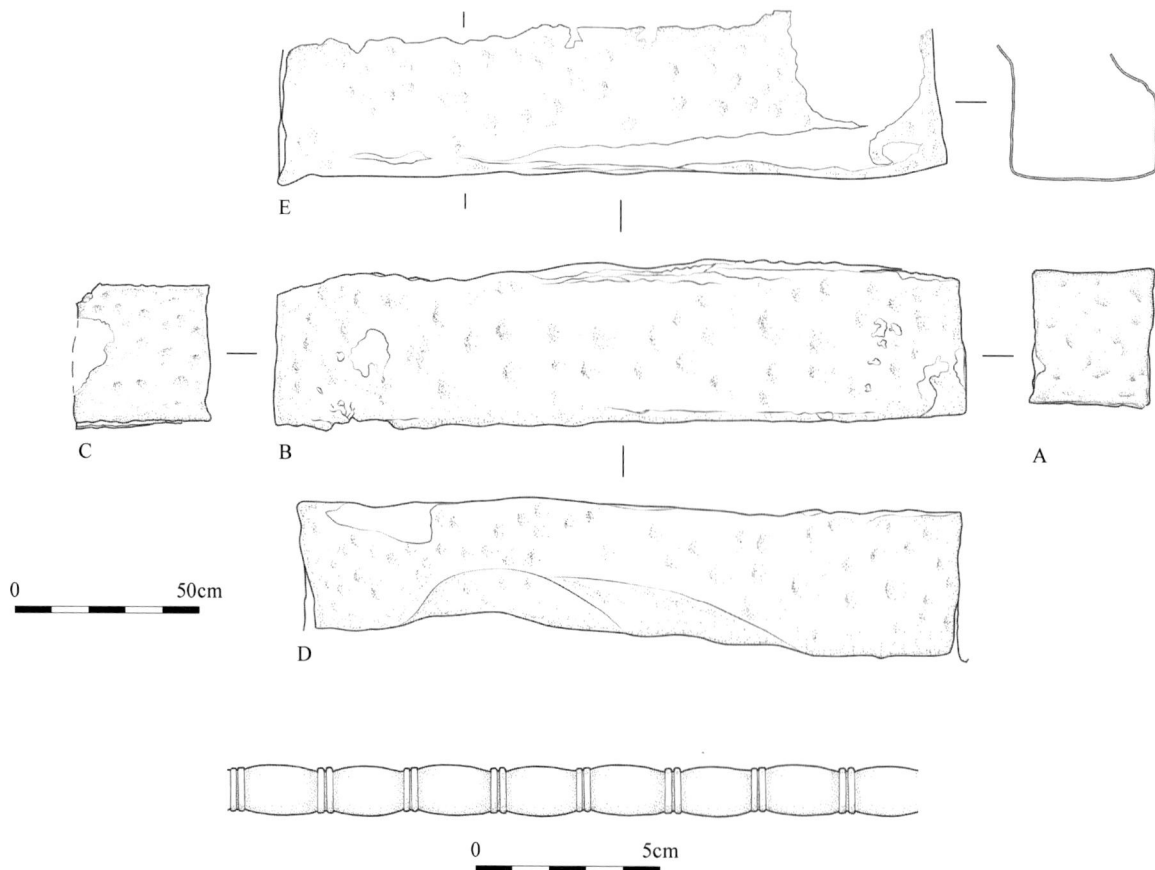

Fig. 3.50   External view of the coffin (top) with detail of internal bead-and-reel decoration shown bottom left (scales 1:20 & 1:2)

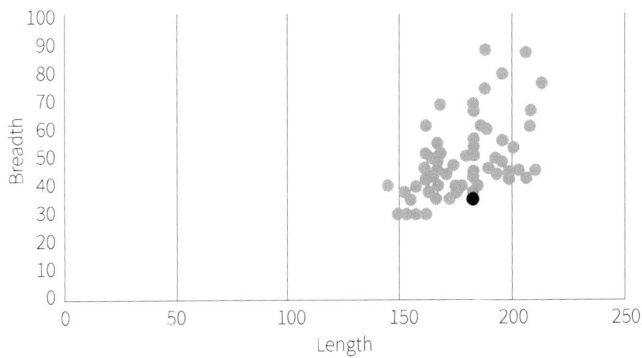

Fig. 3.51   Scatter plot showing the length/breadth of adult or adult-sized coffins recorded by Toller. The black spot denotes the Grange Farm coffin

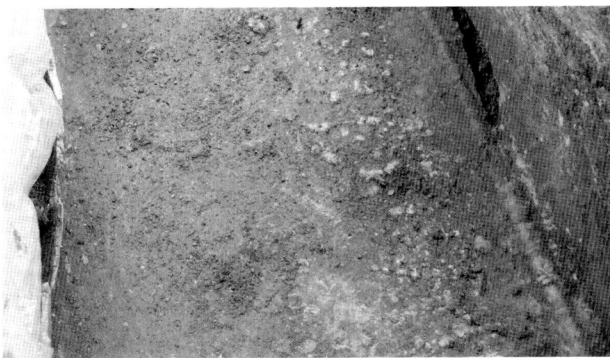

Fig. 3.52   Internal view of coffin during conservation; the double reel decorative band can be seen around the base of the coffin

Fig. 3.53   The coffin-lining following conservation, sitting base up on a protective frame and viewed here from the foot end

1977, 21, fig 4.5 and fig 4.17; 67). It comprises a series of 'beads' each just over 150mm long by *c.* 100mm wide, separated by a double band (Fig. 3.52).

Condition

At the time of recording the coffin appeared to be in a stable condition, it does not appear to have suffered any damage since conservation and protection. Details of condition on recovery and subsequent conservation treatment are held with the archive.

The foot end of the coffin (A) has suffered little damage and remains reasonably intact, with some cracking and small holes occurring close to the base at the point where the coffin has been folded. (Fig. 3.53). The head end of the coffin (C) has suffered damage close to the top (Fig. 3.50). The side which would have lain to the right of the body (D) has collapsed in significantly towards the top, cracks and holes are visible where the side meets the base. The left-hand side (E) is badly damaged with a large piece, measuring roughly 0.25m x 0.35m, missing close to the foot end. Extensive cracking and breakage is also apparent where the side meets the base. Generally, the sides and ends abut but are splitting apart close to the top of the coffin.

The base of the coffin (B, Fig. 3.50) appears to have suffered damage in antiquity in several locations. A hole in the base *c.* 0.1m across corresponds with the original position of the head; deposits of lead corrosion product are visible on the base of the skull along with impressions of what may be textiles (see Chapter 3.20 below). A collection of small holes up to 50mm in diameter at the foot end of the coffin might roughly correspond with the position of the feet. Due to the condition of the skeletal remains no assessment of stature was possible (see Langthorne this publication), however, assuming the latter holes do represent the position of the deceased's feet we might assume she was 1.6m in height or taller.

The wooden outer coffin

Staining of the surrounding soil and *in-situ* nails around the ends and side of the lead coffin-lining are all that survive of a wooden outer coffin. These demonstrate that the lead lining was contained within a wooden casket, secured with nails. The length of the nails was not recorded and these do not survive; however, records indicate that the coffin would have been secured by 20 nails in total, corresponding to the average recorded at Poundbury (Mills 1993, 63). Two nails were driven up through the base and into the sides and ends of the coffin respectively while three nails secured the sides to the ends vertically see (Fig. 3.54). Traces of what appeared to be timber within the grave may represent the remains of a wooden lid to the coffin, possibly thrown back in following robbing.

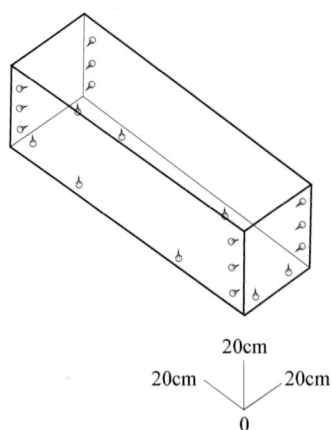

20cm

20cm   20cm

0

Fig. 3.54   The arrangement of coffin nails for the wooden outer coffin

Discussion

Lead-lined coffins are a rare find in Roman Britain constituting *c.* 2% of all known burials (see above); the most extensive survey of lead coffins to date (Toller 1977) records only 243 examples of lead coffins recovered from the province, to which more recently a further 23 have been added (Taylor 1993, 209), excluding the Grange Farm example. Whilst new examples continue to be found, the total number remains low, constituting less that 5% of known burials from the province. It is, of course, possible that lead coffin-linings discovered in antiquity, and perhaps until fairly recently, may have been reused owing to the value of lead as a raw material.

The coffin in the context of Kent and Britain

The distribution of Roman lead-lined coffins across Britain is heavily biased towards lowland Britain. Toller considers that the distribution of these is reflective of the wealth of Roman Britain (rather than the accessibility of lead as a raw material). A concentration is notable around the eastern reaches of the Thames estuary. Of the lead coffins studied by Toller, 55% were directly associated with roads leading out of walled urban centres, among which York, Dorchester and Colchester appear to be the most prolific. There could be some recovery bias in this, suburban areas being particular foci of excavation. Other popular locations include those associated with unwalled settlements and villa sites (Toller 1977, 2). Many of those not associated with urban centres appear to be relatively isolated and it is to this group that the Grange Farm example belongs. Obviously, the relative isolation of such burials may in some cases be misleading, reflecting the extent of investigation or recording in the vicinity of such finds. This may be particularly relevant to antiquarian findings, where a highly decorated lead vessel may have received greater attention than less readily obvious features. Kent appears relatively rich in terms of recovery of lead coffins (Fig. 3.55), of particular interest here is a group of eleven coffins

from the area around Sittingbourne, located on the line of Watling Street, some 12 miles east of Gillingham, described as 'outstanding' by Toller (1977, 2; see Appendix 3; Fig. 3.55, 6–15 and 19).

The adoption of burial in lead-lined coffins appears to be a late Roman phenomenon, although dating of many of the eighteenth and nineteenth-century discoveries, some curated and many others lost, is uncertain. Evidence from Poundbury, Dorset suggests the practice may have achieved its peak in the early fourth century (Mills 1993, 128). It has been associated with Romanisation, in particular the support for new religious beliefs such as '*humanitas*', the hope for survival of the body into the afterlife, a concept which may have gained ground during the later Principate in south-east England (Toller 1977, 4). How this concept might translate to lead *ossuaria*, in which bones were interred following the transformative of process of cremation, is less clear.

Coffins in mausolea: the significance of the mausoleum

The presence of a mausoleum surrounding a lead-lined coffin burial is exceptionally rare. Three percent, or a total of six individual coffins recorded by Toller (1977) are associated with mausolea; Taylor's more recent update does not record any further lead coffin-linings from mausolea (Taylor 1993, 210–212). Of the known examples to date, distribution is limited to Dorset (Poundbury) and North Kent (Keston and Lullingstone, in addition to the Gillingham example). Whilst some attributes (such as presence of an outer wooden coffin, for example) could be easily missed or assigned to excavator error, particularly when dealing with antiquarian records, the lack of identification of a surrounding mausoleum is less easy to explain away. The rarity of this phenomenon may not be unique to Britain. In an extensive survey of lead coffins from the Amiens region none were found in association with mausolea (Gillet & Bechennec 2017, 88).

Of the six examples known, the Poundbury group comprises four burials from two mausolea dated to the early fourth century (Mills 1993, 128). Both were sub-rectangular stone structures (neither fully exposed in plan) containing two lead-lined coffins each (Sparey-Green *et al.* 1993, 59). One of the mausolea contained additional burials. The two Kentish examples, from Keston and Lullingstone, both at some distance from Gillingham (and not shown on Fig. 3.55), provide geographically closer parallels (Philp nd, English Heritage nd) and appear to be slightly earlier, being dated to the late third century.

Despite their relative proximity, there are few obvious parallels within the Kentish group. The Keston lead coffin was contained within a circular mausoleum buried beneath a carefully constructed tile-built cist. Both coffin and lid were decorated with bead and reel moulding. Satellite tombs had been built on to the original structure. The Lullingstone example comprised the burial of a young man in a lead coffin decorated with scallop shell and cord

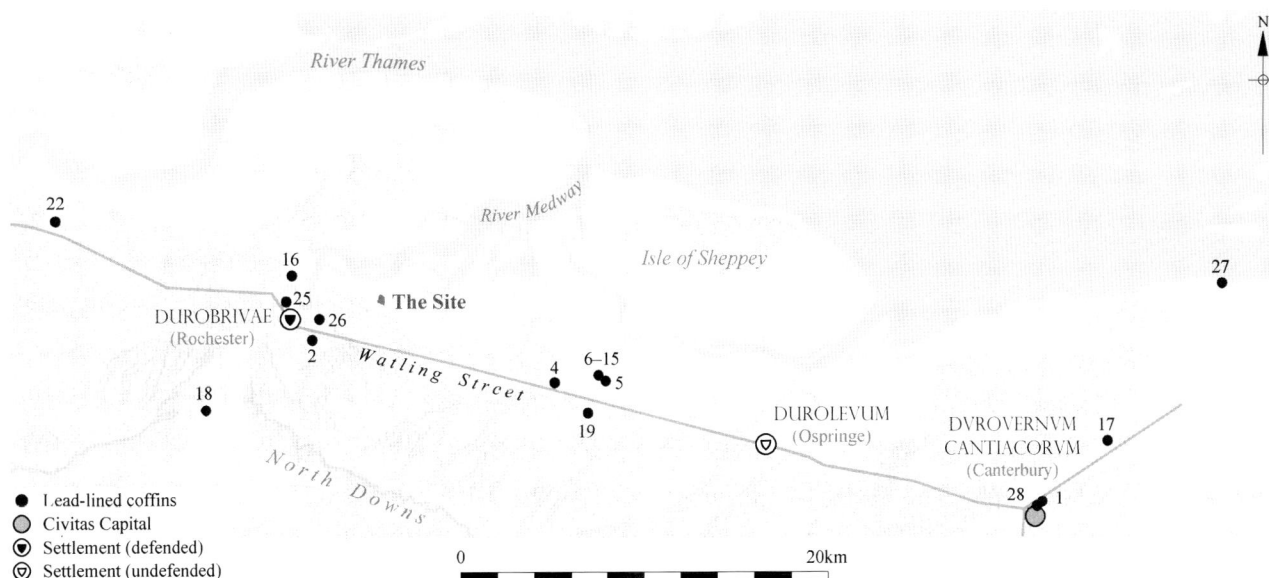

Fig. 3.55   Distribution of lead-lined coffins in the Medway, in relation to known Roman settlements and roads (see Appendix 3) (scale 1: 400,000)

design, within a temple-mausoleum of Romano-Celtic form, accompanied by the burial of a young woman.

The decorative scheme

Decoration, present on many lead coffin linings, is most frequently found on the lid in Britain as in Gaul (Gillet & Bechennec 2017, 94). Even where the sides were decorated the lid is frequently the most highly decorated aspect of the coffin lining and this might accord with its visibility when in the grave. The decorative elements could on occasion be inscribed into the sand-casting base prior to pouring out the molten lead (Mills 1993, 131) but more commonly would first be moulded, then cast and separately applied (Toynbee 1954, 40).

The bead-and-reel moulding, which ornamented the base of the Grange Farm coffin lining, is considered to have apotropaic properties (Toller 1977, 19). It is one of several moulded devices commonly used to accentuate linear elements of coffin linings, divide up panels and to form a St Andrew's Cross. It is a common design element of British, Gaulish, and German examples (Toynbee 1954), appearing as a major design element on the majority of decorated coffin lids from the Amiens region (Gillet 2000).

The Grange Farm lead coffin-lining base displayed no external decoration and had clearly been placed within a wooden outer coffin; outer covers of wood, stone and even lead are known, wood being the most common material in this respect. Some form of outer casing would have been expedient for the handling of coffins, lead being a flexible material lacking tensile strength and it is considered likely that most, if not all, lead coffins had some kind of 'outer' shell (Toller 1977, 1–2). This raises questions concerning the purpose of decoration on lead linings. Toynbee (1954, 39–40) assumes the decoration to be designed for the benefit of the dead,

who might occasionally 'visit' the place where their bones lay. Given the apparent importance of lead for preserving the physical remains of the body, it may be that the decoration was also intended to last long after any wooden casing had perished.

Some aspects of the decoration may also have been visible to the mourners and could have formed a powerful and highly visible decorative element during the funerary ritual, particularly when on the coffin lid, if the closing and sealing of the coffin were a visible part of the funerary ritual. It is, of course, possible that a wooden outer casing could be equally or more highly decorated than the lead lining within, and additionally colour may have been used, forming a notable aspect of the funeral procession.

No evidence for a lead lid to the Grange Farm coffin was found, yet it seems highly implausible that it did not have one. A lidless coffin would be extremely unlikely. Toller (1977, 53, 58) lists one possible and one definite example, both late nineteenth-century discoveries and both now lost, for which the lid did not survive; in both cases the lack of lid is considered most likely to be representative of lack of survival. There is compelling evidence here that the grave was robbed in antiquity (see Chapter 2). Damage to the upper edges of the coffin-lining were ascribed during excavation to the effect of ploughing, however, other explanations may account for this. If, as seems probable, the coffin-lining's lid was removed in antiquity, the damage at the head end of the coffin-lining and particularly the cracking and breakage along the left-hand side (E) may well have been caused as the lid was wrenched off.

Robbing may have partially been intended to remove the lid and if this were highly decorated may have been aimed at recovery for reuse, or for scrap value. Robbing may also have been aimed at retrieving grave-goods from within the coffin, assuming there were any. Against this interpretation is the relative lack of damage or movement to the corpse in antiquity. Alternative scenarios are possible; at Lullingstone offerings had been carefully arranged on the lid of the coffin.

Whatever the potential decoration on the lid or coffin outer, the bead and reel decoration on the inside of the Grange Farm coffin appears to be unique, certainly within Britain. Its presence might suggest that the body may have lain in state prior to burial; however, the likelihood that this decoration woud be visible to mourners remains low. The body of the female within the coffin was very slight (Langthorne, this volume), yet the narrowness of the coffin (at 0.35m) suggests that she would have had to be tightly bound prior to interment. It remains possible that the location of this decoration is actually a mistake, the result of a misunderstanding between those commissioning the coffin liner and the craftsman who carried out the work.

Concluding remarks

The Grange Farm lead coffin lining is a noteworthy example of a relatively rare artefact type. It is further distinguished by the (to date) unique characteristics of internal decoration. It is all the more remarkable for being one of only seven lead-lined coffin burials within mausolea from the province and only the third to be found in Kent. This is clearly an exceptional and high-status burial. Whoever the woman was interred within this grave she clearly was of exceptional standing within the community who buried her.

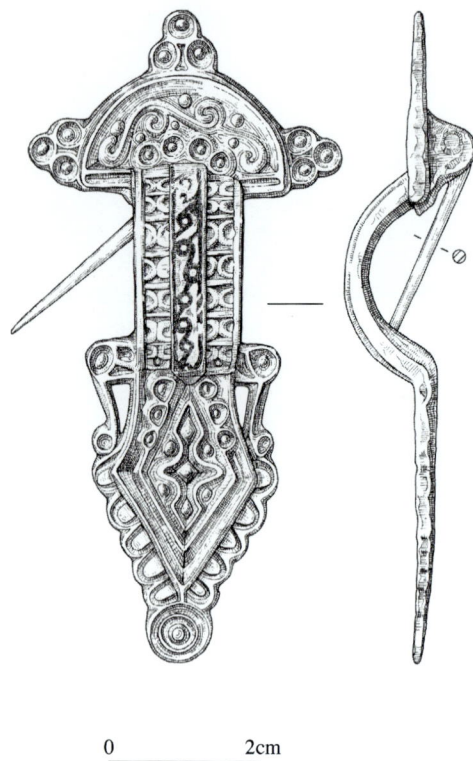

Fig. 3.56   The Anglo-Saxon brooch (scale 1:1)

3.7 The Anglo-Saxon brooch

Märit Gaimster

An early Anglo-Saxon brooch provides an unexpected find from the site. The brooch is interesting in several aspects. Of solid silver, cast in Nydam Style and gilded, it dates from the later part of the fifth century and so may be one of the earliest Scandinavian-style brooches known from England. The finds context of the brooch is also unusual; it was recovered with the aid of metal detectorists on site, just outside the north wall of the Late Roman mausoleum boundary wall. The brooch was initially thought to come from a disturbed burial, but careful excavation of the area found no evidence of a grave cut and no human bone or other grave goods were recovered. Considering its location, the brooch may instead be interpreted as some form of votive offering, with support in both Scandinavian and Anglo-Saxon parallels. This report is a shortened version of a longer article on the Grange Farm brooch and its find context (Gaimster 2016).

The brooch from Grange Farm has a characteristic form with a semi-circular head-plate and a foot plate of lozenge shape, joined by a curved bow. The head plate has three distinct projections, each formed by three lobes arranged as a triangle, around a central panel

Fig. 3.57   The Anglo-Saxon brooch

with curvilinear decoration. On the foot-plate, a central lozenge-shaped field carries a rosette motif while along each side is a frieze of tongue shapes, reminiscent of egg-and-dart design; at the lower end of the brooch is a circular terminal. The curved bow has a central band inlaid with niello, where circles joined by lines form a design reminiscent of the pilcrow, or paragraph, mark. The upper part of the foot-plate, where it joins the bow, is flanked by two openwork animal heads (Fig. 3.56a). The back of the brooch retains an iron pin-bar, set through three evenly spaced lugs, and the silver brooch-pin; the corresponding catch-plate is missing (Fig. 3.56b). A close parallel to the Grange Farm brooch can be seen in a nineteenth-century find held in the Canterbury Museum (Cancm: 2634; Bakka 1958, fig 2). The two brooches differ in some details, in particular in the lower end of the foot-plate where the Canterbury example carries a face-mask terminal flanked by two downwards-facing animals. On the whole, however, they share so many similarities it is likely they were produced in the same workshop (cf. Gaimster 2016 fig. 2). The Canterbury brooch was recognised early on by the Norwegian archaeologist Egil Bakka as a product of the Nydam Style (Bakka 1958, 8–9). The style is closely modelled on Late Roman chip-carved military fittings, with spiral patterns and rosette motifs utilised as surface decoration and moulded animal motifs restricted to the borders (Haseloff 1974, 1–7; cf. Fig. 3.31.3). Another element adopted from Late Roman military fittings is the use of niello inlays to contrast with the deep relief decoration, with examples including the 'paragraph' design, seen on the Grange Farm brooch (Haseloff 1981, 9; cf. Böhme 1986, Abb. 26.1; Behmer 1939, Taf. XXVII 1–3). On the Canterbury brooch, the downward-facing animals and the human face-mask terminal can be recognised as a well-known Roman motif of face masks flanked by animals (Haseloff 1981, 140–41). With the appearance of Style I, conventionally dated to *c.* 475 AD, the Roman motifs were transformed into new and independent designs that were given a central place as surface decoration (Haseloff 1986).

When discussing the Canterbury brooch, Bakka considered it the product of a 'Scandinavian master' (Bakka 1958, 8–9). The view that these early brooches were Scandinavian imports is still broadly held by many scholars of the Anglo-Saxon period and may be supported in a recent find from Uppåkra, an important migration period settlement in south-west Sweden (Magnus 2001, 183–4 and fig 10e). Here the fragment of a very similar gilt-silver brooch was recovered, consisting of a semi-circular head-plate with the same flat, trilobe projections (Magnus 2001, fig 10e). Establishing the provenance of this fragment, however, is not straightforward. In all, some 120 brooches dating from the fifth and sixth centuries were recorded at Uppåkra, with a large proportion broken up and fragmented and interpreted as scrap metal for the workshops on site (Hårdh 2003, 45–59). Many of those brooches were of non-Scandinavian types, including

so-called 'Dreirundelfibeln' that take their name from the characteristic trilobe projections on the head-plate. The brooch type dates from the late fifth and early sixth centuries, and has close parallels on the Continent from where the type is thought to originate (Hårdh 2002, 43–4; Hårdh 2003, fig 8). For the fragment relevant to the brooches from Grange Farm and Canterbury, scholars have pointed to parallels in many different regions, including England (Hårdh 2003, 56–7 and 65). Three brooches from East Anglia, reported through the Portable Antiquities Scheme, also provide support for a regional production outside Scandinavia. Again, these brooches differ in some detail from the Kentish pair, not least in the choice of material as all three are of gilt copper-alloy (cf. Wise 2011). Nevertheless, as a group they share more similarities than with Scandinavian brooches. This is reflected in their small size but also in form and design such as the broad and raised central band on the bow, and in the symmetrical central motif on the foot-plate (for a more detailed discussion of these brooches, see Gaimster 2016). From this perspective, the English brooches may be compared with the gold bracteates from the late fifth and early sixth centuries, where research has confirmed regional productions of these figural and amuletic pendants also outside Scandinavia (Gaimster 1992; cf. Pesch 2004; 2007).

With no obvious connection to a burial, the Grange Farm brooch provides an unusual find. In Anglo-Saxon England, high-status brooches like this were normally deposited as grave-goods. It is of course possible that the brooch was lost; the catch plate at the back is missing, which might suggest it broke and caused the brooch to fall off its owner. However, it would seem unlikely that such a precious object, cast in solid silver, would not be searched for and retrieved. Intentionally breaking or damaging objects, on the other hand, is a phenomenon strongly associated with ritual acts; it is frequently seen in votive offerings, and has been interpreted as a feature marking their transition from this and into the otherworld (Behr 2010, 77–79). This might suggest an alternative interpretation of the brooch at Grange Farm as some form of offering. It is worth noting that closer investigation of its actual find spot recorded an irregular patch of flint nodules and other rounded stones in a clay matrix. This was probably a patch of demolition rubble but might have been a clay-lined pit, something that may also be indicative of a ritual deposit. The careful preparation of pits, in the form of clay lining or layering with cobbles, has been noted as a feature of placed deposits, for example of animal bone (Morris & Jervis 2011, 74–77). In this context the location of the brooch, close by the ruined Late Roman mausoleum, must also be of significance. The choice of ancient monuments as a site for Anglo-Saxon cemeteries is a well-recorded phenomenon that has been discussed from the perspective of both ritual and social considerations. Pre-existing cult places may have been considered appropriate spaces for communicating with ancestral or supernatural powers, but they may also signify connections with the past and serve to legitimise claims over land (Williams 1997). At Grange Farm, the mausoleum represents a ritual space that would not have been so distant in time, if culturally very different, for the owner of the brooch. The later construction of Anglo-Saxon churches over the remains of mausolea, as was the case at both Lullingstone and in Canterbury (Meates 1979, 123; Blockley 2000, 75–78 and 123), indicates the visual presence of these structures, and an awareness of their meaning and function. The brooch, too, is not isolated as a possible votive offering at Grange Farm; as discussed elsewhere in this volume, other ritual activities may have taken place on site throughout the sub-Roman period.

As a placed deposit, the brooch at Grange Farm may be unusual in an Anglo-Saxon context. In South Scandinavia, on the other hand, precious-metal brooches of this type are known in hoards dating from the late fifth and early sixth centuries. Here they are associated with beads and amuletic pendants in the form of gold bracteates, and generally interpreted as votive offerings (Hedeager 1991; Gaimster 2001, 147). Gold bracteates and decorated brooches in the new Germanic animal style were used in many regions around the North Sea and on the continent, but the manner in which these objects were deposited indicates regional differences. Votive offerings have long been recognised as a specific phenomenon of south Scandinavia and northern Germany, while outside this core area they were placed in burials; only in south-west Norway and on the Baltic islands in the east are both forms of deposits known (cf. Gaimster 1992, fig 2). However, the recent discovery of the first known certain Anglo-Saxon bracteate hoard, at Binham in Norfolk, has modified this picture. The hoard consisted of five bracteates, all damaged or deliberately folded prior to deposition, along with two bracelets, one of gold and the other of copper alloy, both of which were chopped and twisted (Behr & Pestell 2014). The find has confirmed the indication of other similar votive offerings in England, suggested by finds of bracteates that were intentionally folded before deposition. This is a phenomenon never encountered in burials, where the bracteates were deposited as actual pendants (Behr 2010, 77–79). These discoveries change our understanding of ritual behaviour in Anglo-Saxon England and show that an interpretation of the Grange Farm brooch as a votive offering would not be out of place. Importantly, they also challenge the perceived contrast to ritual practices in the Iron Age and Roman period, when personal objects are known from both burials and votive deposits (Crawford 2004, 90; Behr 2010, 80).

3.8 The Anglo-Saxon spearheads

Jon Allison, James Gerrard and Andrew Welton

Two complete iron spearheads were recovered from layer [201]. Their presence in this deposit is intriguing because both are of types usually seen as being 'Anglo-Saxon'.

Description

Fig. 3.58, Fig. 3.59 <212> (Phase 9 deposit [201]) A complete iron, lanceolate spearhead with a fullered or 'corrugated' cross section and a split socket.

Typologically the lanceolate spearhead <212> can be classified using Swanton's (1973, fig 47) scheme as part of his I2 group (see also Dickinson 1976, 316). The more recent classification, based on ratios between different elements of the spearhead, by Høilund Neilsen (2013, 163–166, fig 5.95 and table 5.58) would place this as a SP5. Welton, who recently refined Høilund Neilsen's spearhead types, has classified this spearhead as Leaf-Bladed Fullered (2018, 114–117, fig 3.9).

0   5cm

Fig. 3.58 Spearhead <212> showing fullered or 'corrugated' surface

Fig. 3.59 Spearhead <212> showing socketing and end view of fullered or 'corrugated' surface

Fig. 3.60, Fig. 3.61 <542> (Phase 9 deposit [201]) A complete iron, angular spearhead with a concave-profiled blade,. The blade is separated from the socket by a 'neck'. The socket is split and contains a transverse rivet about a third of the way from the base.

Typologically the angular spearhead <542> can be classified using Swanton's (1973, fig 39) scheme as part of his H2 group (see also Dickinson 1976, 310–311). Høilund Neilsen's (2013, 163–166, fig 5.87) typology would describe this example as a SP2–B1A2, and Welton has classified it as Angular-5 (2018, 114–117, fig 3.9).

Date

The date of these spearheads presents an interesting conundrum. Both appear to be 'Anglo-Saxon' spearhead types typically found in the earliest weapon burials of the late fifth and early sixth centuries. Their presence alongside Late Roman finds in layer [201], however, raises the question of when these putatively 'Anglo-Saxon' spearhead types first appeared in Britain. There are relatively few spearheads found in well-dated fourth- and early-fifth-century contexts in Britain or northern Gaul and Germany, and the recent study of Anglo-Saxon graves and gravegoods, of which Høilund Neilsen's (2013) work forms a part, focused on the sixth and seventh centuries AD (Hines & Bayliss (eds.) 2013). Understanding how 'early' in the Anglo-Saxon period, or 'late' in the Roman period, these spears could be, therefore presents a challenge.

Spear <212> has a fullered profile and split socket typical of spearheads found in graves in Britain and along the Rhine dated AD 450–550. There are, however, small numbers of similar spearheads from very late-fourth- and early-fifth-century graves in Gaul and the lower Rhine (Böhme 1974, 101, Taf 60.15). A very good parallel comes from Donderberg Grave 18 (Netherlands) (Wagner & Ypey 2011, 582–584) which is almost certainly to be dated to the first half of the fifth century (Dr Andreas Rau pers. comm.).

Spear <542> can be paralleled by a number of spearheads in Anglo-Saxon contexts in Britain. Swanton dated this style to between AD 450–550, and Hines and Bayliss identified it with their first two phases (AS-M(o)-p, before AD 570; 2013, fig 8.16, table 10.1). There is, however, a continental parallel from Grave 2086 at Bordeshom (Schleswig-Holstein), associated with a very late fourth- or perhaps just fifth-century brooch (Saggau 1981, 87). There is thus a possibility that this spearhead might just be very late-fourth-century.

If the two spearheads are treated as a single closed find and placed into the 'Anglo-Saxon' burial sequence, this assemblage dates to the very beginning of the 'Anglo-Saxon' period. Although the recent study of Anglo-Saxon grave goods (Hines & Bayliss 2013) focused particularly on the sixth and seventh centuries, their catalogue included burials that dated back to the first appearance of furnished inhumation during the fifth century. Spearheads

<212> and <542> can be dated within Hines and Bayliss' chronological sequence by adding the spearheads to their catalogue (2013, e-fig 6.6) and repeating their correspondence analysis (cf. Austin 2014). The result identifies the spearheads as belonging to Hines and Bayliss' earliest phase AS-M(o), which their study dated primarily to the fifth century, but no later than AD 550 (Hines & Bayliss (eds.) 2013: fig 8.16). When this analysis is repeated using Welton's refined spearhead typologies (2018, 114–117: fig 3.9), which distinguish subtypes of fullered spearheads and refine the angular types, the spearheads are placed at the very beginning of the funerary seriation (fifth century) as one of the earliest 'Anglo-Saxon' spearhead assemblages in the study's catalogue.

0   5cm

Fig. 3.60 Iron spearhead <542>

Fig. 3.61 Iron spearhead <542> showing socketing and riveting

Discussion

Both spearheads are types common in 'Anglo-Saxon' burial assemblages dating to the late fifth century, but both might date as early as *c.* AD 400–450. Their recovery from layer [201] in association with a single sherd of Anglo-Saxon pottery, a large number of late fourth-century coins – of which four were struck later than AD 388 and one later than AD 395 (Gerrard this volume) –, a Hawkes and Dunning belt fitting (<532> Gerrard this volume), two finger-rings manufactured from cut down late fourth-century bracelets (Swift 2012, Gerrard this volume) and an extensive group of late Roman pottery (Gerrard & Hudak this volume) is of considerable interest.

Both spearheads are intact and extremely well-preserved. If they had been recovered from a grave then this might be explicable, but their deposition in the upper fill of a holloway is extremely unusual. While most 'Anglo-Saxon' type spearheads are found in burials, these spearheads' well-preserved state makes it inconceivable that they have been ploughed out from a burial and redeposited. A handful of 'Anglo-Saxon' type spearheads have been recovered from Late Roman sites (cf. Swanton 1974). One, a leaf-bladed spearhead, was found in the subsoil at a Romano-British site next to a holloway at Coldswood Road (Ramsgate, Kent) (Andrews *et al.* 2009, 117), although this spearhead's shape (consistent with Swanton's C2/C5 types) is more likely to date from the sixth or seventh century than earlier.

No spearheads with fullered or concave-sided angular blades like <212> and <542> have hitherto been found in Late Roman contexts. Further, while these spearheads types are typical for late-fifth-century 'Anglo-Saxon' cemeteries, both are uncommon in Kent. Swanton's type H2 spearheads comprise 12% of the spearheads found in Early Anglo-Saxon funerary contexts, but only 5% of those recorded from Kent in the Anglo-Saxon Kent Electronic Database (Harrington and Brookes 2012). Spearhead <212> is the only type I2 spearhead ever recorded in Kent. We might therefore wonder how they came to find their way into this deposit.

The discovery of these spearheads in layer [201] is therefore of interest. Do the spearheads date the fill to the early 'Anglo-Saxon' period? Or do the stratigraphy and associated finds provide an early date for the spearheads? Here we are adrift, but the Romano-British finds from [201] are an assemblage that could fit the early fifth-century AD (Gerrard 2013).

3.9 The cross-staff terminal

Märit Gaimster

An openwork copper-alloy mount, recovered from ploughsoil deposits, is of particular interest for the site in the earlier part of the Middle Ages (Fig. 3.62) <321>. The mount belongs to a well-established group of fittings broadly identified as cross-staff terminals, comparable to spherical mounts shown at the base of cross-staffs in medieval pictorial sources (Bailey 1994, 174; cf. Meddens & Draper 2014, 23). Broadly similar in decoration, the terminals feature openwork lattice patterns, sometimes incorporating star- or cross-designs, and with frequent projecting knops connecting the decorative elements. Stratified finds suggest a date in the late eleventh to twelfth centuries for these mounts (Bailey 1994, 173–74; cf. Blockley 1988, 117; Hunt 2011, 77). The Grange Farm terminal is formed by two discs joined by a broad circumferential band. At one end are the remains of a rectangular socket, sufficient for the mount to be attached to a slender shaft; terminals that retain the socket normally show two opposing holes for fixing. The most complete of the discs displays a central openwork equal-armed cross within a circle, surrounded by short arms divided by openwork triangles in opposing directions. Numerous small knops decorate the surfaces, with a larger projecting knop at the centre of the cross. The broad circumferential band also carries an openwork design of opposing triangles. The mount is virtually identical to a complete example in the British Museum, showing that both discs on the Grange Farm mount would have been identical in design (Ward Perkins 1940: fig. 2 no. 2).

As a category of finds, cross-staff terminals await full publication and dissemination; however, a recent overview of around 35 further examples, drawing in particular on finds continuously recorded within the Portable Antiquities Scheme, suggests three recurring forms (Gaimster 2020a, 478–79). Most frequent among

0 2cm

Fig. 3.62   Cross-staff terminal <321>

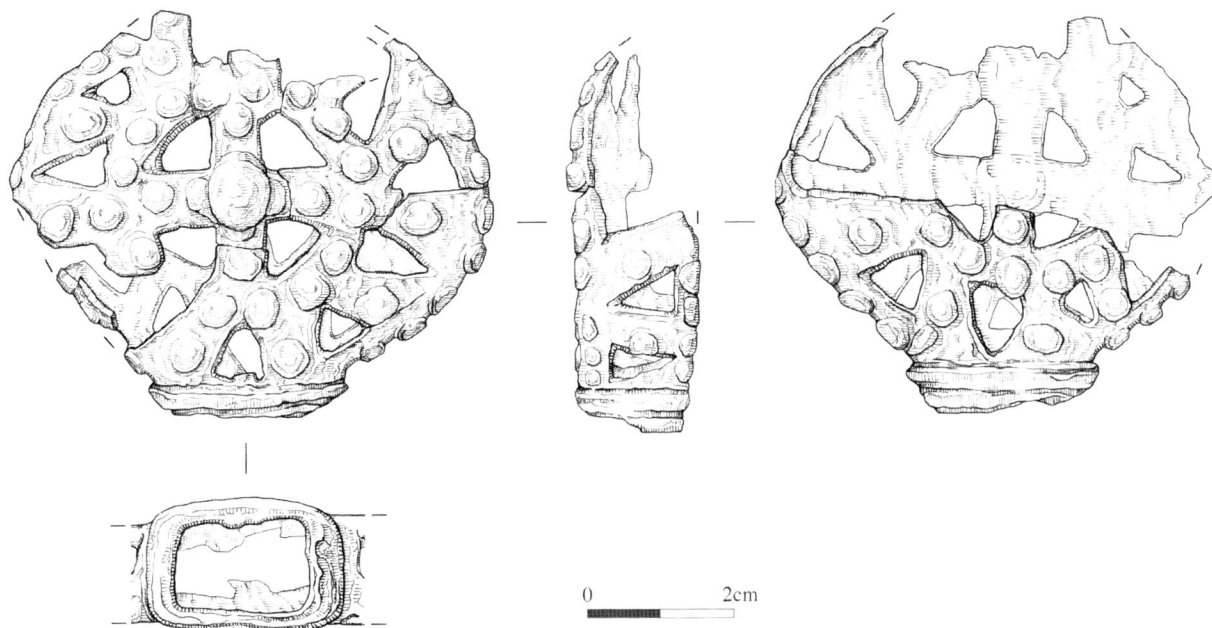

Fig. 3.63   Cross-staff terminal <321> (scale 1:1)

the finds are spherical terminals, which tend to have circular sockets, followed by the disc-shaped form seen at Grange Farm, where the socket is usually rectangular. This suggests the form of the mount related to the shape of the wooden staff it was fixed to. Besides these two forms of cross-staff terminals is also a third and more elongated version. This has a narrow, pointed openwork body, topped with a knop finial, above a round socket. The form has been considered Late Saxon (cf. PAS: NMS-F5B414, NMS-01DEB6 and HER28254, all from Norfolk), a date that is supported by a recent find from a Late Saxon context at Stoke Quay in Ipswich, Suffolk (Gaimster 2020b, 225, fig.5.33). A Late Saxon date is also established for a disc-shaped terminal with zoomorphic decoration, from Fishamble Street in Dublin. The terminal was recovered from a context dated to *c.* 1020–30 but the decoration, in Winchester Style, suggests a date for the manufacture of this object in the early to mid-tenth century (Halpin 1988).

At Grange Farm, the cross-staff terminal provides important physical evidence for a chapel here at the time when Bishop Odo, brother of King William I, held Grange Manor. The standing remains of a late medieval chapel, constructed in the later part of the fourteenth century, survive to the south of the area excavated by PCA, but the earliest record of a chapel at Grange dates from the late eleventh century (Meddens & Draper 2014, 11). A close association with churches and chapels is sometimes supported in the finds context of cross-staff terminals, including examples discovered in the close vicinity of Wixford Church in Warwickshire (Bailey 1994, 173) and Southwark Cathedral, recorded as a minster in the 1086 (Gaimster 2020a, fig. 11.1). At Stoke Quay in Ipswich, the cross-staff terminal was retrieved from an area just to the south of the recorded remains of the Late Saxon Church of St Augustine (Gaimster 2020b, 225).

3.10 The lead *crux ansata* pendant

Märit Gaimster

A small and crudely cast lead cross of an unusual form, with the upper part formed by a flattened disc (<335>; Fig. 3.64), was recovered from ploughsoil deposits. The form is known as *crux ansata* or Coptic cross. Derived from the Egyptian *ankh*, the symbol of life, this cross originates in the developments of the Coptic church in the fifth and sixth centuries. While it presents a surprising find in this context, the Grange Farm cross does have a parallel in the so-called Alban cross, associated with the Romano-British St Alban and itself considered unique in Britain. The Alban Cross is known from both documentary and pictorial medieval sources and has been discussed in depth by Birthe Kjølbye-Biddle (2001). The story of the martyrdom of Alban, based on earlier descriptions of an unnamed saint, originate with Germanus, Bishop of Auxerre, who visited Britain in the fifth century (cf. Wood 2009; Sharpe 2001). It was later elaborated on by other writers, notably Bede. The first reference to a cross in association with St Alban, however, dates from the late-twelfth-century writings of the monk William at St Albans (Kjølbye-Biddle 2001, 96–97). The idea of a cross, given to Alban by Amphibalus, the man who converted Alban and in whose place Alban offered himself to be executed, was developed by Matthew Paris, a monk at St Albans 1217–1259. In his writings, notably the illustrated *La Vie de Seint Auban*, Paris describes the cross as strange and special, 'the first brought to Britain' (Kjølbye-Biddle 2001, 98). Liberally illustrated in *La Vie*, it is clear that the Alban cross is based on the *crux ansata*; like the cross from Grange Farm, the fourth arm is formed by a flat

Fig. 3.64   Lead *crux ansata* pendant <335>

disc although the Alban cross is sometimes shown plain, and sometimes with a crucifixion at the centre or marks indicating stains of blood (Kjølbye-Biddle 2001, figs 2–9). It is also from Matthew Paris we learn that this wonderful cross, having been long hidden in London, was acquired by Abbot William of Trumpington (1214–1236). In fact, it may be more likely that it was Matthew himself who 'found' the cross, likely to have been made made of wood, which would have represented an important relic for the monastic house (Kjølbye-Biddle 2001, 97–100). A cross of this same unusual form is subsequently mentioned in a fourteenth-century reliquary list from St Albans (Kjølbye-Biddle 2001, 95). Whether the cross was a contemporary fake or not, its form clearly corresponded to an idea or understanding of what a very early cross would have looked like. Kjølbye-Biddle here draws attention to the widespread use of the *crux ansata* in the Coptic church, from the earliest period and into the tenth century, and to the contacts with and influences from North Africa seen in Coptic metalwork and textiles and other Egyptian imports in Anglo-Saxon England (Kjølbye-Biddle 2001, 105).

The apparent absence of the *crux ansata* in Anglo-Saxon and Insular imagery undoubtedly strengthens the connections between the cross from Grange Farm and the cult of St Alban, suggesting it may represent a pilgrim souvenir. The appearance of the cross in the story of St Alban fits well into the flourishing of pilgrimage from the twelfth century onwards, a phenomenon that saw a mass-production of lead-tin souvenirs. In Britain, these objects were initially in the form of *ampullae* and, later, pilgrim badges (Spencer 1998, 1–7). The cult of St Alban, as it appears in the writings of Matthew Paris, was clearly given a boost in the thirteenth century with the acquisition

of a wonderful relic in the form of the Alban cross, but this particular imagery was apparently short-lived. The latest reference to the cross is a fifteenth-century oak carving in the watching loft of the St Alban Abbey church, and it seems to have disappeared entirely from the story by the early 1500s (Kjølbye-Biddle 2001, 105). Known pilgrim badges of St Alban, dating from the fourteenth and fifteenth centuries, are all variations of the same theme showing the execution of Alban, his decapitated head caught in the branches of a tree with his body slumped below. No depictions of the wonderful cross are known, although another defining detail of the story is usually included, in the eyes of the executioner shown popping out of his head; thus, he would never benefit from seeing the virtues that would arise from St Alban's martyrdom (Spencer 1990, 44 no. 90 and figs 121–22; cf. Spencer 1998, 175 and cat. no. 196b; Egan 2001). As a probable pilgrim souvenir, the cast Grange Farm cross is unique in many ways. Its crude character is at variance with known signs and badges, which are far more delicate and were designed to be sewn onto clothing, in particular hats and headgear. The cross has a small perforation near the upper edge of the disc-shaped head, indicating that it could have been worn as a pendant; however, it could also have been attached with a nail to a wall or a larger, probably wooden, object. While there are currently no parallels to this unique object, it is also worth remembering that the pilgrim badges known to us are just a drop in the ocean in relation to the vast numbers that were produced at the time. As an example, the short-lived pilgrimage at Regensburg in Bavaria saw the production of over 100 000 badges in one year, celebrating a new miracle-working altarpiece of the Virgin and Child; of these badges only two are known to remain, along with a few moulds (Kjølbye-Biddle 2001, 14).

3.11 The later medieval metal finds

Märit Gaimster

with a contribution on coins and jetons by Murray Andrews

Around thirty later medieval objects were recovered from the excavations, mainly as residual or unstratified finds. The most frequent category is represented by belt accessories, including three complete copper-alloy buckles with buckle-plates. An oval buckle has an ornate outer edge with a notched lip for the pin and an offset bar for the buckle-plate; the plate is short and retains three of its original five sturdy rivets that would have fixed it to the leather strap (Fig. 3.65.1). The buckle dates from the late thirteenth to fourteenth centuries (cf. Egan & Pritchard 1991, 76–78; Whitehead 2003, 22 no. 89). A fragment of the outer frame of a similar buckle was also recovered (Fig. 3.65.2). A later date, from the mid-fourteenth and through to the early fifteenth centuries, can be assigned to a buckle with a characteristic integral plate (Fig. 3.65.3). The buckle has a forked spacer, to which separate sheets were soldered to form the buckle plate (cf. Egan & Pritchard 1991, 78–82). An incomplete, and possibly unfinished, example shows the forked spacers to which the buckle-plate was fixed (Fig. 3.65.4). A third complete buckle has a more unusual trapezoid frame with expanded corners and a central lip, forming an engrailed front edge (Fig. 3.65.5; cf. Whitehouse 2003, 30 no. 175). The buckle-plate is short with the back slightly narrower than the front; it retains two sturdy rivets for fixing. Trapezoidal buckles, too, are a late medieval form, with the engrailed edge considered a feature of the fifteenth century (Whitehouse 2003, 26). Three smaller buckles were also among the finds. Two are rectangular with a widened outside frame that is either plain or furnished with transverse grooves (Fig. 3.65.6–Fig. 3.65.7); these small buckles date from the late fourteenth century (cf. Egan & Pritchard 1991, fig 61; Griffiths *et al.* 2007, 96–97). The third buckle has a small oval frame and collared pin; the offset bar has a small knop at either end (Fig. 3.65.8). The form may belong above all to the thirteenth and fourteenth centuries (Egan & Pritchard 1991, fig 42 nos 271 and 274; Griffiths *et al.* 2007, 86 nos 452–60). A wide single-framed rectangular buckle is also likely to be late medieval in date (Fig. 3.65.9), with examples dating from the thirteenth–fifteenth centuries (Ottaway and Rogers 2002, fig 1469 no. 15189; cf. Whitehead 2003, 26 no. 132).

Two late medieval strap-ends of copper alloy were also identified. One, like the buckles above, has plates soldered to a forked spacer; the strap-end has a circular base with an acorn knop (Fig. 3.65.10; cf. Egan & Pritchard 1991, fig 92). The other, which is more fragmentary, is an openwork cast form with a trefoil terminal, stamped with a fine zig-zag pattern formed by opposing triangles along the centre and sides (Fig. 3.65.11). Parallels suggest it was originally rectangular with two circular openings below the oblong slots, and that it was fixed to the strap with a fine rivet at each end (cf. Egan & Pritchard 1991, fig 85 no. 608). The strap-end from Grange Farm retains a small rivet through the trefoil but only one of the circular openings above has been drilled through, suggesting it might be an unfinished piece. Associated with belts and straps is also a fine pentagonal strap loop with an internal rivet at the base (Fig. 3.65.12). The arched frame would have provided room for mounts and hole reinforcements on the strap (cf. Egan & Pritchard 1991, 231 nos. 1250–53 and figs 143 and 147). A strap-mount in the form of a scallop shell with a single internal has parallels in mounts dating from the late fourteenth to early fifteenth centuries (Fig. 3.65.13; cf. Egan & Pritchard 1991, fig 126 no. 1083; Griffiths *et al.* 2007, 119 nos 1136–42). Two unstratified buckle-plates may also be medieval (Fig. 3.65.14–Fig. 3.65.15).

Other characteristic medieval finds are provided by two horse-harness pendants. One consists of a simple triangular pendant still attached to its mount or swivel, which has a single internal rivet for fixing to the harness; both the pendant and the mount retain liberal traces of gilding (Fig. 3.65.16). The other harness-pendant is represented by the swivel only, which has an oval plate decorated with an enamelled equal-armed cross with rounded finials and two holes for rivets at the top and bottom (Fig. 3.65.17). These well-known horse accessories are known from pictorial sources at least from the twelfth century onwards; they were produced in many different forms, and were used in particular on the breast-band (Griffiths 1986; 1995). Beside these objects, a few finds relate to buildings or activities on site in the later medieval period. An iron pintle, for hanging a small door or shutter was associated with pottery dating from 1150–1400 (Fig. 3.65.18). Two small and crudely made copper-alloy rotary keys with hollow shanks are probably for caskets (Fig. 3.65.19; Fig. 3.65.20). They have parallels in other medieval finds, in particularly in a large thirteenth-century assemblage from the infirmary hall at the Augustinian priory and hospital of St Mary in Spitalfields, London (Egan 1997, 202 no. <S12–S44> and figs 26 and 74; cf. Egan 1998, 111–12). The iron blade of a short whittle-tang knife has a straight edge and curved back, with the tang in line with the back of the blade (Fig. 3.65.21). The blade was recovered from the tertiary fill of well [563], together with pottery dating from 1290–1320. Two cylindrical fishing-weights, or net-sinkers, are of rolled lead sheet, one partially unravelled (Fig. 3.65.22; Fig. 3.65.23). Net-sinkers of this type are known from Roman and Late Iron Age sites, so it is possible that they are residual here (cf. Parfitt 2000, fig 10 nos 5–6); they are however frequent finds from medieval contexts, with numerous examples recovered from the Cinque Port of New Romney (Steane & Foreman 1991, 97; Riddler 2009, 101–3). Administration is reflected in a copper-alloy jeton, for calculating sums on a chequered board or cloth (Fig. 3.65.24). The jeton was manufactured in Tournai, a central source for these reckoning tokens in the late fourteenth and fifteenth centuries. It carries the device of four *fleurs-de-lis* in a lozenge on the obverse, and the inscription AVE MARIA GRACIA around; the reverse shows a triple-stranded cross with rosettes in the centre and quarters. It dates from *c.* 1475–1500 (cf. Mernick & Algar 2001, 237 and no. 164). Three medieval silver coins were also recovered. The earliest is a cut farthing of John, minted 1205–1207 (<621>: not illustrated). A heavily worn and severely altered sterling type penny of Edward III–Edward IV (1351–1464) reveals almost the entire legend cut away to form a smooth round disc (Fig. 3.65.25). At the centre is a small drilled or punched hole, with a larger circular opening in one of the quarters; attempts to produce a third hole can be seen in the opposite quarter. These very even perforations were almost certainly done in the late post-medieval period. The third coin is a mostly illegible standard-type penny of Edward IV–Henry VII (1465–1509; <1>: not illustrated).

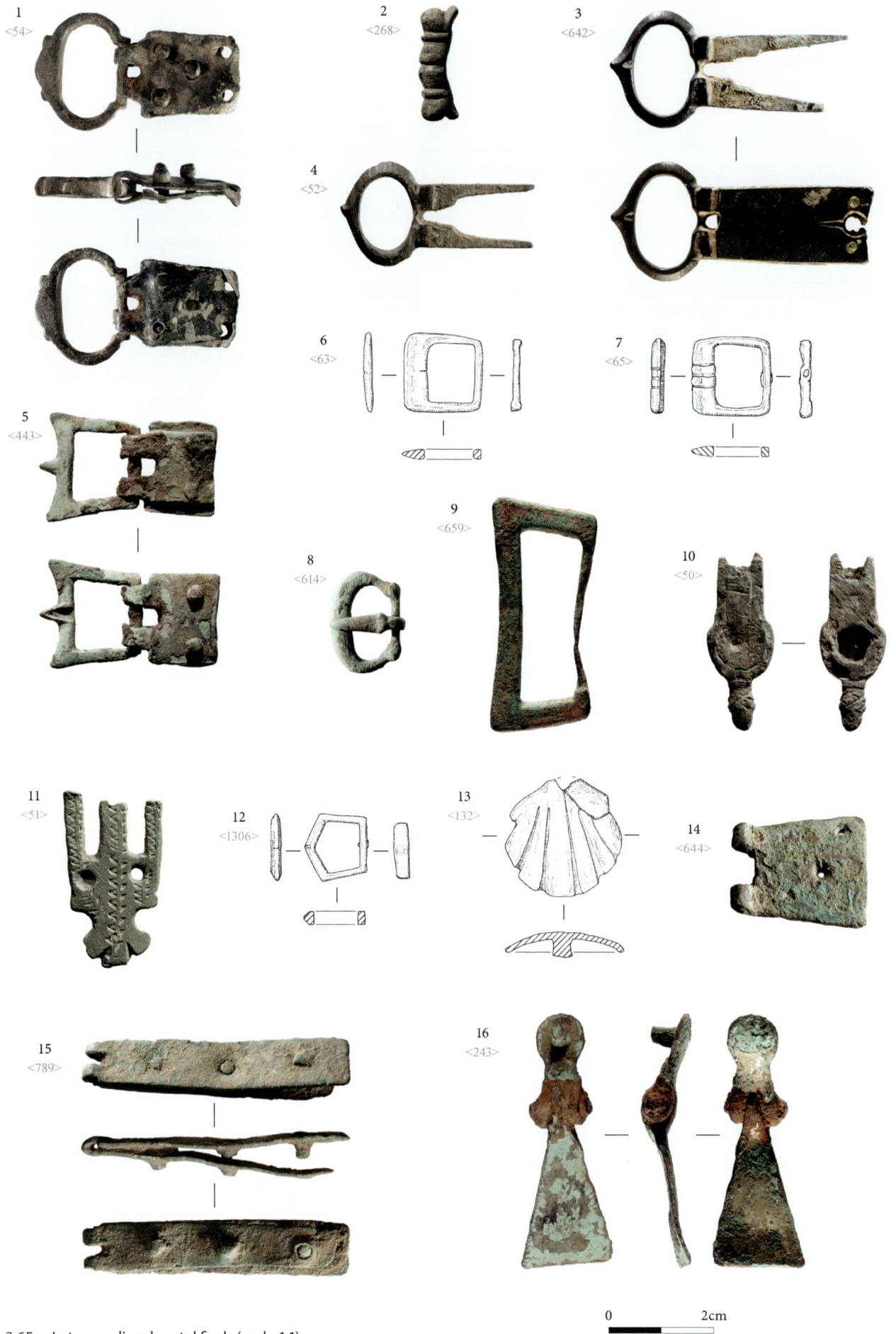

Fig. 3.65   Later medieval metal finds (scale 1:1)

Illustrated later medieval metal finds

Fig. 3.65.1 <54> Complete buckle.

Fig. 3.65.2 <268> Fragment of buckle.

Fig. 3.65.3 <642> Complete buckle.

Fig. 3.65.4 <52> Component of buckle as above.

Fig. 3.65.5 <443> Complete buckle.

Fig. 3.65.6 <63> Small buckle with widened plain frame.

Fig. 3.65.7 <65> Small buckle with widened frame with transverse grooves.

Fig. 3.65.8 <614> Small buckle with oval frame.

Fig. 3.65.9 <659> Wide single-frame buckle.

Fig. 3.65.10 <50> Forked-spacer strap end with acorn knop.

Fig. 3.65.11 <51> Openwork strap-end.

Fig. 3.65.12 <1306> Pentagonal strap-loop.

Fig. 3.65.13 <132> Scallop-shell mount.

Fig. 3.65.14 <644> Trapezoid buckle-plate.

Fig. 3.65.15 <789> Long narrow buckle-plate.

Fig. 3.65.16 <243> Harness pendant.

Fig. 3.65.17 <271> Harness pendant swivel with enamel cross.

Fig. 3.65.18 <1279> Iron pintle.

Fig. 3.65.19 <361> Complete copper-alloy key.

Fig. 3.65.20 <223> Copper-alloy key.

Fig. 3.65.21 <904> Iron knife.

Fig. 3.65.22 <49> Lead net-sinker.

Fig. 3.65.23 <791> Lead net-sinker, partly unravelled.

Fig. 3.65.24 <322> French copper-alloy jeton.

Fig. 3.65.25 <618> Silver long-cross penny with two circular openings.

Fig. 3.65   Later medieval metal finds (scale 1:1)

0   2cm

3.12 The post-medieval metal and small finds

Märit Gaimster

With the aid of metal-detectorists on site, some 150 post-medieval metal objects were recovered, almost all of which were unstratified or from topsoil layers. Only a selection of more interesting finds or categories will be discussed here. They include a small assemblage of early modern dress accessories and other objects from the sixteenth or seventeenth centuries, a substantial group of lead tokens likely to date from the eighteenth century, and a handful of Georgian dress accessories. The latest finds are represented by five Russian lead bale seals from the early nineteenth century.

The sixteenth and seventeenth centuries

Four copper-alloy buckles are of characteristic early modern forms. Two double-oval buckles have moulded decoration on the outer frames and at either end of the strap bar. One features a petalled flower on each frame (Cunningham & Drury 1985, fig 26 no. 11–12; Whitehead 2003, 66 no. 407; Fig. 3.66.1; cf. Egan 2005 fig 17 no. 88), while the other has a lobed knop at each corner (Fig. 3.66.2; cf. Whitehead 2003, 63 no. 382). Both buckles have a date range *c.* 1550–1650 and both show visible traces of a now-black lacquer, originally thought to have been a warm reddish-brown colour, fashionable on dress accessories at the time (Egan & Forsyth 1997, 217). A rectangular buckle with a central bar has pointed outer frames dates from the seventeenth century (Whitehead 2003, 82 nos 511–13: Fig. 3.66.3; cf. Mann 2008, fig 6 no. 8). Another seventeenth-century buckle is trapezoidal, with the wider end finished in two outwards-curled knops (Fig. 3.66.4; cf. Whitehead 2003, 84 nos 526–27). The buckle has lost its narrow half, but other buckles of this form have been found with a hooked plate on the central bar indicating their use as spur buckles (Whitehead 2003, 81). The twisted fragment of an iron rowel spur of the same period was also among the finds; the spur has broad sides that would have curved gently down under the wearer's ankle, and a short neck (Cunningham & Drury 1985, fi. 35 no. 94; Fig. 3.66.5; cf. Mann 2008, fi. 45 nos 216–17). A small group of buckles have a drilled frame for a separate spindle, to which a metal chape would have been fitted; the chape had a buckle pin at one end with the other end formed to be hooked into the leather or fabric. Some of these smaller two-piece buckles were used for shoes in the late seventeenth century, as buckled shoes came back into fashion after the Restoration; this is indicated by the curved frames on two of the Grange Farm examples. One of these retains its chape, with an anchor-shaped finial (Fig. 3.66.6; cf. Whitehead 2003, 100 nos 628–30). Another small curved buckle has a frame decorated with transverse grooves with traces of white metal showing it was originally tinned (Fig. 3.66.7). Two

further frames of this type, for shoe or knee buckles, may date from the late seventeenth or early eighteenth centuries; both have characteristic concave bifid sides which appears as a recurring decorative element at this time (Fig. 3.66.8; Fig. 3.66.9; cf. Whitehead 2003, 98–101).

Two interesting finds relate to arms and armour in the early modern period. One is a small copper-alloy fitting with two iron rivets and an inwards-turned hook (Fig. 3.66.10). Similar hooked mounts are known from early seventeenth-century contexts, and have been interpreted as sword-belt fittings (Margeson 1993, 38 and fig 22 nos 257–58). They have parallels in a complete set from the late sixteenth century, comprising a horizontal bar with loops for a pair of hooked strap-ends for slings (Cunningham & Drury 1985, 43 and fig 26 no. 7). Another is the fragment of a copper-alloy knuckle-guard or quillion from a rapier handle (Fig. 3.66.11). The piece is cast with a foliage pattern, with a flower-like domed protrusion surrounded by nine small knops near the finial; there are traces of a tinned or silvered surface in several places. The fragment has a close parallel in a near-complete rapier knuckle-guard of copper alloy from Meols in the Wirral, cast with figural scenes along the centre (Griffiths *et al.* 2007, 228 and pl. 48 no. 3141). The example from Grange Farm is however more curved, suggesting it may be part of the quillion, or cross guard, instead. The rapier, a gentleman's weapon and very much a fashion accessory, was particularly popular in the late sixteenth and early seventeenth centuries (cf. Blair 1962, 7 and figs 111–20; Patterson 2009, 61 pl. 54).

Besides dress accessories, a few other early modern objects could be identified. They include a corner book-mount with a small raised boss surrounded by a floral design with each petal featuring two minute ?*fleurs-de-lis* flanking two annulets (Fig. 3.66.12). A very similar book-mount from Norwich, with a more crude floral design with petals formed of D-shaped stamps above a trefoil of annulets, was thought to date from the late sixteenth century (Margeson 1993, 74–75 and fig 40 no. 456; cf. also PAS ID: BUC-B3D938). The copper-alloy arm of a pair of scissors is cast with a floral decoration of two vertical and cross-hatched pineapple-like fruits with stylized leaves (Fig. 3.66.13s). The finger loop is formed by an oval flat-section band, and at the base traces of rust show the scissors would have been fitted with iron blades. This composite construction may have contributed to the arm breaking off; several similarly decorated scissor arms of copper-alloy are known from metal-detected finds (PAS ID: DOR-1768BF; NARC3254; cf. Read 1988, fig 25 no. 6). A now-crushed bird-feeder of lead (not illustrated) is of a simple D-shaped form with flat back and curved front; the type is generally dated to the late fifteenth to seventeenth centuries (cf. Egan 2005, 128–29 and fig 124 no. 617).

Copper-alloy jetons continued to be used for calculating sums until the introduction, during the course of the seventeenth century, of Arabic numerals. From the mid-sixteenth century, however, the production of these reckoning counters was dominated by Nuremberg. At this time, and through the early seventeenth century, jetons often carried pious mottoes on the back; this can be seen

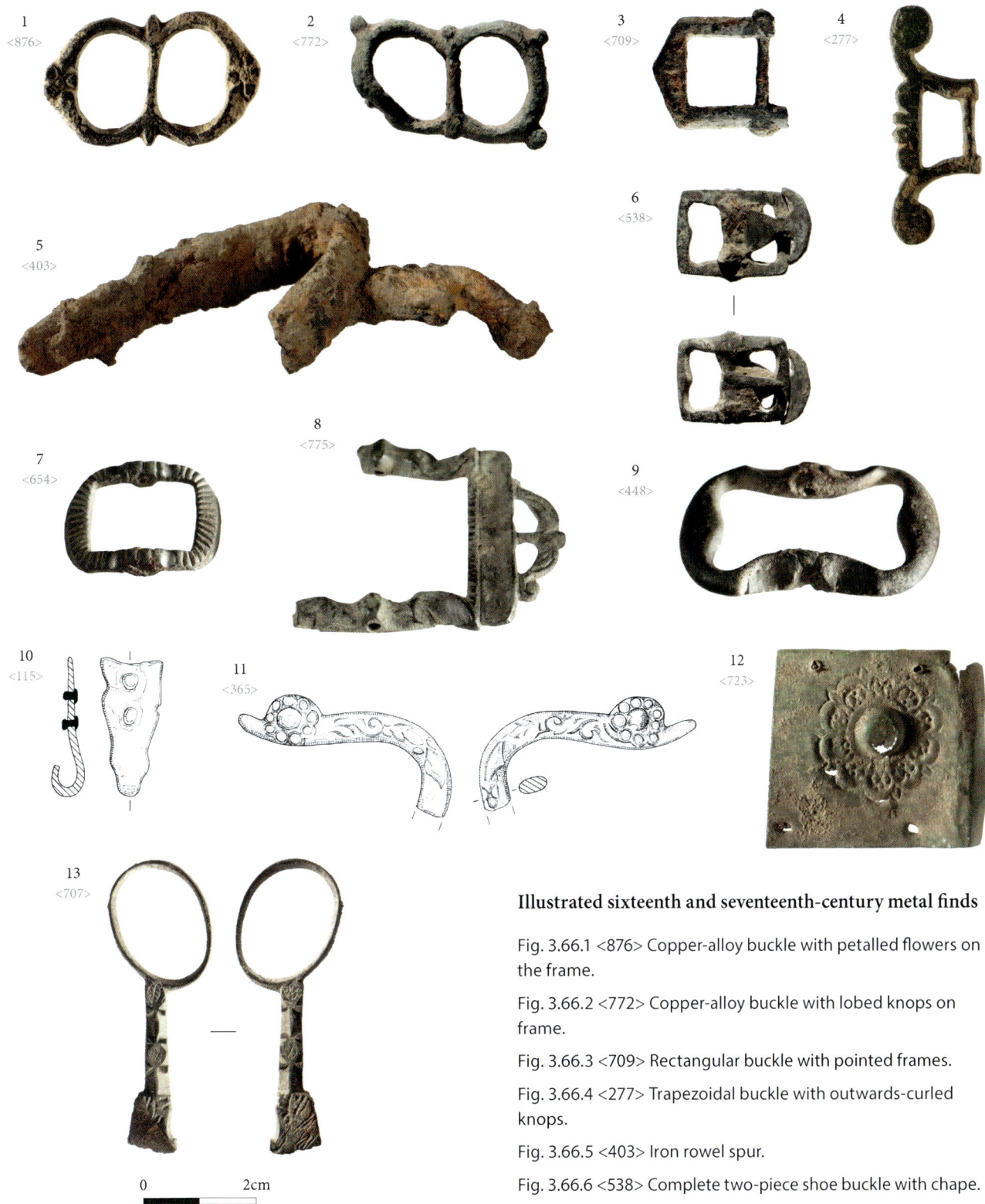

Fig. 3.66   Sixteenth and seventeenth-century metal finds (scale 1:1)

here on a jeton of Hans Krauwinckel II (jeton master 1586–1635) inscribed GOTES SEGEN MACHT REICH ('God's blessing brings riches'; <317>: not illustrated). A further Nuremberg jeton, probably of the common rose-and-orb design, as the one above, was also recovered (<366>: not illustrated).

Illustrated sixteenth and seventeenth-century metal finds

Fig. 3.66.1 <876> Copper-alloy buckle with petalled flowers on the frame.

Fig. 3.66.2 <772> Copper-alloy buckle with lobed knops on frame.

Fig. 3.66.3 <709> Rectangular buckle with pointed frames.

Fig. 3.66.4 <277> Trapezoidal buckle with outwards-curled knops.

Fig. 3.66.5 <403> Iron rowel spur.

Fig. 3.66.6 <538> Complete two-piece shoe buckle with chape.

Fig. 3.66.7 <654> Small two-piece shoe buckle with transverse grooves.

Fig. 3.66.8 <775> Knee or shoe buckle with openwork decoration on outer frame.

Fig. 3.66.9 <448> Knee or shoe buckle with concave sides.

Fig. 3.66.10 <115> Sword-belt fitting.

Fig. 3.66.11 <365> Fragment of ?rapier knuckle guard.

Fig. 3.66.12 <723> Copper-alloy book corner mount.

Fig. 3.66.13 <707> One arm of decorated scissors.

Fig. 3.67   Post-medieval uniface lead tokens

Illustrated lead tokens

Fig. 3.67.1 <631> Token with petal design.

Fig. 3.67.2 <619> Token with geometric design and ?initials D and I/J.

Fig. 3.67.3 <146> Token with heart design.

Fig. 3.67.4 <826> Token with vertical lines, possibly swords.

Fig. 3.67.5 <336> Token with triangular feature.

Fig. 3.67.6 <339> Token with radiating lines/spokes.

Fig. 3.67.7 <823> Token with cross and annulets.

Fig. 3.67.8 <311> Token with initials A I.

Fig. 3.67.9 <337> Token with initials R K.

Fig. 3.67.10 <613> Token with initials R P.

Fig. 3.67.11 <327> Token with initials W D.

Fig. 3.67.12 <828> Token with simple cross.

Fig. 3.67.13 <323> Token with geometric/grid design.

Fig. 3.67.14 <332> Token with fleur-de-lis.

Fig. 3.67.15 <541> Token with geometric/grid design and ?lettering.

Fig. 3.67.16 <331> Token with single initial W.

Fig. 3.67.17 <444> Token with linear design.

Fig. 3.67.18 <279> Token with geometric grid design and initials A M.

0   1cm

Lead tokens

Eighteen lead tokens with legible inscriptions were recovered; all are uniface issues, cast with either lettering or linear/geometric designs on the obverse. Two of the tokens have a high lead content, more similar to earlier, medieval pewter issues; one has a well-executed petal design that resembles that seen on the series of geometric tokens in the late fourteenth and early fifteenth centuries (Fig. 3.67.1; cf. Mitchiner & Skinner 1985, pl. 10 nos 21 and 62). However, these tokens are all bifacial and usually with neat borders; at this time, also, the tokens were produced in pure lead (Mitchiner & Skinner 1985, 36). Uniface tokens, although occasionally found earlier, appears to be a characteristic of issues from the late seventeenth and eighteenth centuries and it is likely that all the tokens from Grange Farm belong to this period (cf. Mitchiner & Skinner 1985, 138–39; Egan 2005, 167–68). Lead or pewter tokens are known from at least as early as the twelfth century and would have had ecclesiastical as well as administrative and economic functions (Mitchiner & Skinner 1985, 29–40; Egan 2006). The latter are particularly clear from the seventeenth century onwards, when lead tokens functioned alongside the copper-alloy farthing, halfpenny and penny tokens that circulated in their tens of thousands between *c.* 1648–1673 in response to the lack of official small change (cf. Mitchiner & Skinner 1985, pl. 16–21; Dickinson 1986, 4–15). While the copper-alloy issues were efficiently suppressed by Charles II in 1672, unofficial lead tokens continued in use until the early nineteenth century. Private and corporate copper-alloy denominations were also struck during short periods at the end of the eighteenth and beginning of the nineteenth centuries, again in response to the lack of official change (cf. Dykes 2011).

Among the finds from Grange Farm, a group of small tokens with diameters of 15–17mm are of a size comparable with seventeenth-century private farthing tokens. They include the lead-tin token with the petal design (Fig. 3.67.1; cf. Mitchiner & Skinner 1985, pl. 22 no. 47–49) and a further lead-tin example with a geometric design that could possibly represent the initials D above I or J (Fig. 3.67.2). All other tokens are of seemingly pure lead. Three carry motifs such as a single heart (Fig. 3.67.3; cf. Mitchiner & Skinner 1985, pl. 21 no. 8) and three vertical lines with pellets between, possibly three swords (Fig. 3.67.4; cf. Noël Hume 1969, fig 62 no. 6); a triangular feature with angled base or handle would have been recognisable as a tool, object or symbol for the user (Fig. 3.67.5). Two tokens carry recurring stock designs such as radiating lines or spokes (Fig. 3.67.6; cf. Mitchiner & Skinner 1985, pl. 17 no. 99; Egan 2005, fig 165 no. 932) or a cross with annulets in the quarters (Fig. 3.67.7; cf. Egan 2005, fig 165 no. 936). Slightly larger tokens, with diameters of 18–20mm, might correspond with either seventeenth-century private halfpennies or eighteenth-century farthings. They fall into two main groups with one displaying initials and the other featuring geometric or stock designs. Tokens with initials include 'A I', 'R

K', 'R P' and 'W D' (Fig. 3.67.8–11). This format differs from the usual representation on the main series of seventeenth-century copper-alloy tokens and which show three initials with that of the surname above those for the husband and wife; however, both formats were used on lead issues (cf. Mitchiner & Skinner 1985, pl. 16–22). Stock designs include a simple cross (Fig. 3.67.12), a geometric or grid design (Fig. 3.67.13) and a probable *fleur-de-lis* (Fig. 3.67.14; cf. Egan 2005, fig 165 no. 935 and Mitchiner & Skinner 1985, pl. 21 no. 15 for late seventeenth-century examples; Noël Hume 1969, fig 62 no. 9 for a token dated 1707). The design of one token possibly combines a geometric or grid design with a horizontal band of ?lettering at the centre (Fig. 3.67.15). Three considerably larger and chunkier tokens, finally, have diameters of 25 (two tokens) and 28mm. This size is closer to to a seventeenth-century token penny but not as large as the halfpennies of the late seventeenth and eighteenth centuries. Of the three tokens one carries the single initial 'W' (Fig. 3.67.16), while the second shows a linear design (Fig. 3.67.17). The third, and largest, token combines a geometric grid design with the overlaid initials A and M (Fig. 3.67.18).

The eighteenth and nineteenth centuries

Later post-medieval finds include some characteristic and fashionable Georgian dress accessories in the form of two large rectangular copper-alloy shoe buckles; both are highly decorative, with one featuring floral motifs and the other, which is also tinned, of openwork with scallop designs at the centre of the sides (Fig. 3.68.1; Fig. 3.68.2; cf. Whitehead 2003, 105 no. 671 and p. 107). Equally large and fashionable, if plain, is a so-called dandy button (Fig. 3.68.3; cf. Bailey 2004, 42 and 61). More unusual among archaeological finds, although prolific in metal-detected collections, is a small copper-alloy clog fastener. These fittings consisted of two pieces. One solid plate with a hook and the other with a series of rectangular openings to adjust the tension; both plates had anchor-shaped finials to fix them into the leather. The solid plate from Grange Farm, which has lost its hook, is cast with a floral design (Fig. 3.68.4). It probably dates from the eighteenth century (cf. Bailey 1992, 13–7). Alongside dress accessories other eighteenth-century finds included a small lead-alloy drawer or door handle cast in the shape of a petalled flower (Fig. 3.68.5; cf. Bailey 1995, 16 no. 7) and a miniature copper-alloy rat-tail miniature spoon (Fig. 3.68.6). This could be a plaything as toy spoons were made in both lead and copper alloy (cf. Forsyth & Egan 2005, 139 no. 3.13) or a similarly small snuff spoon (Moore 2005, 32).

Among the latest finds from Grange Farm is also a group of five lead seals testifying to the voluminous Anglo-Russian trade in flax and hemp during the late eighteenth and nineteenth centuries (Sullivan 2012). Vast amounts were imported into England and Scotland, in particular to feed the textile mills in the north. The

Fig. 3.68   Eighteenth and nineteenth-century small finds (scale 1:1)

raw material was transported in large bales which were controlled and sealed by the port inspector. Two of the seals from Grange Farm, dated 1821 and 1822 respectively, can be identified as flax seals; they are marked NP which was the state control used by all ports before 1829, with the Arabic lettering denoting non-Russian traders (Fig. 3.68.7). A third seal, dated 1823, carries instead the state control lettering SPB which was used for hemp during the same period. A state custom seal was also among the finds, dated 1798 and carrying the possible arms of St Petersburg (Fig. 3.68.8). Once the raw material was processed, the waste was spread in the fields as manure, as reflected in the recovery of vast amounts of these Russian bale seals through metal-detecting. Another interesting find is the central part of a gilded copper-alloy shako plate with the Order of the Garter encircling a G R cipher (Fig. 3.68.9). This device was used on uniforms from the time of the Napoleonic wars at the very start of the nineteenth century and, with the great Napoleonic Fort Amherst at marching distance, may reflect the use of land at Grange Farm for army practising.

Illustrated eighteenth and nineteenth-century small finds

Fig. 3.68.1 <706> Shoe buckle with floral designs.

Fig. 3.68.2 <660> Shoe buckle with openwork design.

Fig. 3.68.3 <806> Copper-alloy dandy button.

Fig. 3.68.4 <1307> Copper-alloy clog fastener with floral design.

Fig. 3.68.5 <388> Lead-alloy drawer handle.

Fig. 3.68.6 <708> Copper-alloy miniature spoon.

Fig. 3.68.7 <362> Russian lead flax seal.

Fig. 3.68.8 <325> Russian lead state custom seal.

Fig. 3.68.9 <555> Copper-alloy shako badge.

3.13 The post-Roman pottery assemblage

Chris Jarrett

The excavation produced a total of 920 sherds of post-Roman pottery representing 270 Minimum Number of Vessels (MNVs); 52 sherds were unstratified. The condition of the material is generally good, showing no or very little abrasion and so was generally deposited soon after breakage, although few vessels with complete profiles are represented and there was a certain degree of residuality or intrusivity. Early medieval/Saxon pottery (25 sherds, 8 MNVs) is noted amongst the assemblage. The coding of the Saxon pottery types used here is site specific but follows the criteria used by Macpherson Grant (1996).

The bulk of the assemblage dates to the period *c.* 1050–1350 (with a small quantity of fifteenth/sixteenth-century material), medieval wares accounting for 825 sherds in total, representing some 185 MNVs. A large group of late thirteenth- to early fourteenth-century pottery came from a well and may be associated with the Grinch/Grange manor house. The post-medieval pottery was noted as 70 sherds or 63 MNVs and was generally fragmentary and so is not discussed in detail here. The pottery is discussed by phase and the range of pottery types, classified according to the Canterbury Archaeological Trust's coding system, is shown in Appendix 4.

The material by Phase/feature

Intrusive material

A small number of post-Roman pottery sherds were recovered as intrusive finds from Roman contexts. Part of the rim of a vessel in West Kent fine sandy with shell and sparse grits (EM21), dated 1125–1200, was noted in the fill of a 2nd- to 3rd-century field boundary ditch [1184]. The base sherd of a cauldron with a foot decorated with a thumb impression in the North or West Kent hard-fired fine sandy fabric (M38C), dated 1325–1400 was recovered from second/third-century pit [789]. A single, small sherd of EM36 was recorded as an intrusive find in the disturbed third-century grave and contemporary posthole [529] contained a base sherd of early medieval sandy ware with flint temper (EM44), decorated with external stick end marks. Two sherds from green-glazed and white-slip decorated London-type ware jugs (M5) were recovered from late Roman pit [517] and may be of a mid-thirteenth- to early-fourteenth-century date. A simple everted rim from a small rounded jar in the M38A fabric was noted from late Roman pit [403] and a very small body sherd of green-glazed Saintonge ware was recovered from late Roman ditch [608].

The fifth and sixth centuries

Pit [732] was the only cut feature in Phase 9 to produce pottery, the assemblage comprising twenty-one sherds (8 MNVs), of which five are medieval in date (fabrics, EM48, M1A and M38A) and believed to be intrusive. The rest of the pottery comprises early medieval/Saxon wares in the form of three closed shaped vessels in different pottery-types. Six sherds were in EMS1A, but with abundant crushed quartzite and very sparse chert, the surfaces being oxidised and the core grey. Eight sherds are from the base and wall of a rounded jar (Fig. 3.69.1). in a reduced, coarse sand-tempered, micaceous fabric with chalk or calcareous inclusions (EMS1B). Two body sherds are from a jar in a sandy, micaceous fabric (EMS7C) with burnished surfaces and external rustication, formed by finger pinching impressions. Chronologically this type of decoration is largely dated to the fifth century at Mucking and West Stow, although Mucking has fewer sherds from sixth- and seventh-century dated deposits, while at West Stow, the late sixth-century occurrences were thought to be possibly residual (West 1982, 34–7; Hamerow 1993, 34–7,). Further sherds of this rusticated vessel were also noted in medieval well [563]. Vessels with rustic decoration are supposedly rare in Kent (Blackmore 2008, 189), although this has been found on a jar in a coarser version of the EMS1 fabric at the Marlow Car Park, Canterbury (Macpherson-Grant 1995, 838–9, fig 355. 25).

Additionally, Phase 9 layer [537] yielded a single sherd of Saxon pottery as the carination of a vessel in early medieval/Saxon fine sandy ware (EMS1D), though the fabric additionally contained mica and sparse burnt-out organic material. Another sherd of Saxon pottery was recovered from Phase 9 Layer [201]. This was in coarse early medieval/Saxon ware (EMS1A) and from the shoulder of a burnished vessel, possibly a biconical jar or carinated bowl and has a faceted rib above vertical, evenly spaced ribs (Fig. 3.69.2). Faceted decoration on Saxon pottery is dated to the fifth century, but mainly placed into the late fifth and first half of the sixth century (Myers 1977, 18–19; Hamerow 1993, 42, 44) and is known from East Anglia and the London area, although previously unknown in Kent (Blackmore 2008, 190). The applied vertical strip decoration is difficult to parallel on other vessels of this date.

Medieval

The largest quantity of post-Roman pottery was recovered from Phase 10 deposits, the majority of the material being medieval in date. Pit [1173] produced a total of 22 sherds of pottery dated *c.* 1100–1150 by the presence of early medieval shell or shell and sand fabric (EM35 and EM36) and the absence of later M38 wares. North or West Kent shell-filled (EM35) is recorded as five sherds from three vessels and most notably as a crudely-made, small, rounded jar with a slightly thickened upright rim with a thumb print on the top. Amongst the sixteen

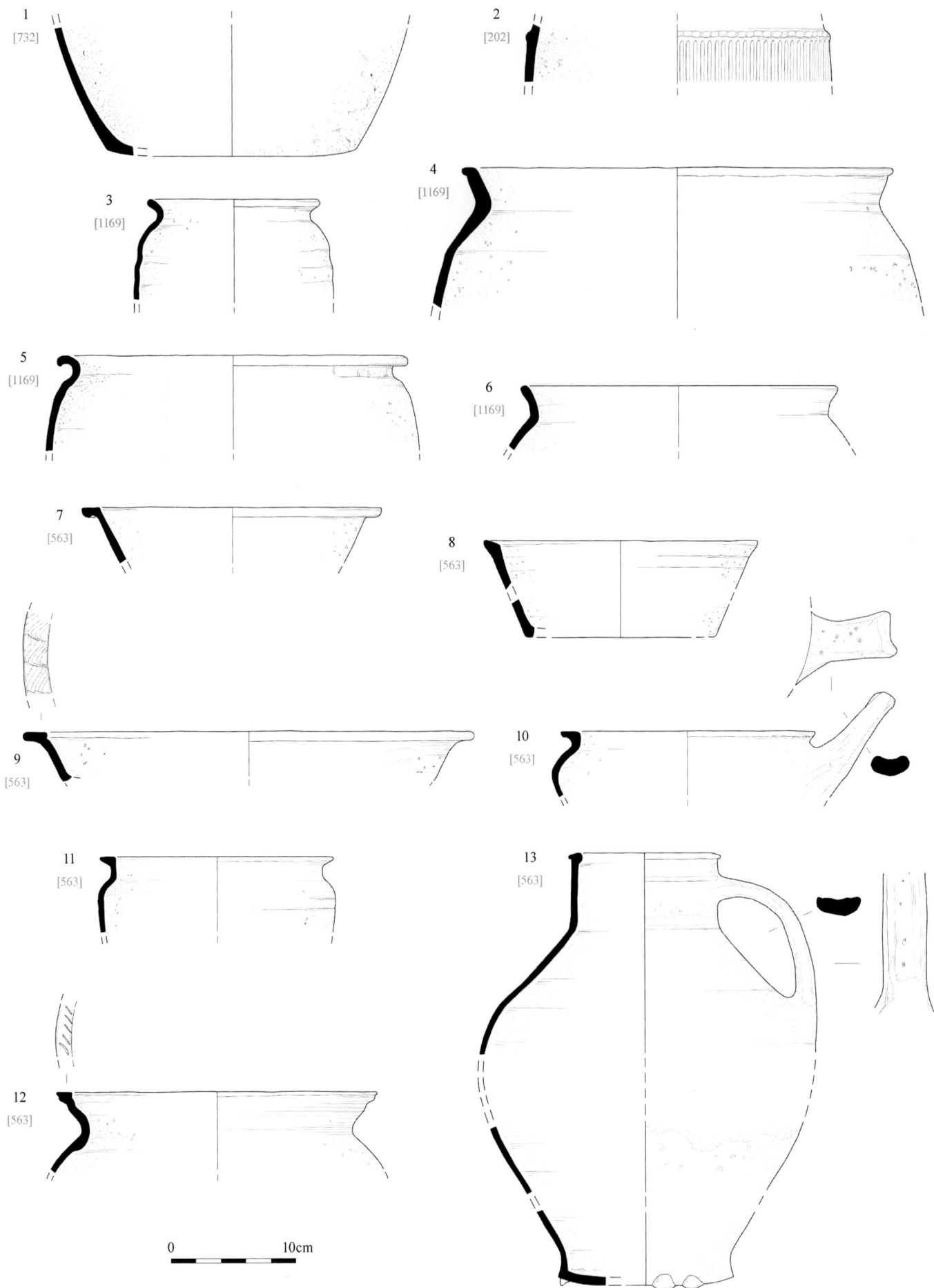

Fig. 3.69   Early medieval/Saxon and medieval pottery (scale 1:4)

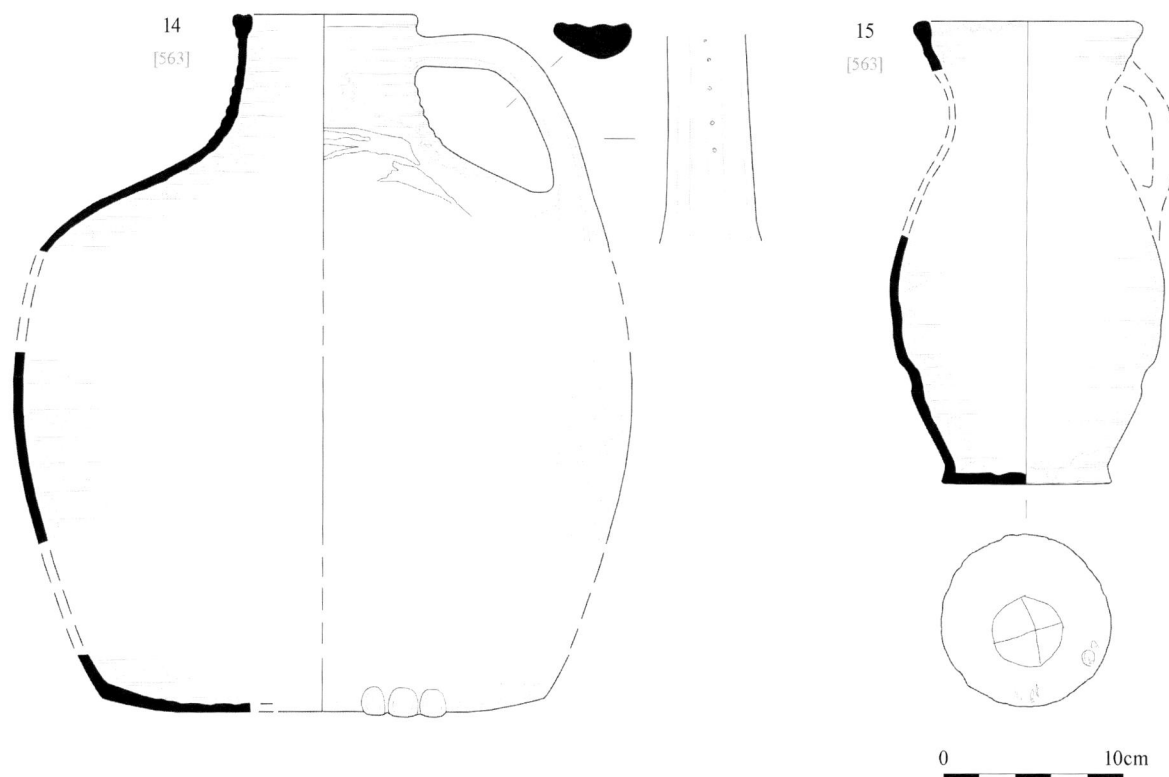

Fig. 3.69   Early medieval/Saxon and medieval pottery (scale 1:4)

sherds (7 MNVs) of North or West Kent sandy and shell-tempered ware (EM36) are two jar rims, one with a simple everted rim and an upright neck, the other having an expanded rim, triangular in profile with a flat top. Five sherds of pottery, from two different fabrics could not be confidently assigned to a type and are classified as EM100, but were all in the form of jars. First, in an abundant, fine clear quartz sand fabric with a simple rim, and secondly in a wheel-thrown ware with very sparse shell and burnt out voids. The form has a rounded rim and short neck. A final, small sherd with leached out shell inclusions from this feature may be prehistoric in date.

Catalogue of medieval and earlier pottery

Fig. 3.69.1 (Phase 9, Pit [732]) EMS1B, jar, 450–700.

Fig. 3.69.2 (Layer [201]) EMS1A biconical jar or carinated bowl with a faceted rib above vertical, evenly spaced ribs, early medieval/Saxon.

Fig. 3.69.3 (Pit [1169]) EM35 cylindrical jar, 1050–1225.

Fig. 3.69.4 (Pit [1169]) EM35 shouldered jar, 1050–1225.

Fig. 3.69.5 (Pit [1169]) EM35 jar with hooked rim, 1050–1225.

Fig. 3.69.6 (Pit [1169]) M38A rounded jar, 1150–1400.

Fig. 3.69.7 (Well [563]) M38A bowl with flat topped, rolled-under rim, 1150–1400.

Fig. 3.69.8 (Well [563]) M38A bowl with triangular rim, 1150–1400.

Fig. 3.69.9 (Well [563]) M38A carinated bowl with flat-topped rim decorated with a combed wavy line and diagonal knife slashes, 1150–1400.

Fig. 3.69.10 (Well [563]) M38A pipkin, 1150–1400.

Fig. 3.69.11 (Well [563]) M38B jar, 1225–1400.

Fig. 3.69.12 (Well [563]) M38B jar decorated with incised lines on the top of the rim, 1225–1400.

Fig. 3.69.13 (Well [563]) M1 rounded jug, 1225–1350.

Fig. 3.69.14 (Well [563]) M1A shoulder jug with white slip decoration and a green-glaze bib, 1225–1350.

Fig. 3.69.15 (Well [563]) M22G jug with batch mark on base, *c.* 1300.

Pit [1169] produced a group of pottery dated 1150–1225. Of the 116 sherds present, 95 sherds or 15 vessels are of the early medieval North or West Kent shell-tempered ware (EM35), dated 1050–1225, as jars and mostly as rounded types, but with single instances of cylindrical (Fig. 3.69.3) and shouldered types (Fig. 3.69.4). Rims are mostly upright or everted simple types, occasionally with beaded edges or slightly thickened, but one jar has a 'hooked' rim (Fig. 3.69.5). A rounded bowl was also noted with a simple rim. The only other pottery type present in the fill is North or West Kent sandy ware (M38A), represented by 21 sherds or 12 vessels and dated 1150–1400. The majority of vessels are rounded jar shapes with simple rims (Fig. 3.69.6). Most of the vessels in the pottery group are sooted and therefore had been used for cooking or heating water, whilst two vessels have internal deposits, probably derived from food.

Backfilling following robbing of masonry from the Roman tomb, produced a single sherd of EM36, dating this activity to the period *c.* 1100–1250 AD. A possible animal burrow within the area of the tomb produced two sherds of M38A ware.

Pit [1347] produced a single sherd of ?non-local coarse sandy ware (EM45) as a rim sherd from an uncertain form. The ridge-and-furrow deposits at the north of the site produced sherds of jugs in North or West Kent sandy ware (M38A) indicating activity *c.* 1150–1400, as well as an unidentified ware.

The largest quantity of post-Roman pottery from a single feature came from well [563] and was interesting for the wide range of local, non-local and imported pottery types and their forms. Two fills produced pottery; the earliest ([713]) contained a jug fragment in Tyler Hill ware (M1A) and twelve sherds from a Saintonge green-glazed jug (M22G), with further sherds noted in the later fill ([562]). The combined quantification of both fills from the well is shown in Appendix 5. Kentish wares dominate the group and these are most frequent as the wheel-thrown North or West Kent sandy ware (M38A), dated 1150–1400 as 412 sherds representing some 31 MNVs. Jars are the main form and two types were noted: medium and tall. The rim profiles are variable but are more often than not narrow, expanded squared types, sometimes down-turned, or occasionally wider, or with an internal bevel. Two rims were rounded in profile. All the jars had short necks, while the only decoration (found on two vessels) consisted of vertical applied thumbed strips. Some of these jars were probably used for storage, while one had an internal limescale deposit, suggesting it had been used for boiling water, while other jars were clearly used as cooking-pots, having external sooting and occasionally internal food deposits.

Bowl forms in M38A were noted as four vessels, three being flared in profile and of a medium or deep size. Rims were either flat-topped and rolled under or triangular in profile (Fig. 3.69.7; Fig. 3.69.8). A medium-sized carinated bowl was also noted with a flat-topped rim and internal bead and was decorated with a combed wavy line and diagonal knife slashes (Fig. 3.69.9). Pipkins were noted as three examples represented by single sherds and two rims survived, both being flat-topped but one has a triangular profile (Fig. 3.69.10). The handles of the pipkins are an oval cross-sectioned, straight type with fine point stabbing and unusually, with a straight strap handle mortised to the body. Jugs were noted as fifteen sherds from five vessels with either a beveled or rounded rims. One handle survived and is a D-shaped section rod type, mortised through the neck and further secured with a finger pushed from inside into the handle. A jug base sherd shows evidence for external thumb decoration.

North or West Kent fine-moderate sandy greyware (M38B), dated 1225–1400 is sometimes known as Dartford rilled ware and it is distinguished by its finer, better-fired quality when compared to that of M38A as well as the distinctive rilling that appears on the Kentish greywares from the thirteenth century. Eight sherds of this ware are represented as two rounded jars. One is of a small size with a narrow, flat-topped expanded rim, short neck and a pronounced shoulder and decorated with incised horizontal lines on the body (Fig. 3.69.11). The second jar contains sparse shell and is tall with an everted rim with an internal beaded bevel, while the neck has finger rilling (Fig. 3.69.12). It has external sooting and was therefore likely to have been used as a cooking-pot. The jars, like those in M38A appear to be of composite manufacture, i.e. the body was handmade and the rims were wheel-thrown.

Essentially pottery types EM36, M38A and M38B are variations in the same sandy fabrics; the M38 wares have sparser, finer shell, if present at all. A number of production centres were likely to have been involved in the manufacturing of these wares in North and West Kent as different manufacturing techniques have been noted at Eynsord Castle when compared to other assemblages. One likely area of production and a possible source for the greywares here may be between Maidstone and Rochester in the Medway Valley (Cotter 2006, 178–80). The M38 wares are part of the Thames basin greyware pottery tradition and were not made in the southern half of Kent.

Tyler Hill ware (M1) occurs as 42 sherds representing nine jugs and most are fragmentary. They are green-glazed with or without a white slip coating. The most complete jug has a bevelled thickened rim, spout and a cordon on the neck and has poor white slip decoration. It has a vertical, loop-strap handle, oval in profile with a central line of point stabbing, and was attached to the lower body of the jug by two fingers pushed through the wall into the handle terminal (Fig. 3.69.13). The base is splayed with continuous thumbing.

Tyler Hill sandy ware with sparse chalk (Fabric M1A) is represented by 31 sherds representing ten, mostly very fragmentary jugs. Two of these could be determined as rounded in shape. The first has a rounded rim with a thickened beaded top, a strap handle, attached in the same manner as the M1 jug above, while the base has discrete groups of three thumb impressions. Decoration consists of a rilled neck and arcaded white-slip decoration below a green glaze. The second jug has a rim that is internally thickened and the top is grooved, while the neck is rilled and the top terminal of the strap handle is attached by mortising. Decoration consists of a poorly-fired white slip and green glaze bib (Fig. 3.69.14).

Tyler Hill is situated approximately two miles to the north of Canterbury and pottery waster dumps have been identified, although it is only the tile kilns that have been excavated (Spillet *et al.* 1942; Cotter 1991). The ware is dated 1175–1525/50, but its core production period was 1225–1350, with a harder, mainly reduced ware known as Late Tyler Hill ware (LM1) being introduced from 1375 onwards (Cotter 2006, 148).

A single sherd of ?Medway chalk-tempered sandy ware (M37) occurs as an undiagnostic body sherd. Non-local pottery is noted as three types from the London and Essex areas and a Surrey whiteware. Fragments of three London-type ware (M5) jugs were noted, one being green-glazed, the others having additional white slip decoration. London-type ware is dated 1080–1350 although the white-slip-decorated jug sherds may belong to a recognised style in production between 1240–1350. Also in this ware is the base sherd and mortised rod handle of a baluster-shaped drinking jug, dated to 1270–1350 (Pearce *et al.* 1985, 41). Fourteenth-century pottery kilns making London-type ware and later sixteenth- and seventeenth-century kilns have been excavated at or in the vicinity of Woolwich Arsenal (Cotter 2008) and indicate probable continuous pottery production at this location from *c.* 1000 to the nineteenth century, although M5 appears to be rare in late fourteenth-century dated London deposits, indicating output of this pottery type was diminished during that period.

Fine red earthenware jugs made in Essex (M6) and usually associated with the Mill Green production centre (Pearce *et al.* 1982) are present as four sherds from three vessels. One jug base has discrete thumbing; a second has a white slip line, while the third is decorated in the Rouen style and has a white slip line and dots. Mill Green ware is recorded in London archaeological deposits dated 1270–1350 and besides its name sake, evidence for production has been found at Noak Hill and wasters of a very similar pottery type were found at Rayleigh (Walker 1990; Meddens *et al.* 2002/2003).

Kingston-type ware (M7) is recorded as four fragmentary jug forms, largely represented by rims or handles, one of which is a large strap type. A drinking jug is also represented. A number of kilns have been found in Kingston dating from the end of the thirteenth century to the late fourteenth century and this Surrey whiteware was traded to London, from where it was probably redistributed *c.* 1240–1400 (Pearce & Vince 1988).

Imported pottery, all from France and the Saintonge area, is present as 51 sherds representing seven jugs. Unglazed wares (M22) include three sherds from two vessels, one of which is decorated with a curving applied strip incorporating diagonal notches. Green-glazed jugs (M22G) are represented by 44 sherds from three vessels, one of which has deep body rilling while the underside of the base has a maker's or batch mark consisting of a circle with a cross (Fig. 3.69.15). This vessel was poorly handled by the potter after being removed from the throwing wheel. The third jug has a mottled green glaze and is represented by three sherds. Polychrome decorated jugs (M22P) are represented by two vessels represented by four sherds and one vessel may have a bird design, a common motif in the decorative repertoire of this ware. This ware has been described as the most western production centre for Mediterranean archaic maiolica. General consensus amongst medieval ceramicists is that Saintonge ware was traded to Britain between 1250 and 1650, while there is some disagreement about the precise dating of the polychrome ware. Generally it is agreed that one or possibly two generations of potters were making this product. Saintonge polychrome ware in London is dated 1280–1350, in Southampton 1250–1350 and at Canterbury 1290–1320: therefore a central date of *c.* 1300 is suggested for this pottery type.

The well produced a number of residual and later, probable intrusive wares: they may have resulted from the final infilling of the feature or levelling of the surface after a hollow was caused by slumping of the well fills. Six sherds of Romano-British pottery were recorded, there are five sherds of Early medieval/Saxon pottery as sandstone tempered ware (EMS1), and two sherds each of EMS1A and a jar with rustication in EMS7C. There is also a sherd of EM36 that is internally sooted.

Late medieval wares are represented by two sherds of Medway hard silty-sandy ware (LM34A), one being oxidised, the other reduced, while its chalk-tempered variant (LM34B) occurs as four sherds from a jug with white slip decoration. These wares are dated 1450–1550. Three sherds of Wealden buff fine sandy ware (PM2), dated 1525–1650 were recovered, representing three vessels, whilst a jug rim with a narrow collared profile, probably sixteenth century in date, is noted.

There are a number of unidentified wares of a medieval or late medieval date. Sixteen sherds (5 MNVs) are in a fine sandy micaceous ware (M100/LM100) with either oxidised or reduced surfaces and occasionally white slip line decorated, but all sherds are unglazed. The forms could not be identified, although a convex base was noted with internal knife paring, while another vessel had a limescale deposit. Six sherds from four vessels are in another fine sandy micaceous fabric but distinguishable by the presence of red clay pellets (M100/LM100 + CL) in an oxidised ware with reduced surfaces. The only identifiable form is a jar with an internal lid-seated rim.

If the later pottery in well [563] is considered intrusive, then this large group of ceramics, with the majority of the wares being contemporaneous, indicates deposition in the late thirteenth to early fourteenth century. The sherds of Saintonge polychrome ware are the most datable pottery type present amongst the medieval wares and probably indicate deposition around *c.* 1300. The source of this pottery may very well be the adjacent manor house, although the presence of Saintonge polychrome jugs should not necessarily be assigned to a high-status property. Pottery had low social status in the medieval period, ranking above wooden vessels and below metal and glassware forms. The presence of imported pottery in the well and elsewhere on the site may be associated with its close proximity to the port of Gillingham, a subsidiary of the Hastings Cinque Port and more to do with availability rather than being close to the manor house.

Such a large group of pottery deserves to be looked at functionally and this has been undertaken with the medieval wares. Jars were assigned to either storage or cooking functions, dependent upon the absence or presence of sooting on the vessels, while other shapes have been allocated to the broad uses expected for certain shapes, e.g. jugs: drink serving; pipkins: cooking. Fig. 3.70 shows the functional uses of the pottery quantified by sherd count (SC) and minimum number of vessels (MNV). If MNVs are taken as the method to discuss the functions, then drinking forms are more common as 42 MNVs (52.5%) and represented by the jug forms, which could have been used in the kitchen and at the table for serving wine or ale. Kitchen wares used for cooking, some here used for heating water, account for 17 MNVs (21.3%) and are mostly in the form of jars/cooking pots besides the three pipkins. Cooking wares are usually over-represented in assemblages as they were subjected to heat and thermal stresses and therefore liable to frequent breakage.

Some indication of the pottery requirements of a peasant's household is understood from the excavation of the Dinna Clerks longhouse, Dartmoor, which burnt down in the late thirteenth or early fourteenth century: the fallen roof sealed the contents of the building. Cooking-pots were found as four small examples next to the hearth, while a larger example had been buried up to its neck in the main living room, and a sixth cooking-pot was found in an inner room (described as a store and sleeping quarters). Jugs consisted of a green glazed example in the living area, while the inner room produced two yellow-glazed examples and a cistern. Two charred wood bowls were also recorded in the main room, while pottery was absent from the byre area (Beresford 1979, 135–6, 148–9, figs 25–6).

The presence of pipkins in the well group may indicate that a wider range of culinary practices were undertaken by the users of the pottery, other than just cooking pottage (the usual meal of peasants) in cooking-pots. The pipkins might possibly imply these vessels came from the kitchen of the manor house. Three of the bowls have sooting marks and were assigned to a cooking function, although during their use life these vessels could have been used in multiple ways, such as for processing food and washing clothes. Storage wares are represented by the unsooted jar shapes and they account for 11 MNVs or 13.8% of the vessel functions. Jars and other storage shapes would have been useful for containing foodstuffs, as well as a wide range of other items. Drink jugs accounted for 2 MNVs (2.5%). Communal use pottery forms were very much the order of the day for most of the medieval period, but from the late thirteenth century in south-eastern England, ceramic vessels for individual use begin to be more common occurrences, becoming more frequent in the later medieval and particularly the post-medieval periods. Food preparation/serving ware (1.3% MNVs) is represented by a bowl without sooting marks. Only one food-processing item is noted (1.3% MNVs), a bowl, which has no evidence for sooting. Vessel sherds that could not be assigned to a shape or showed no evidence for use, e.g. sooting, accounted for 7 MNVs (8.8%).

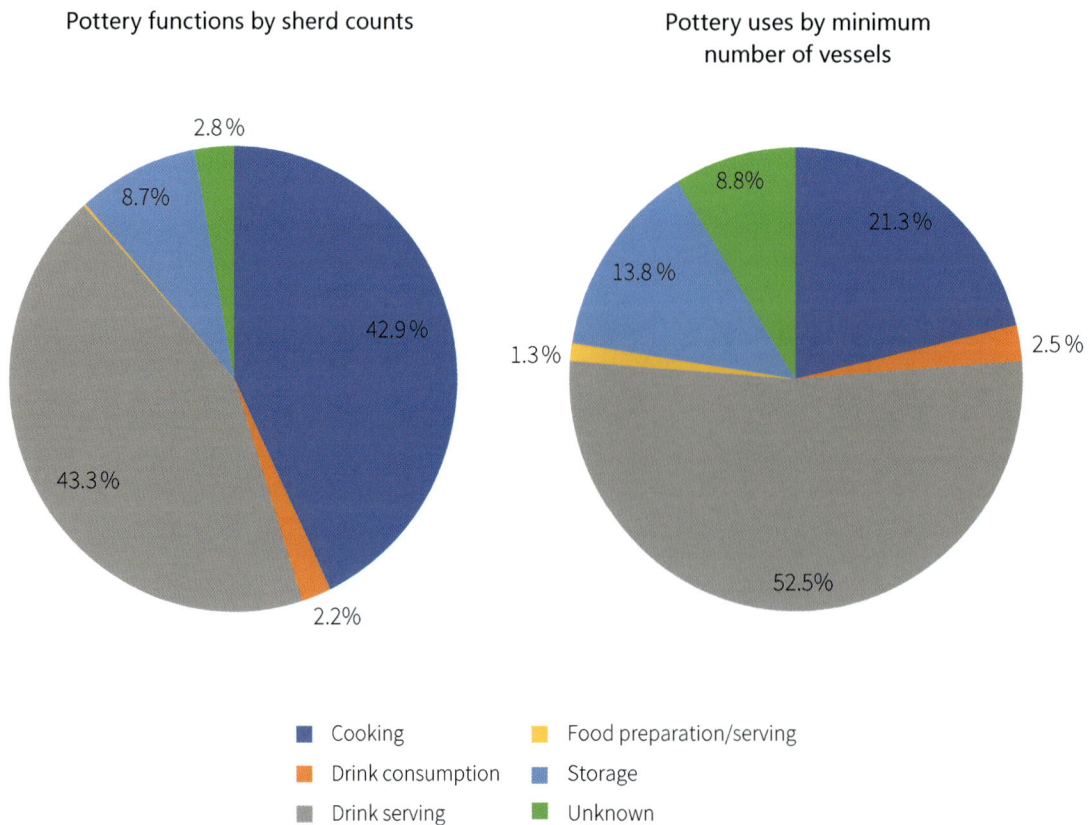

Pottery functions by sherd counts

2.8%
8.7%
42.9%
43.3%
2.2%

Pottery uses by minimum number of vessels

8.8%
21.3%
13.8%
1.3%
2.5%
52.5%

■ Cooking   ■ Food preparation/serving
■ Drink consumption ■ Storage
■ Drink serving   ■ Unknown

Fig. 3.70   Quantification of medieval pottery forms from fills [562]/[713] of well [563]: percentage composition by sherd count (left) and minimum number of vessels (right)

Post-medieval

The pottery from Phase 11 was on the whole very fragmentary with usually one sherd representing a single vessel and residual medieval material noted. The backfilling of the medieval moat produced pottery dated *c*. 1525–1550 by the presence of Wealden orange-buff sandy ware (LM32) and post-medieval redware fabric PM2, both wares including jar forms. Two imported pottery sherds are present, a Saintonge green-glazed ware (M22G) and a salt-glazed German Siegburg stoneware (LM7). One other sixteenth-century-dated pit contained a sixteenth-century redware jug base in fabric LM13. A later-seventeenth-century pit produced pottery dated 1665–1700 by the presence of Surrey-Hampshire Border ware (PM10.1, PM10.2 and PM2.4), delftware (PM9, PM9B, PM9W, PM9BT and PM9P), as well as redwares (PM1, PM1.8) and a slipware dish (PM2WG). The latest pottery type is a Westerwald stoneware sherd with cobalt and purple decoration (PM6CM). A contemporary pit contained similar pottery types; Border ware and redwares but a delftware plate dates the deposition in this feature to *c*. 1675–1700. A later pit is dated *c*. 1775–1900 by the presence of a late red earthenware (LPM1) sherd but a jar rim is also present in late medieval Medway hard silty-sandy ware with chalk (LM34B).

Late post-medieval pottery types were found in tree throws and ditches often as either Creamwares (LPM11], Ironstone-type whitewares and often transfer-printed (LPM14) and Yellow ware (LPM5), dating most of these features to the nineteenth century. A small sherd of Pearl ware and a single sherd of post-medieval Developed Creamware were also recovered. Topsoil deposits produced ten sherds of pottery representing 9 MNVs. The pottery types were wide ranging and consisted of fragmentary sherds of medieval and post-medieval wares (see Appendix 4).

Discussion

The Early medieval/Saxon pottery appears to be of a domestic nature, though possibly one fragment has a decorative element that could be associated with funerary urns: the faceted and rib-decorated sherd. The more datable sherds, those decorated with rustication and the faceted rib could be from the fifth century, possibly early sixth century. This dating therefore raises the question of whether any of the pottery is Jutish in origin or if it has such affinities. Myres (1969) noted that Early medieval/Saxon pottery from Kent could have a Jutish origin, based upon decorative styles (mostly as incised lines) as found on pottery from Jutland, Denmark and Frisia, as well as the micaceous fine sandy, reduced surfaces characteristic of the fabric. Myres also made the connection that Bede in his history claimed that Kent was the main area of Jutish settlement in England. Although it has become unfashionable to

assign pottery to ethnic groups, one sherd maybe of a Jutish type and that is the sherd in fabric EMS1D, but only chemical or petrological analysis could confirm this. Jutish pottery in fabrics EMS1 and EMS2 was noted from the excavations at the Marlow Car Park, Canterbury and other excavations in the vicinity (Macpherson-Grant 1993, 825–7). The sherds decorated with rustication are also in fabric EMS1D, although these and the sherd with a faceted cordon and applied vertical clay ridges, suggest decorative affiliations more so with the London area or north of the Thames. Although the excavation only produced a small quantity of Early medieval/Saxon pottery, the majority of the sherds would appear to be, on decorative grounds, atypical for Kent in the fifth or early sixth centuries.

The distribution of the Early medieval/Saxon pottery is mostly confined to the northern part of Area A and most sherds in the assemblage originated from pit [732], with further sherds of vessels from here being redeposited in the medieval well [563]. This feature indicates one possible focus of Early medieval/ Saxon activity on the site. A small number of sherds were found in deposits in the vicinity of the Roman mausoleum, although no pottery of this date was found associated with the other notable find for this period on the site, a gilded-silver bow brooch <917> dated to the final quarter of the fifth century (see Gaimster, this volume). Both the Early medieval/Saxon pottery and the brooch could be contemporary, although the brooch was recovered from a deposit located between the pit and the mausoleum. No Saxon pottery was recovered from the excavations associated with Grinch Manor (Keller & Chenery 1992, 8; Barber 1998) which indicates the pottery of this period was focussed upon the area around the mausoleum. The evidence is compelling for Early medieval/Saxon society reusing earlier monuments as burial sites (Williams 1998; Semple 2013). Whilst none of the Early medieval/Saxon pottery appears to be of a funerary function, it may reflect a community drawn to the probable upstanding remains of the Roman mausoleum, a structure that may still have had a continuing role in religious observations or, as Williams (1998, 103) suggests, the use of and ownership of an ancient landmark that the community identified with and enforced their tenure of the district. The atypical element of the Kentish Early medieval/Saxon pottery may even imply that people were travelling some distance to the site, perhaps for religious reasons.

The medieval pottery-types from this excavation can on the whole be correlated with those recovered from previous archaeological work on the Grinch manor house (Greatorex 1995; Barber 1998). There cooking pots were noted in Fabrics 1, 2 and 4, (equating to EM2, EM36 and M38B respectively) the latter also producing pitchers, while sherds of Fabric 3 (M38A) could not be assigned to forms. Jugs in oxidised sandy wares (Fabric 5) may relate to London-type or Tyler Hill wares and a small quantity of fine sandy ware (Fabric 6) may correspond with Mill Green ware, while a sherd of a sand and grog-tempered ware was noted. Single sherds of Saintonge ware were noted in both the evaluation and excavation phases of work. In 1991 the Kent Archaeological Rescue Unit also undertook archaeological work within the environs of the manor house and mid-twelfth- to thirteenth-century dated sand and shell tempered wares were recorded as cooking pots with flat-topped rims and applied thumbed strip decoration (probably equating to the M38 fabrics). Later medieval wares were noted during the various investigations.

The excavations at the Grange manor house and its environs therefore all have a similar ceramic profile and may be associated with activities dating back to its earliest history, perhaps during the eleventh century when Bishop Odo was known to have held the estate, and contemporary with pottery types such as the shell wares EM2 and EM35. These were the main pottery types traded to the site from the eleventh to early twelfth century and do not become displaced by the introduction of Early medieval sand and shell-tempered ware (EM36), as they do in other parts of north Kent. This may be reflected by the fact that North Kent was the area for the production of the EM35 shell-tempered pottery. From *c.* 1150 the North and West Kent sandy ware (M38A) became the main type of pottery, providing mostly jar or cooking pot forms, but from *c.* 1225 until *c.* 1350, Tyler Hill was supplying glazed jugs, as were to a lesser extent, London, Mill Green and Kingston.

One reason that Saintonge wares were present on the excavations may be the fact that the Grange Manor was a dependency of the Cinque Port of Hastings. This was brought about in the thirteenth century when Menasses de Hastings was tenant at the Grange. Benefits of being a Cinque port, or being attached to one, were exemption from tax and tolls, self-government and permission to levy tolls. On the basis of this, many of the Cinque Ports were the main controllers of wine from specific regions of France, e.g. Winchelsea was the main handler of wine from Bordeaux for redistribution to London during the fourteenth century. French jugs may therefore have been traded on the back of the wine trade and it has been suggested that these forms were an 'integral part of a wine drinking cultural package', particularly in the polychrome Saintonge ware, and were of a higher social status. This may be the reason why there were several Saintonge jugs recovered from well [563]. Courtney (1997, 102), however, has downplayed the importance of imported medieval pottery and argued that Saintonge wares, including the polychrome-type, follow similar maritime distribution mechanisms as English Bristol wares (Ham Green and Redcliffe types) and Norfolk Grimston wares. These French imports may have been more expensive than plain wares, but were still a low cost item: more costly items may also have been given by the owners, once they were of no interest to them, as 'gifts' to servants or others of a lower socio-economic standing. Additionally, Allan (1984, 67–70) has further normalised the status of imported pottery in reference

to the fact that find-spots for these jugs are found at the residences of people from all levels of socio-economic standing, deflating the idea that French pottery was special.

The presence of Saintonge ware jugs in the well may therefore be attributed to easy access to such a product and this may be because the Manor of Grange was a dependency of Hastings. However, the range of imported pottery from the well is extremely limited when compared to excavated assemblages from other Cinque Ports, even if they were on a larger scale. At Townwall Street, Dover, for example, a lowly fishing community had access to pottery from a number of production centres in France, Belgium and the Low Countries (Cotter 2006), while at New Romney a good range of imported pottery was excavated, although less varied than Dover. Both excavations produced pottery from Yorkshire (Jarrett 2009) and so these major Cinque Ports indicate wider contacts than the present evidence from Gillingham.

3.14 The iron slag and related high-temperature debris

Lynne Keys

Despite the large quantity (100kg) of slag recovered, there was little structural evidence for a focus of iron-working activity. Having said this, all the slag was recovered from close to or overlying the road, much of it redeposited in Phase 9, deposit [201]. No slags diagnostic of smelting (production of iron from ore in a furnace) were recovered although a great deal of slag is described as undiagnostic in this report because its morphology could have been produced by either smithing or smelting.

The diagnostic slags are those of secondary smithing. Although 75 smithing hearth bottoms (the convex-concave slag cakes that built up in the base of a smithing hearth) were recovered, there is no large quantity of hammerscale from the site. The term hammerscale refers to micro-slags produced during smithing which tend to stay in the vicinity of the anvil; it is useful in locating a focus or foci of smithing. The exception to this paucity of hammerscale is Phase 9 layer [537], this context is followed in quantity of micro-slags by Phase 8 layer [616] (trample over road), Phase 7 layer [770] (Open Area 1) and Phase 9 layer [201]).

Many small fragments of iron were recovered from the large dumps of slag and were handed over for examination by another specialist (Gerrard, Chapter 3.3, this volume). Most pieces were straight, thin, flat bars. A second type consisted of thicker, less wide pieces, and a third roughly rounded rods. These iron fragments may be parts of blanks used by smiths to make objects. They may equally be wasters from the smithing process and so be clues as to what was being produced or repaired so intensively.

Table 3.15   *Weights for different slag types*

Slag type	Total wt.(g)	Process
Smithing hearth bottom	17,000	Smithing
Hammerscale	433	Smithing
Microslags	2586	Smithing
Iron-rich cinder	16	Undiagnostic
Iron-rich undiagnostic	159	Undiagnostic
Undiagnostic	73,154	Undiagnostic
Slag runs	151	Undiagnostic
Vitrified hearth lining	3813	non-diagnostic
Fuel ash slag	653	Undiagnostic
Iron	484	non-diagnostic
Cinder	1187	non-diagnostic
Coal	26	non-diagnostic
Charcoal	34	non-diagnostic
Fired clay	35	

Table 3.16   *Statistical data for smithing hearth bottoms*

	Range (g/mm)	Mean	Std. dev.
Weight	35–845	219	126
Length	45–130	83	17
Breadth	35–100	67	13
Depth	15–70	35	10

75 examples; total wt. 17kgs

Fig. 3.71a   Spatial distibution of key contexts containing smithing hearth bottoms in relation to Phase 7 features (scale 1:1000)

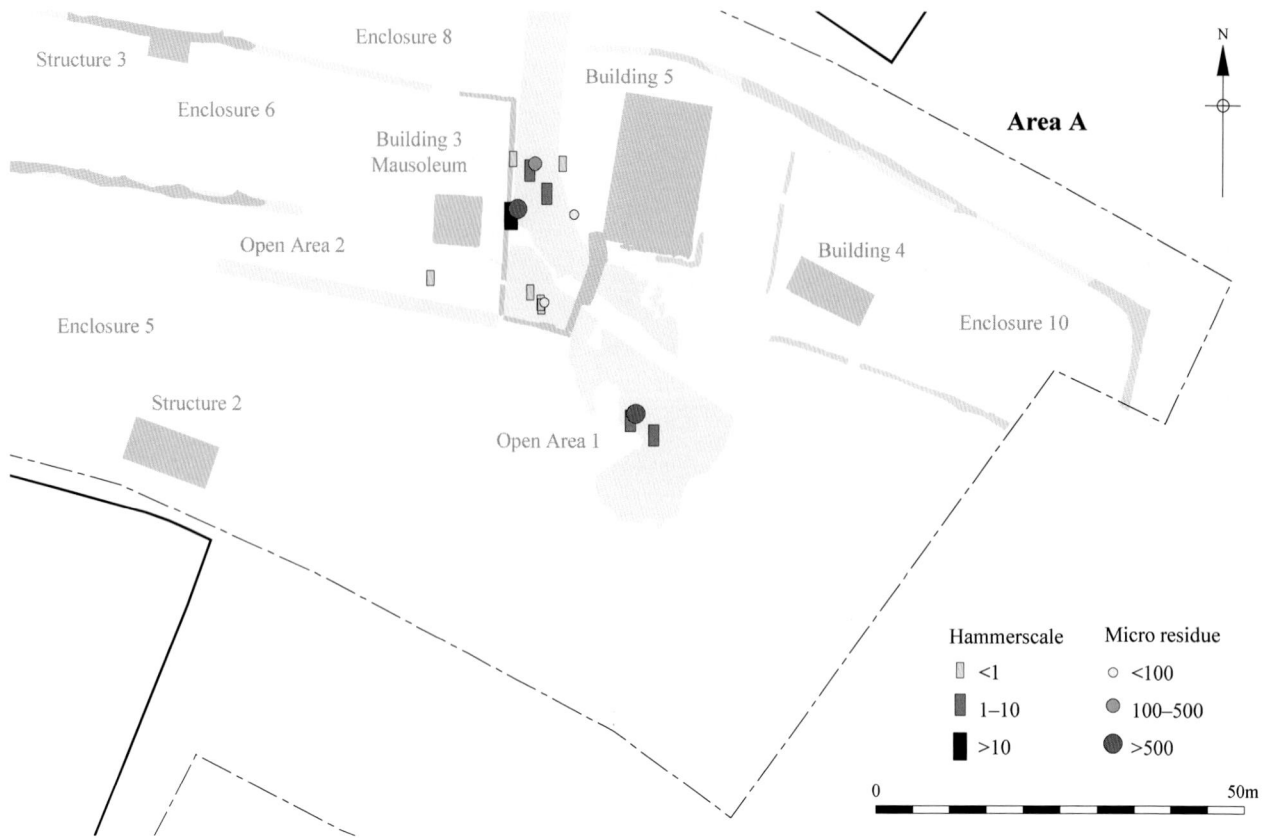

Fig. 3.71b   Spatial distibution of key contexts containing hammerscale and micro residue in relation to Phase 7 features (scale 1:1000)

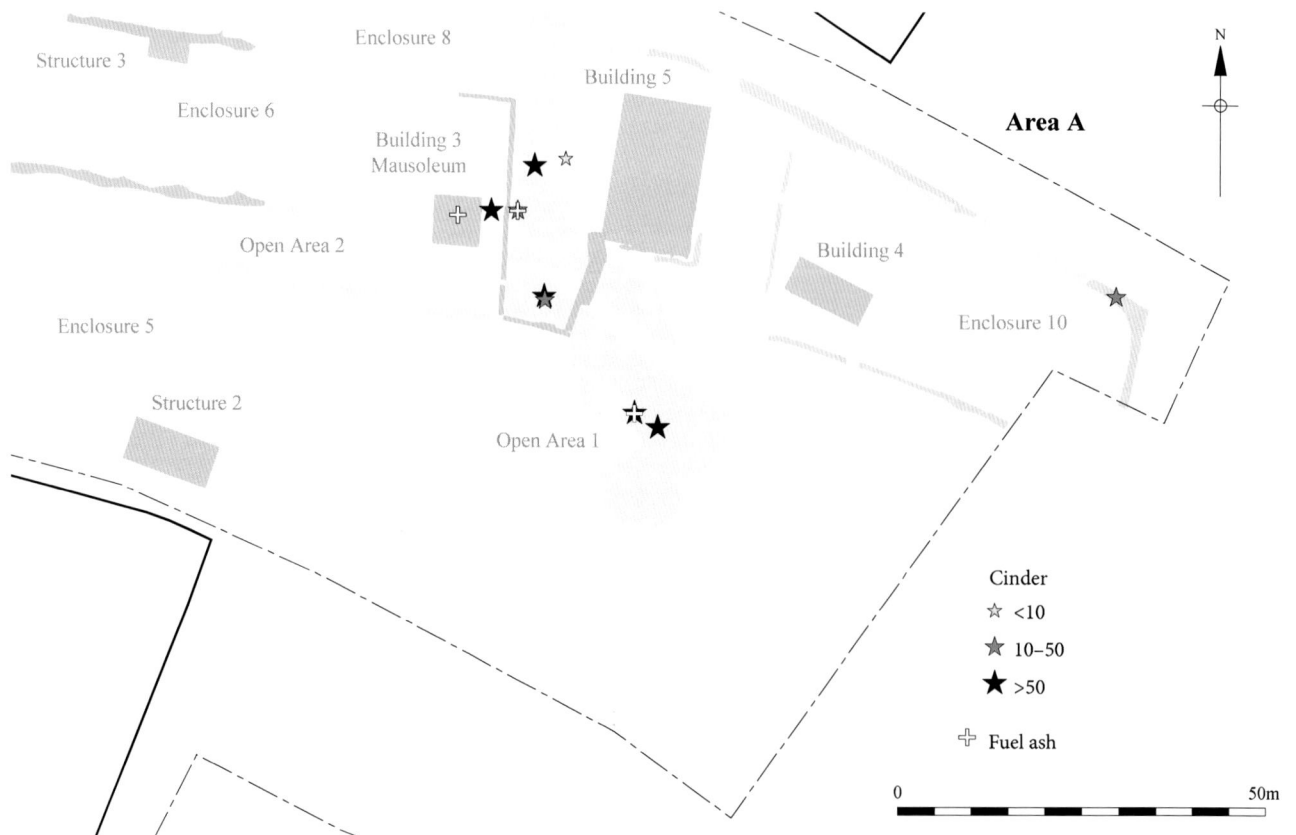

Fig. 3.71c   Spatial distibution of key contexts containing cinder and fuel ash in relation to Phase 7 features (scale 1:1000)

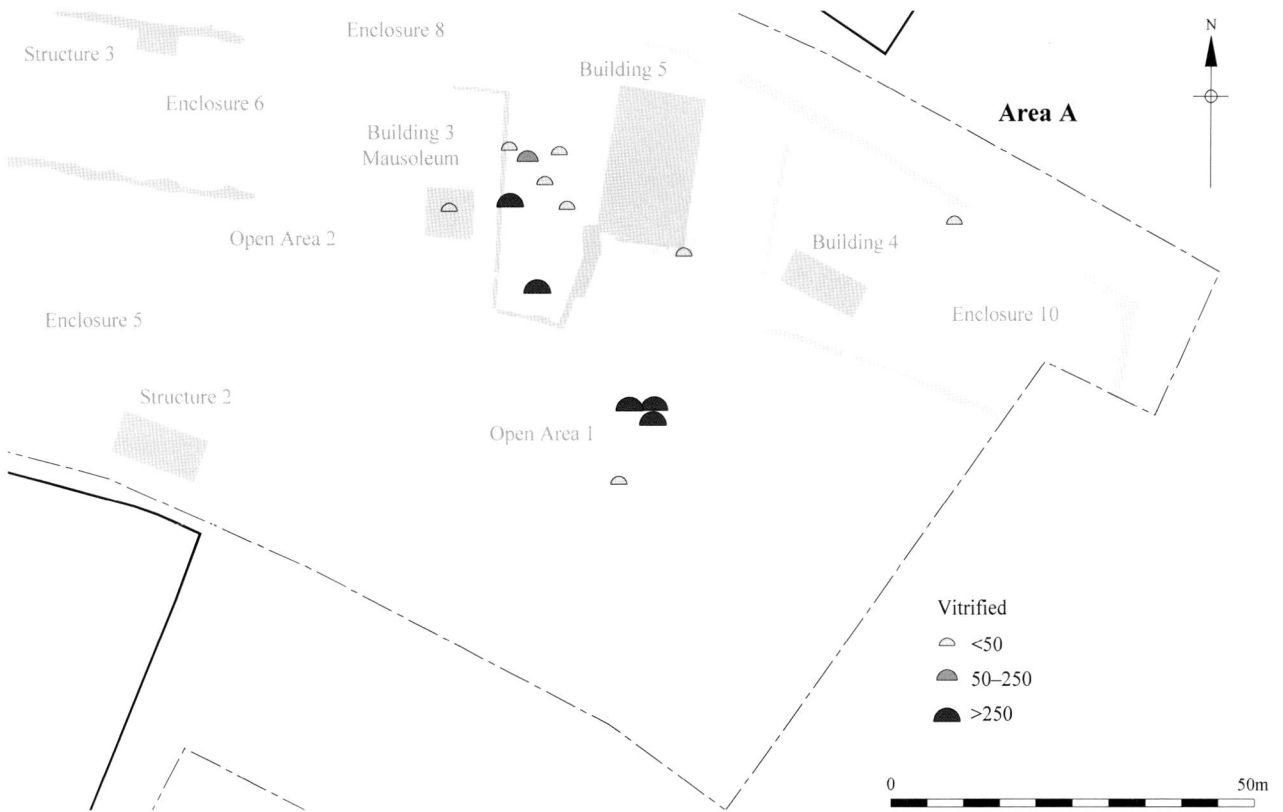

Fig. 3.71d Spatial distibution of key contexts containing vitrified slag in relation to Phase 7 features (scale 1:1000)

Fig. 3.71e Spatial distibution of key contexts containing undiagnostic/other slag in relation to Phase 7 features (scale 1:1000)

Discussion of the assemblage

In Phase 7, associated with oven structure [833], layers [819] and [854] contained a small quantity (just 483g) of iron slag. In the soil adhering to slags from [819], however, large hammerscale flakes (from ordinary hot working of iron to shape or produce simple objects) and some smithing spheres (indicative of high temperature welding to fuse two pieces of iron into one) were found; the size of these flakes indicates they had not been subjected to trampling and had not been moved far from where they were produced. No samples had been taken from this context, so it is not known how much hammerscale was originally present. Whether or not the hearth was a smithing hearth or whether the slag represents nearby activity cannot be ascertained as no other evidence is present to support an identification.

For the rest of the site phases, but particularly Phases 7 and 8, the slag occurs as a series of dumps near to or on the road. Any of these dumps may have been awaiting collection from this deposition point for recycling as reclamation and/or metalling material by a civic or military authority. The slag types evident in Phases 7 and 8 are indicative of a smith or smiths engaged in prolonged and frequent, rather than in one-off small-scale episodes, of ferrous (and possibly non-ferrous) metalworking. Whether the smithy lay on the site or nearby cannot be determined conclusively from the current metalworking evidence, although its distribution in close proximity to hearth [833] (Fig. 3.71) lends weight to suggestions that this might be a focus of smithing (see Chapter 2.6 above).

Phase 7, layer [770] (Open Area 1) contained over 21kg of iron working slag: eleven smithing hearth-bottoms and large quantities of undiagnostic slag (17.3kg), which may be fragments of other smithing hearth-bottoms. Stratigraphically equivalent Phase 7, Open Area 1, layer [694] contained a little more slag (over 5kg) consisting of three smithing hearth-bottoms, some hammerscale, many undiagnostic slag fragments, and lead waste; it also contained fragments of vitrified hearth-lining, two pieces of which have indications they once contained tuyère holes through which air from a bellows entered an industrial hearth.

Phase 8 layer [616] (trample over road) contained just 2.5kg of slag: flake hammerscale, two smithing hearth-bottoms, a quantity of undiagnostic slag, and pieces of iron which may be the waste from smithing or may be fragments of the stock cut and prepared so a smith could more quickly produce commonly required items for customers. This material may well have been dumped or redeposited from Phase 7 activities.

In Phase 9, layer [537] contained 27kg of mixed iron slags including eighteen smithing hearth-bottoms. This layer was in the central area of what was – or had been - the road – but it is not known whether the slag had once formed a metalling on the road or whether it represents a dump on a road that had gone out of use or was re-deposited material from Phase 8. This layer was rich in hammerscale, indicating the bulk slags (larger fragments)

had not been moved far from where they were produced or had been shovelled up and deposited here, allowing the tiny microslags to remain among the bulk material rather than being shed during movement. Phase 9, layer [456] produced four smithing hearth-bottoms and other slag; this deposit was in the central section where the road had been and was close to [537] and so may well be re-deposited.

Slag from Phases 8 and 9 is probably re-deposited material from earlier phases. Some confirmation of this is a piece of iron recovered from Phase 9 layer [462] in this phase can be joined to a piece from layer [694] Open Area 1, west of the road in Phase 7. Similarly, layer [464] contained only one complete smithing hearth-bottom but five fragments which may represent others and very little in the way of flake; it is probably re-deposited or disturbed material. Phase 9 'dark earth' layer [201] contained 21 smithing hearth-bottoms (a total of seventy-five were recovered from the site) and a substantial quantity of hammerscale (at least 10g). The latter was found in the soil adhering to some of the slags and no samples were available for examination.

3.15 The evidence for silver-working

David Dungworth, Marina Vaggi and Lynne Keys

The archaeological excavations yielded 15kg of litharge that provides evidence for silver-working in the late Roman period. This material is described and a brief account is given of its chemical composition and microstructure in relation to comparable material from elsewhere in England.

Background

Litharge is a lead (II) oxide (PbO) and is used (loosely) to indicate lead-rich material generated during a process of cupellation, where silver (or silver and gold) is extracted from lead, copper and other base metals by oxidising the base metals. The oxidised metals are absorbed into a hearth lining which is termed litharge.

Three distinct cupellation processes are known to have been employed during the Roman period and each produced a different type of litharge: primary cupellation, secondary cupellation and cupel assaying. Primary cupellation was used to produce silver (by extracting it from freshly mined and smelted lead, which contained little or no copper) and left primary litharge as a waste product. This process is known from only two Roman sites in Britain, both in rural locations close to outcrops of lead ores in Shropshire and Somerset (Bayley & Eckstein 1998; Dunster & Dungworth 2012). Secondary cupellation was used to recover/refine silver from debased silver alloys (which contained varying levels of copper and sometimes other metals) and left secondary litharge as its waste product (Bayley & Eckstein 1997; 2006; Girbal 2011). Primary litharge can usually be identified by its relatively large size — especially where the litharge cakes are not too fragmented (Dungworth 2015, fig 45). Primary litharge cakes are commonly 0.5m in diameter and 40mm thick, while secondary litharge cakes are 150mm in diameter and 10–20mm thick. Litharge usually weathers in a burial environment with a powdery surface rich in lead carbonate; this can be white, cream, grey or brown in colour. The presence of copper in secondary litharge usually gives this a green colour (Dungworth 2015, fig 47). Cupellation could also be carried out on a small scale to assay or test a sample to determine its silver content (Bayley 2008). Later medieval cupels were usually made from bone ash but earlier medieval cupels were often fashioned from fragments of domestic pottery (there is little evidence for cupel assaying in the Roman period).

Secondary cupellation is discussed in medieval and later sources (*eg* Theophilus in the twelfth century, Hawthorne

& Smith 1979). The debased silver alloy was mixed with excess lead and melted in a hearth or container lined with clay, ashes and/or bone ash (Hawthorne & Smith 1979, 96–97). The melting (unlike most metallurgical operations) requires excess air to oxidise the base metals (in particular, lead and copper). These oxides are then absorbed by the lining while the metallic silver (and any gold) is not oxidised and forms a pool on top of the litharge. Girbal's investigation of secondary litharge from Roman and medieval contexts showed that this can be divided into two categories based on the nature of the lining materials: bone ash or clay/plant ashes (Girbal 2011). Girbal also confirmed earlier suggestions (Bayley & Eckstein 1997; 2006) that the efficiency of the process was determined by lead-copper ratios; cupellation where insufficient lead was used, often resulted in silver remaining in the litharge. Girbal found no correlation between lead-copper ratios and the type of hearth lining (bone or clay/ash), or with date of production.

Fig. 3.72   Spatial distribution of contexts containing litharge in relation to Phase 7 features (scale 1:1000)

Results

The excavation recovered approximately 15kg of litharge (Table 3.17). This litharge is often stained green due to the presence of copper and, as detailed below, all samples contained appreciable levels of copper which indicate that this is secondary litharge. There is no evidence for primary cupellation (or cupel assaying).

The stratified contexts with the most litharge include [201] and [756] (see Fig. 3.72). A little over 3kg of the litharge was recovered from late-third-century to early-fourth-century contexts, but most was recovered from post-Roman or unstratified contexts.

The extent to which the litharge in these later contexts was redeposited from earlier phases of occupation is uncertain but no hearths certainly linked to cupellation (of any date) were identified during excavation. In the absence of any positive evidence for continued cupellation after the end of the fourth century, it is perhaps safest to assume that the litharge from post-Roman contexts is residual.

Secondary litharge is known from at least fourteen other Roman sites in Britain (Table 3.18). Most of this material has been recovered from urban sites and much of it from late Roman contexts. Nevertheless, litharge has been found on some early Roman sites and on a few

Table 3.17 Summary of litharge (in some cases the recorded weights are low as material was retained by Thilo Rehren)

Context	Description	Phase	Count	Wt (kg)	Comments
	unstratified	-	40	3.8	sample retained by Thilo Rehren (UCL)
203	unstratified	-	1	0.1	
200	ploughsoil	-	13	2.0	
562	fill	10	1	0.3	
201	dark earth	9	15	4.4	
453	demolition	9	1	0.4	
456	demolition	9	1	0.4	
867	layer	8	5	0.5	sample retained by Thilo Rehren (UCL)
937	layer	8	1	?	sample retained by Thilo Rehren (UCL)
719	spread	7	4	0.7	
756	spread	7	4	2.1	
769	fill	7	1	0.2	
770	spread	7	2	0.3	sample retained by Thilo Rehren (UCL)

Table 3.18   Other sites in Roman Britain from which litharge has been recovered

Site	Quantity	Reference	Date	Context
Canterbury	2 fragments	Heywort, 1988	Roman	Urban
Doncaster	1 fragment?	Tylecote 1986	Second century	Urban
Southwark	8 fragments	Budd 1987; Yule 2005	Late Roman	Urban
Chester	1.75kg	Gardner 2009	Roman	Urban
Leicester	hearth	Wacher 1975	Late fourth century	Urban
Silchester	hearth	Gowland 1900	Late Roman	Urban
Exeter	hearth	Fox 1968	First century	Urban
Winchester	2 fragments	Starley 1993	Roman	Urban
Dorchester	1 fragment	McDonnell 1993	First to second century	Urban
Lincoln	25 fragments	Bayley 2008; Girbal 2011	Roman (and some medieval?)	Urban
Elms Farm	3 fragments	Mortimer 1996	Late Roman	Small town
Dunkirt Barn	5 fragments	Girbal 2011	Roman	Rural
Tiddington	1 fragment	Wilthew 1986	Roman	Rural
Uley	2 fragments	Bayley 1993	Roman	Rural

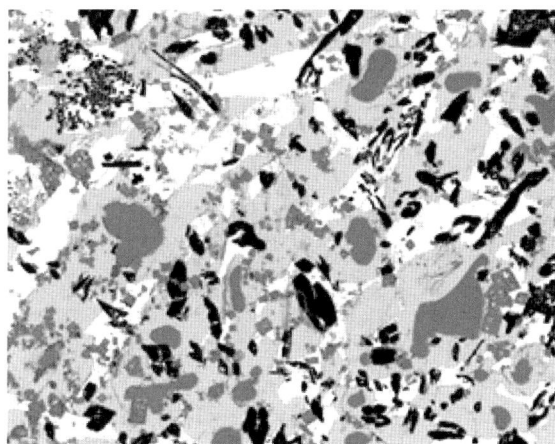

Fig. 3.73   SEM image of sample 200–844 showing white laths of PbO in a matrix of (light grey) $PbCu_2O_2$. The mid grey droplets are Cu_2O and small very dark grey crystals are calcium silicates

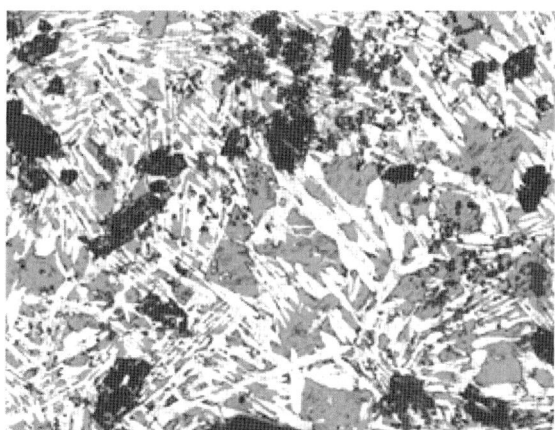

Fig. 3.74   SEM image of sample 201–ore showing light grey laths of PbO in a matrix of (darker grey) $PbCu_2O_2$ with some very dark grey calcium silicates

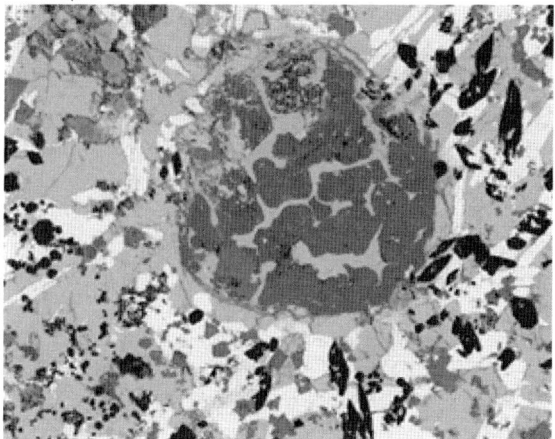

Fig. 3.75   SEM image of sample 200–844 showing a copper-silver alloy droplet in a litharge matrix (laths of PbO in $PbCu_2O_2$ with calcium silicates)

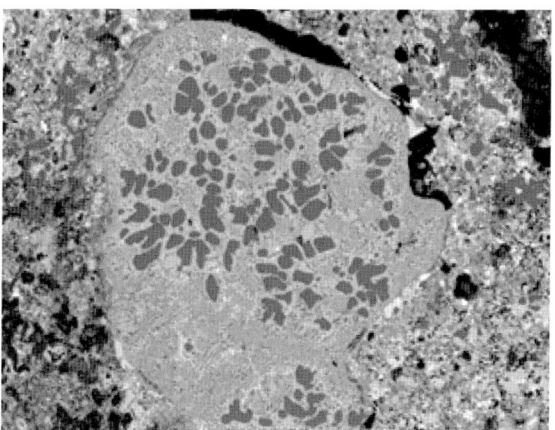

Fig. 3.76   SEM image of sample from the west of Area A(1) showing a large copper-silver alloy droplet in litharge

rural sites. Some of the reports of secondary litharge were published many years ago and lack detailed quantification; however, most of these sites produced fewer than ten fragments of litharge. Despite the limited quantification of litharge from other sites, it is clear that the assemblage of litharge from Gillingham is probably the largest so far known from Roman Britain.

Twenty-two samples of litharge from Gillingham have been examined in detail (21 by Vaggi [2008] and one by Girbal [2011]) using scanning electron microscopy (Fig. 3.73–Fig. 3.76). In addition, samples have been analysed to determine their chemical composition (a combination of x-ray spectrometry techniques, see Vaggi 2008 and Girbal 2011 for further details).

The litharge is composed mainly of lead oxide (PbO), copper oxide (Cu_2O) and copper-lead oxide ($PbCu_2O_2$), with a wide range of minor phases (Fig. 3.73 and Fig. 3.74). The minor phases include metallic copper-silver alloy droplets (Fig. 3.75 and Fig. 3.76) and various calcium silicates (the latter in some cases also contain aluminium, phosphorus and/or lead).

The litharge is chemically heterogeneous and the composition (Table 3.19) was determined from an average of 4–9 areas (SEM-EDS analysis). The litharge is rich in lead (48–68wt% PbO) and copper oxides (12–35wt%); these two oxides together account for 73wt% to 86wt% of the litharge (minor amounts of silver and tin were also detected). The copper would have been present in the original copper-silver alloy, while the lead represents a deliberate addition to the silver-copper alloy during cupellation to aid the separation of the silver and the copper (see below for further details). The litharge also contains a range of other oxides, in particular the oxides of silicon, calcium, phosphorus, aluminium, potassium and magnesium. There are no clear differences in the chemical composition of litharge from Roman and post-Roman contexts.

The litharge contains modest proportions of calcium and phosphorus, suggesting that bone ash was not a significant component of the cupellation hearth lining material. Girbal's (2011) study of litharge samples showed a clear separation into those with relatively high levels of calcium and phosphorus and those with low levels of these two elements (Fig. 3.77). This separation was further reinforced by a consideration of the microstructure: the former contained easily recognisable fragments of bone while the latter did not. All of the Gillingham litharge falls into Girbal's

Table 3.19   Chemical composition of Gillingham litharge (after Vaggi 2008; sample 201–19 after Girbal 2011)

Sample	Phase	MgO	Al_2O_3	SiO_2	P_2O_5	K_2O	CaO	MnO	Fe_2O_3	CuO	AgO	SnO_2	PbO
W of area A(2)	-	0.7	0.5	7.3	1.3	0.3	5.5	<0.1	<0.1	29.4	3.5	0.3	51.2
W of area A(1)	-	0.6	0.8	6.0	1.3	0.5	5.4	<0.1	<0.1	35.4	0.7	<0.2	49.1
SW of area A(2)	-	0.6	0.6	7.8	2.7	1.3	7.3	<0.1	0.2	19.4	0.3	0.8	58.9
SW of area A(1)	-	1.7	1.9	8.8	1.2	1.4	9.9	0.3	0.3	12.3	0.1	0.8	61.2
S of area A (6)	-	0.5	1.2	7.8	2.2	0.5	3.0	<0.1	0.1	21.3	3.5	<0.2	60.0
S of area A (5)	-	1.0	1.2	7.6	0.7	1.4	6.9	<0.1	0.1	19.6	0.4	0.6	60.4
S of area A (4)	-	0.6	1.2	5.7	0.4	1.1	4.1	0.1	<0.1	25.6	0.2	0.2	60.8
200–844	-	0.4	0.6	6.0	0.8	0.7	6.2	<0.1	0.5	20.4	0.3	1.0	63.1
200–843	-	0.9	1.8	7.9	2.2	1.0	4.1	<0.1	<0.1	32.8	0.7	0.3	48.4
200–842	-	0.8	0.4	4.7	0.9	0.6	6.7	0.2	<0.1	33.4	1.5	0.2	50.6
200–281	-	0.9	1.0	9.4	2.2	0.8	3.9	<0.1	<0.1	30.5	0.2	<0.2	50.9
200–280	-	0.7	0.6	6.5	0.6	0.6	7.7	<0.1	<0.1	19.5	0.1	0.7	63.0
453	9	1.0	0.7	6.7	0.7	1.0	8.0	<0.1	0.2	13.0	0.4	0.9	67.4
456–90/260	9	0.6	1.2	8.2	1.3	1.6	7.3	<0.1	<0.1	28.5	0.3	0.3	50.7
201–851	9	0.8	1.4	5.9	3.2	0.4	6.4	<0.1	<0.1	26.8	0.5	<0.2	54.5
201 (ore)	9	0.5	0.7	4.3	1.4	0.7	5.1	0.6	<0.1	14.4	0.5	6.8	64.9
201 (lith19)	9	1.2	1.1	6.1	1.2	1.0	5.4	0.1	0.3	22.0	0.6	0.5	60.4
937–1213	8	1.3	1.5	5.9	1.4	0.7	5.6	0.1	1.0	14.5	0.5	0.7	66.8
770–125–235	7	0.9	0.4	6.9	1.5	0.5	6.1	<0.1	<0.1	31.3	3.0	0.2	49.3
770–1052	7	1.0	0.6	6.7	0.6	0.8	8.1	<0.1	0.1	13.1	0.3	0.6	68.0
719–914(2)	7	0.3	0.8	6.9	3.1	0.6	4.0	<0.1	0.4	17.3	0.9	0.6	64.9
719–914(1)	7	0.5	1.1	8.9	1.5	1.3	7.9	<0.1	<0.1	17.5	0.4	0.8	60.1

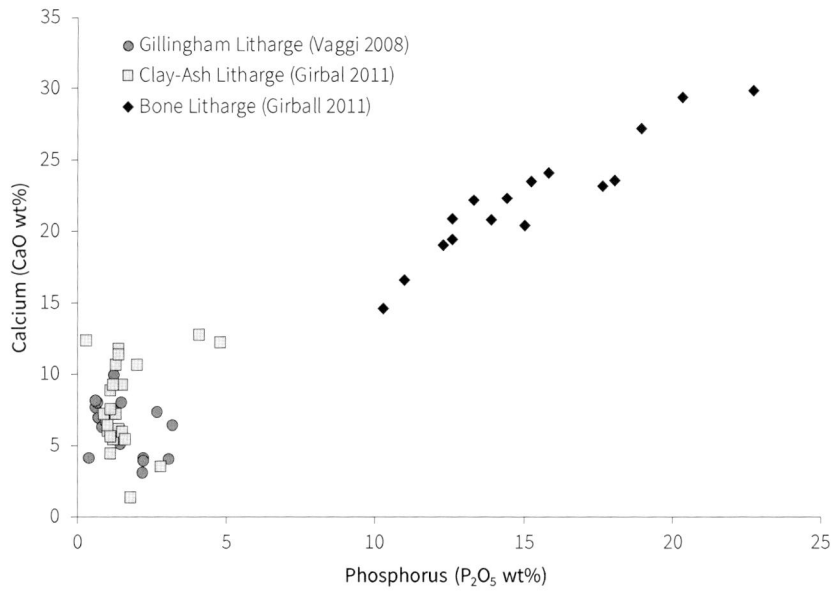

Fig. 3.77   Plot of calcium and phosphorus content of the Gillingham litharge (after Vaggi 2008) compared to the litharge analysed by Girbal (2011)

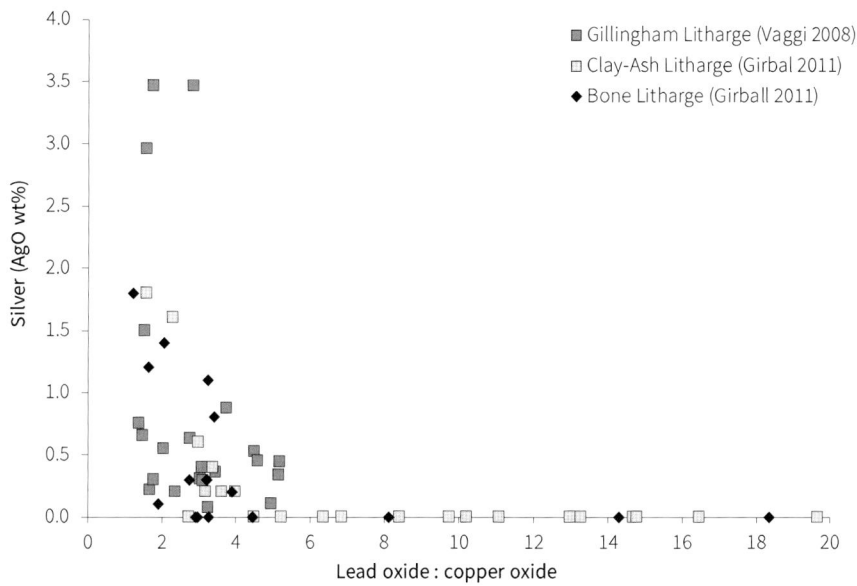

Fig. 3.78   Plot of silver against lead:copper ratios for Gillingham litharge (after Vaggi 2008) compared to the litharge analysed by Girbal (2011)

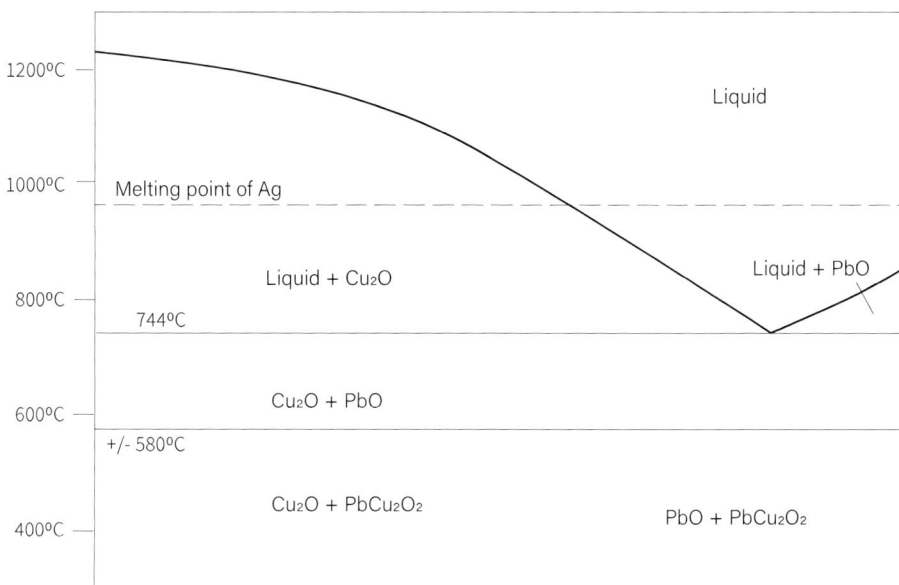

Fig. 3.79   PbO-Cu2O phase diagram (after Čančarević *et al.* 2005)

latter group. Although the low calcium and phosphorus litharge occasionally contains calcium phosphate compounds (and in the past these have been interpreted as evidence for the use of bone ash in cupellation hearth lining) these are likely to derive from materials other than bone ash. The low calcium and phosphorus litharge shows that this hearth lining material was produced using a combination of earthy materials (in particular clay) and plant ashes (the latter are often rich in calcium and phosphorus).

Bayley & Eckstein (2006) and Girbal (2011) explored the lead:copper ratios in litharge as a guide to the efficiency of cupellation. If silver content is plotted against lead:copper ratios (Fig. 3.78), it can be seen that litharge can be separated into two groups. The first group has low lead:copper ratios (<5 $PbO:Cu_2O$ as wt%) while the second has high lead:copper ratios (>5). The former group of litharge almost always contains detectable amounts of silver but the latter does not. The absorption of silver by litharge clearly represents a degree of inefficiency as the aim of secondary cupellation was to separate the silver from the copper.

For litharge, the relationship between silver on one hand and lead:copper ratio is explained by a consideration of the solubility of silver in the different materials used and produced during cupellation. Firstly, silver is completely soluble in lead (Karakaya & Thompson 1987) but is not soluble in lead oxide (PbO) and hardly soluble in copper-lead oxide ($PbCu_2O_2$); however, copper oxide (Cu_2O) can accommodate up to 44% silver (Bayley & Eckstein 2006). This is supported by SEM-EDS 'spot' analyses of phases in litharge (Vaggi 2008; Girbal 2011) which show that any silver in litharge cakes is concentrated in copper oxides (and occasional mechanically trapped metallic particles).

Cupellation of a silver-copper alloy with low levels of lead will tend to produce copper oxide (Cu_2O) which will encourage loss of silver to the litharge, while cupellation with more lead will produce lead oxide and so the silver will not be absorbed. The PbO-Cu_2O phase diagram (Fig. 3.79) shows that a PbO-Cu_2O eutectic forms at 82wt% PbO (18wt% Cu_2O, comparable to a lead:copper ratio of 4.6, caluclated using oxide weights); lower concentrations of lead oxide will tend to encourage the formation of Cu_2O (which will absorb some silver).

Therefore, the efficiency of silver recycling by secondary cupellation is clearly linked to the proportion of lead added to the debased silver. Where insufficient lead was added to the debased silver, some silver was lost in the litharge. The Gillingham litharge consistently shows low lead:copper ratios and some loss of silver in the litharge; however, this relative inefficiency is shared by the majority of Roman (and medieval) litharge from England (Girbal 2011).

Discussion

The recovery of litharge from Gillingham shows that the inhabitants were engaged in silver-working. The presence of high levels of copper in the litharge confirms that the process employed was secondary cupellation in which the aim was to recover pure silver from debased copper alloys. While pure silver has often been employed for the manufacture of coins and ornaments, this has often been alloyed with a proportion of copper. There are a number of reasons why silver might be alloyed in this way. Pure silver is a relatively soft metal and the addition of even small amounts of copper will make a much more durable metal. Perhaps more importantly, the addition of a little copper to silver does little to change its colour (a copper-silver alloy with up to 30wt% copper still has a 'silvery' colour, although it will tarnish more quickly). The use of silver can also be extended when it is alloyed with copper; the use of copper-silver alloys for this purpose in coinage (often referred to as debasement) has a long history (Ponting 2009). The late Roman period sees a rise in the use of pure silver as a medium of exchange between the empire and the increasingly active groups beyond the borders (Hunter & Painter 2013). The use of secondary cupellation to recover pure silver from debased silver alloys may have been a widespread activity in the late Roman period. It is unlikely that the copper-silver alloy that was to be refined was obtained from coins, as late Roman copper-alloy or 'billon' coins contain very low levels of silver (Harl 1996, Table 7.2 and 7.3). The silver:copper ratios in the litharge are comparable to an alloy containing 3.5wt% silver (and 96.5wt% copper) and so it is likely that the alloy to be refined by secondary cupellation contained significantly higher levels of silver (so that the loss of 3.5g of silver per 100g of alloy represented an acceptable loss).

The secondary cupellation process employed at Gillingham is comparable to that used at many other sites in Roman Britain. The copper-silver alloy would be melted with some lead, although at Gillingham they used insufficient lead to completely recover all of the silver. This copper-silver-lead alloy was then placed in a hearth that was lined with a mixture of clay and plant ash. The alloy was heated; however, the details of this are not apparent from the physical evidence recovered. It is likely that a wood fire was built over the cupellation hearth (charcoal would have been unnecessary). While forced draught (*ie* bellows) could have been employed, this was probably not essential. Some sort of hearth superstructure or cover would have aided temperature control; however, the only essential requirement was to maintain the temperature above the melting point of silver (963°C). An open superstructure (or indeed no superstructure) would have helped to provide all of the air needed to fully oxidise the base metals (copper and lead, as well as any tin present).

3.16 The stone

Kevin Hayward

The fabric, geological source and form of a large number (78 examples - 38kg) of worked and unworked examples of Roman stone provide the main focus for this section.

Geological character and source

The geological character and source of the seven different rock types identified from Grange Farm are summarised below (Table 3.20).

Summary

The assemblage can be broadly divided into two groups, first, the large quantity (26kg) of dumped local stone building materials from Phase 9 layer [201]. These are dominated (22kg) by large ashlar blocks (230mm x 170mm x 80mm) made from low-density, calcareous tufa, a geologically recent spring water deposit acquired locally from the catchment area of the Medway. These low-density rock-types were ideal as vaulting materials in bath-houses and they invariably turn up at bath-house sites in London such as at Winchester Palace (WP83) (Yule 2005). Waterproof *opus signinum* fragments were also found bonded to some examples. Quantities of Lower Greensand Kentish ragstone rubble sourced to the Maidstone area would have also benefitted from the proximity of the Medway. The one exotic material from this layer was a partly worked example of Bath-type stone. This material turns up in enormous quantities for use in religious sculpture at sites in London and further downstream such as Greenwich (Hayward 2015) and Springhead, or as funerary stelae (Hayward 2009). In all probability this fragment represents another remnant of the trade in this high-quality stone.

A second group, from Phase 6 layer [874] (Phase 6, Structure 1), Phase 9 demolition layers and Phase 10 well [563] (fill [562]) is dominated by quernstone fragments acquired from outcrops from much further afield. Millstone Grit (200km) probably from South Yorkshire or South Wales, dominates the assemblage supplemented by the occasional fragment of German Neidermendig lavastone (700km) from the Rhineland. Long-distance trade of portable quern-stone objects during the Roman period was commonplace, especially at the coastal/nodal hub of the Medway Estuary, as shown by the identification of these materials at Ebbsfleet and Springhead (Shaffrey 2011).

Table 3.20 Summary of rock-types

MoL fabric code	Description	Geological Type and source	Use at KKGF03
3105	Fine hard dark grey sandy limestone speckles of black iron oxide	Kent ragstone, Lower Cretaceous, Lower Greensand Maidstone District - Kent	Discarded walling rubble some 12 examples 10.9kg most of this from the late Roman soil layer [201]
3109	Banded shelly oolitic limestone	Middle Jurassic (Bathonian) South Cotswolds Cirencester to Bath	Fragment of an undulating part worked block probably sculptural or funerary from phase 9 layer [201] 1 example 0.3kg
3116	Fine white powdery limestone	Chalk Upper Cretaceous (Upper Chalk) London Basin	Rubble stone fragments 10 examples 0.6kg all from phase 9 layer [201]
3117	Hard dark-grey siliceous cryptocrystalline sandstone	Flint – Upper Cretaceous (Upper Chalk) London Basin	Rubble stone fragments 5 examples 0.7kg all from phase 9 layer [201]
3118	White nodular low-density calcareous stone	Calcareous Tufa – Holocene nearest outcrops chalk outcrops Thames Estuary or Medway	Part worked ashlar blocks 38 examples 22kg some degraded as rubble nearly all from phase 9 layer [201]
3123R	Hard dark-grey vesicular lavastone	Neidermendig lava – Tertiary Rhineland	Rotary quernstone fragments (32mm) from (Phase 6, Structure 1) [874]
3130	Hard angular sugary quartz sandstone	Millstone Grit – Upper Carboniferous (Namurian) South Yorkshire or South Wales	Rotary quernstone fragments from Phase 9 demolition layers and fill of Phase 10 well [563]

3.17 The ceramic building material and burnt clay

Berni Sudds

In total 3059 fragments of ceramic building material and burnt clay, weighing just over 513kg, were collected during the evaluation and excavation phases, although due to the agreed site methodology this represents only a proportion of total assemblage present on site. A breakdown of the assemblage by period is presented below (Table 3.21), with the vast majority being of Roman date. Due to time constraints the collected material was further sub-sampled. Of the large Roman assemblage 49% was fully analysed and quantified by fabric and form, with the remaining 51% quantified by form alone.

Fabrics were identified with the aid of a x20 binocular microscope following the Kent fabric series created and curated by Ian Betts. The latter is based upon a number of sites in Kent and makes reference to the Museum of London fabric reference collection where parallels exist. Parallels were also drawn to the large assemblage of building material recovered from two sites in the Ebbsfleet Valley further west along the Thames and from a smaller assemblage from nearby Rochester (Poole 2011; Hayward 2007). Those fabrics thus far unique to Grange Farm, likely to be of relatively localised origin, have been allocated a new number in this series.

Fabric

Sources

A breakdown of the assemblage by fabric type is presented in Table 3.22 both by number and weight. The silty and iron-rich fabrics (K13/LOC3; K41/LOC6) represent by far the most common type together comprising 53% of the overall Roman assemblage by number and 67% by weight.

They represent a distinctive group, containing varying quantities of silt and iron-rich inclusions. The less silty group (K41/LOC6) is slightly more prevalent amongst the two, but there is some overlap between them, with some examples sharing characteristics of both. Indeed, they are perhaps best seen as a continuum, quite distinct from one another at the extremes, but with a blurred area in the middle, effecting a relatively minimal number, where it is difficult to put them in one group or the other. This probably denotes a shared or related clay source for both, but that they were subjected to different treatment of the clay and firing.

As a group K13/LOC3 and K41/LOC6 resemble products of the Radlett kilns in Hertfordshire (MOLA types 3023 and 3060) and are also similar to the description of Group B fabrics identified to the west in the Ebbsfleet valley, which are also likened to the Radlett material (Poole 2011, 327 and 345). Here, though, it was suggested that clays similar to those used at Radlett were also available south of the Thames and that the Ebbsfleet examples probably derive from a more local source (Poole 2011). Less sandy versions of Radlett types have also been found elsewhere in Kent (K13), which could also be local to north Kent. Given that the fabrics of this group dominate the current assemblage, the same is likely to be true of the Grange Farm material. Furthermore, the small number of examples identified as Radlett group (MOLA 3023/3060; 0.5% of the Roman assemblage), whilst potentially originating in Hertfordshire and arriving on site via London and down the Thames, along with the more numerous London 2815 fabrics, could also in fact be locally produced. This could also be the situation in nearby Rochester, where Radlett group material has previously been identified (Hayward 2007).

The fine and sandy red London 2815 group fabrics represent the second most common fabric group on site, although comprising a much smaller component at 9% by fragment count (Table 3.21). Fabrics similar, or equated to, the 2815 group were also identified at Rochester and Ebbsfleet to the west and at Thurnham Villa to the south

Table 3.21 *Ceramic building material by period (weight in grams). P = Present.*

Period and type	Total number	%	Total weight	%
Roman				
Ceramic: brick, roof tile, box-flue tile and tesserae	2,542	83%	483,203	94%
Opus signinum, mortar and wall plaster/render	74	3%	14,038	3%
Burnt clay/briquetage	389	13%	7090	1.5%
Late medieval–post-medieval				
Ceramic: roof tile, brick and floor tile	42	1%	8,485	1.5%
Burnt clay/daub	12	P	188	P
Total	3,059		513,004	

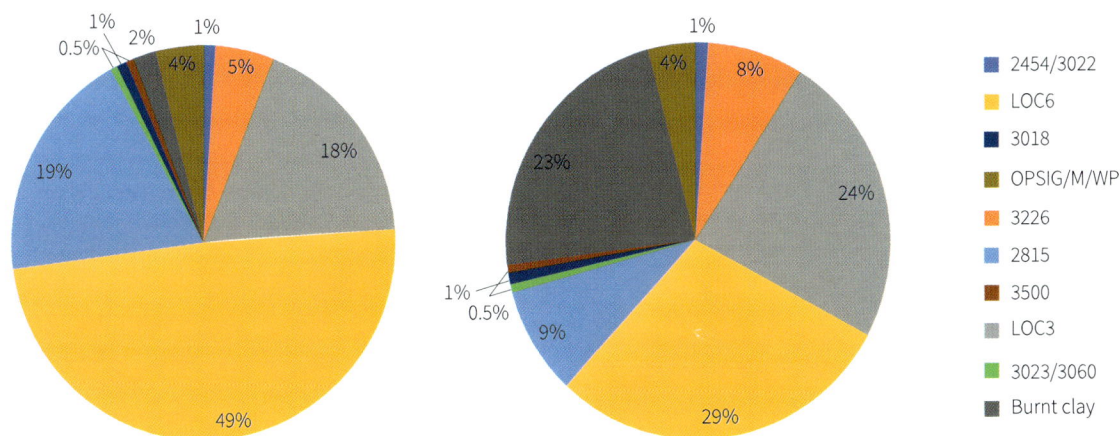

Fig. 3.80   Roman CBM fabric: percentage composition by number of fragments (left) and weight (right); see Table 3.22 for guide to codes used

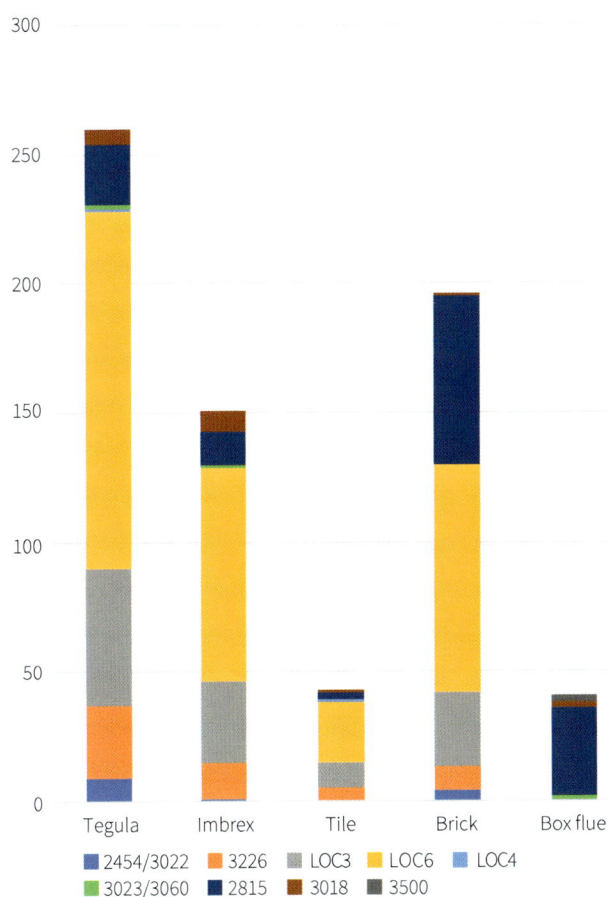

Fig. 3.81   Roman CBM fabric and form breakdown (by number); see Table 3.22 for guide to codes used

near Maidstone (Smith & Betts 2006, 5; Hayward 2007; Group D, Poole 2011, 327). Kilns producing this fabric group have been identified along Watling Street between London and Verulamium, and also more recently in the City near St Paul's, but at both Ebbsfleet and Thurnham the similarity between this material and brick and tile made at Canterbury was noted and some commentators

connect this group to the kilns there (McWhirr 1979; Smith & Betts 2006, 19; Harrison 2008; Poole 2011, 345). It is in fact quite likely that there were a number of tileries in the London area and Thames estuary making 2815 types (I. Betts pers. comm.), and at Ebbsfleet it was suggested that this fabric group could have been made just to the east of Northfleet, where the London clay outcrops.

In the absence of chemical characterisation, it would be difficult to comment on how local the 2815 examples from site are, but some clue to their source may be provided by the form composition of the group. Although the full range of forms is represented, in contrast to the local silty/iron-rich group, box-flue tile and brick are more numerous than roofing tile (Fig. 3.81). Indeed, over 80% of the small assemblage of box-flue tile recovered occurs in the 2815 fabric group. On the face of it this might suggest that certain forms, including specialised hypocaust tile, were being procured from elsewhere as the local tileries were not producing them. However, there is certainly plenty of brick in the local silty/iron-rich group on site, in addition to a couple of box-flue tiles, and the evidence from Ebbsfleet suggests that box-flue tiles were certainly part of the output (Poole 2011, 331). Assuming the 2815 group on site is not very localised, why then would it be needed, if more locally sourced material was available? The suggestion made at Thurnham Villa was that the 2815 group tile arrived as a return cargo on ships transporting Kentish Rag building stone to London down the Medway and up the Thames (Smith & Betts 2006, 5). In the same way the 2815 group material on site could be arriving as a return cargo, or perhaps as ballast, with locally produced commodities returning to London. This argument is explored further below, but even if the 2815 group does not originate from London, it could still be imported to site from another source, say Canterbury, to which the Grange Farm settlement, or broader estate was commercially linked.

Table 3.22 Ceramic building material fabrics (% of total = % total of period assemblage by number)

Kent fabric code	cf MOLA/ other equivalent	Description	Forms	Date range	Source	% of total
K14	MOLA 2454	Cream, yellow and pink, fine fabric with a scatter of colourless or rose quartz. Sparse to moderate iron oxide and calcium carbonate inclusions. Some examples have red moulding sand.	Tegula, imbrex, brick and tessera	50–80/100	Kent, Eccles	1%
	MOLA 3022	Same as MOLA 2454 but with frequent quartz.		50–80/100		
K13	LOC 3 (Poole 2011 fabric Group B)	Fine sandy micaceous orange to orange brown fabric. Moderate to abundant small to large cream to pale yellow silt inclusions (up to 10mm), moderate red/iron rich clay inclusions and sparse blocky orange (unwedged?) clay inclusions from poor blending. Sparse to common fine black iron ore, sparse red iron oxide, ferruginous sandstone, ironstone and calcium carbonate. Some examples with red moulding sand from the ferruginous sandstone/clay. Nr. K13 (less sandy MOLA 3023) and Poole Group B.	Tegula, imbrex, brick and tessera	70–150/200?	Kent, North/ Thames estuary	53%
K41	LOC 6 (Poole 2011 fabric Group B)	Similar to LOC 3 but with fewer or no silt inclusions. Harder and higher fired than LOC3, orange-red/red in colour. Nr. K41 (less sandy MOLA 3060) and Poole Group B.				
K42?	LOC4 MOLA 3024?	Similar to LOC6 but with abundant sand and moderate calcium carbonate and iron oxide inclusions.	Tegula			
	MOLA 3060	Red, orange or brown with frequent fine quartz (up to 0.3mm), common very fine black iron ore (up to 0.1mm) and sparse coarse red iron oxide (up to 2mm).		50–120	Herts/local?	0.5%
	MOLA 3023	Similar to MOLA 3060 but with cream silty inclusions (up to 6mm).	Tegula, imbrex and box-flue			
K7	cf MOLA 2185 Group: 3006 (Poole 2011 fabric Group D)	Fine, slightly sanded red fabric with moderate to common medium quartz (up to 0.3mm) and occasional iron oxide and calcium carbonate inclusions.	Tegula, imbrex, brick, tessera and box-flue	50–160	London/ local?	9%
K40	cf MOLA 2459 (Poole 2011 fabric Group D)	Fine sandy red fabric with sparse quartz above 0.2mm and sparse iron oxide and calcium carbonate inclusions.				
K12	cf MOLA 2452 (Poole 2011 fabric Group D)	Fine red fabric with sparse to moderate quartz (up to 0.5mm) and sparse iron oxide and calcium carbonate inclusions.				

Table 3.22 Ceramic building material fabrics (% of total = % total of period assemblage by number) continued

Kent fabric code	cf MOLA/ other equivalent	Description	Forms	Date range	Source	% of total
K47	MOLA 3226 LOC 1 & 2 (Poole 2011 fabric Group E; Hayward 2007 fabric KR5)	Coarse orange to orange-red fabric. Fine clay laminated matrix with coarse moderate inclusions of grey to reddish-brown ferruginous siltstone/ironstone (mostly up to 5mm but occasionally up to 15mm), iron oxide (1mm), calcium carbonate (up to 2mm). Sparse inclusions of coarse clear, white and pink and iron-stained quartz (up to 2mm), blocky pale orange clay/silt (up to 4mm), red ferruginous fine sandstone (up to 4mm) and creamy clay silty streaks. The fabric is characterised by very coarse moulding sand, comprised of abundant fragments of the same suite of quartz, rock and silt block inclusions that occurs in the matrix.	Tegula, imbrex, brick and tessera	70–100	Kent, Weald/ Maidstone?	8%
K39	MOLA 3018 LOC 5 (Poole 2011 fabric Group E)	Fine, light orange/orange fabric with occasional cream coloured silt inclusions and bands and sparse blocky orange clay/silt inclusions, quartz, iron oxide and calcium carbonate inclusions.	Tegula, imbrex, brick, tessera and box-flue	100–120	Sussex/North Kent/Weald	1%

A distinctive orange rock and calcium carbonate tempered fabric (K47/MOLA3226) accounts for a similar proportion of the Roman assemblage at 8% by fragment count. This fabric occurs on a number of sites in north Kent and in London (Hayward 2007, Smith & Betts 2006, 7 and 22; Poole 2011, 327). The production source remains unknown, but given the greensand inclusions a Wealden source, perhaps somewhere near Maidstone, has been suggested (Hayward 2007). Similarly, the small quantity of the fine orange silty K39/MOLA3018 fabric recovered (1% of the Roman assemblage), although known to be produced at Hartfield in East Sussex, is also found across north Kent, so a more local Kentish source is possible (I. Betts pers. comm.), perhaps further east in the Weald. The final fabric group represented, also comprising just 1% of the Roman assemblage, is the very early Roman cream-pink tiles produced at Eccles (K14/MOLA2454/3022). Again, these occur on many sites in north Kent and were also transported to London in significant quantities for the Neronian building programme (Hayward 2007, Smith & Betts 2006, 6: Poole 2011, 328). These bricks almost certainly arrived on site directly from source, Eccles being located less than 10 kilometres to the south-west, transported via the Medway.

Chronology

A composition of the fabric assemblage by phase is presented in Fig. 3.82. The Eccles group brick and tile K14/MOLA2454/3022) represents the earliest datable material from site and is present in the earliest Roman deposits (Phase 4), increasing slightly in number into Phase 5 and present in small quantities thereafter. In London, this group is dated AD 50–80, and although there is some evidence for later manufacture at Eccles this is probably limited to supplying the local villa (Smith & Betts 2006, 6). Eccles products never represent a significant part of assemblage, as noted at Northfleet further west (Poole 2011, 328), yet they were imported into London in large quantities, passing by the site on route. Rather than the other red and orange tiles, including the abundant silty/iron-rich group, fulfilling the demand for early tile, the relative absence of Eccles material reflects the fact that activity on site was relatively minimal until last decades of first century, as seems to be implied by the other finds assemblages. The London 2815 group and north-Kent/Wealden K47/MOLA3226 fabrics are also present from Phase 4. The former group also dates from *c*. AD 50 but with a longer period of production than the Eccles group, continuing up until

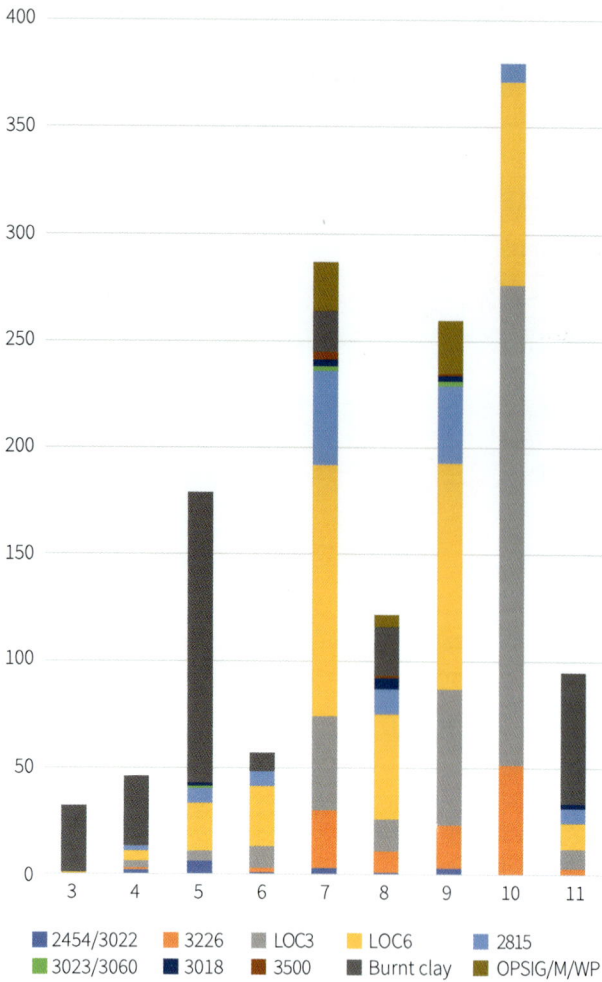

Fig. 3.82   Distribution of Roman CBM fabric by phase, by number

c. AD 160, whilst K47/MOLA3226 are tentatively dated to around AD 70–100 (Smith & Betts 2006, 6; Hayward 2007).

The dating of the local silty/iron-rich fabrics is somewhat speculative. The fact that they occur in Phase 4 deposits alongside early dated types suggest production was under way by the late first century, perhaps post AD 70/80, coinciding with the contraction of output at the Eccles kilns. Due to the widespread practice of re-using building material an end date is much more difficult to pin down. Indeed, all of the fabric groups, including the early types are present throughout the life of the settlement, occurring in increasing quantities (with the exception of the Eccles group). By Phase 7, the most intense period of construction on site, production of the Eccles, K47/MOLA3226, K39/MOLA3018 and London 2815 group fabrics had long since ceased, with brick and tile from these sources being reused. There is a possibility that the local silty/iron-rich fabric continued to be made for longer, but there is no evidence to substantiate this and in size and form it is comparable to other early types.

Given that the greatest evidence for construction post-dates the mid-third century, the total absence of late Roman roof tile on a site is curious. Late Roman types occur on other sites with late Roman activity in the vicinity, including Ebbsfleet and Deerton Street, Sittingbourne (Betts & Foot 1994; Betts 2001; Poole 2011, 327). This must mean that the material required for construction was available on site or in the immediate vicinity. Late Roman tile was also absent from Thurnham villa, where it was concluded that any late structural work must have been confined to the re-use of earlier building material (Smith & Betts 2006, 21). Much of the Phase 7 mausoleum was extensively robbed for building material in Phase 10, but demolition material

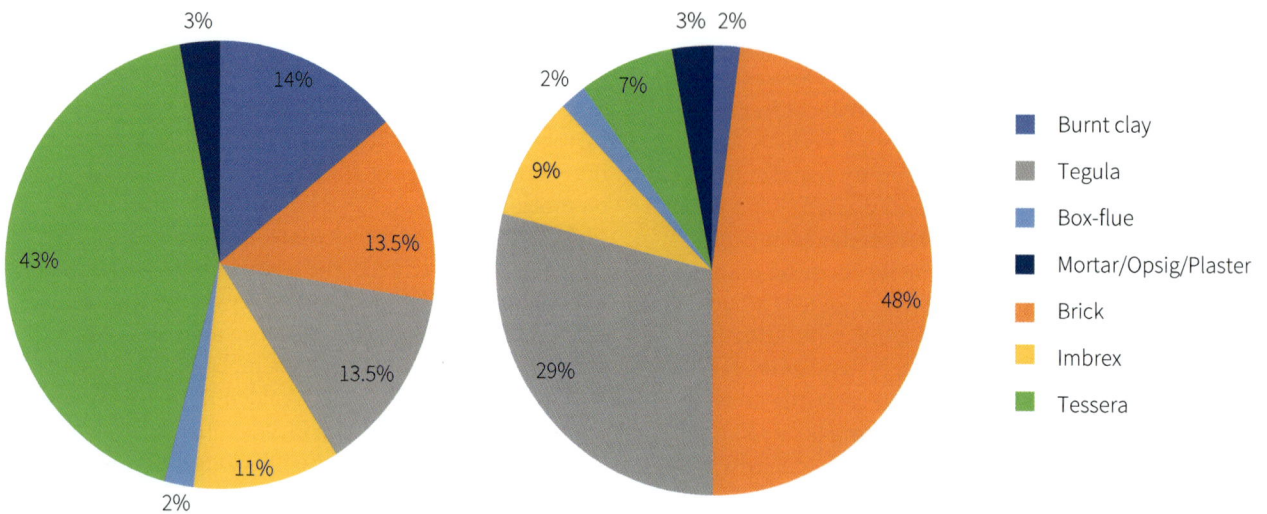

Fig. 3.83   Roman CBM forms: percentage composition by number of fragments (left) and weight (right)

from an episode of disturbance, and possible partial collapse, in Phase 9 would suggest at least some of the building was constructed from re-used early building material. The quantity of tegula and imbrex might also indicate the building had a tiled roof, probably made out of the local silty/iron-rich group, and if not still being produced, these would have to have been carefully salvaged from the roof of an earlier building.

Form

The composition of the assemblage by form type is presented in Fig. 3.83, first by fragment count and then by weight. The former is somewhat skewed by the recovery of a large number of tesserae from the mausoleum, and in the percentages by weight, the heavier brick is proportionally better represented. By fragment count, after the tesserae (43%), roof tile (*tegula* and *imbrex*) represents the next most common group (24.5%), followed by burnt/fired clay (14%) and brick (13.5%). Relatively minimal quantities of mortar/plaster/ *opus signinum* (3%) and box-flue tile (2%) comprise the remainder of the assemblage.

Roofing

By far the greatest majority of the roofing tile on site occurs in the local silty and iron-rich types (K13/LOC3; K41/LOC6), followed by smaller quantities of K47/3226 from a north Kent or possibly Wealden source and in the London 2815 group (K7/K12/K40) (Fig. 3.81). The remaining sources, represented by just a few examples, include Eccles (K14/2454/3022) and possibly Radlett, Hertfordshire (MOLA 3023 & 3060) and Hartfield in East Sussex (K39/3018), although a more local north Kent source for the last two is perhaps more likely (see Fabric discussion above).

The only recordable dimension for the imbrex is thickness. The local silty and iron-rich types (K13/LOC3; K41/LOC6) imbrex are of a similar size and thickness to the 2815 group, typically between 14mm to 18mm, although ranging from 11mm to 24mm. Unusually, one example is covered in pre-firing vertical score marks (Fig. 3.88; see Markings below). The 2815 group examples range in thickness from 13mm to 27mm and the north Kent/Wealden rock-tempered (K47/3226) examples from 13mm to 21mm.

Just one tegula with a complete length was recovered, a local silty (K13) example measuring 415mm. No full widths were recorded in any fabric group but the local silty and iron-rich examples (K13/LOC3; K41/LOC6) range in thickness from as thin as 12mm up to 36mm, although more commonly fall between 18mm and 25mm. The flange depths of this group range from 36mm to 60mm, with most falling between 40mm and 55mm. The 2815 group tegula range in thickness from 12mm to 28mm, with the flange depths from 41mm to 52mm and the north Kent/Wealden rock-tempered (K47/3226)

examples from 18mm to 28mm thick, with flanges ranging from 32mm to 58mm. The smaller number of Eccles examples recovered (K14/2454; 3022) are 20mm to 24mm thick, with flanges ranging from 47mm to 60mm.

The tegula profiles for the local silty and iron-rich group encompass a fairly broad spectrum (see Table 3.22; see Fig. 3.86.1 nr Type 15), although, like the London 2815 group, types 1 and 2 occur most frequently. The remaining flange profiles are consistent with their fabric groups, including K47/3226, composed almost exclusively of the distinctive pointed and ledged profile type 29 (Fig. 3.86.2; Fig. 3.86.3). Both lower and upper cutaways were recorded, the former most frequently comprising of a simple rectangular section cut away from the end of the flange. Amongst the lower cutaways, Type B (composite vertical to top and diagonal to bottom), is the most frequently occurring type across all fabric groups, followed by Type A (diagonal) and Type C (vertical) in equal quantities. The only other group represented was Type E (low diagonal), occurring in the local silty and iron-rich group (K13/LOC3; K41/LOC6), the north Kent/Wealden rock-tempered (K47/3226) group and the Eccles group (K14/2454). Just two end tegula were recovered with nail holes (Brodribb 1987, 10–11).

It is quite probable that much of the roof tile recovered was used for roofing structures on site and in the vicinity, but it is also apparent, as observed on many Roman sites, that it was re-used in masonry lacing courses, floors and hearths/ovens. In all cases tegula, as a flat tile, was favoured over imbrex, with the flange sometimes removed. A smaller quantity of imbrex was also made use of in such features, broken lengthways. Along with a large quantity of single fragments of tegula and brick, three fragments of masonry, formed of a double course of bonded tegula, were sampled from wall [470]. These probably derived from a brick quoin, or abutment framing an opening. A fourth fragment comprised part of a *lydion* or *pedalis* brick, bonded to a non-diagnostic fragment of flat-tile.

Bricks

As with the roof tile, the majority of the brick recovered from site occurs in the local silty and iron-rich fabrics (K14/LOC3; K41/LOC6), although in contrast to the tile, a more significant component occurs in the London 2815 group (K7/K12/K40). The remaining brick is represented by small numbers from north Kent or the Weald (K47/3226), Eccles (2454/3022) and Hartfield in East Sussex (K39/3018), although as explained above a more local north Kent source for the latter is possible (see Fabric discussion above).

The full dimensions of just three bricks were recorded, all bessalis, the smallest of the brick forms, but on the basis of the surviving dimensions and thicknesses from other fragments, it is evident that the full complement of brick types is present in the assemblage. The square *bessales* bricks range in length/width from 172mm to

Table 3.23 Distribution of the sampled tegula flange profiles by fabric group, by number (MOLA: Museum of London Archaeology).

Flange profile (MOLA)		K14/ MOLA 2454; 3022	K13/ LOC3	K41/ LOC6	MOLA 3060	K7/12/40 MOLA 2815	K47/ MOLA 3226	K39/ MOLA 3018
1	Straight inside edge, flat top		21	57		8	1	1
2	Straight inside edge, inward sloping top	1	7	30		2		
4	Straight inside edge, grooved top		1	1				
5	Straight inside edge, groove to top outer edge	1						
6	Tall, thin flange, flat top			1				
7	Undercut inside edge, flat top		1	1				
10	Undercut inside edge, grooved top	1						
11	Undercut inside edge, groove to top outer edge	2						
12	Sloping inside edge, flat top		2	3		1		
13	Sloping inside edge, inward sloping top		3	8	1	2		
15	Sloping inside edge, grooved top		1	1			2	
16	Sloping inside edge, groove to top outer edge			1				
17	Straight inside edge, flat top; sharp inside corner		1	1				
18	Straight inside edge, inward sloping top; sharp inside corner		2	1				1
22	Sloping inside edge, outward sloping top; sharp inside corner						1	
26	Rounded top			2				
29	Straight or sloping inside edge, pointed top with ledge to top outer edge						21	
31	Thin flange with sloping inside edge, inward sloping top		1	2		1		2
32	Tall, thin flange, undercut inside edge and flat top					1		
33	Sloping inside edge, flat top with small bevel to either edge		1					
36	Undercut inside edge, grooved top with bevelled inside corner	1						
39	Straight inside edge, flat top; bevelled inside corner			1				
42	Sloping inside edge, pointed top (bevelled to either side)			1				

195mm and the in thickness from 32mm to 40mm. Bricks with a width of around 290mm are either square *pedalis* types or rectangular *lydions*. Although no complete examples of either type were recovered, *lydions* are identifiable amongst the assemblage when their length exceeds 350mm. The width of *pedalis/lydion* bricks from site ranges from 277mm to 308mm and the thickness from 31mm to 45mm.

The presence of the larger bricks, *sesquipedalis* and *bipedalis* types, is based principally on thickness, with the former generally exceeding 50mm and the latter 60/70mm. Of course, thicker examples of the smaller brick sizes do occur, so thickness cannot be taken to be a definitive means of identification. Nonetheless, of the small sample fully measured, at least 11 large bricks were recorded, including 12 fragments, weighing 27kg, from a probable *bipedalis* (used in wall [470]). A full width could not be reconstructed from the fragments, but the brick was 80mm thick. The vast majority of brick from site, however, falls under 40mm in thickness, suggesting the smaller brick sizes represent the most commonly occurring types, as evidenced at Northfleet to the west (Poole 2011, 332).

Although the different sized bricks were manufactured for specific purposes, they were all used and re-used for a number of different functions. For example, although the primary function of *bessalis*, *pedalis* and *bipedalis* forms were in constructing the *pilae* and suspended floor of hypocaust systems, as with the roofing tile, they were frequently used in bonding/lacing courses and in floors and hearths, as is the case on site (and seen above in wall [470]).

A single example of a *tegula mammata* was recovered from site from Phase 7 layer [1287]. It is of Brodribb's Type A, a brick with added rounded shallow lumps of

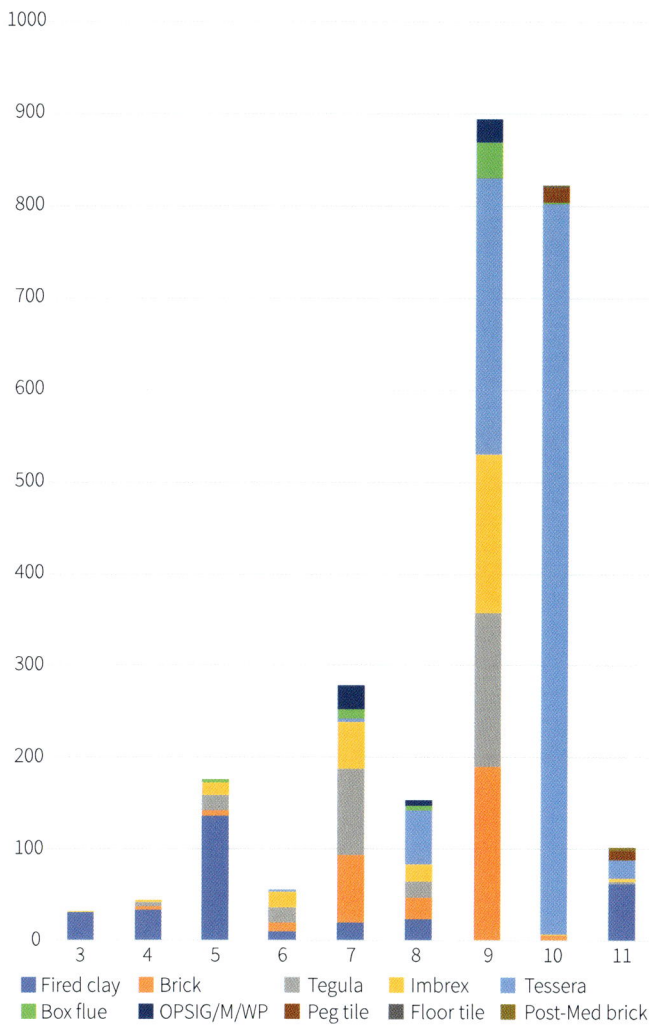

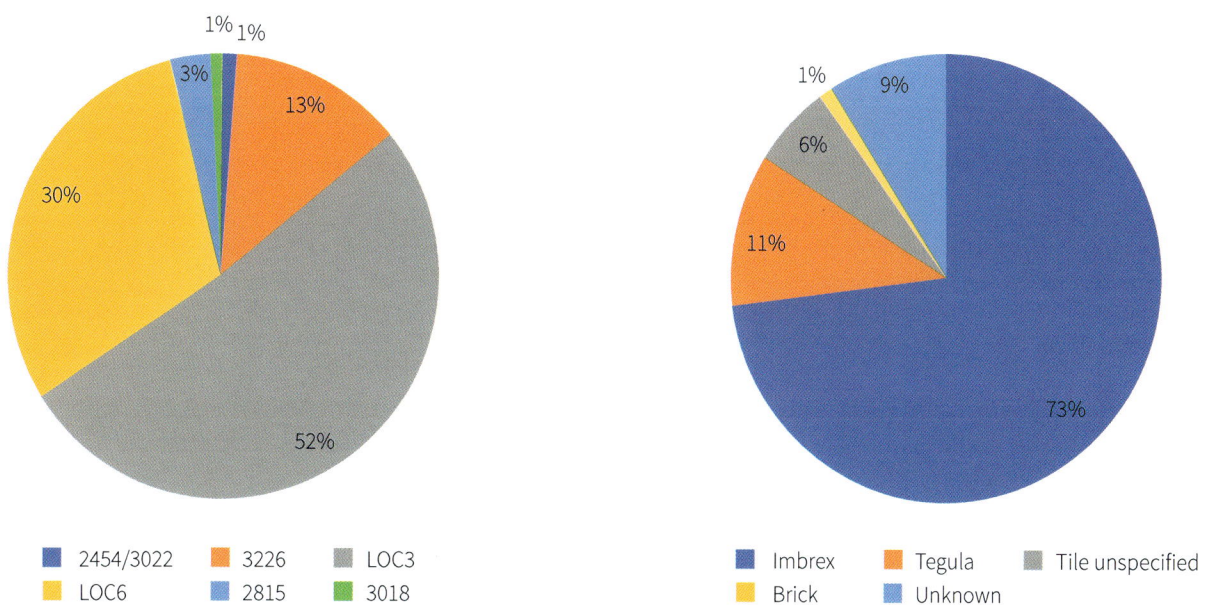

Fig. 3.84   Distribution of Roman and later CBM forms by phase, by number

Fig. 3.85   Ceramic tesserae: percentage composition by source fabric and form, by number

clay or *mammae*, probably used to assist with bonding in walls and floors (Brodribb 1987, 60–62). Just one *mamma* was recorded on the brick fragment from site, close to the corner and fairly small at 35mm in diameter and 10mm in height. Finally, and more unusually, one large brick has a pre-firing hole near to the corner (Phase 9, layer [449]; Fig. 3.86.4). The hole was made from the top and has a conical profile (widest at the top). At 50mm thick the brick is too thick (and thus heavy) to be a *parietalis* (wall tile), and in any case the nail/cramp hole is in the wrong place. Other than providing an added means of fixing or securing, the function of the nail hole remains uncertain.

Flooring

The bulk of the evidence for flooring comes in the form of cut-tile tesserae, 1182 to be precise, the majority originating from the tessellated surface of the mausoleum (Phase 7), although recovered from later episodes of robbing and demolition (Phases 9 & 10; Fig. 3.84). The fabric composition of the parent tile largely mirrors the rest of the material on site, with over 80% cut from the local silty and iron-rich types (K13/LOC3; K41/LOC6), only the more silty and lower fired K13/LOC3 tiles appears to be favoured over the generally harder K41/LOC6 group. This may simply result from the K13/LOC 3 group being easier to cut, which could also explain why imbrex, being thinner, were favoured over other forms of tile or brick (Fig. 3.85). The remaining tesserae were cut from local/north Kent types (K47/3226; K39/3018) and the London 2815 group. The tesserae range in length from 19–49mm, in width from 14–42mm and in thickness from 11–40mm.

The remnants of brick and tile surfaces were also recorded in Building 5 and the smithy area. In both cases large fragments of brick and roof tile, principally tegula used face down or with the flange removed, but also including a few imbrex (broken lengthways), were used to form a surface, sometimes bedded with reused crushed *opus signinum*, mortar or plaster. As with the tesserae these occur most frequently in the local silty and iron-rich fabric (K13/LOC3; K41/LOC6) as the most readily available group for re-use. Fragments of *opus signinum* from the loose assemblage may suggest that 'concrete' surfaces existed in some of the buildings on site, or in the vicinity. A patch of *opus signinum* was recorded in what could be an entranceway to the mausoleum, although this was not sampled.

Box-flue tile

A total of 61 fragments of box-flue tile were recorded in the sample from site, weighing 10,812g, representing 2% of the overall form assemblage by fragment count and weight (Fig. 3.83). Over 80% of those identified to fabric type occur in the London sandy 2815 group. With the remaining examples occurring as MOLA3023/3060 (although these could be local variants), the north Kent/ Wealden fine orange silty fabric K39/MOLA3018 and

the local silty/iron-rich K13/LOC3; K41/LOC6. Combed keying represents the only type identified, including vertical, horizontal and diagonal bands, wavy vertical bands and semi-circles. Unusually, two of the London 2815 group box-flue tiles have civilian tile stamps (see below).

Markings

Tile stamps

Two box-flue tile fragments were recovered with two different and previously unparalleled civilian stamps (Fig. 3.86.5; Fig. 3.86.6). The first is only partially complete, reading '----DNI' and the second complete example reads 'MRTI' or possibly 'IVRTI'. In contrast to official or legionary tileries who stamped to denote ownership or authority, it is thought that private tileries stamped for advertisement, often using personal names (Brodribb 1987, 117). Both the tiles occur in London 2815 group fabric K7/3006, although neither can be paralleled in the small number of civilian stamped tiles identified in London and it is possible they derive from a civilian tilemaker based in north Kent, where a number of production centres are suspected to have been located (I. Betts pers. comm.). The possibility of the London 2815 group material on site being of more local origin is discussed above (see Fabric) and has been raised elsewhere (Poole 2011, 327–8). Whatever their source, to have two such stamps in the same assemblage is rare enough, but to have both on box-flue tile, very few of which are stamped, is remarkable (Brodribb 1987, 124).

Signature marks

A total of 28 'signature' marks have been recorded, predominantly on tegulae but also on a smaller number of bricks (Fig. 3.86.7). Most occur on the local silty/ iron-rich fabric group, with a smaller number occurring on the London 2815 group, no doubt a reflection of the relative proportion of each fabric type in the overall assemblage. The 'local' group signatures include double and triple semi-circles (Fig. 3.86.7), single and double circles, one of the latter also with a dog paw print (Fig. 3.86.8) and single examples of a double parallel wavy line (Fig. 3.86.9) and a horizontal 'S' mark. The London 2815 group marks can all be well paralleled in the corpus, including single, double and triple semi-circles, and one with crossed diagonal lines. The purpose of these 'signature' marks remains ambiguous. It is possible they represent the mark of an individual tiler to identify their own work, a trade-mark of the tilery or even a mark to denote quality or grade. The reason so few were marked is that there is only the need to mark the last in a run of work, or batch. There are problems with all of these suggestions (see Brodribb 1987, 99–105) and the real purpose of these marks could be more complex and regionally or locally dependent.

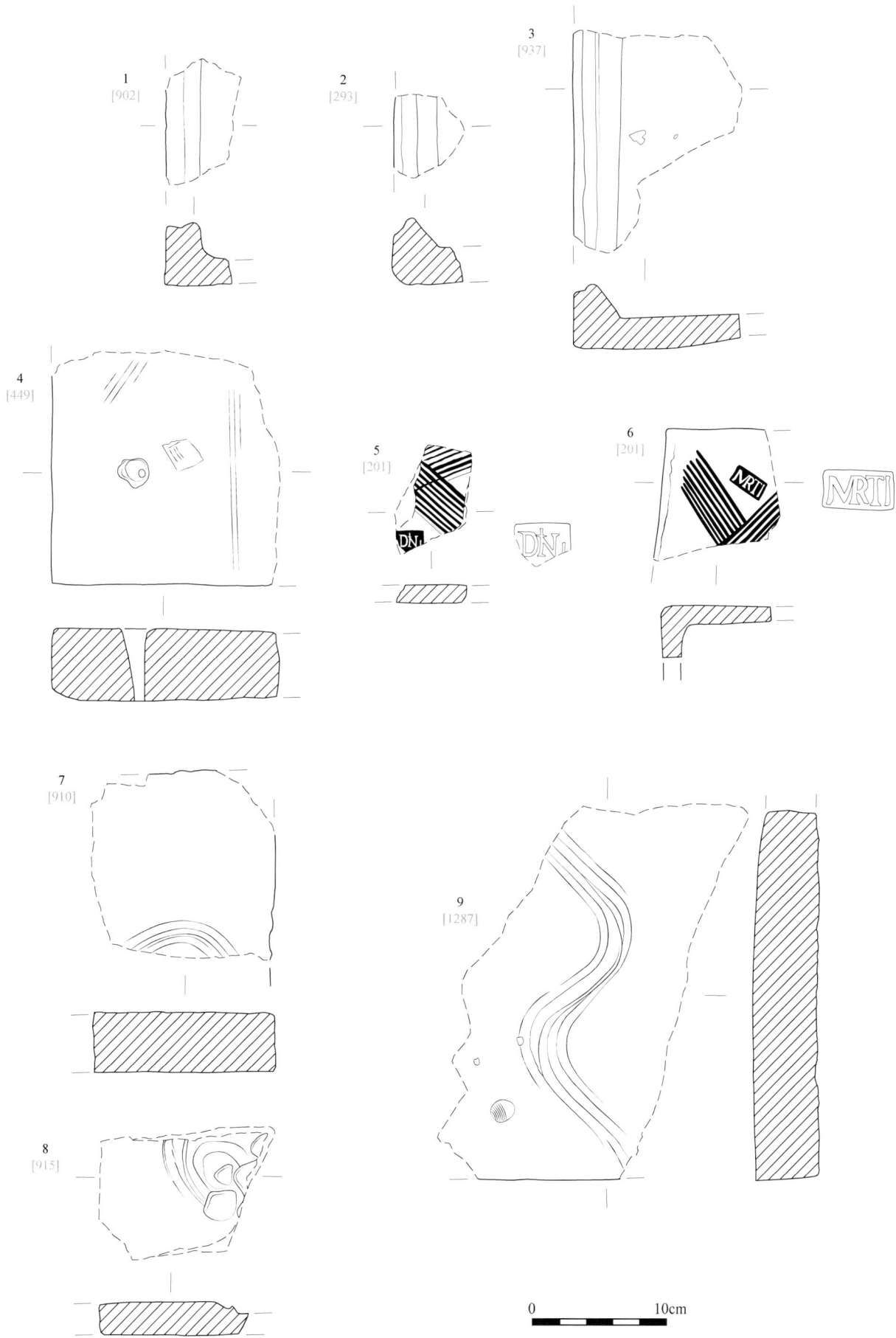

Fig. 3.86   Stamps, signature, tally marks and other markings on brick and tile (scale 1:4)

Tally-marks

One possible tally-mark was recorded, formed of a single vertical line on the edge of tegula (layer [201]). The purpose of tally-marks is also uncertain, but since many take the form of numerals it has been suggested that they relate to quantities or batches of tile, perhaps simply to keep count or track daily output, or to denote loads for firing (Brodribb 1987, 131–135; Poole 2011, 335). It is also not impossible that the different numerals represent an individual tiler's mark.

Scored brick

Fragments of two rare scored bricks were recovered from site from a Phase 7 Open Area 1, layer [694] <971> (Fig. 3.87) and in wall [470] <877>. Both are deeply scored pre-firing in a regular grid pattern. One is a corner fragment but, other than thickness, at 26mm and 30mm respectively, no full dimensions survive. Both examples occur in sandy K7/3006 London 2815 group fabric. Similar examples have been recovered from a handful of other sites (see Brodribb 1987, 114; https://peterborougharchaeology.org/finds-gallery/), but their purpose remains a point for speculation. Brodribb has suggested that the bricks were scored for use as a gaming board, although tiles are usually re-used for this purpose, with the lines of the grid scratched into the surface after firing. Other suggestions made by Brodribb are that the bricks were marked in squares as imitation tesserae, a low-cost, short-cut form of tessellated surface, or that the tile was pre-scored for the production of tesserae.

Of the five broken edges on the examples from site, four have broken neatly along the scored lines, so it could be argued that there is some credibility to the last suggestion. The dimensions of the squares are also in keeping with the cut-tile tesserae on site (*c.* 25mm–35mm), but the deep scoring has left thin ridges of clay on the surface at the edge of the squares and a shallow smooth line at the top when viewing the broken edge (representing the groove). Neither of these features is evident on the cut-tile tesserae from site (most of which are cut from imbrex in any case), or on other examples the author has seen. Both of the fragments from site have been re-used. In the absence of any *in situ* evidence for the primary deployment of such tiles, perhaps the most likely explanation is that the scoring simply represents a form of keying (I. Betts pers. comm).

Scored imbrex

A single fragment of imbrex in the local silty fabric (K13/LOC3) is unusual in being scored, pre-firing, with multiple random roughly parallel vertical lines made with some form of impromptu tool, perhaps a stick (Fig. 3.88). The scoring seems to have no particular design or obvious functional purpose so was perhaps carried out on a whim.

Accidental markings

In addition to the intentionally made markings discussed above, there are a smaller group of accidental impressions. The majority of these take the form of animal paw- or hoof-prints, but also include four hobnail boot or shoe impressions and three finger marks. Of the animal prints twelve are from dogs, one is from cloven-hoofed animal and two are partial indeterminate paw-prints. There is a finger-tip mark to top of one brick and four adjacent finger marks to the underside of a large brick near one corner, possibly suggesting it was moved whilst still soft. In all instances these marks occur on flat forms, namely brick and tegula, with most occurring on the local silty/iron-rich examples and just four, including two of the dog prints and the cloven hoof print, on London 2815 group examples.

Fig. 3.87   Scored brick <694>

Fig. 3.88   Fragment of imbrex scored with multiple random lines

Wall plaster

Just nine fragments of painted wall plaster were recorded, weighing 472g, all from Phase 7 deposits. These include red-painted fragments reused in the Phase 7 smithy area ([1177]), and pink-painted fragments, including chamfered pieces, from deposits overlying the smithy ([694]; [770]). Both have one or more *opus signinum* base coats. The red-painted fragments evidently derive from a building pre-dating the smithy, and possibly from a room where water was integral to use given the waterproof base coats. The pink-painted fragments are also unlikely to be related to the smithy, despite being found overlying the building and may also have originated from a room where water was being used, or being prevented from penetrating. Possible candidates for the painted plaster could be aisled Building 5, although other sources are possible.

Two fragments from a renovated scheme were also recovered from Phase 7 pit [783]. The earlier underlying scheme has one surviving *opus signinum* base coat, although it is not possible to determine if it was painted. The successive, overlying scheme also has an *opus signinum* base coat which is smoothed and red-painted. The red is over-painted with off-white/pale greenish grey, although no pattern can be discerned. One fragment is curved, possibly originating from a door or window recess, or some other internal moulding.

The fired clay and briquetage

A relatively modest quantity of burnt clay was recovered from the site, comprising 13% of the assemblage by fragment count and just 1.5% by weight (Table 3.21). A total of 401 fragments were collected, weighing 7278g. A description of the fabrics identified is held with the archive, but they are characterised by a brickearth matrix with little sand and occasional to moderate flint, organic and/or calcareous inclusions. Colour ranges from pale pinkish-buff, through orange to brown and black (the latter where burnt). A small quantity is marbled fabric, including lenses of lighter clay.

The majority of the burnt clay was recovered from Phases 3 to 5, with smaller quantities collected from features attributed to Phases 6 to 8 and a small group from Phase 11. A proportion of the burnt clay is non-diagnostic, but structural material, likely to derive from clay and timber buildings, was recovered from Phases 5, 7 and 11, and may be represented amongst the non-diagnostic material from other phases. Burnt clay and daub from other features, including a possible oven/kiln or dryer from Phase 4 and hearths from Phase 8 was also recovered, and a small quantity of briquetage from Phases 4 and 5.

The latter is very fragmentary but two groups from the fill of Phase 4 ditch [861] and Phase 5 pit [801] may originate from similar features being approximately

30mm thick, with one curved, roughly smoothed surface and one uneven surface. The fabric is oxidised and tempered with organic inclusions and there are organic impressions and a white bloom, probably representing salt-bleaching, to the curved surface. These probably form part of a heating structure or hearth for the drying of brine to create salt crystals (Morris 2007, 432–435 and fig 4.19; Morris 2012, 239 and fig 3.67.26–29). A curved fragment from a possible cylindrical object was also recovered from Phase 4 ditch [1042], perhaps representing part of a firebar, pedestal or some other form of support also associated with salt production (Morris 2007, 431–432 and fig 4.4–18; Morris 2012, 237–239 and fig 3.67.21–25; Hathaway 2013, 279–281, fig 5.5). Evidence of salt-working and/or onward processing has been recorded or documented at a number of locations in the locality and along the north Kent coast (Morris 2012; Poole 2011; Hathaway 2013, 269–337; Biddulph 2017, 211–217).

Distribution

Ceramic building material was recovered from Phases 3 to 11, although the largest quantities were retrieved from features and deposits attributed to Phases 9 and 10, associated with the robbing and demolition of late Roman masonry structures on the site (Fig. 3.89). Despite being a relatively large assemblage, even representing as it does a sub-sample, the material is not very well preserved with few complete bricks or tiles recovered. A relatively small component was sampled from *in-situ* masonry features, including walls, floors, hearths and metalled surfaces, predominantly relating to Phase 7. The remaining

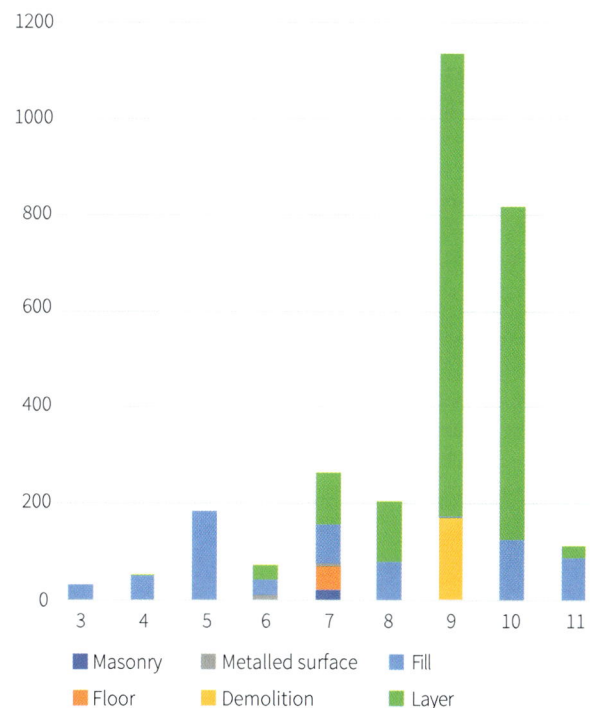

Fig. 3.89   Distribution of the Roman and later CBM by phase and feature type, by number

material was recovered from layers and the fills of discrete features, although through an analysis of distribution, particularly with regard to demolition horizons and robber cut fills, a fairly significant quantity can be attributed to specific structures and can thus inform on their appearance.

Phase 3: Late Iron Age to mid-first century AD

The small Phase 3 assemblage, weighing less than 200 grams, comprises a single fragment of Roman roofing tile (Fabric K41/LOC6 imbrex), ditch [1245] and a small group (31 fragments) of fragmentary burnt daub from ditch [526] in Area A and pit [1352] in Area D (Fig. 3.82; Fig. 3.84). The imbrex is in a fabric that is probably relatively locally, produced from perhaps as early as the mid-first century, with this fragment either being intrusive or deriving from later infilling of the ditch, which was retained into Phase 4.

The small group of daub is not well-preserved with no surfaces or structural impressions and as such can be taken to indicate little more than the likely presence of contemporary clay structures in the vicinity of site.

Phase 4: *c.* AD 43 to *c.* AD 100/120

A slightly larger, but still modest assemblage was retrieved from Phase 4 deposits and features amounting to 46 fragments, weighing just under 4kg. The majority was retrieved from the fill of ditches, pits, post-holes and a single hearth, with a smaller quantity derived from a metalled surface and layer (Fig. 3.89).

Fired clay accounts for the largest proportion of the small assemblage, some of which is non-diagnostic, although there is evidence for the presence of small clay superstructures and salt production in the vicinity (Fig. 3.82; Fig. 3.84). A few curving surfaces were identified in the material from pit [1092]. As these are convex, they may derive from a domed superstructure, perhaps an oven, kiln or corn-dryer, as opposed to a hearth although the evidence is ephemeral. There are also ten fragments (331g) of briquetage from a fill ([804]) of ditch [861]. The latter is oxidised and tempered with organic inclusions, approximately 30mm thick, slightly curved and has one uneven surface, and the other is roughly smoothed and salt-bleached. The fabric differs from much of the remaining fired clay on site, and in addition to a small number of similar fragments recovered from a Phase 5 pit ([801]), could be from a heating structure or hearth for the drying of brine to create salt crystals (Morris 2007, 432–435 and fig 4.19; Morris 2012, 239 and fig 3.67.26–29).

Lastly, the fragments from ditch [1042] include an example with a curved surface, possibly from a cylindrical object. This could be firebar, or perhaps a pedestal for an oven, or also associated with salt production, although the fabric differs to the possible briquetage. It is possible that fragments of wall daub are present in the fragmentary material, although no withy or stave impressions were identified.

The smaller assemblage of ceramic building material includes early fabrics, predominantly from Kent, including examples from Eccles (K14/2454/3022) and other as yet unsourced types likely to be of local or a north Kent origin (K47/3226; K13/LOC3 and K41/LOC6), in addition to a small quantity of London 2815 group types (K12/2452) (Fig. 3.82). The forms identified include brick and roof tile (tegula and imbrex). Single examples of all three types were identified in metalled surface (598), and a single brick from the fill of hearth [1027]. In addition to the examples used in the metalled surface some of the brick and tegula appears to have been used as post-packing and with other potential uses including the construction of hearths or ovens.

With such scant evidence, little can be concluded regarding the likely appearance of the single roomed Building 1. Some of the wall daub recovered from Phase 5 could have originated from the building. It is also possible, but far from certain, that it had a tiled roof. On first appearance, the small quantity of roof tile recovered from Phases 5 and 6 might suggest their use was restricted to the construction of small masonry elements. However, as most building material is subject to salvage and reuse, often more than once, the quantities recovered in subsequent deposits or demolition horizons does not always reflect what was in use at the time. Perhaps more telling are the more significant quantities of roof tile and brick recovered from Phase 7 fills and layers. This material must pre-date the more substantive programme undertaken during that phase and was thus presumably deposited from earlier structures, either on site or in vicinity. The use of such material would be inconsistent with the Phase 5 round house, Building 2 and an analysis of distribution suggests this material is unlikely to have been liberated from flint revetment wall [822] in Phase 6. This leaves Building 1 or as yet undiscovered buildings off site. In either case, the building material would imply there is likely to have been a building with a tiled roof, or tile and brick lacing courses, in the vicinity prior to late third century.

Phase 5: *c.* AD 100/120–150

A further increase in the quantity of fired clay and ceramic building material is evident from Phase 5 features, although the assemblage is still comparatively small comprising 180 fragments, weighing just over 16.5kg (Fig. 3.82; Fig. 3.84). The material is similarly distributed to Phase 4, recovered predominantly from the fill of ditches, pits and postholes, with a few fragments retrieved from the metalled road surface (Fig. 3.89).

As during the previous phase, fired clay accounts for the majority of the material recovered, comprising predominantly wall daub, although a few further fragments of possible briquetage were also recovered.

Two medium to large groups of wall daub were recovered from a construction cut (39 fragments, 1032g) and posthole (81 fragments, 1455g). The former assemblage has multiple withy impressions with fairly well-finished flat surfaces and has been burnt, perhaps suggesting the structure from which it originated was fire-damaged. The larger group is from a posthole forming part of Building 2 in Enclosure 5. No structural impressions survive but the surfaces bear linear wipe marks and cereal stalk impressions. Pit [801] produced three more fragments of possible briquetage (761g), similar to that retrieved from Phase 4 ditch [861].

As during Phase 4 the ceramic building material comprises predominantly Kentish fabrics, dominated by the unsourced silty and iron-rich types (K13/LOC3; K41/LOC6) with smaller quantities from Eccles (K14/2454/3022) (Fig. 3.82). Again, a small quantity of London 2815 group types (K7/3006; K40/2459a) were recovered and also a few fragments potentially from Hertfordshire and Sussex (MOLA 3023; K39/3018), although it is possible these are of more local origin (see fabric discussion). Roofing tile (tegula and imbrex) are most numerous, with a smaller number of bricks and four fragments of box-flue tile. The brick and tile could have been liberated from hearths or ovens although, as noted above, they could also potentially derive from a tiled roof, or even from lacing courses in masonry structures beyond the limit of excavation. The hypocaust tiles could also be taken to suggest the presence of a heated building in the vicinity, although the relatively small number recovered from the site as a whole, coupled with their fragmentary condition and almost exclusively London origin, argue that they may have arrived on site as ballast, rather than as building material (see fabric discussion).

Phase 6: *c.* AD 150–250

The modest Phase 6 assemblage, amounting to 57 fragments, weighing 23.5kg, was recovered largely from layers and the fill of pits, postholes and ditches. A smaller number of fragments came from a metalled surface, forming part of the roadway. For the first time proportionally more ceramic building material is represented than fired clay, although as with all of the statistics quoted, this could reflect a sampling bias (Fig. 3.82; Fig. 3.84). Again, the unsourced 'local' silty and iron-rich types (K13/LOC3; K41/LOC6) dominate, with a smaller number of fragments from elsewhere in Kent (K47/3226; K14/2454/3022). The London 2815 group account for a similar proportion of the ceramic building material to Phase 5.

The small assemblage of fired clay is largely non-diagnostic with just one curved surface fragment from Phase 6, Structure 1, [874]. Amongst the ceramic building material roof tile dominates, with a smaller number of brick fragments and three cut tile tesserae. The latter are likely to be intrusive finds from the later mausoleum (see Phase 7), with much of remaining material associated

with Structure 1, used either as post packing or in made ground. Fragments of roof tile and brick were also recovered from metalled surface (Group 27) and revetment wall [822], reused as building rubble.

Phase 7: *c.* AD 250–325/350

The larger assemblage of ceramic building material recovered from Phase 7, amounting to 288 fragments (150.6kg), reflects the intensification of building on site. The true scale of this, however, only becomes apparent when the large quantity of material from Phases 9 and 10, representing the demolished remains of Phase 7 structures, is taken into consideration (Fig. 3.89). Although a significant quantity was still recovered from the fill of ditches and layers, a sizable group was sampled from masonry elements, including walls, floors and metalled surfaces. Roof tile continues to represent the most common form recovered, although brick accounts for a far greater proportion (Fig. 3.84). There are also smaller quantities of *opus signinum*, mortar, wall plaster, fired clay, box-flue tile and a few cut-tile tesserae.

Boundary and retaining walls (Groups 29, 30, 31 & wall [681])

Relatively little of the Phase 7 boundary and retaining walls survived *in situ*, although some samples were taken from these structures and a significant quantity of the material recovered from later demolition horizons (particularly Phase 9 Group 49) is likely to originate from their collapse. They were largely constructed from unfaced stone rubble, predominantly flint but including Kentish ragstone, bonded in a yellow sandy mortar. Fragments of faced ragstone and unfaced and faced calcareous tufa were present amongst the demolition material, but these are more likely to have been used in the construction of the more substantial mausoleum Building 3 (see below).

Fragments of brick and tile were also recovered directly from the walls, in local/north Kent (K41; K47) and London fabrics (K7; K12; K40). In wall [681] these take the form of small fragments of box-flue tile and imbrex, likely to have been re-used as general building rubble. In Groups 29, 30 and 31, however, they occur (with the odd exception) as larger fragments of brick (*lydion*) and tegula, possibly indicating that these walls had some form of lacing or levelling course.

Structures in Enclosure 10

In the eastern half of Enclosure 10 the remnants of a timber structure were recorded (Building 4). Little building material can be directly associated with this structure, comprising just two fragments of brick (K13; K14) from one of the postholes ([576]), possibly used as post-packing. In the western half of the enclosure the more substantial remains of an aisled building were recorded (Building 5). The masonry footings of 461 were formed of unworked flint nodules and small fragments of brick and roof tile (K13; K47) bonded in a clayey sandy-silt matrix, rather than mortar, possibly suggesting it represented little more than a dwarf wall or footing, supporting a timber superstructure. At least some of the internal timber posts supporting the roof and internal divisions rested on post-pads formed of large fragments of local brick (K41; [1006], [985]).

Traces of a tiled floor were also recorded in the south-east corner of Building 5, adjacent to the walls. A total of 36 samples were recovered, weighing 30.5kg, formed almost entirely of large fragments of brick and tegula (used flange downwards or with the flange removed). The majority is in local/Kentish silty, iron-rich or rock-tempered fabrics (K13; K41; K47), with a smaller quantity in the London 2815 fabric group (K7; K12).

It is possible some of the large quantity of roof tile, and smaller quantity of daub, from later layers and demolition horizons originates from the timber buildings of Enclosure 10. A more significant structure, such as Building 5, may have had a tiled roof, although other sources for this material are also possible, with a least some of the roof tile likely originating from the mausoleum. The small quantity of red-painted wall plaster incorporated into the smithy area ([1177] see below), and the pink-painted fragments from deposits in Phase 7, Open Area 1 ([694]; [770]), could also potentially have originated from Building 461, or again, possibly from the tomb (although the latter is thought to remain standing into Phase 10). The pink plaster includes chamfered fragments from a window recess or doorway.

Possible smithy

The modest assemblage of building material associated directly with the smithing area (Group 34), includes fragments from the hearth structure [833] and possible floor surfaces and make-up layers in Open Area 2. The small group from the hearth includes local/Kentish silty, iron-rich and rock-tempered fabrics (K13; K41; K47) and London 2815 fabric group (K12), formed of re-used fragments of roof tile (tegula and imbrex) and brick. The 'floor' surfaces incorporated fragments of brick and flat roof tile (tegula), all in the local/Kentish silty and iron-rich fabrics (K13; K41), and fragments of re-used painted wall plaster and mortar, presumably used as a bedding agent. A larger group of building material was collected from the make-up layers, with a similar fabric composition. This group is dominated by fragments of roof tile, with some brick and stone rubble (calcareous tufa), representing general building debris reused for consolidation of the floor.

Occupation, accumulation and consolidation deposits overlying the smithy, following the structure's disuse and partial collapse, produced a sizable assemblage of building material (Groups 35 and 36: [694]; [770]; [754];

[755]; [762]). A similar fabric composition is again evident with local/Kentish sources dominant and a smaller quantity of London 2815 group. Roof tile is again the most frequent type, followed by brick. Some of this material may have originated from the walls around the smithy areaor roof, but the composition of the group, including fragments of daub, box-flue tile, painted wall plaster, *opus signinum* and tesserae, as with the earlier make-up layers, are suggestive of a more generalised source. As noted during Phase 6 the few tesserae may be intrusive or stray finds from the construction of the mausoleum, Building 3, and the painted wall plaster and *opus signinum* are unlikely to derive from an industrial building of this nature, but rather other structures in the vicinity.

The mausoleum, Building 3, and subsequent demolition horizons

Flint rubble and mortar footings were all that survived of the mausoleum. The building material assemblages recovered from later episodes of robbing and demolition in Phases 9 and 10 go some way to determining something of the structure's likely appearance, although much of this relates exclusively to the flooring. Indeed, a total of 1182 cut-tile tesserae were recovered from site, over 99% of which derived from robbing and demolition deposits associated directly with, or in close proximity to, the mausoleum, indicating that the structure had a tessellated pavement. Few parallels for tessellated tomb floors survive, or have been discovered, but include an example from a contemporary single chambered mausoleum at Bancroft (Williams and Zeepvat 1994, 259; de la Bédoyère 2001, 226)

The tesserae form a fairly homogenous group, fashioned predominantly from the local/Kentish silty, iron-rich and rock-tempered fabrics (K13; K41; K47), with imbrex being favoured over tegula or brick, presumably due the greater ease with which they could be cut. No stone tesserae were recovered, which might indicate the entire floor was formed of cut-tile examples. It is possible they formed the border to a finer central stone mosaic, but if such existed, even if robbed out, a few stray stone tesserae might be expected in the demolition deposits. A further consideration is that although over 1000 tesserae were found, many thousands more would have been required to cover the entire floor of a tomb with maximum internal dimensions of 4.8m by 4.5m. Although not sampled, a patch of *opus signinum* was recorded in one of the niches, possibly at an entrance point to the tomb. It is presumably therefore also possible that the tomb had an *opus signinum* floor with a central tessellated area. The tesserae are certainly poor candidates for reuse as building material so are unlikely to have been selectively salvaged but with the added vagaries imposed by sampling, it is impossible to be certain how 'complete' the recovered assemblage is.

Little building material could be associated with the with the systematic robbing of the tomb that appears to have taken place in the twelfth century, perhaps as a consequence of the job having been accomplished thoroughly, with only tesserae, worthless for re-use as building material, left behind. A single fragment of imbrex from Group 57 and small quantity of roof, tile, brick and stone rubble, were recovered along with some of the tesserae in a Phase 11 layer ([464]), but the assemblage is too small to draw any firm conclusions about their likely deployment. There were, however, large quantities of roof tile, brick and stone recovered from Phase 9 deposits, particularly 'dark earth' layer [201], that could have originated from the tomb and suggest that, in addition to the burial being disturbed, the structure may have undergone at least partial collapse during the fifth century. Some of this material, including a portion of the roof tile, is likely to originate from other structures, perhaps Building 5 and potentially other truncated timber buildings, but in addition to the tesserae, the large quantity of brick and building stone (see Hayward 2007) is most likely to derive from a masonry structure.

The width and depth of the footings suggest the mausoleum was a substantial structure and potentially quite tall. The unfaced ragstone, flint and chalk amongst the building rubble could have derived from the walls, with some of the brick and flat tile possibly forming lacing/levelling courses, as seen in the tombs at Keston (Philp nd). It was also quite probably internally plastered and externally rendered, although there is scant evidence to verify this.

The strengthened corners could have been added to provide internal niches, but may well have been constructed to support a vaulted roof. Locally available calcareous tufa, as both lightweight and strong, offers the perfect medium for vaulting, with blocks of tufa paralleled in vault of the mausoleum at Lullingstone (Meates 1979; de la Bédoyère 2001, 225). A total of 40 part-worked blocks were collected from layer [201], with a further 25 fragments (from layers [462] and [616]), that could potentially have originated from the tomb, however, fragments of tufa were also recovered from Phase 6 features and in Group 49, associated with the collapse of the boundary walls, so this material could also have been exploited as general building stone. At Thurnham Villa, approximately 10km to the south of Gillingham, blocks of tufa were used in the walls of a number of structures (Smith & Betts 2006, 20).

Likewise, the large quantity of roof tile could have been used in a number of structures, but as a masonry building, the tomb almost certainly had a tiled roof. Given the late third- or early fourth-century construction date of the tomb it is notable that no late Roman roof tile was recovered from site, particularly when it has been identified on other contemporary sites in the vicinity (Betts & Foot 1994; Poole 2011). This either implies that if present it was all robbed for re-use in medieval buildings, which seems unlikely as even if picked clean at least a few stray fragments or breakages are likely to have remained, that production of the local silty and iron-rich roof tile continued into the late third century, or that the temple had a roof made from carefully salvaged and re-used early roof-tile, which although not impossible would be

difficult. At Thurnham, the lack of late Roman tile was taken to suggest that very little construction or repair was undertaken after the mid-to late second century and that any later structural work was restricted to the re-use of earlier building material already present on site (Smith & Betts 2006, 21). On balance, the third option is perhaps most viable, but this would have implications for the wider settlement landscape in which the Grange Farm site is set (see Fabric and Discussion).

Phase 8: *c.* AD 325/50 – 420/450

A small assemblage of 69 fragments, weighing 17.5kg, was recovered from Phase 8 deposits (Fig. 3.82; Fig. 3.84; Fig. 3.89). Very little of this building material is attributed to structures. Two fragments of local iron-rich (K41) roof tile were recovered from postholes in the south-west corner of Enclosure 6 (Group 43), possibly used as post-packing and a single London 2815 fabric group brick and 13 fragments of burnt daub from the fills of hearths within Building 5, both probably used in the construction of the hearth floors.

The bulk of the Phase 8 ceramic building material was recovered from the fill of pits (Groups 44 and 46–48). The material from Group 44 was subject to sampling and only partial recording but included fragments of daub, roof tile, brick, box-flue tile and tesserae. A larger group was sampled from Group 48, although encompassing a narrower range of forms comprising roof tile, brick and daub. Just two bricks each were recorded from Groups 46 and 47, although these include a near-complete *bessalis* brick, typically used in hypocaust *pilae*, although also reused as general building rubble, along with all forms of brick and tile. As observed across the site, the local/ Kentish silty, iron-rich or rock-tempered fabrics (K13; K41; K47) are most common, with a smaller quantity in the London 2815 fabric group (K7; K12; Fig. 3.82). Some of the material from Group 48 could have originated from structure [461] to the immediate east, although as with the remaining material from these discrete features, probably represents general discard from a number of potential sources.

Phase 9 to 11: *c.* AD 400/450 – Post-medieval

Phase 9 and 10 deposits produced the two largest assemblages of building material recovered from site, amounting to some 2002 fragments, weighing 195.3kg, accounting for over 65% of the site assemblage by fragment count (Fig. 3.89). By far the greatest proportion of this material was recovered from large robbing and demolition deposits, originating from Phase 7 structures and as such is discussed above. A smaller assemblage of 109 fragments, weighing 12.6kg was retrieved from Phase 11 features and layers, but again the greatest proportion is of Roman date. Indeed, no contemporary building material was recovered from Phase 9 deposits and a minimal post-Roman assemblage of 19 fragments, weighing 1.5kg, from Phase 10 features, and 26 fragments, weighing 5.9kg, from Phase 11. The small size of the assemblage reflects the cessation of occupation across much of the site, with the land turned predominantly over to grazing and cultivation.

Much of the small post-Roman ceramic building material assemblage was recovered from the backfill of the manorial ditch, comprising largely late medieval/transitional and early post-medieval peg tile. Two fragments of unfrogged brick were also recovered, dating to the sixteenth or seventeenth century and a single fragment of a dark green glazed Flemish floor tile. The latter dates from *c.* AD 1450 to 1600 and most likely originates, along with most of the other material, from the adjacent, well-connected Grange Manor (see Jarrett, Chapter 3.13). From Area C, a further fragment of post-medieval peg tile was recovered from ditch [1362] and from Area D, a small assemblage of daub (12 fragments, 188g) from posthole [1116]. The daub is fresh with well-preserved withy impressions (16–20mm diameter), suggesting the presence of a clay and timber structure in the near vicinity. The dating of this must remain open to question, although the colour and fabric of the daub may distinguish it from comparable material of Roman date.

In Area A, a small assemblage of post-medieval peg tile was recovered from well [563], animal grave [584] as well as pits and French drains. A complete unfrogged stock-moulded orange sandy brick (nr MOLA fabric 3046) was also sampled from wall [653]. The dimensions and forming of the brick suggest it was made during the seventeenth century, or perhaps a little later, although could be reused. A tree throw in Area A also produced 43 fragments of daub, weighing just over 1kg. The assemblage is largely non-diagnostic, with a couple of withy impressions, a few curved surfaces and possible finger marks. As with the daub from Area D, this material could provide evidence for medieval or later clay structures in the vicinity but lies within the area of Roman occupation and may have been cast up from earlier deposits.

Discussion

The significance of the Grange Farm assemblage stems not just from what can be determined about the nature and appearance of the structures on site, but also from what can be inferred about building material supply and consumption in this part of north Kent and the broader Thames estuary in the Roman period. As with other sites in the vicinity much of the building material used is relatively local, both in terms of ceramic building material and stone, but the tentative evidence for salt production, and presence of at least some imported brick and tile indicates the site was part of a broader economic network, at least during the early Roman period.

There is a small quantity of very early tile, but the majority appears to be dated to the late first and second century, and was probably transported to site by water, either down the Medway or from elsewhere in north Kent and London, via the Thames. Indeed, the apparent quantity of early building material, and absence of late Roman tile, is at odds with the limited evidence for structures prior to the late third century and, unless all imported as salvage from elsewhere, potentially suggests that a larger quarry of building material was available to plunder in the immediate vicinity. Therefore, unless production of the local silty/iron-rich tile continued later, Grange Farm could form part of a more significant settlement than the surviving or excavated remains suggest.

Some consideration needs to be given to the box-flue tiles recovered, and whether their presence suggest a heated building formed part of this settlement. If it is accepted that they arrived on site from London on ships that returned loaded with produce, the existence of a heated building near site would depend on whether they came as ballast or cargo. The presence of the London 2815 group material, including box-flue tile, at Thurnham villa was suggested to represent a return cargo for Kentish rag limestone being quarried in the Maidstone area and shipped via the Medway and Thames (Smith & Betts 2006, 5).

The box-flue tile on site is fragmentary, with only one example having two recordable dimensions. There is also evidence for their re-use, with mortar over broken edges and a few examples sampled from wall structures as general building material. However, on some an earlier *opus signinum* mortar survives from a prior use, probably in a heated building, and perhaps even a bath-house given the use of a waterproof mortar. Whether this was salvaged for re-use from such a structure in close proximity to site that had been constructed from a cargo of box-flue tile or represents reused ship ballast from demolished buildings in London is somewhat difficult to determine on the current evidence. Although, few in number, the presence of box-flue tiles from other sources more local to site, might, however, suggest they were being actively procured. Indeed, if arriving as ballast, the proportion of forms represented in the London 2815 group should be more generally representative of the demolished buildings from which it originated, rather than biased in favour of box-flue tile and brick, perhaps intimating the latter were specifically ordered.

Box-flue tile comprises just 2% of the total assemblage by fragment and weight, but at both Northfleet and Thurnham, both of which have bath-houses, it comprised a similarly small component (1.3% by fragment and 1.6% by weight, Smith & Betts 2006, 5; 2% by fragment and weight at Northfleet, Poole 2011, 326) Of course, there is no voussoir tile, typically found on bath-house sites, but the assemblage has been subject to sampling, and in any case, this would not rule out the presence of another form of hypocausted structure.

3.18 The animal bones

Kevin Rielly and Philip L. Armitage

A large animal bone assemblage was recovered from various features which have been assigned to the occupation sequence outlined above. Animal bones were recovered from deposits dating to each of these phases, the vast majority recovered by hand, although with some bones taken from a variety of bulk samples.

Quantity and methodology

A total of 8,066 hand-collected and 90 sieved animal bones were recovered from phased deposits, of which 4,438 and 15 fragments respectively (55.0% and 16.7%) have been identified to taxon and anatomy (body part). Identifications of the bone specimens were undertaken using the authors' modern comparative osteological collections. Published osteological manuals were also consulted that included (among others) the atlas of animal bones by Schmid (1972), the guide to domestic neo-natal and juvenile mammals by Amorosi (1989) and the bird bone identification manual of Cohen and Serjeantson (1986). Measurements were taken following the system of von den Driesch (1976). Study of the faunal assemblage followed standard zooarchaeological methodological and analytical procedures (see Armitage 1999, 102–103). In addition an attempt was made to incorporate a weighted quantitative method, here using the Epiphysis Only method, essentially following Grant (1975) except that no skull pieces were included and no attempt was made to take account of expected frequencies. Note that the total counts using this method incorporated a straight count of limb bone articular ends (counting whole bones twice apart from phalanges) and then using a minimum number of element method for mandibles (counting the best represented tooth), atlas, Axis and sacrum. The ageing methods employed include mandibular tooth eruption and wear following O'Connor (1991, 250) as well as epiphysis fusion, this method facilitated by placing the various epiphyses within three age groups, as follows: Early – proximal (P) scapula, distal (D) humerus, P radius, pelvis acetabulum and P 1st phalange; Intermediate – D tibia and D metapodials; and Late – P humerus, D radius, P and D femur, P tibia and P calcaneus. Ages appropriate to the various mandibular and epiphyseal sequences are taken from Schmid (1972, 75 and 77) and Amorosi (1989, 98 and 99). Further age information concerning equid teeth employed crown heights following Levine (1982) and also incisor wear as described in Goody (1976, 38–40). Finally, the extrapolation of limb bone lengths to shoulder heights used factors described in Harcourt (1974) and Boessneck and von den Driesch (1974).

Table 3.24 The percentage of weathered, burnt and dog gnawed bones within each hand collected phase collection, where N is the number of bones per phase

Phase	Weathered	Burnt	Dog gnawed	N
3	7.5			67
4	1.2		0.6	168
5	1.1		2.0	460
6	1.0		0.4	671
7	0.9	0.3	1.4	1747
8	1.5	0.1	0.6	1715
9	1.3	0.1	1.0	2723
10	2.3	0.9	0.6	350
11	3.5	0.6	0.6	172

Condition of the bones

There would appear to be a greater level of surface damage amongst the bones taken from the earliest and latest levels (Phases 3, 10 and 11) as shown in Table 3.24. A slight level of damage can be seen throughout the phase collections but in general, even within the aforementioned phases, the condition of the bones can be described as fair to good. It is suggested therefore that the bone assemblage from this site is essentially composed of a series of collections which were rapidly buried/incorporated into the archaeological deposits and had not lain exposed on the surface for any length of time. However, the soil conditions had clearly resulted in very many of the bones becoming brittle and as a consequence highly susceptible to fragmentation both *in situ* (in antiquity) and during excavation/post-excavation handling. This high frequency of ancient/recent breakage/fragmentation is particularly noticeable in the skulls and in the shafts of the long bones of the cattle and the horses.

The proportion of burnt bones is generally less than 1%, and where they do occur, they do not appear to follow any discernible spatial distribution. The single exception is the singed sheep bone (from [1154]) the fill of hearth [1155] (Phase 8). No other bones from the other hearth deposits are burnt however. Gnawed bones are somewhat more prolific, represented by proportions equal or greater than 1% in three phases. This in fact represents a moderately high proportion and, in comparison to the relatively good condition of the bones (the weathering evidence), may suggest that such bones were fed to dogs (and then deposited) rather than representing food waste scavenged from middens.

Distribution of faunal assemblage by phase

Phase 3: Late Iron Age to mid-first century AD

Animal bones were taken from four ditches, all part of Enclosure 1 in Area A, and a linear ditch (Group 2) traversing Area D. These produced a rather small collection of bones mainly composed of cattle but also with equid, pig and dog (Table 3.25). There were a range of parts amongst the major domesticates, including a near complete pig skull (in several pieces) from a subadult individual found in ditch [1245].

Phase 4: Earliest Roman *c.* AD 43 to *c.* AD 100/120

A greater distribution and diversity of features, principally in Area 1, provided a larger collection, here comprising 168 bones with an additional three from a single sample. The animal bones were relatively widespread but most were derived from ditches and pits (see Table 3.26) the former especially from features at the eastern end of Enclosure 2, while much of the pitfill assemblage was taken from a single feature, pit [432] just to the east of Building 1 with 43 bones. There was a general pattern across these features, with a predominance of cattle and

Table 3.25 Distribution of hand collected (H) and sieved (S) bones by species and phase

Species/Site phase	3	4	4	5	5	6	6	7	8	8	9	10	11
Recovery:	H	H	S	H	S	H	S	H	H	S	H	H	H
Mammals:													
Horse	2	22		5		11		44	131		75	4	6
Cattle	15	73		180		154	1	626	646	4	898	121	58
Sheep		7		43		68		144	110	8	124	50	8
Goat								1	1		1		
Pig	8	9		37	1	100		68	51		144	27	19
Dog	2			4		64		16	66		4	4	2
Cat				3				3	2				
Hare								2					
Rabbit												1	
Red Deer								5	5		11	1	1
Roe Deer						2		5	1		2	1	
Badger								34	14				
Otter								35					
Small mammal:											12		
Birds:				9		4		10	3	1	20	2	
Fish:												1	
Amphibian:											1		
Unidentified mammal:													
Cattle sized fragments	7	35	1	87		70		353	251	1	784	51	42
Sheep/goat sized fragments	2	3		23		56		132	44	1	87	26	6
Indeterminate 'scrappy' fragments	31	19	2	69	0	143	21	265	394	49	558	61	30
Unidentified bird								2			3		
Total	67	168	3	460	1	671	21	1747	1715	64	2723	350	172

cattle-size bones, followed by small quantities of sheep and pig. In addition, there is no obvious indication of differential deposition, cattle were represented by a wide range of parts, as exemplified by one of the largest collections, from pit [432]. There is a good representation of equid (22 bones) but almost all these were taken from an Enclosure 2 ditch with 18 fragments. These came from a single adult individual with an estimated age of 8–9 years comprising mainly head parts but also with a pair of pelves, an ulna and a metatarsus (see Table 3.31).

Table 3.26 *Distribution of animal bones by phase, recovery and feature type*

Phase:	3	4		5		6		7	8		9	10	11
Recovery:	H	H	S	H	S	H	S	H	H	S	H	H	H
Feature type													
Ditch	67	88		159		189		204	135			3	65
Pit		65	3	296	1	49	22	38	1159	23	1	332	16
Posthole		8		2		6		2	1				3
Beam Slot						3							
Grave												2	
Coffin											34		
Wall								23					
Construction cut								5					
Cut											7		
Hearth		2						7	75	41			
Tree throw													3
Robber trench									35			12	
Layer		5				393		1352	302		2222	1	77
Disturbed natural											9		
Metalled surface				3		31		21					
Raft/foundation								95					
Demo layer									8		450		
Indeterminate													8
Total	67	168	3	460	1	671	22	1747	1715	23	2723	350	172

Table 3.27 *Percentage abundance of cattle, sheep/goat and pig based on hand collected total fragment counts where N is the combined number of bones from all three species (excluding ABGs)*

Phase	4	5	6	7	8	9	10	11
Cattle	82.0	70.6	71.3	74.6	86.8	76.9	61.1	75.3
Sheep	7.9	16.9	20.8	17.3	6.3	10.7	25.3	10.4
Pig	10.1	12.5	7.9	8.1	6.9	12.3	13.6	14.3
N	89	255	216	839	744	1167	198	77

Table 3.28 *Percentage abundance of cattle, sheep/goat and pig based on hand collected Epiphyses Only counts where N is the combined number of bones from all three species (excluding ABGs)*

Phase	4	5	6	7	8	9	10	11
Cattle	71.9	61.3	64.4	77.2	76.1	72.4	51.1	51.1
Sheep	9.4	17.0	20.3	13.2	12.6	10.8	33.3	6.7
Pig	18.8	21.7	15.3	9.6	11.3	16.8	15.6	42.2
N	32	106	59	219	159	399	45	45

Phase 5: Early to mid-second century *c*. AD 100/120 to *c*. AD 150

This phase provided a reasonable assemblage (460 by hand collection and one bone from a sample), the majority arising from just four features, three of which are in Area A. These include ditch [1404] (82 bones) part of Enclosure 5, a ditch in Group 18 to the north-east with 26 bones, ditch [1001] to the south in Area B (33 bones) and, in particular, from pit [801] (Group 13) at the north-west corner of Enclosure 5 with 292 bones plus a single fragment from a sample. Each of these ditches/pits feature a wealth of cattle bones with a good proportion of sheep/goat and pig; plus some equid throughout, dog, cat, chicken and raven. A cat mandible, radius and ulna in [1001] are all probably from the same adult animal. The four dog bones are each from different ditchfills, however, these may also belong to the same individual, comprising a loose upper tooth, a mandible, a metatarsus and one other.

Fragmentation is a problem amongst the site collections (see Methodology). It is likely in this case that cattle is over-represented relative to the smaller and less robust bones of sheep/goat and pig. The use of a weighted quantitative method (here employing Epiphysis Only, after Grant 1975 and 1982) is intended to counter the effects of differential survival and retention, at least to a limited extent. Comparing the results of this method to Total Fragment Counts (see Table 3.27 and Table 3.28), does increase the proportion of the two smaller species but undoubtedly leaves cattle in the predominant position. Note that the good proportion of pig (at 21.7%) may relate in part to a partial skeleton recovered from pit [801], this comprising five bones, a mandible, humerus, radius and two pelves. All of the limb bones are unfused while the mandibular teeth include a just worn deciduous fourth premolar and an unerupted 1st adult molar, thus indicative of a piglet about 1 month old (after Simonds 1854, 102).

A small quantity of salt production waste (briquetage) was found in [801], which could suggest the possibility of salt curing taking place at this site at this time. Similar waste was found at the Roman site at Stanford Wharf Nature Reserve in Essex and a potential link to curing was extrapolated based on concentrations of near-complete cattle scapulae, several with mid-blade perforations (after Strid 2012, 5). An over-representation of cattle scapulae has been interpreted elsewhere 'as waste from specialized preparation of smoked or salted shoulder of beef for consumers' based on evidence from York (O'Connor 1988, 82–4). Otherwise, Maltby (2002, 117–122) referring to Iron Age salt curing, mentions another indication is a greater than average proportion of pig, in particular those aged 18 months or older. A number of cattle scapulae have been found at this site, most notably in Phase 7, but there are no obvious concentrations of this skeletal part. Indeed in this phase, as elsewhere, all three major domesticates are represented by a general mix of such parts. Neither is

pig well represented, although it should be mentioned that 33 out of the 37 pig bones dated to Phase 5 were recovered from pit [801]. The significance of this is only slightly undermined by the aforementioned presence of the piglet part skeleton. The presence of older pigs will be explored later in this report. It should also be mentioned that pig is better represented than sheep/goat (looking at the Epiphysis Only data) following Phase 4 (although there is a problem here regarding sample size) and not seen again until Phase 9.

Phase 6: Mid-second to mid-third century *c*. 150 to *c*. 250

Phase 6 provides a moderately large assemblage with 671 by hand collection and 21 from the bulk samples, from a broad range of feature types, including layers, beam-slots and metalled surfaces. Unusually for such rural sites, a large proportion was taken from layers (392 bones), the majority of the remainder from ditches (189) and then pits (49 hand collected and all sieved bones). The principal layers, both associated with Phase 6, Structure 1, produced 280 and 102 bones respectively. Most of the ditch collection derives from [1077] and [1184] with 86 and 78 bones; while pit [789] (16 hand-collected/21 sieved bones) provided most of the bones from this feature type. These collections are all, with one exception, rather close together, within and adjacent to the road in the central/ southern part of Area A, with layers (Phase 6, Structure 1) within the road, beneath and overlying the posthole Structure 1 positioned across the road respectively, and from associated ditches and pits. The exception is a pit located close to the north-western corner of Enclosure 5.

This central area provided a notable concentration of Associated Bone Groups (ABGs), here including the major part of a subadult female pig from the fill of retained Phase 5 ditch [1077] (these accounting for 83 out of the 86 hand collected bones in this feature); plus 60 bones from the fill of ditch [1184] (out of a total of 78 bones) representing two dogs (1 adult and 1 juvenile). Notably each of these ABGs is highly fragmented.

General waste was clearly best represented amongst the pits and the layers of which by far the largest collections came from the layers associated with the road and Structure 1. These include a high proportion of cattle but with some subtle differences: [874] (Phase 6, Structure 1) 84/32/11 (total fragment counts) and [902] 30/7/3 translating to 66.1/25.2/8.7% (N=127) and 75.0/17.5/7.5% (N=40). Such differences may relate to differential deposition, although this might carry greater significance if the total number of bones were more comparable. There is no obvious difference in skeletal representation to inform on a possible reason for this apparent variation in species abundance. The overall domesticate representation has cattle again predominant with a subtle change to the previous phase where sheep/goat is now better represented than pig. Of interest regarding the latter species was the recovery of two foetal bones, a tibia and a metapodial, these from [874] (Phase 6, Structure 1), indicative of on-site pig breeding. A variety of other food species were recovered, including poultry (chicken) and wild game. The latter was represented by two roe deer bones – a skull fragment from an adult male and a fully fused metatarsus, both from [874]. One unusual find was a tibiotarsus of an owl from [874], this most probably from a tawny owl. It can be supposed that this is a chance find although some ritual connection cannot be entirely ruled out.

Phase 7: Late third century to early to mid-fourth century *c.* AD 250 to 325/350

Phase 7 produced one of the largest assemblages, alongside that from Phases 8 and 9 (see below). It is composed of 1,742 fragments, all hand-collected. As with the previous phase, these bones were derived from a variety of features/deposits but again mostly from layers (1,445 bones) with much of the remainder taken from ditches (201 fragments) and pits (38 bones). The similarity continues with a major concentration in the southern central part of Area 1, here with the notable exception of pit [783] (38 bones) this within Enclosure 5. The aforementioned layers were all found in association with a series of revetment walls, in turn adjacent to the remains of the road. A small part of this collection dated to the use period of these walls, notably the bones from Open Area 2 (120 bones), though the majority postdated these structures, starting with the major spreads of Phase 7, Open Area 1, followed by numerous smaller deposits.

The ditch collection was mainly taken from ditch [264] (133 bones), the northern boundary of Enclosure 10 and located just north and east of the walls and road; and also ditch (eavesdrip gulley) [912] (34 bones) adjacent to one of the revetment walls [949]. Approximately half of the bones recovered from [264] comprise the remains of at least two adult badgers plus two otters, one juvenile and one subadult/adult (Table 3.31). These bones were taken from the lower fill and the upper fill, the latter placed in Phase 8. There is a definite crossover of parts from the same individual in each fill, which would suggest that these animals were deposited in the earlier phase and later disturbed. There was also a couple of badger bones, an ulna and a tibia, from layer [770], potentially indicative of a third individual. Notably the elder of the two otters has skinning marks on one of its tibias. It is conceivable that the otters and badgers may constitute a dump of small mammal skinning-waste. The remainder of the bones from this ditch, in combination with the other ditch fills, is largely composed of cattle fragments with small quantities of sheep/goat, pig, chicken and dog.

The major collections from the layers are similar to those from the ditches, mainly composed of cattle with good proportions of sheep/goat and lesser amounts of pig. There is also a moderate quantity of equid, some dog (principally in [845], Open Area 2 where the ten bones may be part of the same adult individual) as well

as minor amounts of red and roe deer (five fragments each), cat, hare, chicken, goose and mallard. The equid is mainly from [770], possibly the same animal, while deer is represented by antler (two red and one roe), skull, radius, pelvis and metatarsus (all roe) and two radii and metatarsus (red deer). These deer bones constitute a reasonable quantity (even when the possible antler working waste is excluded) and may be indicative of some affluence (following Cool 2006, 114). Each of the major domesticates comprise a general mix of skeletal parts.

Phase 8: Late fourth to early fifth century *c.* AD 325/50–AD 420/450

This equally large collection (1712 hand-collected/64 sieved fragments) was also centrally derived and principally taken from layers (302 bones) and pits (41 bones) with reasonable quantities from hearths (23 bones) and a single ditch (134 bones). The latter formed the upper fills of ditch [264] (see Phase 7) and most of the hearth bones were found in [1046] (74/23). There are numerous pits with animal bones but the best represented include [909] (Phase 8, Group 48) (236) and [1231] (with 689/41 bones). A focal point of this phase is the smithing area, just east of the road, in which was found a series of hearths including [1046] and a large part of the layer collection in dump [462] with 147 bones. Much of the remaining layer assemblage was found in trample [616], with 132 bones, this overlying part of the road [463], while the major part of the phase collection, from the pits, was located within two pit groups just north and west of Structure 461, the closer group including both [909] and [1231].

There are several ABGs including two sheep from [1046], these making up most of the bone collection, with an adult comprising 52 bones (most parts) and a young adult with 12 bones (fore and hindlimb parts); plus a dog from pit [1231], making up 54 out of the 55 dog bones in this deposit, this from a fully adult individual with a fragmented skull. Then there are the horses, including a partial articulation comprising seven bones of a lower hindleg and foot from pit [909] (Phase 8, Group 48), this belonging to an adult animal; as well as at least two adults from the from pit [1231] comprising 79 fragments i.e. all the equid bones in this feature. These two individuals were aged at about 6 years (based on the upper incisor and cheekteeth rows) and about eleven years following the crown heights of a pair of loose maxillary adult third molars. Finally there is a continuation of the badger bones from the last phase with twelve bones from an upper layer in ditch [264] as already mentioned above.

Throughout these deposits, as elsewhere, the major food species are dominated by cattle bones with substantially less sheep/goat and pig. These are accompanied by slight collections of deer (red and roe, five and one bone respectively), chicken and mallard. The red deer bones are divided into three antler pieces and two metapodials while there is a single roe deer mandible (see Table 3.38 and

Table 3.39). While suggestive of a limited use of venison (again excluding the antler pieces), their continued use may be significant. There is no indication amongst the larger food species collections (particularly from [1231]) of anything other than mixed waste deposition.

Phase 9: Early medieval *c.* AD 400/450–1000/1066

This phase provided the largest collection, 2,719 fragments (all hand-collected), mainly taken from layers (2,213 bones) with much of the rest from demolition levels (450 bones) and a minor quantity from coffin [221] with 34 fragments. The demolition layer collection is essentially from deposits ([456], [468] and [469]), with 257, 72 and 54 bones, all within the road/holloway; these in turn covered by a humic 'dark earth' layer [201] with 2,156 bones, directly beneath the topsoil. The stratigraphic evidence clearly shows that these deposits post-date the Roman occupation, however, the dating evidence would appear to suggest that the associated bones do principally derive from earlier i.e. Roman levels. This includes layer [201], which undoubtedly provided a range of post-Roman finds but also close to 4,000 sherds of very late Roman (AD 370–420) and earlier pottery. An argument could be made for the exclusion of these collections and certainly the bones from [201] on the basis of their likely redeposited and/ or residual status. Yet, while undoubtedly disturbed as shown by the dating evidence, there is no obvious indication that the 'dark earth' bones are either less well preserved or more fragmented in comparison with collections from previous phases. The general condition is the usual fair to good while just 0.7% of the collection is weathered (compare the results in Table 3.24). There are a number of root etched bones which is not surprising considering how close this layer is to the topsoil. It was suggested that this large collection may have derived from a Phase 8 rubbish heap or midden (See Chapter 2: Phase 9). The condition of the bones may not necessarily confirm this scenario (a midden-like deposit as well as redeposition would surely have provided a less well preserved and/or more fragmented collection), it can perhaps be assumed that the great majority of the bones from [201] and indeed from the underlying demolition deposits are very likely to be Late Roman in origin.

Cattle is again the predominant food species with, as previously mentioned, a change returning to the pattern observed in Phase 5 with a greater proportion of pig compared to sheep/goat (Table 3.28). The total fragment counts tend to show an above-average proportion of both lesser species (Table 3.27), a pattern which can be seen across each of the deposit types within this phase as well as within the aforementioned larger collections. There are again no obvious dumps of specialized waste, the various deposits clearly containing concentrated dumps of mixed refuse. Other food species are present but in very minor quantities, including deer (red and roe) and poultry (chicken), all from layer [201]. The deer remains comprise eleven red deer and two roe deer fragments, with seven of the former collection comprising antler pieces, all sawn and obviously representing antler working waste. Considering the size of the collection, the few post-cranial deer remains clearly suggest venison was poorly exploited. However, as previously mentioned, the mere presence of these species could well suggest a degree of affluence. This same deposit [201] also provided a large number of equid bones (all parts of the body), some undoubtedly representing at least semi-articulations as there were a number of paired elements. A few bones with cut-marks show that a proportion of these equids were skinned and potentially further utilized.

A small faunal collection was retrieved from the grave-fill deposit ([237]) associated with the lead coffin [221] within the mausoleum. This provided some chicken bones alongside an assortment of wild bird, small rodent, amphibian and bat remains (see Table 3.41). The weight of evidence strongly suggests that these bones, although not the chicken, represent the remains of one or more owl pellets. These could have been dropped into the open coffin by a bird using the ruins of the mausoleum as a roost. The species range and a comparison of pellet structural aspects strongly suggest that these bones derived from a tawny owl (see below).

Phase 10: Medieval AD 1000–1550

The bones dating to this phase were principally taken from pits and in particular from [563] a well in the northernmost part of Area A (194 bones) and pit [1169] in Area C with 123 bones. The fills of these two features are dated between AD 1250 and 1350 and AD 1150 to 1225 respectively. Within these features and indeed within this phase in general, cattle is clearly dominant followed by sheep and then pig. There is a minor quantity of wild game, including the first instance of rabbit (from well [563]), accompanied by some bird (chicken) and fish (cod) bones. The major domesticates are again represented by a general mix of skeletal parts.

Phase 11: Post-medieval

This is one of the smaller collections. It is approximately equally derived from ditchfills and a single layer, the former largely from Area C, while the layer ([464]) was associated with the Roman road in Area A. Dates for these deposits appear to cover a major part of this period – sixteenth to nineteenth centuries. The species abundance pattern generally follows the previous phase with cattle pre-eminent although here followed by pig and then sheep. In addition, there was a sawn red deer antler fragment and two dog bones from different ditches, both representing rather small animals.

Descriptions of the animals

Equids

The range of withers heights (see Table 3.29) calculated from lateral length measurements taken on complete long bones (method of Kiesewalter 1888, see von den Driesch and Boessneck 1974) reveal the presence of a range of 'pony-sized' animals, presumably all horses rather than donkeys or mules. Transcribing millimeters to hands following Rackham (1995, 169), the smallest and largest equids represented equal 12 and 14.2 hands respectively (noting here that the number after the decimal point refers to the number of inches with 4 inches equal to 1 hand). This evidence is essentially referring to Late Roman equids, here assuming that the Phase 9 data are Roman (see above). Thus the community dating to this period clearly employed a variety of small to medium-sized equids, no doubt used mainly as pack animals with the larger animals perhaps also used for riding. As discussed by Luff (1982, 136) 'a farmer would gain a considerable advantage from being seated on a tall horse', possibly employed in rounding up and controlling the movement of cattle and sheep. This size range is very similar to that shown in Roman London (Rackham 1995, 170) although some larger horses, up to almost 15 hands were found at Late Roman Drapers' Gardens (Rielly in prep b). Note also that a similarly large equid was found at Northfleet Roman villa (Grimm & Worley 2011, 48). Ages at death in the Grange Farm equid teeth (principally calculated from crown heights using the method of Levine 1982) are summarized in Table 3.30. No foal deciduous teeth are present in the submitted samples, however, there are three bones (two radii and a metacarpus) probably representing the same young juvenile individual (one of the radii has an unfused proximal end), all found in layer [201] Phase 9. This would suggest that horse-breeding took place at this site, presumably in the Roman era. In addition, there is an unworn adult premolar representing an immature animal (aged 2 to 3 years) from Phase 8. This equid is certainly too young to have been either worked or ridden and would therefore suggest that some horses were certainly trained in this locality during this period if not bred. The older ages fall somewhat short of the expected working life of a draft or riding animal, this at least 18 to 20 years. This shortfall may be explained in economic terms, with animals unable to perform adequately due to overwork, maltreatment or disease (after Rackham 1995, 173–4).

Though a large proportion of the equid collection is rather sparsely distributed and these bones were certainly found for the most part within dumps of food waste, it cannot be clearly ascertained whether these equids had been exploited for their meat. There

Table 3.29 Cattle and equid shoulder heights (in millimeters) where N is the number of specimens

Species	Phase	N	Mean	Min.	Max.
Cattle	5	4	1247.6	1171.8	1322.3
	6	1			1275.3
	7	6	1170.7	1125.5	1199.3
	8	3	1166.3	1128.2	1220.8
	9	9	1175.6	1100.9	1220.8
	10	1			1191.9
Equid	5	1	1326.9		
	6	1	1353.8		
	7	2	1423.6	1385.8	1461.5
	8	6	1329.2	1237.1	1465.7
	9	4	1341.5	1230.7	1465.7
	11	1	1220.8		

Table 3.30 Equid age and sex distribution based on the maxillary and mandibular teeth using crown heights and/or incisor wear (after Levine 1982 and Goody 1976, 100–103) with the exception of the mandible from [263] based on the eruption sequence (following Schmid 1972, 77)

Phase	Context	Age (yrs)	Sex
4	Fill ([808]) of ditch [864]	8 to 9	
5	Fill ([1202]) of ditch [1285]	7 to 8	
6	Fill ([788]) of pit [789]	11 to 14	
7	Layer [762]	12 to 13	
8	Fill ([263]) of ditch [264]	2 to 3	
8	Fill ([1234]) of pit ([1236])	9 to 10	male
8	Layer [462]	9 to 12	
8	Fills ([1229]/[1230]) of pit [1231]	6	
8	Fills ([1229]/[1230]) of pit [1231]	*c.* 11	male
9	Layer ([937])	13 to 14	

is evidence for skinning, as shown by the knife cuts adjacent to the proximal and distal ends of a metatarsus and at the midshaft anterior surface of another metatarsus, both from [201] Phase 9. However, on the basis of this evidence it is difficult to establish whether or not the skinning of horse carcasses was routine or merely an occasional act.

Articulated/associated Bone Group (ABG)

A few parts assumed to be part of the same adult individual were recovered from the fill ([808]) of the Phase 4 ditch [864], these including a highly fragmented skull, though with complete incisor and cheekteeth rows, a pair of pelves as well as an ulna and a metatarsus. Both the incisor wear pattern (after Goody 1976, 38–40) and the upper cheek teeth crown heights provided an estimated age of 8 to 9 years. In addition, there are the remains of two adults (aged 6 and about 11 years) mixed across the two fills ([1229] and [1230]) within pit [1231], this dated to Phase 8 (see Table 3.31). Notably, each skeleton has most of the axial parts, here including the skull/mandibles, vertebrae, ribs and pelves. This contrasts with the limbs where individual parts tend to be either absent (radius, ulna and metatarsus) or represented by no more than one bone, with the exception of a full complement of tibias. None of the bones were sufficiently complete to estimate their lengths, however, it can be seen that these horses are within the range of those already described from the Roman levels.

Cattle

Appearance and size

A small number of Short and Medium horned cattle are represented by horn cores from Phases 5, 6 and 7 (classification of Armitage & Clutton-Brock 1976). These essentially represent cores varying in length between 96 and 200mm. Withers heights (Table 3.29) are calculated from greatest lengths (GL) measurements taken on 24 complete adult limb bones (methods of Fock 1966 and Matolcsi 1970, see von den Driesch and Boessneck 1974). These reveal the presence of a rather large individual, at 132.2cm within Phase 5 and thence an approximately similar range of sizes and mean values, the latter between 116.5 and 117.5cm, here referring to Phases 7 to 9 (again assuming the latest phase is principally Roman). The size of the cattle is certainly larger than those found at earlier sites, as shown for example at Stone Castle near Gravesend (Rielly in prep a) with a range of 95.2 to 116.7cm with a mean value of 104cm (Late Iron Age to first century AD, N=7). Similarly, small sizes

Table 3.31 Associated bone groups where N is the number of identified bones and M and F (in Age) are male and female with yrs equal to years; under Description – H is skull, Mand is mandible, V+R is vertebrae and ribs (while with V, T is thoracic and L is lumbar), FL and HL is fore and hind legs, MP is metapodial, mtc is metacarpal, mtt is metatarsus, phal is phalange, hum is humerus, pel is pelvis and tib is tibia

Phase	Context	Species	N	Age	Description
4	Ditch [864] fill [808]	equid	18	8–9 years	H, FL (ulna), HL (pelves and mtt)
6	Ditch [1184] fills [1183	dog	50	adult	H, Mand, V+R, HL (no foot bones)
6	Ditch [1184] fills [1183	dog	8	less than 8 - 9 months	H, Mand, V+R, FL (hum and rad), HL (fem and tib)
6	Ditch [1077] fills [1296]	Pig	83	about 2 yrs(F)	H, Mand, V+R, FL+HL+Feet
7	Layer [754]	cattle	3	adult	Foot (mtc and 2 phal)
7	Layer [845]	dog	10	adult	Mand, R, FL(No feet), HL (pel)
7	Ditch [264] fill [278]	otter	33	1 to 2 yr	H, Mand, V+R, F and HL (no feet)
7	Ditch [264] fill [278]	otter	2	less than 1 yr	Mand
7/8	Ditch [264] fills [300]/[301]/[271]	badger	32	adult	H, Mand, V+R, F and HL (no tibias), MP
7/8	Ditch [264] fills [300]/[301]/[271]	badger	2	adult	Left FL
7	Layer [770]	badger	2	adult	Left ulna and Right tibia
8	Pit [909] fill [908]	equid	7	adult	Lower HL+Foot
8	Hearth [1046] deposit [1044]	sheep	52	adult(F)	F and HL (no mtt or phal), V+R
8	Hearth [1046] deposit [1044]	sheep	12	2 to 3 yrs	F and HL (no ulna or mtt)
8	Pit [1231] fills [1229]/[1230]	equid	79	2 adults(1M)	H, Mand, V+R, F+HL
8	Pit [1231] fill [1230]	dog	54	adult	H, Mand, V+R, FL (hum and phal)
9	Layer ([937])	horse	4	adult	FL+Foot (radius, mtc and 2 phal)
10	Pit [1169] fill [1168]	cattle	10	adult	V(3T and 7L)

Table 3.32 *Cattle astragalus and metacarpal measurements (in millimeters) where Dim is dimension, GL is greatest length and Bd is the maximum breadth at the distal end*

Bone/Dim.	Phase	N	Mean	Min.	Max.
Astragalus/ GL	4	3	61.9	57.2	68.8
	7	4	67.3	63.5	73.3
	8	3	67.1	63.2	72
	9	13	66.2	60.4	74.3
	10	1			66.8
	11	1			64.2
Metacarpus/ Bd	5	1			68.8
	6	1			65.9
	7	8	59.1	52.6	65.8
	8	2	60.1	56.2	64
	9	7	60	53.3	68.2
	11	1			67.2

are shown within early Roman London, thence rising to the mean values shown at this site from the latter part of the second century (data from PCA and MOLA archives and see Rielly in prep b). Large individuals, in excess of 130cm, tend to appear from the same period, although a single animal with a height of 139.9cm was found in a mid-second century deposit at the Guildhall (Liddle 2008). A rural assemblage at Swanscombe near Dartford, this dating from the late second into the third century also provided similar evidence with a mean value of 117.6cm (N=5), including a single large individual of 130cm (Rielly 2010). In addition two notably large individuals (in excess of 130cm) were found at Northfleet Roman villa (Grimm & Worley 2011, 44), unfortunately not mentioning the date, with size extrapolated from a group of 4 large and robust (wide at the distal end) metacarpals. These were interpreted as representing male individuals (probably oxen) which had been used for draught activities. A notably similar metacarpus was found at this site with GL equal to 215mm and a distal breadth of 68.8mm. Notably large cattle are also represented amongst the astragalus measurements (see Table 3.29), lengths greater than 70mm occurring rather sparingly at other Roman sites and then only from the third/fourth centuries (see Maltby 1981, 187 and individual sites in Levitan 1994, 546, Rielly in prep b, Dobney *et al.* 1996, 151 and Maltby 2010, 348–9) with the notable exception of a first/second century example from Elms Farm in Essex (Johnstone & Albarella 2002, 183).

Ages and sexes

The ages at death of the cattle can be established from the dental eruption and wear in their jawbones (Table 3.28), the dataset amounting to 38 mandibles plus sixteen loose teeth (deciduous fourth premolars and adult third molars) within the Roman levels (including Phase 9) but then just five mandibles and one loose tooth from the medieval and post-medieval levels (Phase 10 and 11). The Roman evidence clearly shows a predominance of older (adult) individuals, principally within the A3 and E age groups, the former conforming to animals aged five to eight years, while the latter group is represented by examples equal or beyond 10 years old within Phases 5 to 9 (latest ages after Jones & Sadler 2012, 18). The oldest individual (from Phase 6) with an adult first to third mandibular wear pattern of 'm', 'm' and 'm' (after Grant 1982) could be aged as high as 15 to 16 years. However, there is also a good proportion of first- and second-year animals (Juvenile, Immature and Sub-Adult) in Phases 7 and 9, as well as third-/fourth-year cattle (A1 and A2), in particular within Phase 9. The abundance pattern between Phases 7 and 9, despite the variation shown in Phase 8 (perhaps related to sample size) would appear to suggest the culling/ consumption of younger individuals alongside a rather greater use of older animals. While the quantities are not large it can be seen that the older individuals include a preponderance of elderly and probably senile cattle up to and including Phase 6, with thence a greater proportion of animals in the A3 group. The epiphysis fusion evidence offers complimentary data, as shown in Table 3.33 and Table 3.34, with first year animals restricted to the later phases (unfused early epiphyses) and a significant wealth of adult cattle (fused intermediate epiphyses) throughout. The presence of unfused late epiphyses would suggest that young adults (A1 and perhaps A2) are better represented than indicated by the mandibular evidence while the high proportion of fused late epiphyses clearly show that most of the cattle survived beyond their fourth year and in particular within the latest 'Roman' levels (Phase 9). A small number of bones from rather young calves, probably up to a few weeks old, were found within levels dated to Phases 3 (one), 4 (two) and 9 (one fragment). These may well represent the remains of infant mortalities and therefore indicative of cattle breeding. Combining the two datasets it can be proposed that there is some culling of younger stock in most phases (generally 2nd year animals), this perhaps best seen in Phases 7 to 9, followed by culls of third- and fourth-year individuals, again in all phases, the majority then slaughtered in excess of five years with a notable proportion (especially in the earlier phases) surviving beyond 9 to 10 years. The cattle at this site were clearly exploited first and foremost for their secondary products, here referring to milk production and/or their use as work animals. The sex evidence (Table 3.36) based on the shape of the pelves (after Grigson 1982) suggests a mix of males (most

Table 3.33 Cattle kill-off profile based on epiphyses fusion dividing the articular ends into three main age groups (see Methodology); where N1 is the number of fused epiphyses in that age group, N2 the total number (fused and unfused) and %F is the proportion of fused epiphyses

Age Group:	J	I	SA1	SA2	A1	A2	A3	E	Total
Species/Phase									
Cattle									
4								3	3
5								2	2
6							1	4[1]	5[1]
7	3	1	2			1	3[1]	3	13[1]
8							4[1]	2[1]	6[2]
9	1		3[3]	1	1[1]	[3]	2[4]	1[1]	9[12]
10		1							1
11		1					1[1]	2	4[1]
Sheep/Goat									
4							[1]		[1]
5		1					5[1]		6[1]
6	1					2	4		7
7	1		3			3	4[1]		11[1]
8					1	1	2[1]		4[1]
9			2			3[3]	3[2]		8[5]
10		1					2		3
11							1		1

Table 3.34 Cattle and sheep/goat kill-off profile based on dental eruption and wear in mandibles using age categories after Bond and O'Connor (1999: 346); Key to categories: J = juvenile, I = immature, SA = sub adult, A = adult, E = elderly; numbers in brackets equal loose teeth – deciduous fourth premolar and adult third molar

	Phase					
Age Group	4	5	6	7	8	9
Early						
N1	8	30	11	61	56	114
N2	8	30	11	63	59	121
%F	100.0	100.0	100.0	96.8	94.9	94.2
Intermed.						
N1	3	6	9	32	11	35
N2	3	9	10	36	16	46
%F	100.0	66.7	90.0	88.9	68.8	76.1
Late						
N1	3	8	3	16	10	29
N2	6	15	6	33	26	50
%F	50.0	53.3	50.0	48.5	38.5	58.0

probably castrates) and females, particularly within the latest phase. This evidence essentially applies to second-year or older cattle (all the pelves used in this method are fused), however, as older animals are more prevalent, it can be assumed that beef was essentially supplied by surplus milch cows and plough oxen. The latter are undoubtedly represented amongst the larger cattle found at this site (see above).

Butchery and body parts

Evidence of skinning (hide removal) in the form of knife cut marks is seen on the frontal bone of a cattle skull from Phase 6 and on the proximal end of a metacarpus from Phase 8. Anatomical (body part) distributions in each phase indicate the cattle bones are waste from all stages of slaughtering and carcass preparation (disjointing) as well as kitchen/table refuse.

Pathologies

A cattle rib shaft from Phase 5 has a partially healed break (traumatic injury). From Phase 8 there is a femur with an eburnated (highly polished) articular surface of the distal medial condyle in combination with bony outgrowths (exostoses) most probably denoting osteoarthritis (after Baker & Brothwell 1980, 115). This condition can be linked to traction stress as would occur in the bones of heavily worked draught/plough animals (Baker & Brothwell 1980; Groot 2005).

Sheep/Goat

Apart from the three horn cores/part skulls described below, all of the ovicaprid elements are ascribed to sheep based on the criteria of Boessneck *et al.* (1964) and Payne (1985).

Sheep

Appearance and size

Polled (naturally hornless) sheep are represented by crania from Phase 5 and Phase 7 [770] (two specimens). Evidence for horned sheep dating to the Roman era is provided by a yearling cranium with horn buds from Phase 6, Structure 1, [874] and a horn core from a young adult male from the Phase 7, Open Area 1 deposit [694]. All the Grange Farm sheep appear to have been small, gracile creatures. Based on greatest length GL measurements taken on complete long bones the withers heights in three sheep are calculated (method of Teichert, see von den Driesch and Boessneck 1974) as follows: 66.7cm dated to Phase 5 and then two heights of 56.7 and 60.9cm from Phase 8 deposits, the former representing the older of the two ABGs described below. These values fall within the size-ranges documented for the majority

of sheep from Romano-British sites, here including those from Springhead and Northfleet (Grimm & Worley 2011, 35). Notably, unlike the cattle size data, there is no evidence for the larger sheep (with heights ranging between 69 and 76cm) noticed at other Late Roman sites, as for example found at Godmanchester, Colchester and London (see Armitage 1983, 90). It should be noted, however, that such large sheep are rather rare, with very few examples from Roman London. Indeed, these tend either to be totally absent, as for example from a selection of sites in Roman Southwark (Liddle *et al.* 2009, 248) or represented by single examples, as at 1 Poultry, Tabard Square and Winchester Palace (with data taken from PCA archives as well as Rielly 2005, 165; Hill and Rowsome 2011, CD Table 91).

Articulated/associated Bone Groups (ABGs)

Two partial skeletons were recovered from the secondary fill of hearth/furnace [1046] dated to Phase 8 (see Table 3.32). The more complete skeleton represents a fully mature individual identified from the pelvis as a female; while the other skeleton can be identified as a young adult, based on the fusion of the intermediate and lack of fusion of the late epiphyses (see Methodology).

Ages

The age profile, following the mandibular method used for cattle (see above), reveals a majority of adult individuals within the Roman levels (Table 3.28) with a notable prominence of older adults. This would clearly suggest the importance of milk and/or wool production with surplus animals eventually culled for their meat. There is however, a minor incidence of first- and second-year sheep throughout, the culling of younger lambs (juveniles) enabling ewes to be milked for human consumption and perhaps also for cheese making. The epiphysis fusion evidence is rather slight (see Table 3.34) but it does at least show, referring to the late Roman phases, a majority of adults and perhaps of older adults (Phases 7/8) as shown by the proportion of fused intermediary and late epiphyses respectively.

Goats

Goats are represented by three horn cores, all from adult female individuals: from Phase 7, one left horn core, chopped/hacked from the skull; from Phase 8, one right horn core and part of skull; from Phase 9, one right horn core (complete) and portion of skull with knife (skinning) cut marks (LOC 136mm BC 83mm). It is perhaps significant that all three specimens are identified as female. These animals probably had been kept primarily for milking (? used in cheese making) and only later, when no longer productive in this capacity, killed for their meat and hides.

Pig

Types and sizes

The majority of the pig bones are believed to be from domestic animals. However measurements taken on three particularly large, robust bone elements fall within the size-range of comparative specimens from modern *Sus scrofa* documented by Clason (1967), Noddle (1980, 407 & 408) and Payne & Bull (1988, 41) and may therefore derive from hunted wild pigs. These larger examples comprise: from Phase 5, Pit [801], pit group 13 (Fill [802]) a metacarpus IV, GL (greatest length) 78.0mm, giving an estimated withers height 82.1cm; from Phase 9 [201] a metatarsus IV, GL 90.6mm, giving an estimated withers height 80.1cm and an innominate bone LAR 38.6mm, LA 43.1mm.

Pig withers heights (above) are estimated from GL using the factors of von Cornelia Becker (1980, 27). A comparison concerning recent pigs can be made with the partial pig skeleton found in a modern pit [584] within Area A. This had several complete limb bones, the radius with a length of 159.4mm providing a withers height of 83.4cm (after Teichert, see von den Driesch and Boessneck 1974).

Ages and sexes

The overall age distribution of the pigs (Phases 4 to 7) based on tooth eruption/wear stage in the jawbones (Table 3.33) indicates the majority of them had been killed/consumed just before the end of their second year (i.e. when they had reached prime/optimum butchering/ carcass weight). The older individuals (the adult component) could include adult baconers (the A1 and perhaps the SA2 contingent) as well as surplus breeding stock (A2). A notable proportion of suckling pigs, as represented by juvenile animals, undoubtedly indicate on-site breeding, as indeed does the recovery of several similarly aged post-cranial bones from deposits dating

Table 3.35 Pig kill-off profile based on dental eruption and wear in mandibles using age categories after Bond and O'Connor (1999, 346) and see Table 3.27 for abbreviations used

Age Group:	J	I	I1	I2	SA1	SA2	A1	A2	Total
Phase									
5	2				1				3
6	1								1
7	2		1	1		1			5
8		1					1	1	3
9		2		5	3	[1]	3		13[1]
11							2		2

to Phases 6, 7 and 8. An approximately similar age distribution is shown by the epiphysis fusion data (Table 3.34) although perhaps indicative of a greater proportion of adults. Determination of the overall sex ratio based on the canine teeth (Table 3.36) reveals a higher proportion of males to females within the Roman levels (2 males : 1 female in Phases 4 to 8 and 1.6:1 adding the Phase 9 data).

Articulated/associated Bone Group (ABG)

Of special interest is the skull and associated post-cranial skeletal elements of what appears to have been a complete carcass of a two-year-old female domestic pig buried in the tertiary fill ([1296]) of the roadside ditch [1077] dated to Phase 6. Based on the signs of weathering/leaching/ cortical erosion of the bones and root-etched surfaces, it would appear the skeleton had lain for some while after disposal at a relatively shallow depth in the ditch fill. There is no evidence of butchery and together with the distinctive pale orangey/yellowish colour of the bones it is suggested the carcass still had its flesh/muscle/soft tissues when thrown into the ditch. Evidently the animal had not been eaten and perhaps was a natural mortality or culled diseased animal considered not fit for human consumption. An old, partially healed break (traumatic injury) is noted in the left fibula, which had not knitted together.

Dog

The majority (121/156 = 78%) of the dog bone elements recovered from the Roman levels (including Phase 9) at the site are from four partially-complete skeletons (ABGs) representing three adult animals and a puppy (see Table 3.32). A fifth adult animal could be added to this list with an assortment of bones including skull, atlas, radius, tibia and calcaneus, all probably from the same animal taken from fills of ditch [264] dated to Phase 7. From measurements of greatest length (GL) taken on the complete humerus and tibia from the certain and probable partial skeletons recovered, as well on disarticulated, scattered limb bones of other dogs from other contexts, the shoulder heights have been calculated (Table 3.37).

These values may be compared against the sizes of the second- to fourth-century dogs from Drapers' Gardens in London with a range of 20.3cm to 67.3cm plus a mean value of 40.1cm based on 45 bones (Rielly in prep b); as well as those from the ritual shaft at Springhead, Kent (shoulder heights 33cm to 52cm) documented by Grimm (2007, 55); and the average shoulder height (45cm) established for 26 dog bones from the Late Iron Age/Romano-British site at Margate (Grimm 2011, 11). The smallest dog, at 28.4cm is of particular interest, this actually falling into a group of small-legged dogs (less than 31cm in height) which form a substantial proportion of the dogs found at numerous sites across

Table 3.36 Cattle, sheep/goat and pig kill-off profile based on epiphyses fusion using combined phase data; following the abbreviations described in Table 3.34 and see Methodology

Species	Age Group	Phase					
		4–6		7–8		9	
		N1/N2	%F	N1/N2	%F	N1/N2	%F
Cattle	Early	49/49	100	117/122	95.9	114/121	94.2
	Int	18/22	81.8	43/52	82.7	35/46	76.1
	Late	14/27	51.9	26/59	44.1	29/50	58
Sheep	Early	8/8	100	8/8	100	8/8	100
	Int	¼	25	10/11	90.9	5/9	55.5
	Late	1/3	33.3	4/7	57.1	1/1	100
Pig	Early	2/7	28.6	12/15	80	22/24	91.7
	Int	3/10	30	1/4	25	5/12	41.7
	Late	0	0	0	0	1/8	12.5

Table 3.37 Estimated shoulder heights for dogs (calculated using the formulae of Harcourt 1974). Overall range 28.4 to 62.8, mean 44.7cm

Phase	Context		Bone element	GL (mm)	est. Shoulder height (cm)
7	[770]	Open Area 1	humerus	158.0	51.5
8	[300]	Fill of ditch [264]	tibia	201.0	59.6
7	[691]	Fill of [717]	radius	83.1	28.4
8	[1234]	Fill of ([1236])	tibia	107.2	32.2
8	[908]	Fill of [909]	tibia	212.0	62.8
8	[1230]	Fill of [1231]	humerus	107.0	34.0

Table 3.38 A comparison of archaeological, domestic and wild cat radii measurements from a variety of sources (all measurements in millimeters); where NC refers to the Newton collection

Measurements:	GL	Bp	SD	Bd
Site/Source				
Grange Farm (691) - Phase 6	101.6	8.7	5.8	-
Winchester (VRW14) - well F43	101.2	9.0	-	13.4
Modern wild cat (female), NC	106.5	9.1	5.5	13.3
Modern domestic cat (male), BMNH C6	109.7	10.6	7.1	15.7
Modern domestic cat (sex unknown), NC	96.0	8.4	6.8	12.1

Roman Britain (Clark 2012, 165–6). While originally thought of as a house or lap-dog (after Harcourt 1974, 164), their frequency and distribution suggest they were more likely to have been used or developed as work animals, most probably as hunters of vermin. It is perhaps no coincidence that the spread of such small dogs is contemporary with the introduction and rapid infestation of the black rat in this country (Clark 2012, 167–8).

Cat

Bones of cats are identified from Phases 5, 7 and 8. Phase 5 provided a mandible, radius and ulna from the same adult individual. The jawbone is from an animal of similar size to the average, modern domestic cat and is comparable to the robust second-century AD specimen identified from the Billingsgate Buildings

Table 3.39 Distribution and description of red deer bones

Phase	Context	Bone element(s) & description(s)
7	Layer [694] Open Area 1	1 radius, immature (dist. epiphysis unfused)
7	Layer [770] Open Area 1	1 naturally shed antler (with coronet and portions of beam & tines), tines sawn.
	Layer [770] Open Area 1	1 radius, adult; shaft spiral fractured (marrow extraction)
	Layer [770] Open Area 1	1 metatarsus, adult
7	Layer [719]	1 red deer antler with end of beam/terminal points sawn through
9	Demolition layer [462]	1 naturally shed antler, beam sawn
	Demolition layer [462]	1 proximal metacarpus
	Demolition layer [462]	1 metacarpus shaft piece
8	Fill [908] of pit [909], (Group 48)	1 tip of antler, sawn
8	Fill [1019] of pit [1020]	1 piece of tine
9	Layer [201]	1 cranium (portion), chopped
9	Layer [201]	1 naturally shed antler
9	Layer [201]	6 sawn pieces of antler
9	Layer [201]	1 metatarsal shaft piece
9	Layer [201]	1 tibia shaft
9	Layer [201]	1 loose mandibular molar
10	Fill [236] of pit [264]	1 antler, sawn
11	(Layer [464])	1 antler, sawn

Table 3.40 Distribution and description of roe deer bones

Phase	Context	Bone element(s) & description(s)
6	Dumped layer [874] Structure 1	1 portion of skull, including pedicles (= male)
6	Dumped layer [874] Structure 1	1 metatarsus, adult
7	Layer [694], Open Area 1	1 radius, adult
7	Layer [770], Open Area 1	1 skull (portion) with antler (= male)
7	Layer [770], Open Area 1	1 innominate (= female - criteria of Lemppenau 1964)
7	Layer [770], Open Area 1	1 metatarsus shaft fragment
7	Layer [719]	1 antler beam fragment
8	Fill [908] of pit [909] (Group 48)	1 jawbone fragment
9	Layer [201]	1 jawbone fragment
9	Layer [201]	1 radius, adult
10	Fill [1168] of pit [1169]	1 radius, adult

site, City of London (Armitage 1980, 155). Another large cat is represented by a radius from [717] (fill [691]) dated to Phase 8, matching in size a specimen from the skeleton of an adult cat excavated from a Roman well in Winchester (Maltby 2010, 218 – 219). As discussed by Maltby, it is assumed that all cat bones from Roman sites are from domestic animals although the presence of native wild cat *Felis silvestris* at this period cannot be ruled out (see comparison of radius size from this site and from Winchester alongside modern wild and domestic specimens in Table 3.38).

Deer

Fifteen red deer elements are identified from Phases 7, 8 and 9, with another one each from Phases 10 and 11 (Table 3.39). These provide evidence of hunted animals utilized as sources of meat and antlers for working. An additional source of antlers came from naturally shed specimens collected from the surrounding landscape. Roe deer are represented by nine elements from Phases 6 to 9 and then one from Phase 10 (Table 3.40). Unlike the red deer, there is no evidence that antlers from these animals were being utilised as a raw material at this site. As discussed by Riddler (2003) the much smaller antlers compared with those of red deer and pronounced guttering greatly limited the range of objects that could be fashioned from them.

Otter

The fill ([278]) of ditch [264] dated to Phase 7 produced a part-complete skeleton of an otter as well as a pair of mandibles from a second animal (see Table 3.31). Examination of the tooth wear and epiphyseal fusion in the limb bones (criteria of Zeiler 1988) indicated the more complete skeleton was from an animal aged between one and two years, while the second individual was somewhat younger – less than one year old. It can be supposed that both animals may have been hunted for their fur, noting the presence of knife marks on the left tibia of the older individual. These include cut marks on the medial surface, two towards the distal end of the shaft and three along the mid shaft. Notably both the right and left tibiae have their distal articular ends missing (broken/splintered) and there are no foot bones. This breakage pattern and skeletal part absence may suggest the manner of removal of the skin with the foot bones still attached. The processing of the skin may have been undertaken elsewhere, the remaining bones perhaps deposited at this place or else incorporated within the finished product. Otter is a rather rare find and there is no Roman-period reference to this species in Fairnell's description, principally using archaeological data, of the utilization of fur-bearing animals in Britain (2003, 38–39).

Badgers

This site provided 48 badger bones divided between the fills of ditch [264] with 46 bones and the additional two from layer [770] in Open Area 1. All of these deposits date to Phase 7 with the exception of the later fill ([300]) of ditch [264] in Phase 8, however, the clear mix of parts from the same individuals across these ditchfills suggests they all date to Phase 7. There is a minimum of two adult individuals within the ditch, one represented by most part of the skeleton and the second by most of the major bones of the left foreleg. The bones from layer [770] include an ulna and a tibia, again from adult animals, and while the tibia may conceivably belong to one of the badgers in the ditch, the ulna clearly does not. Thus the overall count of badgers is at least three. Although all the badger bones have every appearance of being contemporary with the associated Roman bone elements from their respective contexts, the presence of a badger sett at the site presents the possibility that these remains are intrusive (i.e. are natural casualties of burrowing animals). Badger remains have been recorded elsewhere in Roman contexts, including Exeter (Maltby 1979, 65), Claydon Pike, Upper Thames Valley (Sykes 2007, 151, 203), and Cambourne New Settlement, Cambridgeshire (Hamilton-Dyer 2009, 98). All such occurrences present the same problem of interpretation but it is worth considering that ditch [264] at Grange Farm also produced evidence of at least one hunted otter apparently utilized for its skin (see above) and it is documented that badgers in the past have likewise been exploited for their fur (Fairnell 2003). Of interest in this respect was the badger skull found at Northfleet Roman villa (dated to the mid-Roman era) with skinning cuts, these anterior to the orbit on the left-hand side (Grimm & Worley 2010, 49 and Plate 6). Yet badgers have also been used for their fat and their meat (Neal & Cheeseman 1996; Fairnell 2003, 40), with Roman evidence for this use demonstrated by dismemberment cuts observed on badger bones from a second-/third-century level at Caister-on-Sea (Darling & Gurney 1993, 226). It follows, irrespective of the evidence for a sett, that these badgers may well represent food and/or skinning waste.

Small mammals

The small mammal assemblage includes include hare, wood mouse, field vole and a bat species. The first is represented by two bone elements, a single chopped pelvis from [694] (Open Area 1) and a radius from [719], both dated to Phase 7. The small rodents are represented by bones belonging to two adult and three immature wood mice as well as a mandible and a tibia identified as field vole (at least one adult), all recovered amongst the micro-faunal remains recovered from a collapsed layer/fill ([237]) within coffin [221] dated to Phase 9 (see

Table 3.41). One of the adult wood mice was identified as a male (after Lawrence & Brown 1973, 198–9). This same deposit also provided a right humerus identified by bat specialist John Kaczanow as the forearm bone of a Brown (common) long-eared bat (pers. comm. 2007). The length of this bone at 20.09mm suggests it is possibly a male with a forearm length of approximately 37mm.

Birds

Domestic fowl

Phases 5 to 9 yielded a combined total of 25 bone elements of domestic fowl *Gallus gallus* (domestic) with an additional bone dated to Phase 10 (see Table 3.42). Apart from an immature coracoid from Phase 8, all the

Table 3.41 *Species represented within the fill ([237]) of grave [221], where N is the number of bones and MNI is the minimum number of individuals*

Species	N	Bone element(s)	MNI
Mammal:			
Wood mouse	4	2 innominates (both left), 1 right femur & 1 left tibia	2
Wood mouse	5	2 femur & 3 tibia	3
Field vole	2	1 right mandible & 1 left tibia	1
Brown long-eared bat	1	1 right humerus	1
Bird:			
Snipe	1	1 coracoid	1
Robin	1	1 tibiotarsus	1
Song thrush	3	1 scapula, 1 ulna & 1 tibiotarsus	1
Thrush family	9	2 coracoid, 1 scapula, 4 ulna & 2 femur	? 4
Unidentified small wild bird	3	2 scapula & 1 tarsometatarsus	? 3
Amphibian:			
Toad	1	1 ilium	1

Table 3.42 *Distribution of hand collected (H) and sieved (S) small mammal (rodent), bird, fish and amphibians by species and phase*

Species/Site phase	5	6	7	8	8	9	10
	H	H	H	H	S	H	H
Wood mouse						9	
Field vole						2	
Brown long-eared bat						1	
Domestic fowl	8	2	7	1	1	6	2
Greylag/domestic goose		1	1				
Mallard/domestic duck			2	2			
Raven	1						
Owl (sp. Indeterminate)		1					
Snipe						1	
Song thrush						1	
Robin						3	
Turdus spp.						9	
Cod							1
Toad				1			

bones are from adult birds, which by modern standards would appear somewhat scrawny, similar in size to modern bantams. Nonetheless they are well within the size range for Roman chickens (comparing data in the PCA archives). A tarsometatarsal from coffin [221] (fill [237]), Phase 9 and another from [770] in Phase 7 are both recognized as females on the basis of the absence of spurs (criteria of West 1982). The greatest length (GL) of these bones at 67.3 and 72.9mm is comparable to the range of female birds from Drapers' Gardens with a range of 64mm to 82mm and a mean value of 72.2mm (N=12), taken from Rielly (in prep b). The specimen from the fill of the lead coffin [221] is of interest in the light of discussions among zooarchaeologists concerning the significance of domestic fowl bones found in association with female graves, which often are interpreted as food offerings for the deceased. However as reviewed by Lauwerier (1993a, 77) unless there is clear proof the chicken bones in question were grave gifts (i.e. found in vessels), whenever such bones are lying loose/scattered there is the possibility that they were intrusive domestic food waste that had accidentally fallen into the grave.

Geese and ducks

Goose is represented by just two bones, a humerus from the fill (1278) of ditch cut [1280] in Phase 6 and a furculum (wishbone) from layer [770] in Phase 7. Although by Roman times goose husbandry was well established (Albarella 2005, 253) these two bones probably represent wild caught greylag geese rather than domestic reared geese. Four duck bones were recovered, including a carpometacarpus and a humerus from layer [770] in Phase 7; and a sternum and synsacrum from a fill ([962]) of pit [909] in Phase 8 (pit group 48). As discussed by Albarella (2005, 255) there is no evidence for domestic duck breeding in Roman Britain and it must therefore be assumed any ducks consumed at the site were wild-caught mallards.

A variety of other bird species are also represented, with three out of a total of five derived from the aforementioned Phase 9 grave-fill ([237]) in coffin [221]. These include snipe, robin and song thrush. This same deposit also provided another twelve bird bones, nine of which could be identified as thrush family and the remaining two as unidentified small wild birds (see Table 3.41). The avian bones from other deposits include a raven ulna from the fill ([802]) of pit [801] dated to Phase 6; and an owl tibiotarsus from layer [874], in Phase 6 Structure 1. The latter bone could not be identified beyond stating it was not a barn owl.

Amphibian

An ilium of toad was recovered from grave fill (237) of grave [221]. This may well represent the remains of an individual that had lived and died at the site following abandonment of the mausoleum or, as described below,

a possible prey item (along with the described small mammals & birds) introduced onto the site in a voided pellet (see below).

Fish

The site produced a single isolated cod precaudal vertebra from a fill ([1168]) of a Phase 10 pit [1169].

Evidence of a roosting tawny owl in the mausoleum ruins

The micro-faunal remains recovered from the Phase 9 fill ([237]) of grave [221], as described above and shown in Table 3.41, merited special attention and the results of the study are presented below.

Small mammals

Three explanations were considered to account for the presence of the concentration of skeletal remains of mice and voles in the grave fill: 1) these animals had lived and died in the vicinity and their remains were incorporated into the deposit when the layer above collapsed into the coffin, 2) the bones derived from prey taken by mammalian predators such as weasels, foxes, cats and dogs and left at the site in a scat(s), or 3) the bones were from prey taken by an owl and left at the site in a regurgitated pellet when this bird was roosting in the mausoleum ruin. The second explanation was eliminated by closer inspection of the mice and vole specimens, which failed to detect any sign of the erosion and pitting of bone surfaces that are indicative of bones that have passed through the digestive tract of mammalian predators (see Andrews & Evans 1983). Whilst the first explanation could not be entirely ruled out it was the association of the small mammal bones with the group of bones of small wild birds from the same context that seemed to fit the prey spectrum of a tawny owl (explanation 3 - as discussed further below). It was also noted that the Brown (common) long-eared bat (represented in the grave fill by a humerus) is the bat species most vulnerable to predation by tawny owls (Kaczanow pers. comm.).

Wild birds

Viewed in isolation from the other micro-faunal evidence, the presence of a concentration of skeletal elements of several thrushes, a robin, and a snipe were initially interpreted as possible food offerings given to the deceased during a funerary rite. As discussed by Lauwerier (1993a) although the principal birds found as grave goods are domestic fowl, small wild birds occasionally are present. Thrushes especially would have made an apposite offering as these birds were highly esteemed as a delicacy in Roman times (Lauwerier

1993b, 18). However, this explanation had to be dismissed as it became clear that none of the bird bones were found in vessels in the grave as would be expected of meals prepared for the dead person and no other grave goods had been found. An alternative explanation was provided by reference to modern studies of prey taken by tawny owls, which frequently comprise a variety of small wild birds (including thrushes), especially whenever there is locally a scarcity of small mammalian prey, or by the owls opportunistically switching to taking fledgling birds during their own breeding season because they are easier to catch for their young than mice or voles (see Sparks & Soper 1970, 79 & 110; Lawrence & Brown 1973, 268 – 273; Beven 1982; Kirk 1992). Additional supporting evidence for the pellet being produced by a tawny owl rather than a barn owl is provided by the noticeable absence of bones of common shrew, the primary prey of the barn owl. By contrast, in rural landscapes, the preferred primary prey of tawny owl is wood mouse, with field vole as the secondary prey species: significantly both species feature in the Grange Farm assemblage. It should also be mentioned that barn owl pellets tend to be harder, more compact, while those of tawny owl exhibit a looser texture, less resistant to post-depositional taphonomic processes. This undoubtedly accounts for the dispersed distribution of the micro-faunal skeletal elements in the grave fill. In summer months such pellets break down rapidly among moist ground vegetation exposing the undigested remnants of the prey (bones & fur etc.) and rendering these vulnerable to post-depositional disturbance (Glue 1970, 54–56).

Discussion and conclusions

Roman

There is a notable similarity in domesticate abundance throughout the occupation periods, here including Phase 9, marked by the predominance of cattle bones. The fragmentation of the various collections has been alluded to with reference to the possible over-representation of cattle. However, it has also been mentioned that the level of preservation is generally good and that the level of breakage has more to do with their recovery than soil conditions. Thus, there can still be a bias towards cattle bones but this is only partially related to their degree of survival prior to excavation. Recovery bias can be reduced to a certain extent by the use of a weighted quantitative method and the notably comparable results of the total fragment and Epiphyses Only methods would appear to show, the level of fragmentation notwithstanding, that the recovered collection is rather similar to that in the ground prior to excavation. The importance of this conclusion takes on a special significance when the domesticate abundance pattern at this site is compared to those from other Roman sites in northern Kent (see Table 3.43). With the exception of Grange Farm, each of these sites/collections (with the notable exception of Early Roman Springhead, see below) features cattle (>50%) followed by a good proportion of sheep/goat (30–35%). It is notable that none of the samples provided fish bones. A shortfall may relate to a great extent to the sampling strategy and yet the apparently poor use of fish may also reflect the local diet, comparing for example

Table 3.43 *The percentage abundance of cattle, sheep/goat and pig bones from Late Iron Age (LIA) and Roman sites in Kent, where N is the total number of fragments. Broader categories referring to Springhead and Northfleet include Early (E), Mid (M) and Late (L) Roman with date ranges of mid-1st to early 2nd, early 2nd to mid-3rd and mid-3rd to late fourth centuries respectively. The Grange Farm periods ER (Phase 4) and MR (Phases 5 and 6) follow the previous date ranges, while also using late 3rd to early 5th (Phases 7 and 8) and ?late 4th to early 5th (Phase 9).*

Site	Period	Cattle	Sheep/Goat	Pig	N	Ref
Stone Castle	LIA-1c	52.7	33.3	14	1476	Rielly (in prep a)
Grange Farm	ER	82.0	7.9	10.1	89	
Springhead	ER	34.6	55.1	10.2	2069	Grimm & Worley (2011)
Gravesend	L1c-4c	50	39	11	133	Armitage (2004
Swanscombe	L2-E3	56.7	37.3	6	67	Rielly (2010)
Grange Farm	MR	70.9	18.7	10.4	471	
Springhead	MR	52.9	36.0	11.0	408	Grimm & Worley (2011)
Northfleet	MR	63.3	27.8	8.9	169	Grimm & Worley (2011)
Springhead	LR	53.8	30.7	15.5	251	Grimm & Worley (2011)
Northfleet	LR	60.2	27.5	12.3	334	Grimm & Worley (2011)
Grange Farm	L3–E5	80.4	12.1	7.5	1583	
Grange Farm	?L4–E5	76.9	10.7	12.3	1167	

the near total lack of fish from the Late Iron Age and Early Roman levels at Stone Castle, a site which was extensively sieved (Rielly in prep a).

Other aspects of these sites suggest similarities, in particular the presence of large cattle which in part relates to the general utilization of this domesticate. The age profiles from the Ebbsfleet sites (Northfleet and Springhead) feature a high proportion of older individuals as at Grange Farm signifying dairying and/or the use of draught animals (Grimm & Worley 2011, 50–1). These larger animals presumably represent oxen and may be indicative of continued imports and/or an assimilation of earlier larger 'types' dating to the first century as witnessed at sites such as Elms Farm (Johnstone & Albarella 2002, 44). There does appear to be a larger variety in evidence in this part of England from the latter part of the second century (see Cattle, above). The presence of younger individuals, in particular of neonates and infants at this site and also at Northfleet is strongly indicative of a production centre (lambs and piglets at both sites plus lambs at Northfleet). There are notably young lambs, piglets and calves as well as horses at Grange Farm, all evidence of sustainability and self sufficiency. Regarding sheep, there is no evidence for the larger individuals found at other sites in Britain, as for example at late Roman Godmanchester (Armitage 1983, 90), although there is undoubtedly evidence for a mainly adult utilization, thus exploiting milk products and wool. Comparisons can also be made concerning the minimal use of other food species, here including game, poultry and fish. The occurrence of deer is generally poor throughout Roman Britain, apart from a few exceptions (see for example Rielly 2005, 166–7), however, there does seem to be an association with 'high-class dining' (after Cool 2006, 116). Obviously, it is difficult to equate an occasional hunt or perhaps chance find, which could account for the minimal abundance of this species at most sites, with the possibility of affluence. Yet, there is undoubtedly a reasonable proportion of deer (meat waste rather than antler working waste) in Phase 7 which may be significant.

The probable evidence for salt-working, as shown by the fragment of briqeutage from pit [801] suggests the possibility that this site could have been involved in salt curing. Certain aspects of the bone evidence can be used to ascertain this possibility including the over-representation of particular skeletal parts, as cattle scapulae (particularly if they possess mid-shaft perforations) and also of pig bones, again especially if they are well represented by later sub-adult or young adult individuals, the adult baconers. There is clearly no evidence for the former, pig is well represented in [801] but generally makes up a very small proportion of domesticate collections, while the majority of pigs, in all phases, tend to be culled at a younger age. There is, however, a reasonable proportion of animals within the correct age range which could conceivably have provided hams for curing. Another particular animal use is shown by the evidence related to the skinning of small mammals, in this case otter and badger. Dating to the latter part of the occupation sequence, the concentrated nature of these

finds, including whole carcasses, would appear to indicate the presence of a workshop specializing in the production of such skins. Such species are rarely found on Roman sites and it is even rarer to find evidence for their utilization in the form of cut marks. Notably, the otter bones appear to be unique in this case, while badger bones with cut marks are limited to Caister-on-Sea (Darling & Gurney 1993, 226) and Northfleet (Grimm & Worley 2011, 49).

There are a number of bone collections which may contribute to an understanding of the ritual life of the local occupants of this settlement, here referring to the Associated Bone Groups or ABGs. Several of these, however, may be no more than the remains of discarded carcasses, these then undergoing varying levels of disturbance. This interpretation probably accounts for most of the equid remains, most probably those belonging to cattle and certainly the otter and badger bones. This perhaps leaves the dogs, the sheep skeletons from [1046] (Phase 8) and the pig from [1184] (Phase 6). Several such ABGs were found within the ritual shaft at Springhead and it is thought that the large proportion of sheep at the nearby settlement may also relate to ritual activities (Grimm & Worley 2011, 42). However, the same site also provided numerous sheep and dog ABGs, these particularly spread across the mid-and late Roman phase collections. In contrast none were found at Northfleet Roman villa.

Post-Roman

While many of the bones from early medieval Phase 9, in particular those from the possible 'dark earth' layer [201], may be viewed as late Roman in origin, the bone collection recovered from the fill of the lead-lined coffin within the mausoleum is undoubtedly post-Roman. It has been established that these bones are likely to represent the remains of a regurgitated tawny owl pellet. Although tawny owls mostly nest and roost in trees they will occasionally take advantage of disused buildings as alternative sites for these purposes. This is what appears to have happened in the abandoned ruin of the mausoleum. Owl pellets (all from barn owls) have been recorded at several other Roman sites in Britain, notably at the Caerleon Fortress Baths, Gwent (O'Connor 1983), Kingscote late Roman building complex, Gloucestershire (Noddle, referenced by O'Connor 1987), Drayton II Roman Villa, Leicestershire (Baxter 1993), the Roman Basilica, City of London (West & Milne 1993), the Roman signal station at Filey, north Yorkshire (Dobney *et al.* 1996), Gatehouse Roman Villa, Oxfordshire (Sharpe 2006a & 2006b) and the Romano-British circular stone-built shrine at Rutland Water (Armitage 2010). From such archaeological evidence (including that documented at the Grange Farm mausoleum) it would appear many of the more substantially constructed Roman buildings having been abandoned and fallen into a derelict/partially ruinous state at the end of the Roman occupation, provided ideal nesting and roosting sites for owls (tawny as well as barn owls) right through to the medieval period.

3.19 The human bone

James Langthorne

At Grange Farm the mausoleum (Building 3) west of the roadway appeared to have been thoroughly robbed out, potentially during the medieval period, but within the footprint of the building a lead lining was found surrounded by the ephemeral traces of an outer wooden casket. No grave-goods were found within the east-west-orientated inhumation and the lid of the coffin, had it ever had one, was absent, however the coffin's occupant was still present and apparently undisturbed (Gerrard, stratigraphic sequence; Ridgeway, the lead coffin, this volume).

Further disarticulated human bone from at least two individuals was also found within the fill of the robbed-out mausoleum walls, perhaps indicating that other individuals had once been buried within the building. Disarticulated human bone was also encountered within demolition deposits and the 'dark earth' type layer [201], all of which contained Roman material.

The examination of the body in the lead coffin and the other disarticulated skeletal material lay within the province of osteoarchaeology or bioarchaeology, one of the key areas of archaeology for directly understanding the lives of past populations. Aspects of the life of an individual may be exhibited by the bones of their body. Ultimately given a large enough number of contemporaneous skeletons, this archaeological discipline can allow us to trace the life ways of an entire population, ranging from infant mortality rates through occupational related stresses, to levels of interpersonal violence and evidence for medical practices.

The aim of the osteological analysis was principally to provide a description of the demography and pathology of the individual within the lead casket, together with a discussion of the data resulting from assessing the disarticulated human bone.

Methodology

Articulated human bone

The articulated skeleton was fully analysed to provide a complete inventory of every bone, an estimation of completeness, preservation, age and sex of the individual and recording of metric and non-metric traits and pathology. All results were entered onto Pre-Construct Archaeology's PELICAN database.

Inventory

The analysis of the skeleton required recording the presence or absence of each element. For the long bones these elements were sub-divided into five components:

proximal joint surface, proximal third of the shaft, middle third of the shaft, distal third of the shaft and distal joint surface.

Certain elements of adult individuals, specifically the sternum, scapula, clavicle, ilium, ischium, pubis, sacrum, coccyx and patella were categorised as to the percentage of the constituent part that was present: <25%, 25–50%, 50–75% or >75%.

The dentition was detailed using the Zsigmondy system (Hillson 1996) with specific notations made using Brothwell's recording standards and terminology (Brothwell 1981).

Condition and completeness

The condition and completeness of skeletal remains has a direct impact on the quantity and quality of information that can be recovered from them. The condition of the bone was documented following the stages of surface preservation (from Grade 0, very good, through to Grade 5+, very poor) proposed by McKinley (2004).

Completeness of the skeleton was calculated based on the percentage of the entire skeleton extant. Completeness can be affected by a variety of factors including truncation resulting from the intercutting of graves, and by later features as well as the state of preservation of the skeleton itself.

Age estimation

The age of an individual was assessed using a range of complementary variables comprising the stages of epiphyseal fusion (Buikstra & Ubelaker 1994, chapter 4), dental eruption (Ubelaker 1989, chapter 5 or Hillson 1996, chapter 5), and, additionally for adults, dental attrition (Brothwell 1981), changes within the pubic symphysis (Brooks & Suchey 1990) and the auricular surface (Lovejoy *et al.* 1985). This survey allowed the individual to be placed into one of the following age ranges (Based on categories outlined in Buikstra & Ubelaker 1994):

Neonate	birth
Infant	birth – one year
Juvenile	1 – 11 years
Adolescent (Adol)	12 – 20 years
Young Adult (YA)	20 – 34 years
Middle Adult (MA)	35 – 49 years
Old Adult	50+ years
Unspecified Adult	20+ years

The unspecified adult category is applied to adults lacking the necessary attributes which would have allowed for further refinement of the age of that individual.

Sex determination

Sexually dimorphic traits in the pelvis and skull are used to ascertain the sex of adult individuals, based on the work of Acsádi and Nemeskeri (1970), Buikstra and Mielke (1985), Milner (1992) and Phenice (1969). Greater emphasis has been placed on the characteristics of the pelvis than the skull as the former is considered more reliable considering that the variations here are founded in functional differences between the sexes (Mays 2010, 40). The individual was placed into one of six categories: Male (a positively identified male adult individual), Female (a positively identified female adult individual), Male? (an individual which compares favourably to the male sex but not conclusively), Female? (an individual which compares favourably to the female sex but not conclusively), Indeterminate (the survey of the individual has proved inconclusive), Unknown (the individual lacks the necessary elements that would determine its sex).

Biometry and stature estimation

Cranial and post-cranial measurements were recorded using the guidelines established in Buikstra and Ubelaker (1994, chapter 7). One aspect of biometric survey can allow for the estimation of the living stature of the adult skeletons. An individual's stature can, where possible, be calculated from appropriate long bone lengths using the regression equations devised by Trotter, Gleser, Gentry Steele and Bramblett (Trotter & Gleser 1958, Trotter 1970; Gentry Steele & Bramblett 1988). No adult individuals of indeterminate sex or displaying severe pathology of the femur can be used within this part of the analysis.

Non-metric analysis

Every adult individual can be examined for 64 specific non-metric traits using the criteria defined in Buikstra and Ubelaker (1994, chapter 8), these being the ones most commonly used as the standard by human bone specialists active in the field. These traits were previously believed to be principally determined by genetic inheritance, and so an examination of the clustering of traits could be used to indicate familial or other cultural groups. Increasingly however it has become clear that at least some of these traits are influenced more by modification due to activity undertaken by an individual or the environmental circumstances in which they lived (Saunders 1989, Tyrrell 2000 and Mays 2010).

Recording of pathology

All pathological alterations of bones were recorded by describing the type and location of the changes to individual bones, their distribution within the skeleton and potential differential diagnoses. These descriptions are based on the standards defined by Roberts and Connell (2004). Classifications of pathology were based on Roberts and Manchester (1995), Aufderheide and Rodríguez-Martín (1998) and Walker (2012).

Disarticulated human bone

The disarticulated bone recovered from each context was assessed to identify each type of bone, the number of fragments of each bone present in each context, the condition that each bone was in, the presence of any pathological lesions or notable morphological idiosyncrasies and, if possible, the age and/or sex of the individual from which the bone originated. The same criteria for assessing condition, pathology, age and sex in articulated human remains was applied to the disarticulated bone.

After all the disarticulated human bone had been assessed the minimum number of individuals represented in each context was calculated (McKinley 2004). All results were recorded onto PCA's PELICAN database.

Articulated skeleton [231]

Completeness and condition

The skeleton [231] in the lead coffin was assessed as being approximately 80% complete and judged as being in a moderate-poor state of preservation. Whilst most parts of the skeleton were represented, each of the bones themselves displayed some degree of fragmentation, and erosion of the surfaces had resulted in flaking and loss of definition of the articular surfaces.

Both the loss of skeletal elements and the condition they were found in was considered to be the product of the processes of decomposition rather than deliberate disturbance leading to truncation of the remains. The lead coffin itself was in a parlous state. Had it had a lid (as seems likely, see Ridgeway, this volume) this had been removed, possibly looted, leaving the skeleton either exposed or only covered by a wooden lid, potential traces of which were found amongst the deposits contained within the casket.

Demography

The analysis of the sex and age of the articulated skeleton concluded that the individual was probably a woman of more than 35 years of age. Unfortunately, the condition of the skeleton prevented any further refinement of these results and, due to the incomplete nature of the long bones, it was not possible to assess their stature either.

Non-metric traits

Despite the relatively high levels of erosion present on the bones of the skeleton in the lead coffin for the sake of completeness, the results of the survey of non-metric traits shown by that individual are included herein (see Appendix 6).

Skeletal pathology

The articulated skeleton presented some indications of joint disease of the spine and the right hand. Degeneration of this kind is associated with a range of factors such as wear and tear, age, genetic predisposition and occasionally they may be the result of other pathological conditions such as rickets or trauma (Aufderheide & Rodríguez-Martín 1998; Walker 2012). Joint disease can result in pain, stiffness, limited movement within the joint and abnormal appearance of the joint (Roberts & Manchester 1995, 99).

Specific descriptions of the pathological changes occurring on each bone suffering from joint disease are detailed below (Table 3.44).

Dental pathology

The only dental pathology observed on the extant mandible was ante-mortem tooth loss. This condition is commonly caused by the destruction of a tooth by caries or gum disease leading to alteration of the alveolus and the tooth subsequently being lost. The void left then remodels and ultimately becomes filled with new bone (Boston *et al.* 2008, 65). The tooth loss was extensive, bilateral and was focussed in the molar areas of the jaw.

Details of concretion

An extensive white deposit was evident on the outer surface of the occipital part of the skull, where the back of the head would have rested within the casket. The white substance was considered to be the mineralised by-products of the corrosion process that acted upon the lead coffin. These by-products perhaps absorbed or clung to the hair of the body or a textile, such as a burial shroud, in that location producing the irregular concentric pattern of concretion evident on the skull.

Articulated Human Bone Summary

Skeleton [231]

Age: 35+ years (Mid–Old Adult)
Sex: Female?
Stature: Not possible.
Preservation: Moderate–Poor
Completeness: 80%
Pathology: Joint disease. Osteophytosis and eburnation of right finger and ankylosis of T4 and T5.
Comments: White concretion (mineralised lead by-products) on occipital.
   Dentition:

R																L
---	---	---	-5-	---	---	---	---	---	---	---	---	---	---	---	---	---
X	X	X	X	4	3	2	1	1	2	3	4	R	X	X	8	

Key for dentition:
X: Tooth lost ante-mortem.
- -: Tooth present but socket missing.
---: Jaw not present.
R: Only the root of the tooth is extant.

Disarticulated bone

A sizeable amount of disarticulated human bone, notably fragments of skull and femur, was found within the medieval fill of robber cut [909] that truncated the mausoleum. These bones represented a minimum of four other individuals including a child and two adults, a man and a woman, suggesting that there were originally additional burials to that of the lead casket within the mausoleum.

Occasional fragments of disarticulated human bone were also found in a handful of further contexts including Roman demolition layers and a dark earth deposit. A complete catalogue of all disarticulated bone recovered from the Grange Farm site is detailed below (Table 3.45).

Table 3.44 *Pathological changes occurring on each bone suffering from joint disease*

Skeletal element involved	Description of pathological changes
Right middle hand phalanx	Probable osteoarthritis: Eburnation and osteophytic lipping sufficient to slightly alter the profile of the distal joint surface.
4th and 5th Thoracic vertebrae	Severe osteophytic activity leading to the ankylosis (fusion) of the left and right distal articular facets of the 4th thoracic vertebra with the corresponding left and right proximal articular facets of the 5th thoracic vertebrae.

Table 3.45 Catalogue of disarticulated bone (MNI = Minimum number of individuals represented within each context

Type	Skeletal element	Condition	Comments	MNI
Phase 9 'dark earth' type layer [201]	Skull - fragment of parietal bone	Good		1
	Skull - fragment of parietal bone	Good-Moderate		
	Skull - fragments of occipital bone	Good		
	Radius - mid shaft fragment	Good		
Fill of Phase 8 robber cut [909]	Skull - fragments of frontal, parietal and temporal bones	Poor	Male	4
	Skull - fragments of frontal, parietal and occipital	Poor	Female	
	Right mandible - no teeth	Good	Juvenile (*c.* 5 years)	
	Femur - proximal shaft fragment	Moderate		
	Femur - mid shaft fragment	Poor		4
	Left clavicle	Poor		
	Right 1st rib	Good		
	Long bone - 10 x shaft fragments (femur?)	Poor		
	Right femur - complete in 3 fragments	Poor		
	Right femur - head fragment and shaft fragment	Poor		
	Right femur - head and shaft in 3 fragments	Poor		
	Right femur - 2 x proximal shaft fragments	Poor		
	Left femur - head and proximal shaft fragment			
Phase 9 demolition layer [456]	Skull - 2 fragments of right parietal bone	Moderate		1
Phase 9 layer [462]	Skull - frontal bone	Good	Male?	1
	Skull - left parietal bone fragment	Good		1
Phase 8 layer [537]	Foot - proximal foot phalanx	Good		1
	Foot - right 2nd metatarsal	Good		
	Foot - right 5th metatarsal	Good		

3.20 The oyster and marine shell

Rebecca Haslam

An assemblage of whole and fragmented marine shells was recovered during excavations at Grange Farm, the dominant component being the Common European Flat Oyster (*Ostrea edulis* L.). The marine mollusc remains were assessed in order to determine the degree of fragmentation and preservation, to quantify the number of oyster valves by context and to record any other shells that were present in the assemblage. This information was used to determine whether marine molluscs were utilised as a resource by the inhabitants of Grange Farm over time and whether any temporal or spatial trends or changes could be identified.

Methodology

The marine shells from Grange Farm were collected from selected contexts via handpicking on-site. Marine shell species present were identified and quantified and the information collated by Phase and species (Table 3.46). Much of the assemblage was highly fragmented, so in the case of bivalves, only fragments with a complete umbo (i.e. the curved tip or 'beak' of the shell immediately above the hinge) were counted. Marks, cuts and perforations were also noted in order to further determine how the shells were exploited.

Results

The dominant species throughout the assemblage was *Ostrea edulis* L., the Common European Flat Oyster, which is a species native to the British Isles. Three other indigenous species, namely mussel (*Mytilus edulis*), cockle (*Cerastoderma edule*) and whelk (*Buccinum undatum*), were represented in lesser quantities (Table 3.46). Preservation of the oyster shell within the sampled contexts was poor and the number of marine shells recovered from any single context was generally small (not exceeding 100 specimens), the only exceptions being those recovered

from the backfill of Enclosure 2, ditch [860] (Phase 4) and the backfill of pit [801] (Period 5). The former contained a total of 166 oyster valves and four whelks whilst the latter contained two mussel valves, four cockle valves, ten whelks and 348 oyster valves. The morphology and pathology of valves forming part of an assemblage from a single context amounting to over 100 valves can be analysed statistically to deduce geographical origin (see Winder 2011). However, the Grange Farm remains could not be analysed in this way owing to their high degree of fragmentation and poor levels of preservation.

One specimen, recovered from the backfill ([562]) of Phase 10 well [563], is of note on account of a roughly ovoid perforation, measuring 28mm by 16mm, that was found in the approximate centre of the shell. It appeared to have been deliberately created by punching rather than drilling.

Conclusions

The results suggest that marine molluscs, in particular oyster, formed part of the diet of the inhabitants of Grange Farm from the Roman period onwards (i.e. Phases 4 to 11; Table 3.46). Evidence from elsewhere in Britain suggests the oyster was a popular foodstuff in the Roman period (McCloy & Midgley 2008, 62), a finding that is supported by the large percentage of oysters relative to other species of marine Mollusc present in this assemblage.

The shellfish were probably imported to Grange Farm from south-eastern coastal and estuarine habitats, however direct evidence of origin could not be obtained from this assemblage through statistical analysis. The proximity of the River Medway to the site would have provided a means of importing coastal resources quickly and easily, thus maintaining freshness.

Concentrations of shell were generally moderate thus suggesting that such resources did not form a significant component of the diet of the inhabitants of Grange Farm. However, a caveat must be attached to this statement, since some marine shell processing waste could have been discarded elsewhere, for example in shell middens or more general dumps situated beyond the site boundary.

The discovery of two concentrations of oyster shell within the backfill of ditch [860] (Phase 4) and pit [801]

Table 3.46: Quantification of shell, presented by phase

Period		4	5	6	7	8	9	10	Total
	Total Number of Shells/ Valves Collected								
Species Present									
Buccinum undatum		4	12					46	**62**
Cerastoderma edule			4					3	**7**
Mytilus edulis			2		4	2	2	8	**18**
Ostrea edulis L.		168	441	23	96	6	4	81	**819**
Total		172	459	23	100	8	6	138	**906**

(Phase 5) could perhaps each represent a single episode or a series of episodes of consumption that took place at a similar time. Other than this, the quantity and density of the assemblage is too small and its fragmentation and preservation too poor to enable any other spatial or temporal trends or patterns to be meaningfully identified from the data.

The perforated oyster specimen that was recovered from well [563] (Period 10) is worthy of note. It appears to have been punctured rather than drilled, perhaps in order to retrieve mother of pearl that could be used as inlay in jewellery or furniture. Alternatively, it could have been suspended as a pendant.

3.21 The archaeobotanical remains and charcoal

K. Le Hégarat and D.E. Mooney

This report by Quanternary Scientific (QUEST), University of Reading, summarises the results of the assessment and analysis of bulk soil samples taken for the recovery of environmental remains from the site. Post-excavation assessment of 35 samples revealed, primarily, a small assemblage of charred macroplant remains with the exception of three more productive samples. Samples {268}, ([1174]) and {246}, ([1025]), from the basal and upper fills of pit [1092], and sample {270}, ([1199]), from the fill of pit [1197] (all dated to the Roman occupation; Phase 4 and Phase 6 respectively), were recommended for full analysis of their charred macroplant remains on the basis of the abundance of material present and the potential of the material provided for further interpreting the features, the agricultural economy and the domestic activities (Gray 2012). In addition, the analysis of the charred wood remains from ten samples was recommended. These samples spanned three phases of occupation at the site: Phase 5, Phase 6 and Phase 8. Samples were taken from a variety of contexts including pit fills, hearths and floor deposits. Although the quantity of charred wood remains recovered from these samples was generally small, the assemblage was sufficiently large to provide limited information on the woody taxa present in the environs of the site, and the fuel procurement strategies employed by the occupants. The results of this analysis will complement work from other contemporary sites in Kent such as Lullingstone (Meates 1987), Westhawk Farm (Booth *et al.* 2008), and Thurnham (Challinor 2006a) to contribute to an overall picture of the wooded environment and fuel use strategies of Roman Kent.

Methodology

Samples were originally processed by PCA in a flotation tank with the flots and residues captured on 300µm and 1mm meshes. Flots selected for analysis were submitted as dried flots. They were measured and weighed before being passed through a stack of geological sieves of 4mm, 2mm, 1mm, 500µm and 250µm mesh sizes. Each of the size fractions were examined under a stereozoom microscope at x7–45 magnification and any plant remains were extracted and put in glass vials. Identifications were based on morphological characteristics using modern comparative specimens and reference manuals (Cappers *et al.* 2006; Jacomet 2006; Neef *et al.* 2012; NIAB 2004). The term 'seed' is used in the text to encompass a range of fruiting bodies such as nutlets and achenes as well as true seeds. cf. denoting 'compares with' is used to precede identifications that are considered most similar to a specific taxon but that do not display sufficient anatomical features for secure identification. Habitat information and nomenclature used follows Stace (1997) for native species and Zohary and Hopf (2000) for macrobotanical remains of cultivated taxa.

For the charcoal analysis, samples were selected for analysis on the basis of their charcoal content, as established in the preliminary assessment (Gray 2012). The ten samples selected comprised all samples containing greater than ten fragments of charcoal >4mm in size, recovered from both the residues and flots. All fragments of suitable size from each sample were fractured along three planes (transverse, radial and tangential) according to standardised procedures (Gale & Cutler, 2000). Specimens were viewed under a stereozoom microscope for initial grouping, and an incident light microscope at magnifications up to 400x to facilitate identification of the woody taxa present.

Taxonomic identifications were assigned by comparing suites of anatomical characteristics visible with those documented in reference atlases (Hather 2000; Schoch *et al.* 2004), and by comparison with modern reference material held at the Institute of Archaeology, University College London. Identifications have been given to species where possible, however genera, family or group names have been given where anatomical differences between taxa are not significant enough to permit satisfactory identification. Where identifications were uncertain due to poor preservation or limited size of charcoal specimens the identification is preceded by cf., denoting 'compares with'. Presence of roundwood in the samples was noted, however the fragments recovered were too few to merit quantification and further analysis. Nomenclature used follows Stace (1997).

Results and interpretation of the charred seed and charcoal analysis

The results of the analysis of the charred macrobotanical remains are displayed in Appendix 7; the results of the charcoal analysis are displayed in Appendix 8. Both analyses are summarised below.

Results and interpretation of the charred macrobotanical remains

Phase 4: c. AD 43–c. AD 100/120

Two samples dated to Phase 4 were analysed. They came from pit [1092] (sample {268}, [1174] from the basal fill and sample {246}, [1025] from the upper fill). Both were notable because they produced more charred weed seeds than charred crop remains, although this trend was slightly less evident in the uppermost fill. Preservation was variable. While the crop remains were generally poorly preserved, the preservation of the small weed seeds was better. A large proportion of the grains consisted of grains which were either too pitted or too fragmentary to be identified. Wheat (*Triticum* sp.) made up the vast number of the identifiable grains. Oat (*Avena* sp.) was also relatively frequent in the basal fill and barley (*Hordeum vulgare*) was present in low numbers in both samples.

Although it is often difficult to identify charred wheat grains to species level (Jones 1998), eight short grains with a rounded appearance were characteristic of short bread-type free-threshing wheat (*Triticum aestivum* – type). Seven grains were more typical of glume wheat species, either emmer or spelt wheat (*Triticum dicoccum/spelta*), although distinguishing these based on the grains alone is difficult. Nonetheless, spelt wheat was probably included as the species was identified from a glume base. While grains of hulled barley (*Hordeum vulgare*) were infrequent, grains of oat (*Avena* sp.) were commonly recorded in the basal fill [1174]. However, no diagnostic floret bases were found, and it was therefore impossible to confirm if the remains represented the wild and/or cultivated taxa.

Pulses were recorded in both samples although they were more numerous in the primary fill. They included seeds of small surface dimension (<3mm) but also larger ones which indicate the presence of cultivated species. A possible garden pea (cf. *Pisum sativum*) was tentatively identified from its shape, size as well as a round and short hilum. The remaining large-sized pulses that are likely to be vetch or pea (*Vicia/Pisum* sp.) were insufficiently preserved and could not be securely identified. Seeds of elderberry (*Sambucus nigra*) could indicate foods gathered from the wild.

An extensive assemblage of weed flora was recovered from the pit. The assemblage of charred weed seeds which accounted for 60.1% of the total charred macroplants in the basal fill ([1174]) and 57.7% in uppermost fill ([1025]) comprised typical species of arable/wasteland habitats such as black-bindweed (*Fallopia convolvulus*), field penny-cress (*Thlaspi arvense*), goosefoot (*Chenopodium* sp.), knotgrass/dock (*Polygonum* sp./*Rumex* sp.), possible mayweed (cf. *Matricaria* sp.), bedstraw (*Galium* sp.), scentless mayweed (*Tripleurospermum inodorum*) and vetch/vetchling/tare (*Vicia* sp./*Lathyrus* sp.). While the latter (which were particularly prominent) are often seen as indicators of nutrient-poor soils, goosefoot and small nettle (*Urtica urens*) occur on nitrogen-enriched disturbed ground around settlements. Sheep's sorrel (*Rumex acetosella*) is usually associated with acidic soils. Grasses including small-sized taxa such as cat's tail (*Phleum* sp.) and possible meadow-grass (cf. *Poa* sp.) as well as larger grasses such as oat and possible fescue/rye-grass (cf. *Festuca* sp./*Lolium* sp.) were also numerous.

Seeds of damp and wet environments were also represented including meadow/creeping/bulbous buttercups (*Ranunculus acris/repens/bulbosus*), sedges (*Carex* spp.) and possible common spike-rush (*Eleocharis* cf. *palustris*).

Phase 6: c. AD 150–c. 250

Sample {270}, ([1199]), from the fill of pit [1197] contained a moderate quantity of material which was fairly similar to the macroplant remains present in the previous feature. Crop remains were limited and weed seeds were more plentiful. A few grains of wheat were recovered of which eleven were characteristic of emmer/spelt wheat (*Triticum dicoccum/spelta*) and three were typical of free-threshing variety (*Triticum aestivum* – type). Grains of hulled barley and oat were infrequent. Two wheat glume bases including spelt, a barley rachis fragment and a bread – type wheat rachis fragment were recovered. No edible pulses were present in this sample. However, two walnut (*Juglans regia*) nutshell fragments were recorded.

Weed seeds were very common comprising mainly grasses (Poaceae) followed by a moderate quantity of knotgrass/dock (*Polygonum* sp./*Rumex* sp.). Additional less numerous seeds included goosefoot (*Chenopodium* sp.), vetch/vetchling/tare (*Vicia* sp./*Lathyrus* sp.). These represent typical species of disturbed or cultivated soils. Seeds of wet and damp grounds were also recovered including sedges (*Carex* spp.) and meadow/creeping/bulbous buttercups (*Ranunculus acris/repens/bulbosus*).

Results and interpretation of the charcoal assemblage

Preservation

Although no more than 60 identifiable charcoal fragments were recorded in any of the samples analysed, the charcoal was generally well-preserved. Material from some contexts across Phases 5 to 8 exhibited low levels of sediment concretion and infiltration related to fluctuations in groundwater level, but this did not in general have adverse effects on the interpretative value of the assemblage as a whole. In some cases, fragments of charcoal were unable to be assigned taxonomic identifications either due to poor preservation, or to distortion of the anatomical structure of the wood associated with the carbonisation process. These fragments, along with the taxonomic identifications assigned to the identifiable fragments recovered, are recorded in Appendix 8.

Summary of recorded taxa

The anatomical structure of the charcoal fragments analysed from the site was consistent with the following taxa:

Identified to species:
Aceraceae: *Acer campestre*, field maple
Aquifoliaceae: *Ilex aquifolium*, holly
Betulaceae: *Corylus avellana*, hazel
Oleaceae: *Fraxinus excelsior*, ash

Identified to genus:
Betulaceae: *Alnus* sp., alder; *Betula* sp., birch
Fagaceae: *Quercus* sp., oak
Rosaceae: *Prunus* sp., cherry, blackthorn, plum; *Rosa* sp., rose
Ulmaceae: *Ulmus* sp., elm

Identified to subfamily:
Rosaceae: Maloideae, including *Crataegus monogyna*, hawthorn; *Malus* sp., apple; *Pyrus* sp., pear; *Sorbus* sp., rowan, whitebeam

In some cases, the differences between genera are not significant enough to conclusively identify wood remains to genus level. For this reason, no further division is given of the Maloideae subfamily. Furthermore, in some cases poor preservation or small size of the charcoal did not permit the differentiation of hazel (*Corylus* sp.) and alder (*Alnus* sp.), hence the taxonomic category *Corylus/Alnus* (hazel/alder). Taxa are referred to in the following text by their English common names, with the exception of the Maloideae which are given their subfamily name.

Phase 5: c. AD 100/120–c. AD 150

A single sample from Phase 5, from the fill of pit feature [276], in pit group 17, produced a small charcoal assemblage comprising oak, elm and birch.

Phase 6: c. AD 150–c. 250

Four samples were analysed from Phase 6. The two samples from fills of pits [789] and [1196] produced small assemblages containing oak, ash, elm, Maloideae, hazel, field maple and holly charcoal. The assemblage from the fill of pit feature [1197] was larger and more varied. This sample was dominated by oak and cherry/blackthorn charcoal, but fragments of ash, elm, rose, Maloideae, hazel, alder and birch were also recorded. The sample from a Phase 6 layer ([1335]) produced a similar assemblage, composed of oak, ash, Maloideae, birch and hazel/alder. Fragments of roundwood were recorded in all samples, but did not comprise a significant proportion of any of the assemblages.

Phase 7: c. AD 250–325/350

The only sample from Phase 7 A was from the fill of a pit [210], which produced an assemblage of moderate size, containing only oak charcoal.

Phase 8: c. AD 325/50–AD 420/450

Phase 8 of the occupation of the site was represented in the charcoal analysis by four samples. A sample from the fill of pit feature ([1236]) produced a small charcoal assemblage dominated by oak, but also containing small quantities of Maloideae, cherry/blackthorn and hazel/alder charcoal. The remaining three samples from Phase 8 originated from the fills of hearths. Varied assemblages were recovered from the fills of hearths [1136] and [1155], containing mostly oak charcoal but also ash, Maloideae, cherry/blackthorn, hazel and alder. The charcoal remains from the fill of hearth [982] comprised predominantly Maloideae charcoal, but also produced a smaller quantity of oak charcoal. As with the samples from Phase 6, these samples contained small quantities of roundwood charcoal from a variety of taxa.

Discussion and conclusions

The remains from the three samples analysed for their macrobotanical remains are likely to represent waste material deriving from a number of charring events corresponding to various activities carried out in various locations. While some of the remains would have been deliberately deposited in the pits, others might have accumulated over an extended period.

The agrarian economy of the site

The charred macroplant remains have given an insight into the range of crop plants used on the site during the Roman period. The results appear to show very small changes through time but given the small size of the assemblage (based on three samples) and the relatively poor preservation of the crop remains it is difficult to confirm if they represent a comprehensive picture for the site. Even though the quantity of cereal remains is very small, the range of cereals, with the apparent dominance of spelt, is typical of the Romano-British period. During this period, in southern England, spelt is often the principal cereal found followed by smaller amount of hulled barley and free threshing wheat (Greig 1991). Nonetheless, numerous recent excavations in Kent including Thurnham Roman Villa (Smith & Davis 2006) and Saltwood Tunnel (Stevens 2006) have revealed that although spelt was the dominant hulled wheat cultivated, emmer was also an important localised crop during the Romano-British period. Pelling (2008) has suggested that in the south-east both hulled wheat species could have been cultivated side by side or even together. Bread wheat is sometimes interpreted as representing a contaminant (Campbell 1998).

Spelt wheat, bread wheat and barley were recorded in both pits, but in terms of variations over time, cultivated pulses were only recorded in Phase 4 pit [1092]. It is likely that their cultivation would have complimented the existing cereal diet. Another observation is the paucity of oat in Phase 6 pit [1197].

Walnut (*Juglans regia*)

Two fragments of walnut (*Juglans regia*) nutshell recovered from the Phase 6 pit [1197] could indicate a new cultivar for the site during this period. Van der Veen *et al.* (2008, 34) explain that while some foods introduced during the Roman period were only consumed by a select few, walnuts, which have been recorded in Britain since the first century AD, were actually available to a large part of the rural population. They add (2008, 27) that remains of walnuts are present on rural sites from the start of the second century only. No records of walnut nutshell from published Kentish sites could be found. It is impossible to tell if the remains from pit [1197] were cultivated locally in an orchard and they could simply have been imported to the site.

Crop processing activities

The chaff assemblage was very small; nonetheless, the presence of glumes and rachis fragments together with charred weed seeds are indicative of crop-processing activities. For hulled wheat species, chaff adheres tightly to the grains; and, in order to release the caryopses various stages of threshing, winnowing, pounding and sieving are undertaken (Hillman 1981; 1984). Chaff is fragile, and the low number of chaff remains in both features could relate to preservation bias. The presence of large and small weed seeds could indicate that the remains represent several processing stages using sieves with varying mesh sizes (Hillman 1981).

When considering the ratio of grain, chaff and weed seeds in the samples, it is clear that weeds dominate these assemblages. They represent 60.1% of the total assemblage of charred macroplants in sample {266}, 57.7% in sample {246} and 55.7% in sample {270}. The abundance of grasses together with vetches and sedges suggest that part of the remains could represent burnt fodder or stable waste such as bedding and/or dung. Oat, recorded in pit [1092] could have also been used as fodder.

Woodland exploitation

The range of taxa represented in the charcoal remains analysed from Grange Farm shows little variation over the period of occupation of the site, suggesting that the wooded environments utilised for fuel procurement were fairly constant in their species composition. The range of woody taxa identified indicate that firewood was sourced from oak-dominated deciduous woodland, with other large trees such as ash also present, and an understorey of smaller trees and large shrubs including elm, hazel, alder, birch, cherry/blackthorn and Maloideae taxa.

Two species, field maple and holly, were only recorded in a single sample from Phase 6, indicating that they were present in the landscape but perhaps were more rare, or not routinely selected as fuel. The presence of alder in samples from Phases 6 and 8 suggests that damp woodland or wetland margin environments were also present in the landscape, and exploited for fuel procurement. A similar range of taxa was also recorded in charcoal assemblages from Westhawk Farm (Challinor 2008), Thurnham Villa (Challinor 2006a) and Northumberland Bottom (Challinor 2006b), and cherry/blackthorn seeds were also recorded at Lullingstone villa (Meates 1987), suggesting a level of uniformity in wooded vegetation across Kent during the Roman period.

The majority of the samples analysed from Grange Farm originated from contexts such as pits and floors, and the charcoal remains present will have arrived in these deposits by dumping or accidental deposition rather than as the consequence of primary burning events. These contexts, therefore, have the potential to provide information on the choice of fuel wood for a variety of purposes across the site, rather than for particular domestic or industrial activities. The exceptions to this are the hearth fills from Phase 8, which are the result of primary *in situ* burning. Although these assemblages may be the result of more than one burning event, they do represent wood taxa chosen as domestic fuel, as opposed to the pit fills which are likely to comprise amalgams of fuel remains.

The charcoal assemblages from the vast majority of contexts analysed were dominated by oak, which might be expected considering both its excellent quality as a fuel wood (Taylor, 1981) and the predominance of this taxon in published archaeological charcoal assemblages from south-east England. Most of the other taxa identified in the samples are known to be good fuel woods, and those that are not (such as elm, maple and holly) are rare in the assemblage. This suggests that a selective firewood collection strategy was employed focusing on woody taxa known to make efficient fuels, and generally excluding those woods known to be poor burners. Although small quantities of roundwood were present in many of the samples, these were too few in number to give an indication of whether fuel wood resources were managed systematically, for example by coppicing or pollarding. The assemblage from Phase 8 is much less varied than those from the earlier phases of occupation at the site. This may be indicative of an increased emphasis on the use of oak in preference to other fuel woods, however as the three hearth samples from these phases may represent only the result of one or two burning events this can only be a tentative interpretation – it may indicate a specific choice of fuel almost entirely limited to oak, or merely that the final burning event or events in the hearths primarily utilised oak as fuel. Considering the value placed on oak as a timber resource (Taylor 1981), the continued predominance of this taxon in the charcoal assemblage is likely to indicate its abundance in the landscape, as has also been noted at Thurnham and Westhawk Farm.

3.22 Pollen sampling and the coffin

Nick Branch, Rob Batchelor and Gemma Swindle

This report summarises the findings arising out of the pollen assessment of sub-samples taken from the fill of lead coffin [261], within the late Roman mausoleum. The pollen analysis was conducted on samples obtained from the general fill of the coffin (samples {29} to {42}), and from the general area of the stomach, small and large intestine (samples {1} to {28}). The aim of this analysis was to evaluate the potential of the samples for providing information on: (1) Roman diet, in particular the last meal(s) of the individual, (2) the plants flowering in the general area, and (3) the possible presence of an 'exotic preparation' e.g. special drink, which may have given to the individual prior to death.

Methodology and sampling strategy

The lead coffin was removed from the site and excavated under controlled conditions in a laboratory at Chatham Dockyards. Because the recovery of bioarchaeological remains, other than human bone, from graves and coffins is relatively rare, it was decided from the outset to remove small samples for pollen analysis from the fill of the coffin in a grid pattern (Fig. 3.90), with the aim of providing some information on diet, environment and ritual/religious practices (see Dickinson 1976; Whittington 1993; Clarke 1999). The grid (5cm intervals (x-axis) by 10cm intervals (y-axis)) was laid out over the stomach and intestinal area of the skeleton using matchsticks and each grid square numbered (Fig. 3.90). Squares 5 and 6 lay directly over the stomach, with squares 10, 11 and 12 directly over the small and large intestine.

1	2	3	4	5	6	7
8	9	10	11	12	13	14
15	16	17	18	19	20	21
22	23	24	25	26	27	28

Fig. 3.90 Grid pattern used to sample the fill of the coffin in the stomach and intestinal areas of the skeleton

In addition samples were taken randomly from areas around the skeleton such as the feet ({29} to {31}), the pelvis ({32}), the skull (sample {33}), fill [237] ({34} to {37}), from the position of a possible necklace? ({38}), around the top of the skull ({39} to {41}), and from demolition deposit [205] {42}) (Appendix 9). These samples were not expected to yield interesting information, but instead provided 'control samples' for comparison with samples {1} to {28}.

All samples were assessed for their pollen content. The pollen was extracted from these as follows: (1) Sampling a standard volume of sediment (1ml); (2) Deflocculation of the sample in 1% Sodium pyrophosphate; (3) Sieving of the sample to remove coarse mineral and organic fractions (>125μ); (4) Acetolysis; (5) Removal of finer minerogenic fraction using Sodium polytungstate (specific gravity of $2.0g/cm_3$); (6) Mounting of the sample in glycerol jelly. Each stage of the procedure was preceded and followed by thorough sample cleaning in filtered distilled water. Quality control is maintained by periodic checking of residues and assembling sample batches from various depths to test for systematic laboratory effects. Pollen grains and spores were identified using the Royal Holloway (University of London) pollen type collection and the following sources of keys and photographs (Moore *et al.* 1991; Reille 1992). Plant nomenclature follows the *Flora Europaea* as summarised in Stace (1997). The assessment procedure consisted of scanning the prepared slides at 2mm intervals along the whole length of the coverslip and recording the concentration and state of preservation of pollen grains and spores, and the principal pollen taxa (Appendix 9).

Results

The results of the pollen assessment are presented in Appendix 9.

Samples {29} to {31} Only sample {31} from the feet area contained a very small amount of pollen, which was identified as pine.

Samples {32} to {42} The remaining samples ({32} to {42}), from the pelvis, skull, context [237], area of the possible necklace, top of the skull and from context [205], contained no pollen grains.

Samples {1} to {28} The results clearly indicate that the samples removed from the stomach and intestinal areas contain a higher pollen concentration. However, the proportion of grains having high sporopollenin content and complex, thickened exine suggests that the assemblage is biased in favour of grains that are more resistant to decay. Nevertheless, despite the evidence for differential preservation, and based on the assumption that these grains are representative of plants growing on or around the settlement during the Roman period, they indicate the presence of weeds belonging to the daisy (*Lactuceae*) and carrot (*Apiaceae*) families, as well as bindweed. These pollen grains would have been incorporated within the coffin either as a component of airborne pollen that settled on the surface of the body, or as a component of those pollen grains ingested, either as part of a meal or within swallowed mucous. The presence of cereal pollen is especially interesting because this may indicate that cereals were not only being cultivated locally, but that the pollen was ingested as part of a meal e.g. bread.

Conclusions

The results indicate that pollen found within the stomach and intestinal area of the body is clearly better preserved and in higher concentration that the 'control samples'. However, the results also indicate that the assemblage is biased in favour of grains that are more resistant to decay. Nevertheless, the results provide some useful information on the former local vegetation cover and possibly the diet of the adult female. There is no evidence for an 'exotic preparation' in the stomach or intestinal contents, which would have possibly been suggestive of special ritual/religious practices prior to death.

3.23 The strontium and oxygen stable isotope analysis

Jane Evans

Given the unusual nature of the burial in the mausoleum it was considered desirable to pursue isotopic analysis of the human remains, in order to answer questions about the possible childhood origins of this individual. Accordingly, a second molar was submitted to the British Geological Survey for oxygen and strontium isotope analysis. Such analysis does not routinely feature in developer funded projects of this sort, although it is becoming more common, and this work was not part of the original research design for this project. Fortunately the 'Empires and After Research Strand' in History, Classics and Archaeology kindly provided a small grant to enable this work.

Methodology

Sample preparation

The enamel surface of the tooth was abraded from the surface down to a depth of >100 microns, using a tungsten carbide dental bur, and the removed material discarded. Enamel was cut from the cleaned area using a flexible diamond edged rotary dental saw. All surfaces were mechanically cleaned, with a diamond bur, to remove adhering dentine. About 30 milligrams of enamel were taken for Sr and O isotope analysis, 3 milligrams of which was ground to a power in an agate mortar and Pestle for carbonate oxygen analysis. The enamel for Sr was transferred to a class 100 clean suite for further preparation. The sample was rinsed twice in de-ionized water, and left

to soak in water for an hour on a hot plate set at 60° C. Following this, the samples were placed in dilute (1% HNO_3) for 5 minutes and then rinsed twice using de-ionised water, dried and weighed into a pre-cleaned Teflon© beaker.

Sample chemistry for Sr isotope and concentration analysis

The sample was mixed with [84]Sr tracer solution and dissolved in Teflon© distilled 16M HNO_3. After evaporation to dryness, the sample was converted to chloride form by addition of Teflon© distilled 6MCl and taken up in 2.5MHCl. Sr was collected using Eichrom© AG50 X8 resin (Dickin 1985). Strontium was loaded onto a single Re Filament following the method of (Birck 1986) and the isotope composition and strontium concentrations were determined by Thermal Ionisation Mass spectroscopy (TIMS) using a Thermo Triton multi-collector mass spectrometer. The international standard for [87]Sr/[86]Sr, NBS987, gave a value of 0.710262 ± .000020 (2SD, n=8) during the analysis of these samples and the data are corrected to the accepted value of 0.710250. Data are presented in Table 3.47.

The chemical preparation and isotope analysis of oxygen in structural carbonate

For the isotopic analysis of phosphate carbonate oxygen, approximately 3 milligrams of prepared enamel was loaded into a glass vial and sealed with septa. The vials are transferred to a hot block at 90°C on the GV Multiprep system. The vials are evacuated and 4 drops of anhydrous phosphoric acid are added. The resultant CO_2 was collected cryogenically for 15 minutes and transferred to a GV IsoPrime dual inlet mass spectrometer.

$\delta^{18}O$ is reported as per mil (‰) ($^{18}O/^{16}O$) normalized to the PDB scale using a within-run calcite laboratory standard (KCM), calibrated against NBS-19 IAEA reference material. Values were converted to the SMOW scale using the published conversion equation of (Coplen 1988): SMOW = (1.03091 x $\delta^{18}O_{VPDB}$) +30.91. Analytical reproducibility for the laboratory standard calcite (KCM) is: $\delta^{18}O_{SMOW}$ = ± 0.03‰ (1σ, n=14) and $\delta^{13}C_{PDB}$ is ± 0.01‰ (1σ, n=14). The external reproducibly is estimated from the duplicate sample pairs run during the analysis, whose average reproducibility was ± 0.18‰ (2SD, n=7). The carbonate oxygen results $\delta^{18}Ov_{SMOW(c)}$ are additionally converted phosphate values $\delta^{18}Ov_{SMOW(p)}$ using the equation of (Chenery *et al.* 2012): ($\delta^{18}Ov_{SMOW(p)}$ = 1.0322*$\delta^{18}Ov_{SMOW(c)}$ – 9.6849). Data are presented in Table 1.

Table 3.47 Result of the Sr and O analysis

Name	Chemistry code	Sr ppm	87Sr/86Sr	δ13C (‰) PDB	δ18O (‰)carb SMOW	δ18O (‰)phos SMOW
KKGF-03	P914:2	116	0.70852	-12.0	25.9	17.0

Results

The results are presented in Table 3.47. Fig. 3.91 is based on an interactive Isotope Biosphere Map (Evans *et al.* 2018) to highlight, in dark grey, the areas of Britain that cannot be excluded as possible site of childhood origin for this individual. The uncertainties associated with this interpretation are documented in Evans *et al.* (2018). In summary, the oxygen isotope domains represent the 1SD (66%) of the data used to define the domain and the Sr data uses the IQR of the Sr data allocated to the domains based on the relationship between plant and human data given in Evans *et al.* 2012.

The strontium isotope composition of this tooth enamel is indicative of spending a childhood on a Chalk based area, when considering English origins. Such values can also be found in areas underlain by basalt but these do not exist with sufficient spatial extend in southern Britain to provide a realistic option (Fig. 3.91).

The oxygen isotope composition of $\delta^{18}O$ (‰)$_{phos\ SMOW}$ = 17.02 is within the 2SD range of oxygen British isotope compositions (Evans *et al.* 2012). More specifically the value is with the range given for this part of Britain (Evans *et al.* 2018) albeit very much on the margin of this oxygen zone. Ringlemere, Kent provides the nearest Anglo Saxons dataset for comparison, giving $\delta^{18}O$ (‰)$_{phos\ SMOW}$ 18.24 +/- 0.48 (Brettell *et al.* 2012) however there is uncertainty as to whether these values indicate a non-local origin. It should be noted that while the sample value is consistent with a British origin it does not rule out origin in much of Europe (Lightfoot and O'Connell 2016).

Fig. 3.91 Areas in England (shaded dark grey) that cannot be excluded as the childhood origin of this individual based on combined strontium and oxygen isotope composition

The combined strontium and oxygen isotope results show that areas close to the excavation site cannot be excluded as a childhood origin for this individual; however, it should be noted that such values are not exclusive and can be found elsewhere in Europe.

Chapter 4

Discussion

Phase 2: Prehistoric

The site was occasionally visited and utilised by people in the millennia from the Mesolithic until the Late Iron Age. Evidence for the character of those activities is lacking, but it is reasonable to assume that the area was utilised for hunting, gathering and later farming and grazing. Flint cores demonstrate that some flint-knapping took place and the burnt stone from pit [638] might suggest the heating of water and preparation of food.

Phase 3: Late Iron Age

During the Late Iron Age Kent was apparently inhabited by a group known to us from Classical sources as the *Cantii* (for the challenges of understanding Late Iron Age identity and social structure see Moore 2011). In the aftermath of Caesar's invasions, the south-east of Britain and the Greater Thames Estuary became the primary zone of contact between the Roman Empire and indigenous groups (for instance Millett 1990, 9–39; Mattingly 2007, 47–83). Large central places known to archaeologists as *oppida*, developed at Canterbury and probably Rochester too (Champion 2007, 123) and over the water at Colchester (Essex). These sites seem to have been *foci* of trade, exchange, craft and industrial production combined with elements of settlement, specialised ritual and high-status activities such as coin minting. As the region was drawn into ever closer networks of cross-channel interaction it seems likely that economic production intensified (Champion 2007, 129–132; Hathwaway 2013).

At Grange Farm the Late Iron Age saw the development of the first formal enclosure systems, along with scattered pits containing quantities of occupation debris, stakeholes and hearths that would seem to be indicative of settlement activity. The fragmentary nature of the evidence means that any interpretation must, of necessity, be tentative. The division of the landscape into enclosures was perhaps driven by a need to define the use and ownership, or rights to land in a more intense fashion than had hitherto been the case. It seems also likely that these enclosures may have allowed for a more intensive regime of agricultural production. One of the functions of ditched field systems is to drain the land and drainage,

as evidenced by the post-medieval French drains, was arguably a necessity on the clayey brickearth based soils if arable agriculture was to be practiced.

In summary, the Late Iron Age activity is difficult to define precisely but it can be linked to the increasing intensification of economic activity and settlement in Kent during the Late Iron Age. The position of the site, on the interface between the rich marshes to the north, where wildfowl, rushes, salt and other resources existed in abundance, and the dryland suitable for arable and pastoral farming to the south perhaps explains the choice of location.

Phase 4: Early Roman *c.* AD 43–100/120

The earliest years of the Roman period saw the tide of military conquest sweep through Kent. Watling Street, the major arterial route connecting Canterbury and the Channel ports with the Thames crossing at London, was a major supply route and laid out in the very earliest years of the conquest, probably following a prehistoric route (Millett 2007, 148–149 and fig 5.9). The road passed 2.5 kilometres to the south of the site but crossed the Medway at Rochester, an important Iron Age location (Harrison 1991) and probably the site of a Roman fort during this phase (Burnham & Wacher 1990, 77–78). The presence of the garrison and the traffic along the road probably had a very destabilising effect on the local region. Recent scholarship would emphasise the bloody nature of the conquest and the expropriation of land and resources by the new imperial power (Mattingly 2007, 92–94; James 2011). The so-called 'Battle of the Medway', an opposed river crossing recorded by Dio (*Roman History* LX.20; Cary & Foster 2014, 417–419), may have been a very local manifestation of conquest in AD43.

In archaeological terms the creation of Watling Street and the fort, followed by the development of a town at Rochester represent one manifestation of Roman imperialism. Another manifestation of this process might be the abandonment of the Iron Age settlement at Iwade (11km to the east) (Bishop & Bagwell 2005, 130). Out on the marshes other changes were occurring. In the Late Iron Age the lower reaches of the Medway appear to have been heavily exploited for salt production (Hathaway 2013, 270). There is also evidence for Late Iron Age pottery production in the littoral zone (Monaghan

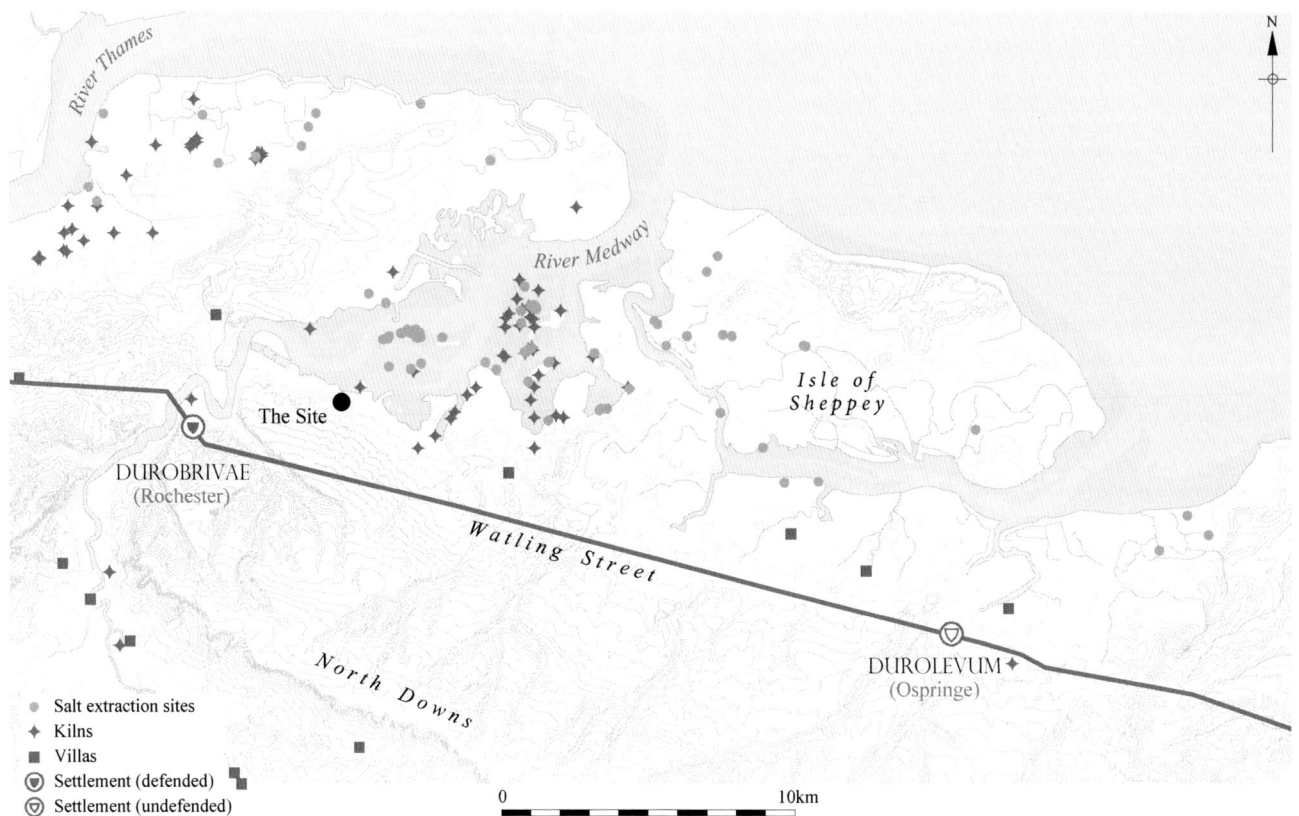

Fig. 4.1   Pottery and salt production sites in the Medway (scale 1:250,000)

1987, 215). Both of these 'industries' are likely to have been the archaeologically visible elements of complex and potentially seasonal economic networks based on foodstuffs and agricultural products (Gerrard 2008; Biddulph 2017). The exploitation of these existing productive networks probably occurred in the first decades of the Roman Conquest. On the Hoo Peninsula a new pottery industry developed, almost certainly due to the transfer of knowledge and labour from Continental Europe, producing specialist fineware flagons with a wide regional distribution (Applegate 2015). Other technological changes, such as the widespread adoption of the potter's wheel and the abandonment of flint-tempering had all occurred by the late first century (Monaghan 1987, 216).

These developments were all within a short distance of the land at Grange Farm and the Nor Marshes, not far to the north-east of the site, contain both evidence of salt working and pottery production (Hathaway 2013, table 5.2 and fig 10.3.5). It seems reasonable to interpret Phase 4 as a consequence of the developing Romano-British interest in the economic potential of the region. The new enclosure systems may point to an increasingly formalised landscape and, possibly, further significant changes in the way that the ownership and rights to land were perceived. The large post-built Building 1 may be indicative of a new architectural style. Potentially these changes may have been accompanied by the relocation of people. Whether those people were from the local area, or further afield within Britain or beyond remains difficult

to ascertain, as does their status. The pottery includes locally-produced material and some small quantities of imported wares; there is nothing in any of the other finds assemblages to suggest a particularly unusual or high-status site, although the zoomorphic mount <896> is a noteworthy piece (Gerrard, small finds, above). Probably we are looking at a situation in which a decision was made by some authority, be that individual, familial, communal or state, to exploit an under-utilised part of the landscape. The need to pay taxes, feed resource-hungry military garrisons and developing urban centres in the region may all have encouraged this re-configuring of the landscape.

Phase 5: AD 100/120–150

The early second century was a time of transformation for the Roman province of *Britannia*. Urban centres were developing apace, and the army was becoming concentrated in the upland regions of Britain. For the Medway estuary the most important development was the importation of ceramic influences from the Black Burnished ware (BB1) producers of south-east Dorset. Thameside pottery producers now set themselves to manufacturing 'BB2': wheel-thrown imitations of these BB1 vessels (Monaghan 1987; Pollard 1988; Tyers 1996). Salt production continued, perhaps now concentrated on fewer more centralised locations (Hathaway 2013, 467), and, as in Dorset (Gerrard 2008), seems to have been intimately linked to pottery production (Fig. 4.1).

From the Hadrianic period onwards both BB1 and BB2 are found in considerable quantities in London (Davies *et al.* 1994, 107) and also on military sites along the Northern Frontier (Gillam 1976). Even the large North Kent Shell Tempered Ware jars are found, not only in London, but also at South Shields, and elsewhere in the north (for instance Davies *et al.* 1994, 101–102; Bidwell & Speak 1994, 230). Traditional interpretations would see this as the pottery producers of Dorset and the Thames Estuary winning 'contracts' to supply the military. More recent research would emphasise the pottery as the archaeologically visible signature of the movement of meat, cereals, salted products and other archaeologically invisible commodities from agriculturally productive parts of the province to support the garrisons in the north and west (Gerrard 2008; Smith *et al.* 2016, 410). The precise mechanism for this movement of goods can be disputed, although it is difficult to argue that the hand of the Roman state and the provincial administration was not involved at some level.

At Grange Farm the second century manifested itself in the form of two large rectilinear enclosures with a north–south alignment that seems to be replicated in the landscape to the modern day (Rippon *et al.* 2015). The seemingly regular and planned nature of these enclosures hints that this development was part of some larger reorganisation of the lower Medway's region's economy. At the western end of Enclosure 5 a large pit full of oyster shells, BB2 and other pottery suggests, along with the plough-truncated remnants of a timber roundhouse, that people were living at the site. Presumably this population exploited both the dryland and the marshes raising crops and grazing animals across these ecological zones.

Even more importantly the large holloway indicates a routeway carrying heavy traffic on a north-south axis. What could this traffic be? The most meaningful explanation is that packhorses, carts and wagons, evidenced by the solitary linch-pin <417>, carried sacks of grain and beans from the dryland to the south to the Gillingham Reach. Alongside this we can probably envisage herds of cattle, sheep and pigs being driven into the littoral zone for slaughter and salting. Salt-producing sites to the north seem to have been preserving beef for export; over the estuary to the west an early Roman droveway on the Hoo peninsula may point to a similar interest in the movement of animals (Jones *et al.* 2011, 19).

If there was a small landing-place, analogous to the 'hythe' or 'creek' of later periods (for which see Jones 2011, 67–70), in the Gillingham Reach as there was during the medieval period (Draper & Meddens 2014) then this would make the site analogous to the setting of Northfleet villa, with its associated buildings and quayside providing access to Ebbsfleet and the Thames (Biddulph *et al.* 2011, 213–230). It may further be supposed that the holloway at Gillingham was a route linking the river ultimately with Watling Street to the south. Such a route would have 'cut the corner' by avoiding Rochester and a long Medway passage. It would have allowed vessels similar to the Blackfriars I boat (Marsden 1994, 33–96), which carried

a cargo of Kentish rag, the opportunity to load cargoes to feed the hungry population of *Londinium* and the voracious appetites of the army in the north. Such cargoes may have been the primary loads, or supplementary cargo piggy-backing on bulky commodities like building stone. In return those same vessels might have travelled ballasted with the bricks and tiles made in the London area (Sudds, this volume) and the various forms of imported pottery.

Phase 6: AD 150–250

The mid-second to mid-third century covers the period time from the reign of Antoninus Pius and the construction of the Antonine Wall to the middle of the period traditionally known as the Third Century Crisis. The most important aspect of this imperial narrative for our site was the continuing demands on resources exerted by the northern frontier. Evidence for the impact of this comes from the quantities of BB2 found on the Antonine Wall and also in Severan deposits in the north. The granaries constructed on the banks of the Tyne at *Arbeia* (South Shields) in the Severan period point to the scale of supplies required to feed a campaigning imperial army (Bidwell & Speak 1994, 28–32). It seems likely that some of the meat, grain, leather, salt, pottery and other commodities were drawn from the Thames Estuary region and travelled northwards by sea along the eastern coast of Britain. The construction of the forts at Reculver, Kent (Philp 2005) and Brancaster, Norfolk (Hinchcliffe & Sparey Green 1985) in the early third century probably also points to the importance of this east coast route. Civilian demand, centred on the major local urban centres of London, Canterbury and Colchester, also continued.

The Phase 6 activity at the site arguably echoes these broader themes of continuity. The Phase 5 enclosures continued in use and there is some evidence for an expansion of agricultural activity with the creation of Enclosure 8. The most striking aspect of this phase is the significant effort that was expended to metal the route through the holloway with many wagon-loads of flint nodules and stones. This stopped the continued downcutting and erosion of the track and converted it into an all-weather road surface, which would seem to indicate that heavy and continuing use was anticipated. If so, then the hypothesized movement of foodstuffs and animals down to the Gillingham Reach must have continued.

The seeming importance of the road is somewhat at odds with the evidence for the erosion of the road surface and the erection of posts across its line in the south. There is a genuine sense, at its most extreme in this phase, that considerable elements of the site are missing, having been ploughed away. The finds assemblages, for instance, would indicate a population living and working at the site but there are no traces of buildings that can be assigned to this phase. To this end, it may be hypothesized that the edges of the road, which were not defined by ditches to the south here, were demarcated by hedgerows. Following the interpretation advocated (albeit with some reservations) above, it might be supposed that the structures crossing the line of the road worked seasonally, or episodically, to block access. The erosion of the road surface suggests large numbers of animals milling around and thus it may be that this was a point where herded animals driven along the road were separated for some reason or reasons. Perhaps the herds were split up here for onward travel to the salterns for slaughter or salting. As part of this process it may be that the number, types or conditions of the animals had to be checked or recorded. All of this could account for the postholes and the erosion of the road surface.

At the end of the phase considerable quantities of occupation debris were deposited over the eroded road surface. This may represent an attempt at consolidating the surface. However, the changes that were to occur in Phase 7 suggest that it may be better to interpret these dumps of pottery, metal objects, animal bone and the like as the clearance of waste that had accumulated during Phase 6. Such a 'tidying up' of the site might occur before a major period of redevelopment.

Phase 7: AD 250–325/350

The changes wrought during the third century resolved themselves in the early fourth century into a recast Roman imperial system (for instance McGill *et al.* 2010). This transition from the *principate* (early Roman period) to the *dominate* (the late Roman period) has been well studied. In Britain fundamental changes in the nature of urban life and the ways in which economic production were organised seem to have occurred, although the reasons for these changes are not so clear (Millett 1990; Mattingly 2007). Recent work has emphasised the third century as a period of settlement contraction in Kent (Andrews *et al.* 2015, 361–364, Smith *et al.* 2016, 81–82, fig 4.7). Major roadside settlements at Springhead and Westhawk Farm (near Ashford) seem to have been abandoned and this has been linked to a decline in urban vitality at London and Canterbury and a consequent decrease in road traffic (Smith *et al.* 2016, 82).

In North Kent changes seem to have been afoot in the marshes. The production of BB2 and TSK seems to have been in decline during the third century (Monaghan 1987, 227–230) and more or less ceased by the early fourth century (Pollard 1988, 176–177). At Oakleigh Farm, 8km to the north-west on the far side of the Medway, the latest excavated BB2 kilns seem to have been producing pottery into the middle of the third century, but not for long after (Catherall 1983). Salt production may also have begun to decline in this region. Far fewer third- and fourth-century salterns are known, although this may simply be a consequence of early Roman salt producing technologies leaving far more archaeologically visible residues (Hathaway 2013, 275–276).

The traditional interpretation of these phenomena would argue that they are symptomatic of late Roman decline (for a discussion of these approaches see Gerrard 2013). In particular, external threats from across the North Sea would be emphasised and seen as a causal factor in the creation of coastal fortifications, the walling of towns (such as Rochester and Canterbury) and the decline of economic production in exposed littoral zones. Such explanations are overly simplistic and other factors were at work in the region. It may well be that dislocations and realignments in long-distance exchange networks from the Rhine to the Thames and from the Thames to the north, caused by transformations in local economic systems and the changing economic status of London, had as much to do with the decline of pottery production in North Kent as extra-systemic threats.

The late Roman period at Grange Farm speaks directly to some of these topics. Instead of evidence for abandonment and settlement retrenchment there seems to be a new settlement pattern involving a monumental funerary structure, as well as far more archaeologically visible and robust styles of domestic architecture. Here, on the fringes of the Medway Estuary, the story of the late Roman period is not one of decline. Instead, significant change and development can be discerned and this activity is of considerable importance.

The western side of the holloway was demarcated and revetted in this phase by a well-built mortared wall of flint, which – the evidence of the Phase 9 demolition spreads suggests – was of some height. To the west of the holloway, the now silted or filled in enclosures of Phases 5 and 6, were recreated with walls. This at the very least would indicate long-standing continuity of landholding and property division. Nevertheless, the decision to use walls, rather than simply recutting the ditches or maintaining hedges, requires some explanation, especially as building stone is not readily available in Kent. As a consequence, these enclosure walls, unlike the boundary/revetment walls demarcating the holloway, may, at least in places, have been built from cob.

The only advantage that a wall holds over a ditch or a hedge is that it provides a solid and impenetrable barrier that also blocks line of sight. Walled enclosures are known from a number of late Roman rural sites and are usually interpreted as bounding settlement *foci* (for instance Maull *et al.* 2005; Chapman & Atkins 2005). One exception to this pattern is the roadside settlement at Catsgore (Somerset), where early Roman ditched enclosures alongside a road were replaced with walls in the late Roman period (Leech 1982). However, Catsgore was a nucleated roadside settlement and each walled plot was densely occupied with domestic buildings fronting the road. Thus it was quite different in character to Grange Farm.

One possible explanation for the walling of Enclosures 5, 6 and 8 is that those enclosures were used to grow fruit trees in the late Roman period. Bullace, cherries, damsons, plums, apples and pears are all Roman introductions and were well-established by the third century (van der Veen *et al.* 2008). Evidence for the large-scale consumption of fruits has been found at some urban sites (Robinson *et al.* 2006, 215; Livarda & Orengo 2015) but evidence for fruit production is less clear-cut and restricted to the interpretation of features as bedding trenches (Allen *et al.* 2017, 72–73). The production of fruit on a large scale might require walled enclosures to protect the trees from the elements. Unfortunately the only archaeological evidence in support of this interpretation are the so-called pruning-hooks (Gerrard, small finds, this volume), all of which are from late Roman or early medieval contexts, and some fragments of charcoal from trees of the *Maloideae* family (Hégarat & Mooney, this volume). A thoroughly Classical reference to walled orchards can be found in Ovid's description (*Metamorphoses* IV.646) of Atlas's fruit trees and orchard, which was enclosed with 'massive walls'. If nothing else, it suggests that a walled orchard is at least a possibility in Roman Britain.

Within a walled orchard it would be usual in traditional agriculture to intercrop or graze the grass beneath the trees. This means that the productive capacity of one piece of land could be increased. Fruits would also be a valuable export commodity when in season, or out of season if dried or preserved in honey. Such a trade occurred during the sixteenth century when orchards in Kent, including land at Gillingham, supplied London and Southwark with fruit. This analogy with a late period does not prove the interpretation advanced above, but it does demonstrate that it was not impossible for such a trade to operate at an earlier date (Mate 2006, 46–47). The walling of these enclosures may thus represent a diversification of economic strategy and a response to the dislocation of the early Roman economic networks.

To the east of the road the enclosure (Enclosure 10) was occupied, almost for the first time, by robust traces of buildings. The eastern half of the enclosure was occupied by a timber building of uncertain plan and function and the western half by a large aisled building. This, although badly ploughed out, would probably have had a multi-purpose domestic function. Current thinking would interpret these structures as a 'hybrid' architectural style and it may have functioned as the major communal domestic residence for an extended kin-group (Taylor 2001, 2013; Wallace 2018). Certainly, the traces of tile flooring at the southern end conform to Taylor's (2001, fig 14) model of the use of space within these buildings. The hearth features have been assigned to Phase 8 (below) but some of these could conceivably have functioned in Phase 7 and their location would also conform to Taylor's model.

The creation of this aisled building marks a major change in the architectural arrangements of the site and it is unfortunate that it was not better preserved. Moving inland from the river a traveller would be funnelled between the aisled building on the left and the substantial revetment and boundary wall on the right. What is most surprising and testament to a fundamental change in the organisation of activity was the creation of a substantial wall [852] that blocked the dog-leg of the holloway,

essentially turning it into a cul-de-sac. Beyond the wall the old metalled surfaces of the road seem to have become little more than rubbish-strewn yard surfaces (Open Area 1) for the inhabitants of the aisled building and the building further to the east. At the end of the road, in the space bounded on three sides by walls industrial type activities associated with heat and metalworking seem to have occurred. It is possible that this space may have been partially roofed. Pentice-roofs supported by upright timbers set on robbed-out post-pads (no traces of which survive) could run along the boundary walls providing open-sided shelters. The excavators considered the deposits in this area to be 'floors' and thus thought that they were internal surfaces. As to the function of this area, the balance of probability would strongly suggest that it may have been a smithy (Keys, this volume).

The location of this potential smithy, close to but separated from the mausoleum (see below), is also of note. To modern eyes the mixing of 'industrial' and 'funerary' practices seems peculiar. Yet in late Roman Britain there is good evidence for metalworking occupying what had previously been high-status locations, particularly in towns (Rogers 2011, 130–148) but also in villas. How this phenomenon should be interpreted is a debate beyond the scope of this volume (Gerrard 2013). Nevertheless, it is worth considering the ambiguous cultural position of smiths in many societies and their wider cosmological importance (Wright 2019). In this case the proximity of a smithy to a high-status burial could be explained by reference to the liminality of both metalworking and funerary ritual and remembrance. Of course, the chronology of the mausoleum is impossible to establish with certainty. If the metalworking ceased *c.* AD 265 and the mausoleum was built *c.* AD 310 the juxtaposition of the two may be irrelevant.

In economic terms the evidence for metalworking, regardless of whether Hearth [833] was actually a smithy or not, is such that it can be considered indicative of 'prolonged and frequent' ferrous metalworking (Keys, this volume). This blacksmithing may have been intended to serve the boats and ships on the river to the north as well as local demand. The blacksmith (or blacksmiths) may also have engaged in, or worked alongside, non-ferrous metalworking and particularly the cupellation of argentiferous bronze alloys to extract silver. It remains uncertain what objects these argentiferous copper-alloys were derived from. Coins seem an unlikely source as after the early third century many hundreds of billon coins would need to undergo cupellation to produce an appreciable quantity of silver. The resulting litharge assemblage, the biggest so far recovered from a Roman site in Britain (Dungworth, this volume), is poorly stratified. Nevertheless, its presence in the upper deposits within Open Area 1 suggests that some of this silver-refining was taking place during this phase and someone on the site was managing the production of silver ingots. What those ingots were destined for remains a mystery. Possibly they were refashioned by silversmiths into late Roman silver plate or used to pay rents or taxes.

The mixed arable/pastoral economy apparent in the biological remains seems to have continued into this phase with little change. However, there is some slight evidence for an increase in hunting in Phases 7 and 8. This may suggest that the inhabitants of the site had aspirations of higher status in these phases (Cool 2006, 111–118). All of the red deer and some of the roe deer bones are from Late Roman contexts and goose, duck and hare bones were found in Phase 7 contexts south of the aisled building and in Open Area 1. The ditch north of that building also produced a skinned otter and parts of two badger skeletons. These animals point to the exploitation of different kinds of habitat. The deer would be found in woodlands and open land; the badgers in woods and hedgerows in farmland, the hares from open land, the otters, geese and ducks from the river and the estuary. The hunting of these animals was probably occasional and opportunistic and points to the ecological zones being visited and exploited by the inhabitants of the site.

The otter and the badger deserve some further comment. Both were presumably hunted for their fur. Fur clothing was traditionally viewed as 'barbarian dress' in the Roman Empire, but during the late imperial period what can be termed 'barbarian chic' was coming into vogue, particularly in the militarized elements of frontier communities (for instance Halsall 2007, 110). Fur might also be worn by those on the fringes of society or used to manufacture specific garments such as hats. Badgers have been identified in Roman deposits in Exeter (Maltby 1979, 65) and were probably hunted for their skins, which were given a low value in Diocletian's *Prices Edict* (*Prices Edict* 8.29–30; Graser 1975, 49) and are known to have been manufactured into hats in the Roman period (Lewis & Llewelyn Jones 2017). Badger meat was also consumed, although it was seen as a mean meal, the poorest game one could eat (Lewis & Llewelyn Jones 2017). Other uses are also plausible: badger fur was used until recently to make brushes and their musk was valued in Gaul during late Antiquity (Lewis & Llewelyn Jones 2017). Otter fur may similarly have been used to make hats.

Alongside the living, the farming, the blacksmithing and the hunting there was also dying. For the generations of people who lived and worked at the site during the Roman period there is very little biological evidence. No cemetery was identified. Instead, during the late Roman period a mausoleum, essentially a house - to insert a category below Brown's 'very special dead' of holy men and martyrs (1981, 69–85) - for the 'special dead', was built. The structure may have been imposing and the form of its foundations suggests that it was tall and visible from the Medway to the north. Other excavated mausolea in Kent and beyond would suggest that the structure would have been rendered with plaster and perhaps decorated internally, although little plaster survived. A painted plaster scheme would certainly be in keeping with the unusual evidence for a plain red tessellated floor within the building. The only other hint of embellishment comes from a block of Bath Stone, which might derive from the mausoleum (Hayward, this volume).

The mausoleum marked the last resting place of a small number of individuals. Of these, there is good evidence for only one: the middle-aged to elderly woman whose mortal remains were contained within a lead-lined coffin. Of this individual we know little, except that she was of a slight build, had lost some of her teeth and suffered from osteoarthritis in her right hand and spine. Isotopic analyses of origins indicate that she grew up on chalkland and thus may well have been born locally to the site although an origin further afield in parts of Europe remains possible. Isotopic analyses of diet are lacking due to resource constraints. It is also impossible to determine her religious beliefs from the surviving evidence. What can be stated with reasonable certainty is that she was held in high esteem by those that chose to bury her in a ostentatious fasion in a lead-lined coffin within a decoratively embellished stone-built mausoleum. Other individuals may have been buried in the mausoleum, in shallower graves, or had their remains stored above ground in sarcophagi contained within the building. One of those individuals may have been buried with two gold necklaces <233> and <234>, which, given the evidence for wear and modification (Hobbs, this volume), were probably heirlooms (for an alternative interpretation see below).

The Late Antique veneration and commemoration of the dead was a phenomenon associated with both pagans and Christians alike. This is perhaps best seen at Lullingstone (Kent) where a mausoleum was closely associated with the important villa complex (Meates 1979, 122–131). In the extra-mural cemetery of Poundbury (Dorchester, Dorset) mausolea seem to have been elite burial locations (Farwell & Molleson 1993), with skeletons producing isotopic values interpretable as evidence of high-status diets (Richards *et al.* 1998). Certainly the lead-lined coffin, tessellated floor and possibly the gold jewellery could indicate that those buried at Grange Farm were 'elite' individuals. Yet, and with the exception of the aisled building, the site has produced no evidence of high-status structures. It is also relevant to note that the mausoleum occupied the south-eastern corner of an enclosure, a location that enabled it to overlook both the sunken road and aisled building. However, the boundary wall that ran along the side of the road would have restricted access to the mausoleum. The mausoleum was thus intimately part of the built environment of the settlement but at the same time physically separated from it.

The evidence allows for two contradictory interpretations to be presented. The mausoleum and its occupant(s) may simply have been members of the landowning elite. The woman buried in the lead-lined coffin would, in this interpretation, be broadly analogous to the 'Lady Juliana' remembered on one of the gold bracelets from the Hoxne Hoard (Johns 2010, 166). She could have been the mother, wife or sister of a local landowner, or the landowner herself, and buried in such a location that her tomb was a constant reminder to her clients in the aisled building and those travelling from the river to the settlement, or up and down the Medway, of her family's power and claim to the land. Alternatively, the woman and the other potential occupants of the mausoleum may have been important members of the community living on the site. Taylor (2001, 2013) has emphasised the 'hybrid' nature of aisled buildings and perhaps the kinds of social structure that accompanied them were different from our perceptions of Romano-British norms. In this situation the occupants of the mausoleum may have been 'elite', not because of their personal power or wealth, but because of their roles within the settlement and local community. This could make the elderly woman a matriarchal type figure, a decision-maker, with a store of knowledge and lore; or someone who was revered because of their piety, intelligence and standards of behaviour (Grey 2011, 45). Under this interpretation the boundary wall would separate the 'special dead' from the hustle and bustle of the aisled building and road. Choosing between these interpretations is a matter of personal preference. A 'third way' might consider that an elderly landowner or patron might be revered by her clients because of her standards of behaviour and wisdom.

Phase 7 shows a thriving and economically successful coastal community, seemingly unhindered by threats of barbarian raiding, and engaging in a variety of economic activities. Farming, metalworking and hunting all functioned as part of the suite of activities that this group of people living by the shores of the lower Meday practised in the late third and early fourth centuries. Their connections to Rochester, the villas of Kent and the Medway Valley, the shore forts at Reculver, Richborough, or the big urban centres of Canterbury, Colchester and London are less clear, but the routeway down to the river continued in use, even if it now terminated at the settlement. This surely shows the continued pre-eminence of riverine communications during this phase.

Phase 8: AD 325/350–AD 400/450

The orthodox narrative of the late fourth and early fifth centuries focusses on political and military instability in late Roman Britain coupled with economic difficulties, culminating in Britain being sundered from the Western Roman Empire *c.* AD 410. From the middle of the fifth century onwards, whatever was left began to fall under the control of various barbarian groups from northern Germany, whom we anachronistically describe as Anglo-Saxons (Gerrard 2013).

At Grange Farm the late fourth and early fifth centuries seem to represent a continuation of the activity visible in Phase 7. At the heart of the site stood the aisled building. This structure may have changed its function, if the hearths really do all belong in this phase, but even so the outlook of the structure remains entirely domestic and in keeping with the way other aisled buildings were used.

Around the building parts of the enclosure system created in Phase 7 seem to have been undergoing modification, this suggests a certain dynamism to activity at the site and it is unfortunate that there is not more evidence of what was happening in the eastern half of the site during this phase.

To the south of the aisled building in Open Area 1 little seems to have been happening. This was covered in occupation debris, perhaps from activities centred on Hearth structure [833], at the end of Phase 7 but this dumping seems to have ceased. Large pits, running parallel to the line of the aisled building's west wall and bordering the road, were dug during this phase and contained assemblages of late-fourth- or early-fifth century material. Possibly these represent a change in standards of waste disposal at the end of the fourth century and an explanation for why rubbish dumping did not continue in Open Area 1. Alternatively, it may be that the material redeposited in Phase 9 layer [201] included the late-fourth-century and early-fifth-century midden spreads generated by the inhabitants of the site.

To the west of the aisled building the road continued in use and still ran down towards the river, with late-fourth-century material culture accumulating on its surface. This surely implies that connections with the river remained important. Some support for this comes from the pottery assemblages, which includes small numbers of imported vessels from the Argonne and Eifel regions. The Oxfordshire wares are also likely to have reached the site by boat via the Thames and London (Fulford & Hodder 1975).

The road remained bounded on its southern and western sides by the walled enclosures. There is little evidence for activity within these boundary walls but that means nothing by itself. As has been argued above, any traces of occupation or other activities must have been ploughed away. Along the eastern edge of Enclosure 8, where the road ran, a number of large pits were dug and filled with animal bone groups and late-fourth-century material culture. It is difficult to determine the function of these features: the articulated animal remains can be interpreted as the product of either mundane, or unusual social practices (Morris 2011). However, the pits and their contents are evidence that occupation within Enclosure 8 probably continued into the early fifth century

In economic terms the inhabitants continued to farm and occasionally hunt as they had in Phase 7. Iron-working seems to have continued if the dump [537] of slag and hammerscale at the southern terminus of the road at the end of Phase 8 or the beginning of Phase 9 is anything to go by. The ceramics from the site continued to include small quantities of material imported from Gaul and, like the rest of Kent at the time, the vast majority of the pottery assemblage continued to be drawn from a diverse range of sources. In keeping with the picture for London and the Thames Estuary this included material sourced from Oxfordshire, Bedfordshire and the Hampshire/Surrey region. For some this dependence on pottery kilns located far away signifies economic fragility, but it better demonstrates how trade and exchange was still taking place over long distances in lowland Britain at the end of the fourth century without fear of hindrance.

Fear is one thing that the site does not display during this or the preceding phase. Yet the inhabitants lived with a stone's throw of the Medway Estuary in the midst of what the *Notitia Dignitatum* described as the *Litus Saxonicum* (the Saxon Shore). Here it is worth considering the small collection of late Roman belt equipment from the site and just possibly the 'Anglo-Saxon' spearheads. Once upon a time these belt fittings and spearheads would have been seen as evidence for the presence of 'Germanic' barbarian mercenaries at the site. The same objects would now be seen as typically late Roman martial accoutrements. The fragment of chip-carved belt-plate may well have been manufactured in the Rhineland for someone in the Roman army. The other fragments of belt-buckle are purely insular types with a steadfastly lowland distribution. They point to individuals wearing military-style belts, but these people were not necessarily soldiers (Halsall 2007; Gerrard 2013). Instead, they were likely to be aping military fashions in a stylistic change that challenged long-standing norms within Romano-British provincial society. During the fifth century these changes would unfold into the shape and form of early medieval Europe.

Phase 9: AD 400/450–1050

The late fourth and early fifth centuries represent one of the most vexing periods in Britain's past (see Gerrard 2013 and references therein). In historical terms the narrative is usually framed in terms of the decline of Roman imperial power or the arrival of barbarian groups from what is now northern Germany who we anachronistically describe as 'Anglo-Saxons'. To say that this period is one of contested interpretations and significant differences of scholarly opinion would be an understatement. The archaeological difficulties surrounding the end of the fourth and the early fifth century are equally problematic. The decline of coin use in Roman Britain and the cessation of most coin supply between AD 388 and AD 402 make dating archaeological sequences and assemblages extremely difficult. The nature of the barbarian settlement and its chronology are also archaeologically contentious (for instance Hills 2006). Yet the volume of research on this period has never been greater and it is beginning to yield dividends. Work on both sites and material culture are beginning to throw the fifth century into sharper focus.

At Grange Farm the point at which Phase 8 ends and Phase 9 begins remains blurred. There is, for instance, no conclusive surviving evidence for when the aisled building was abandoned. It was still standing at the beginning of the fifth century and could have continued to be occupied for some decades after that date. Parallels for this come from Orton Hall Farm (Cambridgeshire) where the excavator consider late Roman aisled buildings

to have still been standing and useable in the early Anglo-Saxon period (Mackreth 1996, 39–41). Other excavations at Faversham (Kent) have produced Anglo-Saxon material from within an aisled structure (Wilkinson 2006) and an aisled-building at Fullerton (Hampshire) has produced an early- to mid-fifth-century supporting-arm brooch (Cunliffe & Poole 2008, fig 3.86 no. 1.15). At the southern end of the road the sherd of early medieval pottery of fifth to sixth century date, securely sealed beneath the collapse of the boundary walls, is the first appearance of the new post-Roman ceramic styles. Its association with sherds of the latest Roman pottery perhaps suggests this material was deposited in the first decades of the fifth century. If so, then the deposition of ferrous slags and hammerscale in this deposit is an indicator that blacksmithing continued into the early fifth century.

Layer [537] also contained 83 ceramic tesserae of the same type and dimensions as those recovered from the robbing of the mausoleum. The presence of these tesserae suggests that the tessellated pavement in the mausoleum had been broken up before the collapse or demolition of the enclosure walls. The deposit also contained human toe bones providing another link with the nearby funerary structure. Together this evidence may suggest that the opening of grave [231] and interference with the lead coffin lining may have occurred during the early fifth century. Why this might have been the case is a matter for debate. One possibility is that the coffin was robbed to remove any grave-goods and to recycle the lead from the lid. This is plausible and finds a parallel in the sequence at Lullingstone (Meates 1979, 124). However, it seems strange that the robbers did not remove the entire coffin. Nor was the burial heavily disturbed. Another possibility is that the coffin was disturbed so that the mortal remains of its occupant could be viewed. If she was a local notable and some memory of this survived into the fifth century it seems possible that elements of her skeleton might have become the focus for veneration. There is abundant evidence for the manipulation of corpses in the Roman period (for instance Crerar 2012) and the transition from this form of social practice to the veneration of relics in the cult of saints was but a small step.

Late Antique and early medieval texts contain some detail that is pertinent to the context of this discussion. Sulpicius Severus' late fourth-century *Life of St Martin*, includes a narrative of how Martin found a group of Christians mistakenly venerating a 'martyr's' tomb outside Tours (France). Martin having prayed, God allowed him to commune with the shade of the deceased, who confessed that he was in fact an executed robber (*Vita Martini* 11; Burton 2017, 107–108). Conversion-period Anglo-Saxon England contains a similar account, which was excluded from Bede's *Historia Ecclesiastica* for political reasons (Foley & Higham 2009, fn 107). St Augustine is recorded as having found a local Christian cult site in Kent, venerating a 'St Sixtus' (Stancliffe 1999, 121–123; Blair 2005, 24). He went on to supress this cult but it suggests that there were people in sixth-century who professed Christian belief in the pagan Kingdom of Kent. A Roman mausoleum and the 'special dead' within could provide a focus for such a cult, even if the dead within it had not originally been Christian (Morris 1989, 23–26). Bede (*Hist. Eccl.* IV.19) also has a story of relevance when he recounts how a magical marble (*ie* Roman) coffin was dug up near Cambridge in the seventh century to be reused as the container for the bones of St Aetheldreda. Interfering with the dead in pursuit of the cult of relics was an early medieval phenomenon.

It is difficult to escape the conclusion that the mausoleum, even if ruinous and haunted by a tawny owl, stood during the early medieval period as an important monument in the landscape. The almost inexplicable presence of a late-fifth-century gilded silver Nydam-style brooch in what was probably a patch of demolition rubble, or perhaps just possibly the fill of a shallow pit, is interpreted as 'some form of votive offering' (Gaimster, this volume), although casual loss remains a possibility. The proximity of the find to the mausoleum suggests that the deposition of the brooch was with reference to the ruined mausoleum in some way.

Votive deposition brings this discussion back to the two, probably third-century, gold necklaces from the robbing deposits of the mausoleum. If these necklaces originally accompanied a burial either within a sarcophagus stored above ground or within a shallow inhumation, it seems strange that these precious objects were not removed during the disturbance of these graves. An alternative is that these were valuable heirlooms deposited either for safe-keeping, or as part of a ritual act within the mausoleum. Hidden with a crack in the masonry it is easy to imagine how they might have been missed during the robbing of the building. When the necklaces were concealed is, of course, impossible to determine but the possibility that they are not disturbed grave-goods is worth considering.

The start of Phase 9 was argued above (Gerrard, the sequence) to be marked by the demolition, or collapse of the boundary walls into the holloway, sealing layer [537] and the road. In common with most rubble deposits sealing late Roman structures it is impossible to distinguish definitively between collapse through natural process and demolition due to human agency. In favour of the latter hypothesis was the lack of any stratigraphy indicative of abandonment between the latest Roman contexts and the extensive spreads of flint rubble. This suggests that little time had elapsed between the cessation of the latest Phase 8/earliest Phase 9 activities and deposition of the rubble. Another way of thinking about this is to consider how the collapse of Roman political and military power would cause boundary walls in Kent to fall over.

If the walls were demolished in the fifth century then it is logical to ask why people would undertake this task? The recycling of stone is the usual explanation, but fifth-century Kent is lacking in stone-built structures and in any case the flint was left where it fell. One possibility, and one that is offered (like so many interpretations advanced in this volume) only tentatively, is that the boundary walls were demolished to make the mausoleum more visible. If the mausoleum structure served as a landmark for vessels on the Gillingham Reach; if the mausoleum also held the remains of some person or ancestor considered to be 'special' and worthy of veneration; then, perhaps, opening up the vistas of that structure, or easing access to it, was important. These changes could apply equally to either indigenous communities or incomers as a means of connecting with ancestral powers to legitimise claims on the land (Williams 1997). The Nydam brooch, recovered from what was probably demolition rubble, could then be interpretable within this context of altering the environs of the mausoleum.

The final aspect of the early part of Phase 9 that needs to be considered is the deposition of the thick layer of 'dark earth' over the demolition rubble within the holloway. It appears most likely that this material was redeposited and then biologically reworked Roman midden and occupation debris. Within the layer a sherd of 'Anglo-Saxon' pottery and two probably fifth- or sixth-century spearheads indicates that its deposition should be placed earlier in Phase 9 than later. Whether this material was moved by natural or human agency is difficult to determine. The presence of the spearheads is something of a puzzle too. Usually fifth- or sixth-century spears are found in grave contexts or recovered from rivers and bogs, so the depositional context of the Gillingham examples is curious. Welton's (2018) recent doctoral study emphasises the spear as an active piece of material culture. In particular he draws attention to the way in which Roman ironwork was recycled and repurposed into post-Roman spearheads. This, he argues (Welton 2018, 181–184), was a conscious decision to appropriate and refashion the remnants of the Roman past into new post-Roman 'tools of social power'. The deposition of these spearheads - over the demolished walls of what had been a late Roman iron working site and close to the ruin of the mausoleum – may have been a conscious symbolic act, acknowledging and possibly appropriating the ancient significance of the place.

The lack of any evidence for settlement, other than the isolated pit in the north of the excavation area, may reinforce this sense of the specialness of the site. It was neither a location for the living or the recent dead. Perhaps it was turned over to grazing land, with the ancient ruins of the mausoleum keeping watch over the boundary between the marshes, perceived by some in the early medieval period as a liminal space of demons and monsters (Rippon 2017, 92–93), and the dry land.

From the sixth century onwards archaeologically visible evidence for human activity at the site ceases. Presumably the land was grazed and farmed with ships continuing to thread their way along the Medway to what was from the seventh century onwards the important ecclesiastical and administrative centre at Rochester.

Phase 10: Medieval AD 1050–1550

The story of the medieval period begins with two documentary sources: the late-eleventh-century Domesday Book and the early-twelfth-century *Textus Roffensis*, containing the cartulary of Rochester Cathedral. The first demonstrates that there was a Late Saxon estate at Grange, although the excavations have provided almost no evidence of its existence. The second document points to the existence of a chapel at *Grenc*, although whether this text is describing a pre- or post-Norman Conquest structure cannot be ascertained (Meddens & Draper 2014, 11–12).

The ruins of the Phase 7 mausoleum were still visible and probably included substantial fragments of standing masonry. These, on the evidence of the pottery from the robber trenches, were not finally removed until the twelfth century. There are two possible and plausible interpretations of this sequence. A minimalist view would simply argue that the ruin was a convenient source of building stone, waiting to be recycled into the buildings of a Norman manorial estate centre. A more speculative interpretation would note the Middle and Late Saxon interest in mausolea (Bell 2005). At Faversham (Kent), St Martins, Canterbury (Kent) and Wells (Somerset) Roman structures, arguably mausolea, were incorporated into Anglo-Saxon churches (Morris 1989). The Late Saxon church at Lullingstone (Kent) also occupied the site of the late Roman mausoleum (Meates 1979). Given this, one wonders what archaeological traces there would be if a ruined mausoleum became the focus of some sort of religious interest or veneration in the eleventh century. Here the cross-head terminal takes on some significance. It is, in Gaimster's words 'important physical evidence for a chapel here at a time when Bishop Odo, held Grange Manor' (this volume, above). If so, then perhaps Odo or an unnamed Late Saxon priest were interested in the ruins, which were then demolished and recycled into the manorial buildings by Odo's successors. Evidence for this reconstruction of events is sadly lacking, but it is a tantalising possibility.

The later medieval history of the manor of Grange has been discussed by Meddens & Draper (2014) and the excavations add only a little to the story. A modest group of medieval finds appears to reflect the importance of the manorial centre. The machine-cut sections across the manor site's moat demonstrated the scale of the feature but failed to ascertain anything about its chronology. Elsewhere the well and the finds contained within it indicates that *villeins* lived nearby and worked the land.

Phase 11: AD 1550 to the present day

The post-medieval and modern periods are mainly concerned with the changing nature of British society in the eighteenth and nineteenth centuries. Agricultural improvements allowed the land to be worked more intensively and productively. The consequent population growth and the development of urban industrialism led to a need for more homes and infrastructure, which in turn was reflected in the development of the Cinque Ports brickfield. Finally, the planting of orchards was a form of agricultural specialisation enabled by the demands of urban populations for fruit. If the interpretation of the Phase 7 enclosures is correct, then these post-medieval orchards would also mark a similar economic strategy to one used in the late third century.

The final element of the history of the site concerns the traces of the Second World War encountered in Areas A, B, C and D. It is somewhat disquieting to consider that when the site was excavated in 2005 World War II was still very much within living memory. More than a decade later those that lived through the 1939–1945 conflict as adults are inevitably growing fewer in number and their memories dimmer. As that war begins to pass from memory and into remembrance it is perhaps worth paying more attention to unexploded ordnance and filled-in bomb craters – the material signature of the world's first total war and a conflict that caused untold death, destruction and misery.

The construction of a housing estate on the land, part of the eastward expansion of Gillingham, marks the most recent phase in the continuing history of the site. It also marks a fundamental discontinuity with what had gone before with the only references to the past memorialised in street names - Conqueror Drive, Herleva Way and Odo Rise - that reference the Normans rather than the Romans. How long the houses on those streets will stand and what will eventually replace them are concerns for the future. What almost ten thousand years of human activity demonstrates is that change is inevitable and will come to the land at Grange Farm again.

Appendices

Appendix 1   Handmade coarse wares

There are a variety of coarse fabrics, mainly dating to the Late Iron Age and first century that cannot be ascribed to a known source with confidence. Most are probably local products and exhibit a wide variety of inclusions, surface treatments, decorative schemes and firings. For ease of analysis they have been divided here into broad fabric groups. They could be split further into smaller groups but as the Late Iron Age and first-century groups are relatively small this has not been deemed necessary. Fabric codes are based on a sequential alphanumeric system. They are all prefixed with 'C.' to indicate that they are coarse fabrics and to distinguish them from the London and Canterbury codes. Following this prefix are a series of letters that indicate the dominant inclusion type (*i.e.* SF: Sand and Flint, MCQ: Multi-coloured quartz). A number after this code represents further subdivision. They are probably broadly analogous to Canterbury fabrics under the M.LIA code.

C.SF1   Handmade, rough-smooth, hard, black with an irregular fracture. Moderate to abundant multi-coloured quartz <1mm and occasional to moderate angular flint, usually but not always calcined <2mm. Common.

C.SF2   Handmade, rough-harsh, hard, brownish-black with an irregular fracture. Abundant angular calcined flint <3mm and occasional quartz <1mm. Rare.

C.SF3   Handmade, rough, hard, orange-black with abundant multi-coloured quartz, occasional angular flint <2mm and occasional angular ironstone <2mm. Rare.

C.SF4   Handmade, rough orange brown with irregular fracture and abundant multi-coloured quartz <1mm also occasional rounded red iron ore <1mm, and angular flint <2mm. Rare.

C.SF5   Handmade, rough, hard, black with irregular fracture and moderate rounded (alluvial?) flint <2mm and multi-coloured quartz <2mm. Rare.

C.F1   Handmade, harsh, hard, black with a hackly fracture. Abundant, angular flint <3mm. The flint inclusions are usually, but not always, burnt. Common.

C.F2   Handmade, hard, rough brownish-orange with irregular fracture and moderate rounded (alluvial?) flint <2mm. Frequent.

C.F3   Handmade, hard, smooth pink orange (occasionally fired scummy white) with occasional angular calcined flint < 2mm. Rare.

C.MCQ1   Handmade, smooth, hard, black with an irregular fracture. Abundant multi-coloured quartz <1mm. Common.

C.MCQ2   Handmade, rough, hard, red-black with a fine fracture and abundant multi-coloured quartz <1mm. Common.

C.SILT   Handmade, smooth, hard. A variety of colours from brownish pink through black with a fine fracture and abundant silt with other occasional inclusions. Rare.

C.Q1   Handmade, rough orange to grey, with fine fracture and abundant quartz <1mm. Common.

C.Q2   Handmade, smooth, orange, with irregular fracture and abundant quartz <1mm and occasional angular shell <2mm. Common.

C.Q3   Handmade, smooth, grey-red to grey-brown with fine fracture and abundant iron stained quartz <1mm. Rare.

C.Q5   Handmade orange brown, with smooth black surfaces and moderate white and colourless quartz <0.5mm. Rare.

C.GL   Handmade, smooth, hard greyish brown with a fine fracture abundant glauconite <0.5mm. Rare. More of this fabric might have been expected given the site's proximity to the Medway Valley (Pollard 1988, 31).

Appendix 2   Roman fabric quantities and expansion codes

Sherd Count	Weight (g)	Fabric Code	Fabric Name	Date
868	18,713	AHFA	Alice Holt/Farnham Ware	LR
8	49	AHSU	Alice Holt/Surrey Ware	ER
42	2881	AMPH	Unsourced amphorae	ER/LR
4	100	ARGO	Argonne Ware	LR
1	1	ARRETINE?	Arretine Ware?	LIA/ER
77	997	B1	Belgic fine grog tempered	LIA/ER
7	109	B1.1	Belgic fine/coarse grog tempered	LIA/ER
102	1997	B2	Belgic coarse grog tempered	LIA/ER
1	3	B2.1	Belgic coarse pale grog tempered	LIA/ER
97	1840	B2/R1	Belgic/Romanised grog tempered	LIA/ER
51	1541	B3	Belgic grog tempered with sparse flint	LIA/ER
1	42	B5	Belgic grog tempered with sand	LIA/ER
21	207	B8	Belgic fine sandy	LIA/ER
27	151	B9	Belgic coarse sandy	LIA/ER
33	5647	BAET	Baetican amphorae	ER
11	1145	BAETL	Late Baetican amphorae	ER
43	868	BB1	Black Burnished 1	ER/LR
3887	46,155	BB2	Black Burnished 2	ER
1	12	BBS	Black Burnished Style	ER
11	222	BER16	Thanet Dry	LIA/ER
1	43	BER6	Early Gaulish White Ware	LIA/ER
194	4318	C.F1	See Appendix 1	LIA/ER
2	32	C.F2	See Appendix 1	LIA/ER
25	327	C.F3	See Appendix 1	LIA/ER
77	905	C.FS1	See Appendix 1	LIA/ER
29	284	C.FS2	See Appendix 1	LIA/ER
1	76	C.GL	See Appendix 1	LIA/ER
47	828	C.MCQ1	See Appendix 1	LIA/ER
16	308	C.MCQ2	See Appendix 1	LIA/ER
86	1454	C.Q1	See Appendix 1	LIA/ER
9	259	C.Q2	See Appendix 1	LIA/ER
6	185	C.Q3	See Appendix 1	LIA/ER
3	31	C.Q5	See Appendix 1	LIA/ER
6	55	C.SF1	See Appendix 1	LIA/ER
1	9	C.SF2	See Appendix 1	LIA/ER
1	17	C.SF3	See Appendix 1	LIA/ER
2	44	C.SF4	See Appendix 1	LIA/ER
1	26	C.SF5	See Appendix 1	LIA/ER
59	1040	C.SILT	See Appendix 1	LIA/ER
70	1636	CALC	Late Roman Shell Tempered Wares	LR
2	16	CGBL	Central Gaulish Blackware	ER
2	4	CGWH	Central Gaulish Whiteware	ER
2	248	COL MO	Colchester *mortaria*	ER
23	281	COLCC	Colchester Colour Coated	ER
157	2435	FINE	Unsourced Fine Wares	ER/LR

Appendix 2 (continued)

Sherd Count	Weight (g)	Fabric Code	Fabric Name	Date
46	999	GAUL	Gauloise amphora	ER
6	133	GBWW	Galo Belgic White Ware	ER
2	15	GROG Burgess Hill	Grog Tempered ware from Burgess Hill	LR
2	391	GROG ESSEX	Grog tempered wares from Essex	ER
700	12,606	GROG LR1	Late Roman Grog Tempered Wares	LR
11	250	HADBS	Hadham Black Slipped	LR
23	323	HADG	Hadham Grey	LR
18	294	HADOX	Hadham Oxidised	LR
675	8747	HOO	Hoo	ER
2	12	KOLN	Cologne Colour Coated	ER
7	51	LR14	N. Kent 'Streak Burnished' Ware	LR
4	103	LRMA GERM	Late Roman Marbled Wares from Germany	LR
3	172	MAYEN	Mayen Ware	LR
356	1849	MISC	Miscellaneous unidentifiable sherds	
2	14	MORT	Unsourced *mortaria*	ER/LR
32	129	MOSL	Moselkeramik	ER
2360	17,840	NKFW	North Kent Fine Ware	ER
1130	27,181	NKSH	North Kent Shell Tempered Wares	ER
2	4	NKWS	North Kent White Slipped Ware	ER
84	764	NVCC	Nene Valley Color Coated Ware	ER/LR
192	2075	OXID	Unsourced oxidised wares	
58	3220	OXMO	Oxfordshire Mortaria	LR
2	8	OXPA	Oxfordshire Parchment Ware	LR
249	3362	OXRC	Oxfordshire Red Colour Coated Ware	LR
28	746	OXWS	Oxfordshire White Slipped	LR
113	1943	PATCH	Patchgrove Ware	ER
1	22	PKGTW	Pink Grog Tempered Ware	ER
87	109	PORD	Portchester D	LR
10	1033	PRESTON	Preston, Canterbury	LR
284	5343	R1	Romanised Native Coarse Ware	ER
3	16	R5	Canterbury Coarse Grey Sandy Ware	ER
5	20	R6.1	Canterbury Coarse Sandy Orange Ware	ER
1	101	R6.3	Canterbury Coarse Buff Sandy	ER
10	101	SAM	Samian	ER
276	3080	SAMCG	Central Gaulish Samian	ER
42	1059	SAMEG	East Gaulish Samian	ER
15	140	SAMSG	South Gaulish Samian	ER
303	3116	SAND	Unsourced Sand Tempered Wares	
10	35	SHELL	Unsourced Shell Tempered Wares	
1	147	THDR	Late Roman Thundersbarrow Ware	LR
1	18	TN	Terra Nigra	ER
1	5	TR	Terra Rubra	ER
6797	68,184	TSK	Thameside Kent Grey Wares	ER/LR
1	213	VCWS	Verulamium Coarse White Slipped Ware	ER
7	122	VRW	Verulamium Region White Ware	ER

Appendix 3   Gazeteer of known Roman lead coffins in Kent (see Fig. 3.55 for locations)

Reference (Fig. 3.55)	Findspot	Reference (secondary)	Current location
1	Canterbury	Toller 1977	lost
2	Chatham	Toller 1977	?
3	Crayford	Toller 1977	reburied
4	Chalkwell, Sittingbourne	Toller 1977	stole
5	Murston	Toller 1977	lost
6	Bexhill, Sittingbourne	Toller 1977	lost
7	Bexhill, Sittingbourne	Toller 1977	lost
8	Bexhill, Sittingbourne	Toller 1978	lost
9	Bexhill, Sittingbourne	Toller 1977	lost
10	Bexhill, Sittingbourne	Toller 1977	lost
11	Bexhill, Sittingbourne	Toller 1978	lost
12	Bexhill, Sittingbourne	Toller 1979	lost
13	Bexhill, Sittingbourne	Toller 1980	lost
14	Bexhill, Sittingbourne	Toller 1977	Maidstone museum
15	Bexhill, Sittingbourne	Toller 1977	British Museum
16	Frindsbury	Toller 1977	lost
17	Sturry	Toller 1977	lost
18	Holborough	Toller 1977	Maidstone museum
19	Highstead, Sittingbourne	Toller 1977	maidstone museum
20	Lullingstone	Toller 1977	Lullingstone Museum
21	Plumstead	Toller 1977	Maidstone Museum
22	Southfleet	Toller 1977	lost
23	Ramsgate	Toller 1977	lost
24	Petham	Toller 1977	lost
25	Rochester	Toller 1977	lost
26	Chatham	Toller 1977	lost
27	Thanet	Kent Her	sold for scrap
28	Canterbury	Kent HER	lost
29	Keston	Philp nd	?

Appendix 4   Distribution of post-Roman pottery types, Phases 9–11, quantified by sherd count (SC) and minimum number of vessels (MNV)

Pottery type	Code	Date	Phase						Residual/ intrusive		Total	
			9		10		11					
			SC	ENV	SC	ENV	SC	ENV	SC	ENV	SC	ENV
Early medieval/Saxon sandy ware	EMS1	450–700			1						1	
Early medieval/Saxon coarse sandy ware	EMS1A	450–650	7	2	2	1					9	3
Early medieval/Saxon sandy chalk - filled (sand dominant)	EMS1B	450–700	8	1							8	1
As above with organics	EMS1D (O)	450–700	1	1							1	1
Early medieval/Saxon sandy chalk-filled (sand dominant)	EMS1F	450–650	1	1							1	1
Early medieval/Saxon micaceous non - local coarseware	EMS7C	625–700	3	2	2	1					5	3
West Kent fine sandy with shell and sparse grits	EM21	1125–1250							1	1	1	1
North or West Kent shell-filled	EM35	1050–1225			100	18			5	3	105	21
North or West Kent sandy and shell-tempered	EM36	1100–1250			16	8			1	1	17	9
Non-local sandy ware with flint-temper	EM44								1	1	1	1
?Non-local coarse sandy ware	EM45				1	1					1	1
Probably North or West Kent shell-filled fine sandy ware	EM48	?1100–1250	1	1							1	1
Miscellaneous Unidentified: ?English	EM100				5	5					5	5
Tyler Hill ware	M1	1225–1350	15	4	42	9	1	1			58	14
Tyler Hill sandy with sparse chalk	M1A	1225–1350	6	2	31	10					37	12
Tyler Hill sandy: moderate sand in a smooth matrix; soft (?under-fired)	M1B	1225–1350	1	1			1	1			2	2
London-type ware: general	M5	1140–1375			13	4			3	2	16	6
London-type: Rouen copies	M5	1190–1250			13	4			3	2	16	6
Essex Mill Green	M6	1270–1350			4	3					4	3
Surrey: Kingston sandy	M7	1240–1400			10	4					10	4
Saintonge	M22	1250–1650			3	2	1	1			4	3
Saintonge: green-glazed	M22G	1250–1400+			44	3			1	1	45	4
Saintonge: Polychrome	M22P	1290–1320			4	2					4	2
?Medway chalk-tempered sandy ware	M37		1	1	1	1					2	2
North or West Kent sandy	M38A	1150–1400	12	12	434	44	13	13	1	1	460	70
North or West Kent fine-moderate sandy	M38B	1225/50–1400			15	2					15	2
North or West Kent hard-fired fine sandy	M38C	1325/50–1400							1	1	1	1

Appendix 4 (continued)

Pottery type	Code	Date	Phase									
			9		10		11		Residual/ intrusive		Total	
			SC	ENV	SC	ENV	SC	ENV	SC	ENV	SC	ENV
?Wealden white/cream/buff sandy	M53	?1250–1400/50					1	1			1	1
Miscellaneous unidentified: ?English	M100		2	2	1	1	3	3			6	6
Miscellaneous unidentified: ?English	M100/ LM100				22	9					22	9
German Siegburg stoneware	LM7	1300–1500					1	1			1	1
Hareplain/Biddenden brown near-stoneware	LM18C	1475–1550+							1	1	1	1
London: Guy's Hospital	LM19	1475–1650					2	1			2	1
Wealden orange-buff sandy ware	LM32	?1375–1550					2	2			2	2
Medway hard silty-sandy ware	LM34A	1450–1550			2	2					2	2
Medway hard silty-sandy ware with chalk	LM34B	1450–1550	5	1	4	1	1	1	1	1	11	4
Post-medieval red earthenwares	PM1	1550–1800					7	7	1	1	8	8
Sandy earthenware	PM1.8	1550–1800					1	1			1	1
Wealden buff fine sandy ware	PM2	1525–1650			3	3	3	3			6	6
?Wealden/London area fine sandy redware with grey core slipped/unslipped	PM2WG	1475–1750					1	1			1	1
Wealden or Surrey/Hants fine pink-buff earthenware	PM2.4	1550–1900					2	2			2	2
German grey Westerwald stoneware with cobalt and manganese	PM6CM	1650–1750					1	1			1	1
English tin-glazed earthenware	PM9	1575–1775					7	6			7	6
Surrey/Hants Border ware	PM10	1550–1725					10	8	3	3	13	11
Staffs-type press-moulded slipware: combed	PM21	1700–1800					3	2			3	2
Staffs 'Butter pot'	PM58	1600–1750	1	1							1	1
Miscellaneous unidentified ?English	PM100	1500–1900					1	1			1	1
	LPM1						2	1			2	1
North-East English (Tyneside) slip-decorated redware	LPM4	1775–1925					1	1			1	1
Yellow Ware	LPM5	1825–1900	1	1			2	2			3	3
Later Creamware: plain	LPM11A	1775–1825	1	1			4	3	1	1	6	5
Pearl Ware: blue feathered/ shell edged	LPM12D	1780–1825					1	1			1	1
Staffs 'Ironstone'-type white earthenware	LPM14	1825–1875	1	1			7	7	1	1	9	9
Black basalt-type ware. unglazed	LPM18AA	1770–1900	1	1							1	1
Total			68	36	773	138	79	72	25	21	945	257

Appendix 5   Quantification of pottery types and forms from fills [562]/[713] of well [563]

The following are quantified by sherd count (SC) and minimum number of vessels (MNV)

Pottery type	Code	Date range	Form	SC	% SC	MNV	% MNV
Early Saxon sandy ware	EMS1	450–700	Unidentified	1	0.2	1	1.0
Early Saxon coarse sandy ware	EMS1A	450–650	Unidentified	2	0.3	1	1.0
Early Saxon sandy chalk-filled (sand dominant)	EMS7C	625–700	Jar	2	0.3	1	1.0
North or West Kent sandy and shell-tempered	EM36	1100–1250	Unidentified	3	0.5	1	1.0
Tyler Hill ware	M1	1225–1350	Jug	8	1.2	8	8.2
			Jug, rounded	34	5.3	1	1.0
Tyler Hill sandy with sparse chalk	M1A	1225–1350	Jug	13	2.0	8	8.2
			Jug, rounded	18	2.8	2	2.0
Sub-total				73	11.4	19	19.4
London-type ware: general	M5	1225–1350	Baluster drinking jug	10	1.6	1	1.0
			Jug	3	0.5	3	3.1
London-type: Rouen copies		1190–1250	Baluster drinking jug	10	1.6	1	1.0
			Jug	3	0.5	3	3.1
Sub-total				**26**	**4.1**	**8**	**1.2**
Essex Mill Green	M6	1270–1350	Jug	4	0.6	3	3.1
Surrey: Kingston sandy	M7	1240–1400	Drinking jug	3	0.5	1	1.0
			Jug	7	1.1	3	3.1
Sub-total				**10**	**1.6**	**4**	**4.1**
Saintonge	M22	1250–1650	Jug	3	0.5	2	2.0
Saintonge: green-glazed	M22G	1250–1400+	Jug	32	5.0	2	2.0
			Jug, rounded	12	1.9	1	1.0
Saintonge: polychrome	M22P	1290–1320	Jug	4	0.6	2	2.0
Sub-total				**51**	**8.0**	**7**	**7.1**
?Medway chalk-tempered sandy ware	M37	Undated	Unidentified	1	0.2	1	1.0
North or West Kent sandy	M38A	1150–1400	?Jug	18	2.8	6	6.1
			Bowl, flared	3	0.5	2	2.0
			Bowl, deep flared	16	2.5	1	1.0
			Bowl, medium carinated	1	0.2	1	1.0
			Jar	288	44.9	4	4.1
			Jar, rounded	30	4.7	3	3.1
			Jar, medium rounded	26	4.1	3	3.1
			Jar, tall rounded	11	1.7	3	3.1
			Jug	6	0.9	2	2.0
			Pipkin	3	0.5	3	3.1
			Unidentified	10	1.6	3	3.1
Sub-total				**412**	**64.3**	**31**	**31.6**

Appendix 5 (continued)

Pottery type	Code	Date range	Form	SC	% SC	MNV	% MNV
North or West Kent fine - moderate sandy	M38B	1150–1400	Jar	7	1.1	0	0.0
			Jar, small rounded	6	0.9	1	1.0
			Jar, tall rounded	2	0.3	1	1.0
Sub-total				**15**	**2.3**	**2**	**2.0**
Medieval/late medieval unidentified: ?English	M100/ LM100	Undated	Jar	1	0.2	1	1.0
			Unidentified	21	3.3	8	8.2
Sub-total				**22**	**3.4**	**9**	**9.2**
Medway hard silty - sandy ware	LM34A	1450–1550	Unidentified	2	0.3	2	2.0
Medway hard silty - sandy ware with chalk	LM34B	1450–1550	Jug	4	0.6	1	1.0
Wealden buff fine sandy ware	PM2	1525–1650	Jug	3	0.5	3	3.1
Total				641	100	98	100

Appendix 6   Non-metric traits shown by burial [231]

Non-metric trait	Observed No.	Total skeletal element present
Metopic Suture	0	0
Supraorbital Notch (L/R)	0/1	0/0
Supraorbital Foramen (L/R)	0/0	0/0
Infraorbital suture (L/R)	0/0	0/0
Multiple Infraorbital Foramina (L/R)	0/0	0/0
Zygomatico-facial Foramina (L/R)	0/0	0/0
Parietal Foramen (L/R)	0/0	0/0
Epipteric Bone (L/R)	0/0	0/0
Coronal Ossicle (L/R)	0/0	0/0
Bregmatic Bone	0	0
Sagittal Ossicle	0	0
Apical Bone	0	0
Lambdoid Ossicle (L/R)	0/0	0/0
Asterionic Bone (L/R)	0/0	0/0
Ossicle in Occipito-Mastoid Suture (L/R)	0/0	0/0
Parietal Notch Bone (L/R)	0/0	0/0
Inca Bone	0	0
Condylar Canal (L/R)	0/0	0/0
Divided Hypoglossal Canal (L/R)	0/0	0/0
Flexure of Superior Sagittal Sulcus (R/L/B)	0/0/0	0
Foramen Ovale Incomplete (L/R)	0/0	0/0
Foramen Spinosum Incomplete (L/R)	0/0	0/0
Pterygo-spinous Bridge (L/R)	0/0	0/0
Pterygo-alar Bridge (L/R)	0/0	0/0
Tympanic Dihiscence (L/R)	0/0	0/0
Auditory Exostosis (L/R)	0/0	0/0
Mastoid Foramen (L/R)	0/0	0/0
Mental Foramen(L/R)	1/1	1/1
Mandibular Torus (L/R)	0/0	0/0
Frontal grooves (L/R)	0/0	0/0
Ethmoidal foramina (L/R)	0/0	0/0
Supratrochlear Notch or foramen (L/R)	0/0	0/0
Trochlear Spine (L/R)	0/0	0/0
Double occipital condylar facets (L/R)	0/0	0/0
Paracondylar process	0/0	0/0
Bridging of Jugular foramen (L/R)	0/0	0/0
Pharyngeal tubercle	0/0	0/0
Clinoid bridges or spurs (L/R)	0/0	0/0
Accessory lesser palatine foramina (L/R)	0/0	0/0

Appendix 6 (continued)

Non-metric trait	Observed No.	Total skeletal element present
Palatine torus (L/R)	0/0	0/0
Maxillary torus (L/R)	0/0	0/0
Divided parietal bone (L/R)	0/0	0/0
Os Japonicum (L/R)	0/0	0/0
Marginal tubercle (L/R)	0/0	0/0
Mylohyoid Bridge (L/R)	0/0	0/0
Atlas Lateral Bridging (L/R)	0/0	0/0
Atlas Posterior Bridging (L/R)	0/0	0/0
Accessory Transverse Foramina in 7th cervical vertebrae (L/R)	0/0	0/0
Septal Aperture	0/0	1/1
Sixth Lumbar vertebrae	0	0
Accessory sacro-illiac articulation (L/R)	0/0	0/0
Supra scapular Foramen or notch form (L/R)	0/0	0/0
Accessory acromial articular facet (L/R)	0/0	0/0
Unfused acromial epiphysis (L/R)	0/0	0/0
Glenoid fossa extension (L/R)	0/0	0/0
Circumflex Sulcus (L/R)	0/0	0/0
Sternal foramen	0	0
Supratrochlear Spur (L/R)	0/0	0/0
Trochlear notch form (L/R)	0/0	0/0
Allen's fossa (L/R)	0/0	0/0
Poirier's facet or extension (L/R)	0/0	0/0
Third trochanter (L/R)	0/0	0/0
Vastus notch (L/R)	0/0	1/1
Tibia Squatting facets (L/R)	0/0	0/0
Talus Squatting facets (L/R)	0/0	0/0

Appendix 7 Charred macrobotanical remains

		Phase	4	4	6
		Sample Number	{268}	{246}	{270}
		Feature Number	[1092]	[1092]	[1197]
		Context Fill Number	[1174]	[1025]	[1199]
		Feature Type	pit	pit	pit
		Flot volume (ml)	8	8	12
		Flot weight (g)	4	4	14
Taxonomic Identification	**English Name**	**Habitat Codes**			
Cereal Grain					
Hordeum vulgare L.	barley - hulled	C*	1		2
cf. *Hordeum vulgare* L.	possible barley - hulled	C*		2	1
Triticum cf. *dicoccum* Schübl./*spelta* L.	possible emmer/spelt wheat	C*	5	3	11
Triticum aestivum - type	bread - type free threshing wheat	C*	3	1	3
Triticum cf. *aestivum* - type	possible bread - type free threshing wheat	C*	2	1	1
Triticum sp.	wheat	C*	9	2	6
cf. *Triticum* sp.	possible wheat	C*	2	4	3
Cerealia indet.	indeterminate cereal - whole grain	C*	13	6	12
Cerealia indet.	indeterminate cereal - frag.	C*	24	22	24
Cerealia indet. /*Poaceae*	indeterminate cereal/grass - large seeded	CG	12	6	4
Chaff					
Hordeum vulgare L.	barley rachis frag.	C*			1
Triticum spelta L.	spelt wheat - glume base	C*	1		1
Triticum dicoccum Schübl./*spelta* L.	emmer/spelt wheat - glume base	C*	2		1
Triticum sp.	wheat - glume base	C*		1	
Triticum sp.	wheat - spikelet base	C*	1		
Triticum aestivum - type	bread-type wheat - rachis frag.	C*			1
Indet. rachis frag.	indeterminate rachis frag.	-		1	
Edible Pulses					
cf. *Pisum sativum* L.	possible garden pea	C*	1		
Vicia sp./*Pisum* sp.	vetch/bean/pea - whole	C*DG	7	1	
Vicia sp./*Pisum* sp.	vetch/bean/pea - halves	C*DG	7	1	
cf. *Vicia* sp./*Pisum* sp.	possible vetch/bean/pea	C*DG	18		
Weed/Wild Plants					
Ranunculus acris L./*repens* L./*bulbosus* L.	meadow/creeping/bulbous buttercups	Gw or GwWRM or Gd		1	2
cf. *Ranunculus acris* L./*repens* L./*bulbosus* L.	possible meadow/creeping/bulbous buttercups	Gw or GwWRM or Gd		2	
Urtica urens L.	small nettle	AD		2	
Juglans regia L.	walnut - nutshell frag. <12mm	C*			2
Chenopodium spp.	goosefoot	AArDn	3	9	2
Stellaria sp.	stitchworts	-		1	
Fallopia convolvulus (L.) Á Löve	black-bindweed - whole	Dar	12	1	
Fallopia convolvulus (L.) Á Löve	black-bindweed - frag.	Dar	4		
Polygonum sp./*Rumex* sp./*Carex* sp. (internal structure)	knotgrass/dock/sedge	AD G or MROw			1
Polygonum spp./*Rumex* spp.	knotgrass/dock	DGEAoa	1		13
cf. *Polygonum* sp./*Rumex* sp.	possible knotgrass/dock	DGEAoa			1
Rumex acetosella L.	sheep's sorrel	EoGAa	2		2
Thlaspi arvense L.	field penny-cress	Dar	3		

Appendix 7 (continued)

Phase			4	4	6
Sample Number			{268}	{246}	{270}
Feature Number			[1092]	[1092]	[1197]
Context Fill Number			[1174]	[1025]	[1199]
Feature Type			pit	pit	pit
Flot volume (ml)			8	8	12
Flot weight (g)			4	4	14
Taxonomic Identification	**English Name**	**Habitat Codes**			
Malva cf. *mochata* L.	possible musk-mallow	G		1	
Malva sp.	mallow	GDY		1	
Vicia spp./*Lathyrus* spp. (2–3mm)	vetch/vetchling/tare - whole	AArDGY	28	2	
cf. *Vicia* spp./*Lathyrus* spp. (2–3mm)	possible vetch/vetchling/tare - halves	AArDGY	11	4	1
Vicia spp./*Lathyrus* spp. (≤2mm)	vetch/vetchling/tare - whole	AArDGY	4	1	
cf. *Vicia* spp./*Lathyrus* spp. (≤2mm)	vetch/vetchling/tare - halves	AArDGY	1	3	1
cf. *Vicia* spp./*Lathyrus* spp.	possible vetch/vetchling/tare	AArDGY	6	5	1
Galium spp.	bedstraw	-		3	
Sambucus nigra L.	elder	HWS	4		
cf. *Matricaria* sp.	possible mayweed	ArDY		3	
Tripleurospermum inodorum (L.) Sch.Bip.	scentless mayweed	DA	3		
Asteraceae	daisy family	-	2		
Carex spp.	sedge - lenticular	GwMWwHSGah	1		3
Carex spp.	sedge - triangular/round	GwMWwHSGah	6		2
cf. *Carex* sp.	possible sedge	GwMWwHSGah			1
Eleocharis cf. *palustris* (L.) Roem.& Schult.	possible common spike-rush	OMGw		4	
Avena sp.	oat - indet. cultivated/wild oat	C or AArDG	16		
cf. *Avena* sp.	possible oat - indet. cultivated/wild oat	C or AArDG	8		1
cf. *Festuca* sp./*Lolium* sp.	possible fescue/rye-grass	DG	2		2
Phleum sp.	cat's tail	GD		3	
cf. *Poa* sp.	possible meadow-grass	DG	4		2
Poaceae	grass - large seeded	AD G	19		
Poaceae	grass - medium seeded	AD G	14	2	1
Poaceae	grass - small seeded	AD G	21	17	49
cf. *Poaceae*	possible grass - stem frag.	AD G			5
Unidentified or Indeterminate Plant parts					
unidentified seed		-		2	2
indeterminate seed (<2.5mm)		-	7		
Total count (fragment or item)			291	123	165
Sample size (in litres)			40	40	20
Processed soil (in litres)			10	20	10
Count density (items per litre of processed soil)			29.1	6.15	16.5

Key: Habitat characteristics: A - Weeds of cultivated grounds, Ar - Arable weeds, C - Cultivated plants, D - Ruderals, weeds of waste and disturbed places, E - Heath, G - Grassland, H - Hedgerows, M -Marsh/bog, R - Plants of running waters, O - Plants of open water, S - Scrub, W - Woods, Y – Waysides; Soils/ground conditions: a – acidic, c – calcareous, d – dry, b – base rich, n – nutrient rich, o – open ground, s – shaded, w – wet/damp soils, h – heavy soils.

Appendix 8   Taxonomic identifications of wood charcoal remains

Taxonomic Identifications

Phase Number	Context Number	Sample Number	Feature	Feature Type	Quercus sp.	Fraxinus excelsior	Ulmus sp.	Rosaceae cf. Rosa sp.	cf. Maloideae group	Prunus sp.	cf. Corylus avellana	Alnus sp.	Betula sp.	Corylus/Alnus	Acer campestre	Ilex aquifolium	indet. Distorted
5	275	111	276	Pit	5	-	1	-	-	-	-	-	4	-	-	-	-
6	788	207	789	Pit	9	-	-	-	5r	-	6r	-	-	-	3	9	-
6	1195	269	1196	Pit	5	1	1	-	2r	-	-	-	-	-	-	-	1
6	1199	270	1197	Pit	6r	1	1	2r	2	8r	3r	2r	1	-	-	-	7
6	1335	284	1335	Floor	8r	8r	-	-	1r	-	-	-	1	5r	-	-	4
7	209	102	210	Pit	47	-	-	-	-	-	-	-	-	-	-	-	1
8	1234	278	1236	Pit	11r	-	-	-	1	2	-	-	-	1	-	-	2
8	981	237	982	Hearth	15r	-	-	-	42r	-	-	-	-	-	-	-	1
8	1135	260	1136	Hearth	16r	3	-	-	2	-	-	6r	-	-	-	-	3
8	1154	261	1155	Hearth	10r	3	-	-	-	1	1r	-	-	-	-	-	5

Key: r = roundwood present

Appendix 9   Pollen assessment of samples from the lead coffin

Location/ context number	Sample number	Main taxa present	Common name	Fungal spores	Microscopic charred particles	Concentration 0 (none) to 5 (High)	Preservation 0(none) to 5 (High)
Grid	1	-	-	Present	2/3	0	0
Grid	2	-	-	Present	2/3	0	0
Grid	3	Apiaceae Lactuceae	Carrot family e.g. Dandelion	Present	2/3	1	1
Grid	4	-	-	Present	2	0	0
Grid/Stomach	5	*Chenopodium* type *Anthemis* type	e.g. Fat hen Chamomile	Present	2/3	1	3
Grid/Stomach	6	-	-	Present	3	0	0
Grid	7	-	-	Present	2/3	0	0
Grid	8	cf Lactuceae *Sinapis* type	e.g. Dandelion e.g. Charlock	Present	3/4	1/2	1/2
Grid	9	*Pinus*	Pine	Present	2	1	1
Grid/Intestine	10	*Sinapis* type, Unknown trizonoporate grain, Lactuceae	e.g. Charlock e.g. Dandelion	Present	2/3	1/2	1/2
Grid/Intestine	11	Lactuceae *Convolvulus* type	e.g. Dandelion e.g. Bindweed	Present	3/4	1	1
Grid/Intestine	12	Lactuceae	e.g. Dandelion	Present	2	1	1
Grid	13	cf *Pinus*	Pine	Present	3/4	1	1
Grid	14	cf *Sinapis* type	e.g. Charlock	Present	2/3	1	1
Grid	15	cf *Sinapis* type	e.g. Charlock	Present	2	1	1
Grid	16	-	-	Present	3/4	0	0
Grid	17	-	-	Present	3	0	0
Grid	18	-	-	Present	3/4	0	0
Grid	19	-	-	Present	1/2	0	0
Grid	20	-	-	Present	3	0	0
Grid	21	-	-	Present	3/4	0	0
Grid	22	Poaceae/*Cereale* type	Grass/Cereal	Present	3	1	1
Grid	23	cf *Sinapis* type	e.g. Charlock	Present	3/4	1	1/2
Grid	24	cf *Sinapis* type	e.g. Charlock	Present	3/4	1	2
Grid	25	-	-	Present	3	0	0
Grid	26	-	-	Present	3	0	0
Grid	27	-	-	Present	3	0	0
Grid	28	-	-	Present	3/4	0	0
[237] organic patch by feet	29	-	-		1/2	0	0
[237] organic patch by feet	30	-	-		2	0	0
[237] feet	31	cf *Pinus*	Pine	Present	2	0	0
[237] pelvis	32	-	-		3	0	0
[320] Backfill	33	-	-	Present	3/4	0	0
[320] Backfill	34	-	-		2/3	0	0
[320] Backfill	35	-	-	Present	2/3	0	0
[320] Backfill	36B	-	-		3	0	0
[320] Backfill	36A	-	-		1/2	0	0
[320] Backfill	37	-	-		3	0	0
Necklace?	38	-	-		2	0	0
Around head	39	-	-		3	0	0
Around head	40	-	-		3	0	0
Around head	41	-	-		3	0	0
(205) Demo	42	-	-		3	0	0

Appendix 10 Radiocarbon determinations

Three samples were submitted for radiocarbon dating: an equid bone from an articulated bone group within a Phase 8 pit [1231], and two samples submitted to different institutions and both taken from rib bones, from burial [231]. Plots are replicated below. Details of calculation for ΔR, marine component and OxCal Code used are held with the archive.

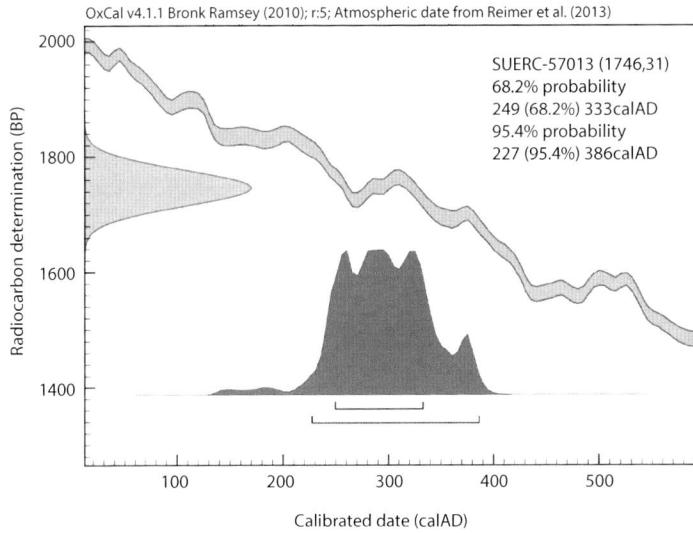

OxCal v4.1.1 Bronk Ramsey (2010); r:5; Atmospheric date from Reimer et al. (2013)

SUERC-57013 (1746,31)
68.2% probability
249 (68.2%) 333calAD
95.4% probability
227 (95.4%) 386calAD

Fig. A10.1 Radiocarbon determination on equid bone from [1230]: SUERC-57013 (GU35812)

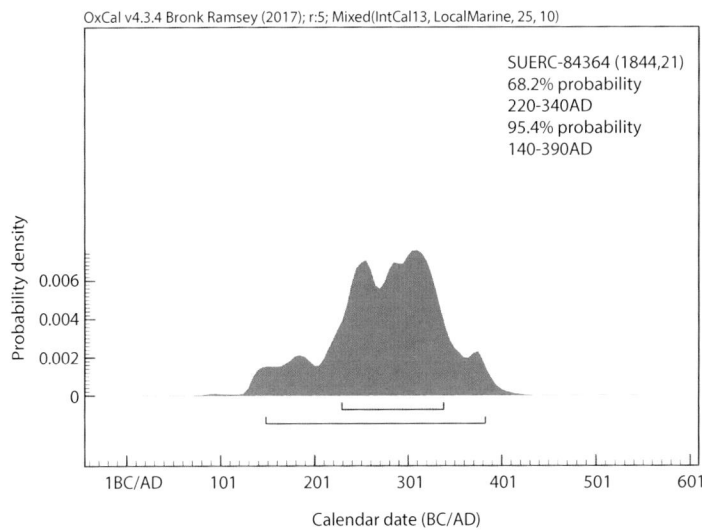

OxCal v4.3.4 Bronk Ramsey (2017); r:5; Mixed(IntCal13, LocalMarine, 25, 10)

SUERC-84364 (1844,21)
68.2% probability
220-340AD
95.4% probability
140-390AD

Fig. A10.2 Radiocarbon determination on human rib bone from skeleton [231]: SUERC-84364 (GU50092)

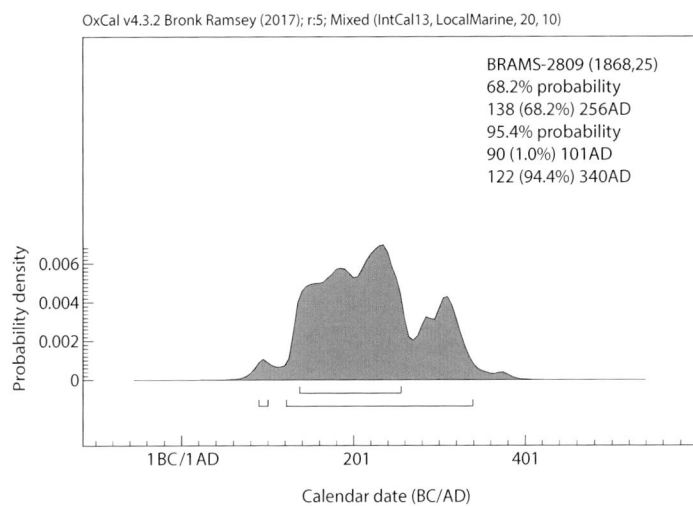

OxCal v4.3.2 Bronk Ramsey (2017); r:5; Mixed (IntCal13, LocalMarine, 20, 10)

BRAMS-2809 (1868,25)
68.2% probability
138 (68.2%) 256AD
95.4% probability
90 (1.0%) 101AD
122 (94.4%) 340AD

Fig. A10.3 Radiocarbon determination on human rib bone from skeleton [231]: BRAMS-2809

Bibliography

Acsádi, G. and Nemeskéri, J. 1970. *History of Human Life Span and Mortality*. Budapest: Akadémiai Kiadó.

Alarcão, J. and Alarcão A., 1965. *Vidros romanos de Conimbriga*. Lisbon: Ministério da Educação Nacional.

Albarella, U. 2005. Alternate fortunes? The role of domestic ducks and geese from Roman to Medieval times in Britain. In: G. Grupe and J. Peters (Eds.) *Documenta Archaeobiologiae III. Feathers, Grit and Symbolism*, 249–58. Munich: VML Verlag Marie Leidorf.

Allan, J. P. 1984. *Medieval and post-medieval finds from Exeter, 1971–1980*. Exeter Archaeological Reports 3. Exeter: Exeter City Council and the University of Exeter.

Allason-Jones, L. 2002. Small finds: copper-alloy. *Archaeologia Aeliana* 31, 211–234.

Allason-Jones, L. 2006. The small finds. In: M. Millett (Ed.) *Shiptonthorpe, East Yorkshire: archaeological studies of a Romano-British roadside settlement*, 220–248. Leeds: Yorkshire Archaeological Society Monograph 5.

Allason-Jones, L. 2011. Recreation. In: L. Allason-Jones (Ed.) *Artefacts in Roman Britain*. Cambridge: Cambridge University Press, 219–242.

Allason-Jones, L. and Miket, R. 1984. *The Catalogue of Small Finds from South Shields Roman Fort*. Newcastle: The Society of Antiquaries of Newcastle upon Tyne.

Allen, M., Lodwick, L., Brindle, T., Fulford, M. and Smith, A. 2017. *The Rural Economy of Roman Britain*. Britannia Monograph 30. London: Society for the Promotion of Roman Studies.

Amorosi, T. 1989. *A Postcranial Guide to Domestic Neo-Natal and Juvenile Mammals*. Oxford: British Archaeological Reports International Series 533.

Anderson-Whymark, H. and Thomas, J. 2012. *Regional Perspectives on Neolithic Pit Depositions: beyond the mundane*. Neolithic Studies Group Seminar Papers 12. Oxford: Oxbow.

Andrews, P. and Evans, E. M. N. 1983. Small mammal bone accumulations produced by mammalian carnivores. *Paleobiology* 9, 289–307.

Andrews, P., Biddulph, E., Hardy, A. and Brown, R. 2011. *Settling the Ebbsfleet Valley: High Speed 1 Excavations at Springhead and Northfleet, Kent: The Late Iron Age, Roman, Saxon and Medieval Landscape*. Aberystwyth: Oxford Wessex Archaeology.

Andrews, P., Booth, P., Fitzpatrick, A. and Welsh, K. 2015. *Digging at the Gateway: archaeological Landscapes of Southern Thanet*. Oxford: Oxford Wessex Archaeology Monograph 8.

Andrews, P., Dinwiddy, K.E., Ellis, C., Hutcheson, A., Phillpotts, C., Powell, A.B. and Schuster, J. 2009. *Kentish sites and sites of Kent: A miscellany of four archaeological excavations*. Wessex Archaeology Report 24. Salisbury: Wessex Archaeology.

Applegate, D. 2015. Hoo Ware: an investigation and comparative analysis of evidence recovered from a first century AD Romano-British site in North Kent. *Journal of Roman Pottery Studies* 16, 23–53.

Armitage, P. L. 1980. Mammalian remains. In: D. M. Jones and M. Rhodes, Excavations at Billingsgate Buildings ('Triangle') Lower Thames Street, London, 1974. *Transactions of the London and Middlesex Archaeological Society Special Paper No. 4*, 149–63.

Armitage, P. L. 1983. The Early History of English Longwool Sheep. *The Ark (the monthly Journal of the Rare Breeds Survival Trust)*, X, No. 3, 90–7.

Armitage, P. L. 1999. Faunal remains. In: I. Soden (Ed.) A story of urban regeneration: excavations in advance of development off St. Peter's Walk, Northampton, 1994–7, *Northamptonshire Archaeology* 28, 61–127.

Armitage, P. L. 2004. The Mammal, Bird and Fish Bones from Archaeological Excavations at Gravesend and North Kent Hospital (site KGEH04). PCA Unpublished Report.

Armitage, P. L. 2010. The Mammal, Bird, Fish and Amphibian Bones from Rutland Water Excavations (sites RWLB08 & RW208). Middle Iron Age and Roman Contexts. Northamptonshire Archaeology Unpublished Report.

Armitage, P. L. and Clutton-Brock, J. 1976. A system for classification and description of the horn cores of cattle from archaeological sites, *Journal of Archaeological Science* 3, 329–48.

Aufderheide, A.C. and Rodríguez-Martín, C. 1998. *The Cambridge Encyclopaedia of Human Palaeopathology*. Cambridge: Cambridge University Press.

Austin, M. 2014. Rethinking Hardown Hill: Our Westernmost Early Anglo-Saxon Cemetery? *The Antiquaries Journal* 94, 49–69 (https://doi.org/10.1017/S0003581514000250).

Bailey, G. 1992. *Detector Finds 1*. Witham: Greenlight Publishing.

Bailey, G. 1995. *Detector Finds 2*. Witham: Greenlight Publishing.

Bailey, G. 2004. *Buttons & Fasteners 500BC–AD1840*. Witham: Greenlight Publishing.

Bailey, S. 1994. Two copper alloy cross-staff heads from Warwickshire. *Medieval Archaeology* 37, 171–75.

Baker, J. and Brothwell, D. 1980. *Animal Diseases in Archaeology*. London: Academic Press.

Bakka, E. 1958. *On the beginning of Salin's Style I in England, Historisk-antikvariske rekke 3*. Bergen: Universitetet i Bergen Årbok.

Barber, L. 1998. The Pottery. In: L. Kirk, *An Archaeological Excavation at Grench Manor, Gillingham, Kent*. Archaeology South-East, unpublished report, 12–14.

Barber, B. and Bowsher, D. 2000. *The Eastern Cemetery: Excavations 1983–1990*. MoLAS Monograph 4. London: Museum of London.

Barfield, L. and Hodder, M. 1987. Burnt Mounds as Saunas, and the Prehistory of Bathing. *Antiquity 61*, 370–379.

Barfield, L. H. 1991. Hot Stones: hot food or hot baths? In: M. A. Hodder and L. H. Barfield, (Eds.) *Burnt Mounds and Hot Stone Technology: papers from the 2nd International Burnt Mound Conference, Sandwell, 12–14 October 1990*, 59–67. Sandwell: Sandwell Metropolitan Borough Council.

Baxter, I. L. 1993. Bones of small animals and birds from predator pellets and scats at Drayton II Roman Villa, Leicestershire. *Organ - The newsletter of the Osteological Research Group. Issue 2*, 5–6.

Bayley, J. 1993. The metalworking evidence. In: A. Woodward and P. Leach (Eds.) *The Uley Shrines. Excavations of a ritual complex on West Hill, Uley, Gloucestershire*. London: English Heritage, 215.

Bayley, J. 2008. Medieval precious metal refining: archaeology and contemporary texts compared. In: M. Martinón-Torres and T. Rehren (Eds.) *Archaeology, History and Science: integrating approaches to ancient materials*, 131–150. Walnut Creek, CA: Left Coast Press.

Bayley, J. and Eckstein, K 1997. Silver refining - production, recycling, assaying. In: A. Sinclair, E. Slater and J Gowlett (Eds) *Archaeological Sciences 1995*, 107–11. Oxford: Oxbow Monograph 64.

Bayley, J. and Eckstein, K. 1998. *Metalworking debris from Pentrehyling Roman Fort, Brompton, Shropshire*. Ancient Monuments Laboratory Report 13/98. London: English Heritage.

Bayley, J. and Eckstein, K. 2006. Roman and medieval litharge cakes: structure and composition. In: J. Pérez-Arantegui (Ed.) *Proceedings of the 34th International Symposium on Archaeometry*, 145–153. Zaragoza: Institución Fernando el Católico- CSIC.

Bédoyère de la, G., 2001. *The Buildings of Roman Britain*. London: Tempus.

Behmer, E. 1939. *Das zweischneidige Schwert der germanischen Völkerwanderungszeit*. Stockholm: Tryckeriaktiebolaget Sve.

Behr, C. 2010. New Bracteate Finds from Early Anglo-Saxon England. *Medieval Archaeology* 54, 34–88.

Behr, C. and Pestell, T. 2014. The Bracteate Hoard from Binham – an Early Anglo-Saxon Central Place? *Medieval Archaeology* 58, 47–82.

Bell, T. 2005. *The Religious Reuse of Roman Structures in Early Medieval England*. Oxford: British Archaeological Reports British Series 390.

Benes, Z. 2018. 'Kování jha doby římské v Čechách'. *Študi Jné Archeologického Ústavu Sav* 63, 107-124.

Beresford, G. 1979. Three deserted medieval settlements on Dartmoor: a report on the late E. Marie Minter's excavations. *Medieval Archaeology* 23, 98–158.

Betts, I. M., 2001. Summary of the building material from Deerton Street Roman villa, Kent, MoLSS unpublished report.

Betts, I. M. and Foot, R. 1994. A newly identified late Roman tile group from southern England. *Britannia* 25, 21–34.

Beven, G. 1982. Further observations on the food of tawny owls in London. *The London Naturalist 61*, 88–94.

Biddulph, E. 2017. The Roman Salt Industry in South-Eastern Britain. In D. Bird (ed.) *Agriculture and Industry in South-Eastern Roman Britain*, 210–235. Oxford: Oxbow Books.

Biddulph, E., Seager-Smith, R. and Schuster, J. 2011. *Settling the Ebbsfleet Valley. High Speed Excavations at Springhead and Northfleet, Kent – The Late Iron Age, Roman, Saxon and Medieval Landscape. Volume 2: Late Iron Age and Roman Finds Reports.* **Oxford: Oxford Wessex Archaeology.**

Bidwell, P. and Speak, S. 1994. *Excavations at South Shields Roman Fort*. Newcastle: Society of Antiquaries of Newcastle upon Tyne and Tyne and Wear Museums.

Birck, J. L. 1986. Precision K-Rb-Sr Isotopic Analysis - Application to Rb-Sr Chronology. *Chemical Geology 56 (1–2)*, 73–83.

Bishop, B. J. 2008a, Appendix 4: Lithic Assessment. In: G. Seddon. An Assessment of an Archaeological Excavation on Land at Grange Farm, Gillingham, Kent, 203–7. PCA Unpublished Report.

Bishop, B. J. 2008b. Excavations at the Former Bexley Hospital, Dartford Heath, Kent. *Kent Archaeological Society eArchaeological Reports*, http://www.kentarchaeology.ac/archrep/dartford01.pdf.

Bishop, B. J. 2014. Worked Flint. In: P. Boyer. *From Prehistory to the Nineteenth Century: excavations on two sites adjacent to Stuarts Road, Gravesend (Site 2)*, 19–22. London: Pre-Construct Archaeology Kent Papers 1.

Bishop, B. J. and Bagwell, M. 2005. *Iwade: occupation of a north Kent village from the Mesolithic to the Medieval period*. London: Pre-Construct Archaeology Monograph 3.

Blackmore, L. 2008. The pottery. In R. Cowie and L. Blackmore (Eds.) *Early and Middle Saxon rural settlement in the London region*, 168–93. London: Museum of London Archaeology Service Monograph 41.

Blair, C. 1962. *European and American arms c. 1100–1850*, London: B. T. Batsford Ltd.

Blair, J. 2005. *The Church in Anglo-Saxon Society*. Oxford: Oxford University Press.

Bland, R., Besly, E. and Burnett, A. 2009. *The Cuentio and Normanby Hoards: a new joint edition*. London: British Museum Press.

Blockley, K. 2000. *The Anglo-Saxon churches of Canterbury archaeologically reconsidered*, Durham theses, Durham University. Available at Durham E-Theses Online: *http://etheses.dur.ac.uk/4320/*.

Blockley, P. 1988. Excavations at No. 41 George Street, Canterbury, 1985, *Archaeologia Cantiana* 105 (1987), 59–178.

Blockley, K., Blockley, M., Blockley, P., Frere S. S. and Stow S. (Eds.) 1995. *The Archaeology of Canterbury, Volume V: Excavations in the Marlowe Car Park and Surrounding Areas*. Canterbury: Canterbury Archaeological Trust Ltd.

Boessneck, J., Müller, H-H. and Teichert, M. 1964. Osteologische Unterscheidungmerkmale zwischen Schaf (*Ovis aries* Linné) und Ziege (*Capra hircus* Linné). *Kühn-Archiv, Bd. 78, H.1–2*.

Böhme, H. 1974. *Germanische Grabfunde des 4. bis 5. Jahrhunderts*. Munich: Beck'sche Verlagsbuchhandlung.

Böhme, H. W. 1986. Das Ende der Römerherrschaft in Britannien und die Angelsächsich Besiedlung Englands im 5. Jahrhundert. *Jahrbuch Des Römish-Germanischen Zentralmuseums Mainz 33, 469–574*.

Bond, J. M., O'Connor, T. P. 1999. Bones from Medieval Deposits at 16–22 Coppergate and Other Sites in York. *The Archaeology of York 15/5*. York: York Archaeological Trust & CBA.

Boon, G. C., 1972–73. Roman glassware from Caerwent 1855–1925. *Monmouthshire Antiquary 3*, 111–23.

Booth, P. 2014. A late Roman military burial from the Dyke Hills, Dorchester upon Thames, Oxfordshire. *Britannia 45*, 243–273.

Booth, P., Bingham, A.-M. and Lawrence, S. (Eds.) 2008. *The Roman Roadside settlement at Westhawk Farm, Ashford, Kent: Excavations 1998–9*. Oxford: Oxford Archaeology.

Boston, C., Witkin, A., Boyle, A. and Wilkinson, D.R.P. 2008. *Safe Moor'd in Greenwich Tier': A study of the skeletons of Royal Navy sailors and marines at the Royal Hospital Greenwich*. Oxford: Oxford Archaeology Monograph 5.

Branch, N., Batchelor, C. R. and Swindle 2008. Appendix 8: Pollen Assessment of Samples Recovered from the Lead Coffin. In: G. Seddon. An Assessment of an Archaeological Excavation on Land at Grange Farm, Gillingham, Kent, 255–61. PCA Unpublished Report.

Brettell, R, Evans, J.A., Marzinzik, S., Lamb, A. and Montgomery, J. 2012. Can Oxygen and Strontium Isotopes Serve as Indicators of Provenance in Early Medieval European Cemetery Populations?. *European Journal of Archaeology 15 (1)*, 117–145.

Brickstock, R. 1987. *Copies of the Fel Temp Reparatio Coinage in Britain*. Oxford: British Archaeological Reports 176.

Brodribb, A. C. C, Hands, A. R. and Walker, D. R. 1968. *Excavations at Shakenoak Farm, near Wilcote, Oxfordshire, Part I: sites A & D*. Oxford: A.R. Hands.

Brodribb, G. 1987. *Roman Brick and Tile*. Gloucester: Alan Sutton Publishing.

Brooks, S.T. and Suchey, J.M. 1990. Skeletal Age determination Based on the OS Pubis: A Comparison of the Acsadi-Nemeskeri and Suchey-Brooks Methods. *Human evolution 5*, 227–238.

Brothwell, D.1981. *Digging Up Bones. London:* British Museum Press.

Brown, A. 1991. Structured Deposition and Technological Change among the Flaked Stone Artefacts from Cranbourne Chase. In J. Barrett, R. Bradley and M. Hall (Eds.) *Papers on the Prehistoric Archaeology of Cranbourne Chase,* 101–33. Oxford: Oxbow Monograph 11.

Brown, P. 1981. *The Cult of the Saints: its rise and function in Latin Christianity.* Chicago: University of Chicago Press.

Budd, P. 1987. Analyses of some "Litharge Cakes" from Southwark Cathedral, London. *Ancient Monuments Laboratory Report 142/87.* London: English Heritage.

Buikstra, J. E., and Mielke, J. H. 1985. Demography, Diet and Health. In: R. I. Gilbert. And J. H. Mielke (Eds.) *The Analysis of Prehistoric Diets.* New York: Academic Press.

Buikstra, J. E. and Ubelaker, D. H. 1994. *Standards for Data Collection from Human Skeletal Remains.* Fayetteville: Arkansas Archaeological Research Series No. 44.

Burnham, C. and Wacher, J. 1990. *The small towns of Roman Britain.* Berkeley and Los Angeles: University of California Press, 77–78.

Burton, P. 2017. *Sulpicius Severus' Vita Martini.* Oxford: Oxford University Press.

Campbell, G. 1998. The charred plant remains. In: A. Boyle and R. Early. *Excavations at Springhead Roman Town, Southfleet, Kent,* 36–39. OAU Occasional Paper 1.

Čančarević, M., Zinkevich, M. and Aldingeret, F. 2005. Enthalpy of formation of Cu_2PbO_2 and revision of the Cu_2O-PbO Phase Diagram. *Materials Science Forum 494,* 67–72.

Cappers, R. T. J., Bekker R. M. and Jans J. E. A. 2006. Digital Seed Atlas of the Netherlands. Barkhuis, Netherlands: *Groningen Archaeological Series 4.*

Catherall, P. D. 1983. A Romano-British pottery manufacturing site at Oakleigh Farm, Higham, Kent. *Britannia XIV.*

Challinor, D. 2006a. *The wood charcoal from Thurnham Roman Villa, Kent (ARC THM 98).* CTRL Specialist Report Series.

Challinor, D. 2006b. *Wood charcoal from Northumberland Bottom, Southfleet, Kent.* CTRL Specialist Report Series.

Challinor, D. 2008. Wood Charcoal. In: P. Booth, A.-M. Bingham. S. Lawrence (Eds.) *The Roman Roadside settlement at Westhawk Farm, Ashford, Kent: Excavations 1998–9,* 343–349. Oxford: Oxford Archaeology.

Champion, T. 2007. Prehistoric Kent. In: J. Williams (Ed.) *The Archaeology of Kent to AD800,* 67–134. Woodbridge Boydell and Kent County Council.

Chapman, A. and Atkins, R. 2005. Iron Age and Roman Settlement at Mallards Close, Earls Barton, Northamptonshire. Northamptonshire Archaeology Unpublished Report 05/031.

Charlesworth, D. 1974. Glass Vessels. In: M. Hassall & J. Rhodes (Eds.) Excavations at the New Market Hall, Gloucester 1966–7', *Trans Bristol & Gloucestershire Archaeol Soc, 93,* 15–100.

Chenery, C. A., Pashley, V., Lamb, A. L., Sloane, H. J. and Evans, J. A. 2012. The oxygen isotope relationship between the phosphate and structural carbonate fractions of human bioapatite. *Rapid Communications in Mass Spectrometry 26(3),* 309–319.

Clairmont, C. W. 1963. *The Excavations at Dura-Europos, Final Report IV, Part V: Glass vessels.* New Haven: D. B. Harden.

Clark, A. 1993. *Excavations at Mucking Vols 1.* London: English Heritage Archaeological Reports 20 and 21.

Clark, K. 2012. A review of the Romano-British dog. In M, Fulford (Ed.) *Silchester and the study of Romano-British urbanism (JRA suppl. 90),* 165–184.

Clarke, C. 1999. Palynological indicators of a Bronze Age cist burial from Whitcome, Scottish Borders, Scotland. *Journal of Archaeological Science 26,* 553–560.

Clason, A. T. 1967. *Animal and Man in Holland's Past,* vol. A. Groningen: J. B. Wolters.

Cohen, A. and Serjeantson, D. 1986. *A Manual for The Identification of Bird Bones from Archaeological Sites.* London: Archetype Publications.

Cool, H. 1990. Roman metal hairpins from southern Britain. *The Archaeological Journal 147,* 148–182.

Cool, H. 2006. *Eating and Drinking in Roman Britain.* Cambridge: Cambridge University Press.

Cool, H. and Price, J. 1987. The glass. In: G. W. Meates. *The Roman villa at Lullingstone, Kent: 2, the wall-paintings and finds,* 110–42, Kent Archaeological Society Monograph, 3.

Coplen, T. B. 1988. Normalization of oxygen and hydrogen isotope data. *Chemical Geology 72,* 293–297.

Cotter, J. 1991. The medieval pottery and tile industry at Tyler Hill. *Canterbury's Archaeology 1990–1991.*

Cotter, J. 2006. The pottery. In K. Parfitt, B. Corke and J. Cotter. *Townwall Street, Dover Excavations 1996,* 121–254. The Archaeology of Canterbury New Series Volume III. Canterbury Archaeological Trust.

Cotter, J. 2008. Medieval London-type Ware Kilns Discovered at Woolwich. *Medieval Pottery Research Group Newsletter* 61, 3–5.

Courtney, P. 1997. Ceramics and the history of consumption: pitfalls and prospects. *Medieval Ceramics* 21, 95–108.

Crawford, S. 2004. Votive deposition, religion and the Anglo-Saxon furnished burial ritual. *World Archaeology* 36, 87–102.

Crerar, B. 2012. *Conceptualising 'deviancy': The fragmentation of the corpse and the dislocation of identity in Romano-British funerary rites. PhD Thesis,* Cambridge University.

Crummy, N. 1979. A Chronology of Romano-British Bone Pins. *Britannia* 10, 157–163.

Crummy, N. 1983. *Colchester Archaeological Report 2: The Roman small finds from excavations in Colchester 1971–9.* Colchester: Colchester Archaeological Trust Ltd.

Cunliffe B. and Poole, C. *1998. The Danebury Environs Roman Programme: A Wessex landscape in the Roman era, Volume 2, Part 2: Grateley South, Grateley, Hants 1998 and 1999.* Oxford: Oxbow Books.

Cunningham, C. M. and Drury, P. J. 1985. *Post-medieval sites and their pottery: Moulsham Street, Chelmsford.* Chelmsford Archaeological Trust Report 5/CBA Research Report 54.

Darling, M. J. and Gurney, D. 1993. Caister-on-Sea excavations by Charles Green, 1951–55, *East Anglian Archaeology* 60, 1–290.

Davies, B., Richardson, B. and Tomber, R. 1994. *A Dated Corpus of Early Roman Pottery from the City of London.* Council for British Archaeology Research Report 98. London.

Dickin, A.P., 2018. *Radiogenic isotope geology.* Cambridge: Cambridge University Press.

Dickinson, M. 1986. *Seventeenth-century tokens of the British Isles and their Values.* London: Seaby.

Dickinson, T. 1976. *The Anglo-Saxon burial sites of the upper Thames region, and their bearing on the history of Wessex, circa AD 400–700.* Unpublished PhD thesis. St Annes's College, Oxford.

Dobney, K. M., Jacques, S. D. and Irving, B. G., 1996. *Of butchers and breeds: Report on vertebrate remains from various sites in the city of Lincoln.* Lincoln: Lincoln Archaeology Ser 5.

Dobney, K., Jacques, D., Carrott, J., Hall, A., Issitt, M. and Large, F. 1996. Biological remains from excavations at Carr Naze, Filey, N. Yorkshire: Technical report. *Reports of the Environmental Archaeology Unit, York 96/26:* 14 – 37.

Dowker G. and Roach Smith C. 1878. Roman Remains at Preston next Wingham. *Archaeologia Cantiana,* 12. 47–48.

Driesch, von den, A. 1976. *A Guide to the Measurement of Animal Bones from Archaeological Sites.* Peabody Museum Bulletin 1.

Driesch, von den, A. and Boessneck, J. 1974. Kritische Anmerkungen zur Widerristhöhenberechnung aus Langenmassen vor-und frühgeschichlicher Tierknochen. *Saugetierkundliche Mitteilungen 22,* 325–348.

Dungworth, D. 2015. *Archaeometallurgy: Guidelines for Best Practice.* Historic England.

Dunning, G. C. 1966. Neolithic Occupation in East Kent. *Antiquaries Journal 46 (1),* 1–25.

Dunster, J. and Dungworth, D. 2012. *St Algar's Farm, Frome, Somerset. The analysis of lead-working waste.* Research Report 15/2012. Portsmouth: English Heritage.

Dykes, D. W. 2011. *Coinage and Currency in Eighteen-Century Britain. The Provincial Coinage.* Malta: Spink & Son Ltd.

Eckardt, H. 2014. *Objects and Identities: Roman Britain and the North-West provinces.* Oxford: Oxford University Press.

Edmonds, M. 1995. *Stone Tools and Society.* London: Batsford.

Egan, G. 1997. Non-ceramic finds. In C. Thomas, B. Sloane and C. Phillpotts. *Excavations at the Priory and Hospital of St Mary Spital, London,* 201–10. London: Museum of London Archaeology Service Monograph 1.

Egan, G. 1998. *The Medieval Household c. 1150 – c. 1450. Medieval finds from excavations in London 6.* London: The Stationery Office.

Egan, G. 2001. 'Pilgrims' Souvenir Badges of St Alban. In: M. Henig and P. Lindley (Eds.) *Alban and St Albans; Roman and Medieval Architecture, Art and Archaeology*, 213–17. Leeds: BAA Conference Transactions XXIV.

Egan, G. 2005. *Material culture in London in an age of transition. Tudor and Stuart period finds c 1450–c 1700 from excavations at riverside sites in Southwark.* London: Museum of London Archaeology Service Monograph 19.

Egan, G. 2006. The earliest English lead tokens? 589–600. In: B. Cook and G. Williams (Eds.) *Coinage and History in the North Sea World, c. AD 500–1250; Essays in Honour of Marion Archibald*, Leiden/Boston: Brill.

Egan, G. and Forsyth, H. 1997. Wound Wire and Silver Gilt: changing fashions in dress accessories c. 1400 – c. 160. In: D. Gaimster and P. Stamper (Eds.) *The Age of Transition. The Archaeology of English Culture 1400–1600*, 215–38. The Society for Medieval Archaeology Monograph 15. Oxbow Monograph 98. Exeter: Oxbow.

Egan, G. and Pritchard, F. 1991. *Dress Accessories c. 1150–c. 1450. Medieval finds from excavations in London 3.* London: Boydell Press.

English Heritage (nd). *History of Lullingstone Roman Villa.*

Evans, C., Appleby, G., Lucy, S. and Regan, R. 2013. *Process and History: Romano-British communities at Colne Fen, Earith: an inland port and supply farm.* Cambridge: Cambridge Archaeological Unit Landscape Archives Series.

Evans, J. 2001. Material approaches to the identification of different Romano-British site types. In: S. James and M. Millett (Eds.) *Britons and Romans: Advancing an Archaeological Agenda*, 26–35. Oxford: British Archaeology Research Reports No. 125.

Evans, J. A., Chenery, C. A. and Montgomery J. 2012. A summary of strontium and oxygen isotope variation in archaeological human tooth enamel excavated from Britain. *Journal of Analytical Atomic Spectrometry 27(5)*, 754–764.

Evans, J. A., Chenery, C. A. Mee, K., Cartwright, C. E., Lee, K. A. Marchant, A. P. and Hannaford, L. 2018a. Biosphere Isotope Domains GB (V1): Interactive Website. British Geological Survey. (Interactive Resource).https://doi.org/10.5285/3b141dce-76fc-4c54-96fa-c232e98010ea

Evans, J., Mee, K., Chenery, C., Cartwright, C., Lee K. and Marchant, A. 2018b. User guide for the Biosphere Isotope Domains GB (Version 1) dataset and web portal. British Geological Survey Open Report OR/18/005, 21pp.

Fairnell, E. H. 2003. *The Utilisation of Fur-bearing Animals in the British Isles.* M.Sc. Thesis: University of York.

Farwell, D. and Molleson, T. 1993. *Poundbury Volume 2: The cemeteries.* Dorchester, Dorset Natural History and Archaeological Society Monograph 11.

Foley, W. T. and Higham N. J. 2009. Bede on the Britons. *Early Medieval Europe 17*, 154–85.

Ford, S., Bradley, R., Hawkes, J. and Fisher, P. 1984. Flint-Working in the Metal Age. *Oxford Journal of Archaeology 3*, 157–173.

Forsyth, H. and Egan, G. 2005. *Toys, Trifles and Trinkets: Base Metal Miniatures from London 1200–1800.* Museum of London. London: Unicorn Press.

Fox, A. 1968. Excavations at the South Gate, Exeter, 1964–5. *Proceedings of the Devon Archaeological Society 26*, 1–20.

Frere, S. 1972. *Verulamium Excavations.* London, Reports of the Research Committee of the Society of Antiquaries 28.

Friendship-Taylor, R. and Greep, S. 2012. A Claudian group of bone hinges and box fittings from a 'military' latrine pit beneath the Piddington phase 1b proto-villa. *Lucerna 42*, 2–9.

Fulford, M. and Hodder, I. 1975. A regression analysis of some late Romano-British pottery: a case study'. *Oxoniensia 39*, 26–33.

Gaimster, M. 1992. Scandinavian Gold Bracteates in Britain: Money and Media in the Dark Ages. *Medieval Archaeology 36*, 1–28.

Gaimster, M. 2001. Gold bracteates and necklaces. In: B. Magnus (Ed.) *Roman Gold and the Development of the Early Germanic Kingdoms: Aspects of Technical, Socio-Political, Socio-Economic, Artistic and Intellectual Development, A.D. 1-550*, 143–55. Kungliga Vitterhets Historie och Antikvitets Akademien, Konferenser 51, Stockholm: Almqvist & Wiksell International.

Gaimster, M. 2016. A snapshot of the Dark Ages: the finds context of a fifth-century gilded silver brooch from Gillingham in Kent. In I. Riddler, J. Soulat and L. Keys (eds), *The Evidence of Material Culture: Studies in Honour of Professor Vera Evison*, 197–207. Europe Médiévale 10, Autuns: Editions Mergoil.

Gaimster, M. 2020a. Metal and small finds. In A. Fairman, S. Teague and J. Butler, *Bridging the Past: Life in Medieval and Post Medieval Southwark; Excavations along the route of Thameslink Borough Viaduct and at London Bridge Station*, 477–88. London and Oxford: OAPCA.

Gaimster, M. 2020b. Small Finds from the Settlement. In R. Brown, S. Teague, L. Loe, B. Sudds, E. Popescu, *Excavations at Stoke Quay, Ipswich*. Norwich: East Anglian Archaeology 172.

Gale, R. & Cutler, D. 2000. *Plants in Archaeology*. Otley/London: Westbury/Royal Botanic Gardens, Kew.

Gardner, C. 2009. *Chester, Cheshire. Assessment of evidence for metalworking from Chester amphitheatre*. Research Department Report Series 26–2009. Portsmouth: Historic England.

Garrow, D. 2006 Pits, Settlement and Deposition during the Neolithic and Early Bronze Age in East Anglia. *British Archaeological Report (British Series)* 414.

Garrow, D., Beadsmore, E. and Knight, M. 2005. Pit Clusters and the Temporality of Occupation: an earlier Neolithic Site at Kilverstone, Thetford, Norfolk. *Proceedings of the Prehistoric Society* 71, 139–57.

Gelling, M. 1984. *Signposts to the Past*. Chichester: Phillimore.

Gentry Steele, D. and Bramblett, C. A. 1988. *The Anatomy and Biology of the Human Skeleton*. Texas: A&M University Press, College Station.

Gerrard J. 2008. Feeding the army from Dorset: pottery, salt and the Roman state. In: S. Stallibrass, and R. Thomas (Eds.) *Feeding the Roman Army: The Archaeology of Production and Supply in NW Europe*, 116–130. Oxford: Oxbow Books.

Gerrard, J. 2011. New Light on the End of Roman London. *The Archaeological Journal* 168, 181–194.

Gerrard, J. 2013. *The Ruin of Roman Britain*. Cambridge: Cambridge University Press.

Gerrard, J. and Lyne, M. 2008. Assessment of the Romano-British Pottery. In: G. Seddon. Grange Farm, Gillingham, Kent. Assessment of an Archaeological Excavation. PCA Unpublished Report, 165–191.

Gerrard, J. and Ridgeway, V. 2018. A Romano-British graffito of a ship from Gillingham, Kent, UK. *International Journal of Nautical Archaeology* 1–2.

Gibbard, P.L. 1986. Flint Gravels in the Quaternary of Southeast England. In: G. De C. Sieveking and M. B. Hart (Eds.) *The Scientific Study of Flint and Chert*, 141–149. Cambridge: Cambridge University Press.

Gillam, J. 1976. Coarse fumed ware in North Britain and Beyond. *Glasgow Archaeological Journal* 4, 57–80.

Gillet, P. A. 2000. Sarcophages en plomb Gallo-Romaines Decouverts a Amiens et Dans ses Environs (Somme). *Revue Archeologique de Picardie*, 77–118.

Gillet, P.-E., Bechennec, J. 2017. Sarcophages en plomb de la necropole Nord Gallo-Romaine de la Citadelle d'Amiens. *Revue Archaeologique de Picardie*, 69–106.

Girbal, B. 2011. *Roman and Medieval Litharge Cakes. A Scientific Examination*. Research Department Report Series 51–2011. Portsmouth: Historic England.

Glue, D. E. 1970. Avian predator pellet analysis and the mammalogist. *Mammal Review 1 (3)*, 53 – 62.

Goody, P. C, 1976. *Horse anatomy. A pictorial approach to equine structure*. Tonbridge: J.A. Allen & Co. Ltd.

Gowland, W. 1900. Remains of a Roman silver refinery at Silchester. *Archaeologia* 57, 113–124.

Grant, A, 1975. The animal bones. In: B. Cunliffe. *Excavations at Portchester Castle Volume I: Roman*, 378–408. Reports of the Research Committee of the Society of Antiquaries of London No. XXXII.

Grant, A, 1982. The use of toothwear as a guide to the age of domestic ungulates. In Wilson, B. Grigson, C, S Payne, S. (Eds) *Ageing and sexing animal bones from archaeological sites*, 91–108. Oxford: British Archaeological Series.

Graser, E. 1975. The Edict of Diocletian on Maximum Prices. In T. Frank (Ed.) *An Economic Survey of Ancient Rome Vol. V: Rome and Italy of the Empire*. New York, Octagon, 305- 421.

Gray, L. 2012. Grange Farm, Gillingham, Kent (Site Code: KKGF03): Environmental Archaeological Assessment – Interim Report. PCA Unpublished Report for QUEST.

Greatorex, C. 1995. An Archaeological evaluation at Grench Manor, 348 Grange Road, Gillingham. South Eastern Archaeological Services Unpublished Report.

Greep, S. 1987. Lead sling-shot from Windridge Farm, St. Albans and the use of the sling by the Roman army. *Britannia* 18, 183–200.

Greep, S. 1995. Objects of Bone, Antler and Ivory from C.A.T. Sites. In: K. Blockley, M. Blockley, P. Blockley, S.S. Frere and S. Stow (Eds.) *The Archaeology of Canterbury, Volume V: Excavations in the Marlowe Car Park and Surrounding Areas, Part II: The Finds, 1112–1169.* Canterbury: Canterbury Archaeological Trust Ltd.

Greig, J. R. A. 1991. The British Isles. In: W. van Zeist, K. Wasylikowa and K.-E. Behre (Eds.) *Progress in Old World Palaeoethnobotany: A Retrospective View on the Occasion of 20 Years of the International Work Group for Palaeoethnobotany,* 299–334. Rotterdam: A.A. Balkerma.

Grey, C. 2011 *Constructing Communities in the Late Roman Countryside.* Cambridge, Cambridge University Press.

Griffiths, D., Philpott, R. A. and Egan, G. 2007. *Meols. The Archaeology of the North Wirral Coast. Discoveries and observations in the 19th and 20th centuries, with a catalogue of collections.* Oxford: Oxford University School of Archaeology Monograph 68.

Griffiths, N. 1986. Horse Harness Pendants. *London: Medieval Finds research Group 700–1700,* Datasheet 5.

Griffiths, N. 1995. Harness pendants and associated fittings. In: J. Clark (Ed.) *The Medieval Horse and its Equipment, Medieval Finds from Excavations in London 5,* 61–71, London.

Grigson, C. 1982. Sex and age determination of some bones and teeth of domestic cattle: a review of the literature. In: B. Wilson, C. Grigson and S. Payne (Eds.) *Ageing and Sexing Animal Bones from Archaeological Sites,* 7–23. Oxford: British Archaeological Reports Series 109.

Grimm, J. M., Worley, F. 2011. Animal Bone. In: C. Barnett, J. I. McKinley, E. Stafford, J. M. Grimm and C. J. Stevens. *Settling the Ebbsfleet Valley: High Speed 1 Excavations at Springhead and Northfleet, Kent, The Late Iron Age, Roman, Saxon and Medieval Landscape, Vol. 3: Late Iron Age to Roman Human Remains and Environmental Reports,* 15–52. Oxford: Wessex Archaeology.

Grimm, J. M. 2007. A dog's life: animal bone from a Romano-British ritual shaft at Springhead, Kent (UK). *Beiträge zur Archäozoologie und Prähistoischen Anthropologie Bond VI,* 54–75.

Groot, M, 2005. Palaeopathological evidence for draught cattle on a Roman site in the Netherlands. In: J. Davis, M. Fabiš, I. Mainland, M. Richards and R. Thomas (Eds.) *Diet and health in past animal populations,* 52–57. 9th ICAZ Conference, Durham. Oxford: Oxbow Books.

Guest, P. S. W. 2005. *The Late Roman Gold and Silver Coins from the Hoxne Treasure.* London: British Museum Press.

Guido, M. 1978. *The Glass Beads of the Prehistoric and Roman periods in Britain and Ireland.* London: Society of Antiquaries Research Report 35.

Halpin A. 1988. A 'Winchester-style' bronze mount, *Miscellanea 1, Medieval Dublin excavations 1962–81,* Series B 2, 7–12. Dublin: National Museum of Ireland.

Halsall, G. 2007. *Barbarian Migrations and the Roman West 376–568.* Cambridge: Cambridge University Press.

Hamerow, H. 1993. *Excavations at Mucking, Vol. 2: the Anglo-Saxon settlement, excavations by M U Jones and W T Jones.* English Heritage.

Hamilton-Dyer, S. 2009. Animal bone. In: J. Wright, M. Leivers, R. Seager Smith and C. J. Stevens Cambourne. *New Settlement. Iron Age and Romano-British Settlement on the Clay Uplands of West Cambridgeshire,* 82–133. Wessex Archaeology Report No. 23.

Harcourt, R. A. 1974. The dog in Prehistoric and early historic Britain. *Journal of Archaeological Science 1,* 151–175.

Harden, D. B. 1936. *Roman glass from Karanis found by the University of Michigan archaeological expedition in Egypt 1924–29.* Univ. of Michigan Stud, Humanistic Series, 4.

Hårdh, B. 2002. The Contacts of the Central Place. In: L. Larsson and B. Hårdh (Eds.) *Centrality – Regionality: The Social Structure of Southern Sweden during the iron Age,* 27–66. Uppåkrastudier 7, Acta Archaeologica Lundensia series in 8°, no. 40. Lund: Almqvist & Wiksell International.

Hårdh, B. 2003. Uppåkra i folkvandringstiden. In: B. Hårdh (Ed.) *Fler fynd i centrum: Materialstudier i och kring Uppåkra,* 41–80. Uppåkrastudier 9, Acta Archaeologica Lundensia series in 8°, no. 45, Lund: Almqvist & Wiksell International.

Harl, K. 1996. Coinage in the Roman Economy 300BC – AD700. London: Johns Hopkins University Press.

Harrington, S. and Brookes, S. 2012. ASKED – the Anglo-Saxon Kent Electronic Database. *Journal of Open Archaeology Data* 1: e2. http://doi.org/10.5334/4f33a7b040dd1.

Harrison, A. 1991. Excavation of a Belgic and Roman site at 50–54 High Street, Rochester. *Archaeologia Cantiana* 109, 41–50.

Hartley, B. and Dickinson, B. M. 2010. *Names on Terra Sigillata: an index of makers' stamps & signatures on Gallo-Roman Terra Sigillata (Samian ware)*, Volume 5 L to Masclus I, Bulletin of the Institute of Classical Studies Supplement 102. London: Institute of Classical Studies.

Haseloff, G. 1974. Salin's Style I. *Medieval Archaeology* 18, 1–15.

Haseloff, G. 1981. *Die germanische Tierornamentik der Völkerwanderungszeit: Studien zur Salin's Stil I*, Band I–III, Berlin, New York: Walter de Gruyter.

Haseloff, G. 1986. Bild und Motif im Nydam Stil und Stil I. In: H. Roth (Ed.) *Zum Problem der Deutung Frühmittelalterlicher Bildinhalte*, 67–110. Veröffentlichungen des Vorgeschichtlichen Seminars der Phillips-Universität Marburg a. d. Lahn, Sonderband 4. Sigmaringen: Jan Thorbecke Verlag.

Haslam, A. 2003. An Archaeological Evaluation of Land at Grange Farm, Gillingham, Kent. PCA Unpublished Report.

Hasted, E. 1798. *The History and Topographical Survey of the County of Kent.* 2nd Edition: Volume 4.

Hathaway, S. J. E., 2013. *Making the invisible, visible. Iron age and Roman salt-production in Southern Britain.* Unpublished Doctoral Thesis. Bournemouth University. http://eprints.bournemouth.ac.uk/21381/10/5_Kent.pdf.

Hather, J. G. 2000. *The Identification of the Northern European Woods: A Guide for archaeologists and conservators.* London: Archetype Publications Ltd.

Hawkes, C.F.C. 1951. Bronze-workers, cauldrons, and bucket-animals in Iron Age and Roman Britain. In: W.F. Grimes (Ed.) *Aspects of Archaeology in Britain and Beyond: Essays presented to O.G.S. Crawford*, 172–199. London: H.W. Edwards.

Hawkes, S. and Dunning, G. 1961. Soldiers and settlers in Britain: Fourth to fifth century. *Mediaeval Archaeology* 5, 1–70.

Hawkins, D. 2002. Archaeological Desk Based Assessment. Land at Grange Farm, Gillingham, Kent. CgMS Consulting Unpublished Report.

Hawthorne, J. G. and Smith 1979, C. S. *Theophilus on Divers Arts: the foremost medieval treatise on painting, glassmaking and metal-work.* Translated from the Latin with introduction and notes. New York: Dover Publications.

Hayward, K. 2007. Rochester Riverside (RRS04) The Building Material. Unpublished report for AOC Archaeology.

Hayward, K. M. J. 2009. *Roman Quarrying and Stone Supply on the periphery – southern England. A geological study of first century funerary monuments and monumental architecture.* Oxford: British Archaeological Reports Series 500, Archaeopress.

Hayward, K. M. J. (2015). Types and sources of stone. In Coombe, P. C. Grew, F., Hayward, K. And Henig, M. 2015. *Roman Sculpture from London and the South-East.* Oxford: Oxford University Press.

Hedeager, L. 1991. Gulddepoterne fra aeldre germanertid. In: C. Fabech and J. Ringtved (Eds.) *Samfundsorganisation og Regional Variation, Norden i romersk jernalder og folkevandringstid*, 203–12, Jysk Arkaeologisk Selskabs Skrifter 27, Aarhus: Jysk Arkaeologisk Selskab.

Herne, A. 1991. The Flint Assemblage. In: I. Longworth, A. Herne, G. Varndell and S. Needham. *Excavations at Grimes Graves Norfolk 1972 - 1976. Fascicule 3. Shaft X: Bronze Age flint, chalk and metal working*, 21 - 93. Dorchester: British Museum Press.

Heyworth, M. 1988. *Non-Ferrous Metalworking Evidence from St Jon's Lane, Canterbury, Kent.* Ancient Monuments Laboratory Report 18/88. London: English Heritage.

Hill, J. and Rowsome, P. 2011. Roman London and the Walbrook Crossing: Excavations at 1 Poultry and vicinity, City of London, MOLA Monograph 37. London: MoLA.

Hillman, G. 1981. Reconstructing crop husbandry practices from charred remains of crops. In R. Mercer (Eds.) *Farming practice in British prehistory*, 123–62. Edinburgh: Edinburgh University Press.

Hills, C. 2006. *The Origins of the English.* London: Duckworth.

Hillson, S. 1996. *Dental anthropology.* 3rd Edition. New York: Cambridge University Press.

Hinchcliffe, J. and Sparey Green, C. 1985. *Excavations at Brancaster 1974 and 1977.* Dereham: East Anglian Archaeology 23.

Hinds, K. 2018. *HAMP-CE1119: A Roman Dodecahedron.* https://finds.org.uk/database/artefacts/record/id/895851.

Hines, J. and Bayliss, A. (Eds.) 2013. *Anglo-Saxon Graves and Grave Goods of the 6th and 7th Centuries AD: a chronological framework.* London: Society for Medieval Archaeology Monograph 33.

Høilund Neilsen, K. 2013. 'SP Spearhead'. In: J. Hines and A. Bayliss (Eds.) *Anglo-Saxon Graves and Grave Goods of the 6th and 7th Centuries AD: a chronological framework*, 163–181. London: Society for Medieval Archaeology Monograph 33.

Humphrey, J. 2003. The Utilization and Technology of Flint in the British Iron Age. In J. Humphrey (Ed.) *Re-searching the Iron Age: selected papers from the proceedings of the Iron Age research student seminars, 1999 and 2000*, 17–23. Leicester Archaeology Monograph 11.

Hunt, G. 2011. Along the eastern defences: excavations at 8–14 Cooper's Row and 1 America Square in the City of London. *Transactions of the London and Middlesex Archaeological Society* 61 (2010), 41–80.

Hunter, F. and Painter, K. (Eds.) 2013. *Late Roman Silver. The Traprain Treasure in Context.* Edinburgh: Society of Antiquaries of Scotland.

Isings, C. 1957. *Roman Glass from dated Finds.* Groningen/Djakarta.

Isings, C. 1971. *Roman glass in Limburg.* Archaeologica Traiectina IX, Groningen.

IWM 2018 *B1E 1kg incendiary bomb.* https://www.iwm. org.uk/collections/item/object/30021484 [date accessed: 10/6/2018].

Jackson, R. 2010. *Cosmetic sets of Late Iron Age and Roman Britain.* London: British Museum Press.

Jacomet, S. 2006. *Identification of cereal remains from archaeological sites.* 2nd ed. Archaeobotany laboratory, IPAS, Basel University Unpublished Report.

James, R. 2006. A Prehistoric Flintworking Site at Berengrave Nursery, Rainham. *Archaeologia Cantiana* 126, 375–380.

James, S. 2011. *Rome and the Sword.* London: Thames and Hudson.

Jarrett, C. 2009. The ceramics: pottery consumption and trade. In: G. Draper and F. Meddens. *The sea and the marsh. The medieval Cinque Port of New Romney*, 71–83. Pre-Construct Archaeology Monograph 10.

Johns, C. 2010. *The Hoxne Late Roman Treasure: Gold jewellery and silver plate.* London: British Museum Press.

Johnstone, C., and Albarella, U. 2002. *The Late Iron Age and Romano-British Mammal and Bird Bone Assemblage from Elms Farm, Heybridge, Essex (Site Code: Hyef93-95).* Centre for Archaeology Report 45/2002

Jones, G. 1998. Wheat grain identification, why bother?. *Environmental Archaeology* 2, 29–34.

Jones, G. and Sadler, P. 2012. Age at death in cattle: methods, older cattle and known-age reference material, *Environmental Archaeology*, 17:1, 11–28.

Jones 2012 Howell, I., Henderson, M. and Spurr, G. 2011 Excavations of prehistoric, Roman and Saxon remains by the Medway Estuary at Kings North. London, MoLA .https://www.kentarchaeology.org. uk/10/041.pdf.

Karakaya, I. and Thompson, W. T. 1987. The Ag-Pb (Silver-Lead) system. *Bulletin of Alloy Phase Diagrams 8, (4)*, 326–334.

Keller, P. and Chenery, M. 1992. *Gillingham, Grinch Manor, Summary Report of an Archaeological Rescue Excavation January, 1992.* Kent Minor sites Series, No. 7. Kent Archaeological Rescue Unit.

Kirk, D. A. 1992. Diet changes in breeding tawny owls (*Strix aluco*). *Journal of Raptor Research 26 (4)*, 239–242.

Kjølbye-Biddle, B. 2001. The Alban Cross. In: M. Henig and P. Lindley (Eds.) *Alban and St Albans; Roman and Medieval Architecture, Art and Archaeology*, 85–110. Leeds: BAA Conference Transactions XXIV.

Lauwerier, R. C. G. M. 1993a. Bird remains in Roman graves. *Archaeofauna* 2, 75–82.

Lauwerier, R. C. G. M. 1993b. Twenty–eight bird briskets in a pot: Roman preserved food from Nijmegen. *Archaeofauna* 2, 15–19.

Lawrence, M. J. and Brown, R. W. 1973. *Mammals of Britain Their Tracks, Trails and Signs.* London: Blandford Press. Revised Edition.

Leech, R. 1982. *Excavations at Catsgore 1970–73: A Romano-British village.* Bristol: Western Archaeological Trust Monograph 2.

Lemppenau, U. 1964. *Geschlechts-und Gattungsunterschiede am Becken Mitteleuropäischer Wiederkäuer.* Dissertation: München Universitat.

Levine, M. A. 1982. The use of crown height measurements and eruption-wear sequences to age horse teeth. In B. Wilson, C. Grigson and S. Payne (Eds.) *Ageing and Sexing Animal Bones from Archaeological Sites*, 223–50. British Archaeological Reports Series 109.

Levitan, B. 1994. The vertebrate remains from the Villa. In: R. J. Williams and R. J. Zeepvat. *Bancroft - A late Bronze Age/Iron Age settlement, Roman villa and temple-mausoleum, Vol 2, Finds and Environmental evidence*, 536–549. Buckinghamshire Archaeological Society Monograph Series, No 7.

Lewis, S. and Llewellyn Jones, L. 2017. *The Culture of Animals. Antiquity* (co-author). London: Routledge.

Liddle, J., Ainsley, C. and Rielly, K. 2009. Animal bone. In: C. Cowan. *Roman Southwark settlement and economy: Excavations in Southwark 1973-91*, 244-248. MOLA Monograph 42. London: Museum of London Archaeology.

Liddle, J, 2008. The animal bones. In: N. Bateman, C. Cowan and R. Wroe-Brown. *London's Roman amphitheatre: excavations at the Guildhall.* MoLAS Monograph 35. London: Museum of London Archaeology Service.

Lightfoot E. and O'Connell T. C. 2016. On the Use of Biomineral Oxygen Isotope Data to Identify Human Migrants in the Archaeological Record: Intra-Sample Variation, Statistical Methods and Geographical Considerations. PLoS ONE 11(4): e0153850. https://doi.org/10.1371/journal.pone.0153850.

Livarda, A. and Orengo, H. 2015. Reconstructing the Roman London flavourscape: new insights into the exotic food plant trade using network and spatial analysis. *Journal of Archaeological Science 55*, 244-252.

Lodwick, L. 2017. Evergreen plants in Roman Britain and beyond: movement, meaning and materiality'. *Britannia 48*, 135-173.

Lovejoy, C. O., Meindl, R. S., Pryzbeck, T. R. and Mensforth, R. P. 1985. Chronological metamorphosis of the auricular surface of the ilium: a new method for the determination of the adult skeletal age at death *American Journal of Physical Anthropology 68*, 15-28.

Lucy, S. 2016. Odd goings on at Mucking: interpreting the latest Romano-British pottery horizon. In: J. Gerrard (Ed.) *Roman Pottery in the Fifth Century.* Internet Archaeology.

Lucy, S., Tipper, J. and Dickens, A. 2009. *The Anglo-Saxon Cemetery at Bloodmoor Hill, Carlton Colville, Suffolk.* Cambridge: East Anglian Archaeology 131.

Luff, R. M. 1982. *A Zooarchaeological Study of the Roman North-western Provinces.* Oxford: British Archaeological Reports International Series 137.

Lundock, J. 2014. *A study of the deposition and distribution of copper-alloy vessels in Roman Britain.* Unpublished Kings College London PhD Thesis.

Lyne, M. 1999. The pottery. In: J. Sawyer. The excavation of a Romano-British site at Burgess Hill. *Sussex Archaeological Collections 137*, 49-58.

Lyne, M. and Jefferies, R. S. 1979. *The Alice Holt/Farnham Roman pottery industry,* Council for British Archaeology Research Report No. 30. London: Council for British Archaeology.

Mackreth, D. 2011. *Brooches in Late Iron Age and Roman Britain.* Oxford: Oxbow.

Mackreth, D. 1996. Orton Hall Farm: a Roman and Early Anglo-Saxon farmstead. Nottingham: *East Anglian Archaeology 76.*

Macphail, R., Galinié, H. and Verhaeghe, F. 2003. A future for dark earth? *Antiquity 77(296)*, 349-358.

Macpherson Grant, N. 1995. Part II: The Pottery. II: Post Roman. In: K. Blockley, M. Blockley, P. Blockley, S.S. Frere and S. Stow. *Excavations in the Marlow car park and surrounding areas, Part II: The finds,* 815-920. Canterbury Archaeological Trust, volume 5.

Magnus, B. 2001. Relieffspenner fra Uppåkra og andre funnsteder i Skåne. In: B. Hårdh (Ed.) *Uppåkra, Centrum och sammanhang,* 175-85. Uppåkrastudier 3, Acta Archaeologica Lundensia series in 8°, no. 34, Lund: Almqvist & Wiksell International.

Maher, D. and Makowski, J. 2001. Literary evidence for Roman arithmetic with fractions. *Classical Philology 96(4)*, 376-399.

Maltby, M. 1979. The Animal Bones from Exeter 1971-1975. *Exeter Archaeological Reports volume 2,* University of Sheffield.

Maltby, M. 1981. Iron Age, Romano-British and Anglo-Saxon animal husbandry - a review of the faunal evidence. In: M. Jones and G. Dimbleby (Eds.) *The environment of man: The Iron Age to the Anglo-Saxon period,* 155-203. Oxford: B.A.R. British Series 87.

Maltby, M., 2002. Animal bones in archaeology: how archaeozoologists can make a greater contribution to British Iron Age and Romano-British archaeology. *Bones and the Man: Papers in Honour of Don Brothwell, Oxbow Books, Oxford,* 88-94.

Maltby, M. 2010. *Feeding a Roman town – Environmental evidence from excavations in Winchester 1972-1985,* Winchester: Winchester Museums & English Heritage.

Mann, J. (Ed.) 2008. *Finds from the Well at St Paul-in-the-Bail, Lincoln.* Lincoln Archaeological Studies No. 9. Llandysul: Oxbow Books.

Manning, W. 1976. *Catalogue of the Romano-British ironwork in the Museum of Antiquities, Newcastle upon Tyne.* Newcastle: Newcastle University.

Manning, W. 1985. *Catalogue of the Romano-British iron tools, fittings and weapons in the British Museum.* London: British Museum Press.

Margary, I. 1955. *Roman Roads in Britain: Vol I, South of the Foss Way–Bristol Channel*. London: Phoenix House.

Margeson, S. 1993. *The Medieval and Post-Medieval Finds from Norwich Survey Excavations. East Anglian Archaeology* 58.

Marsden, P. 1994. *Ships of the Port of London. First to Eleventh Centuries*. London: English Heritage Archaeological Report.

Martingell, H. 1990. The East Anglian Peculiar? The 'Squat' Flake. *Lithics* 11, 40–43.

Martingell, H. 2003. Later Prehistoric and Historic Use of Flint in England. In: N. Moloney and M.J. Shott (Eds.) *Lithic Analysis at the Millennium*, 91–97. London: University College London Institute of Archaeology Publications.

Mate, M. 2006. *Trade and economic developments 1450-1550: the experience of Kent, Surrey and Sussex*. Woodbridge, Boydell and Brewer

Mattingly, D. 2007. *An Imperial Possession: Britain in the Roman Empire*. London: Penguin.

Maull, A., Masters, P. and Chapman, P. 2005. A Roman settlement and early Saxon farmstead at Glapthorne Road, Oundle, Northamptonshire. *Northamptonshire Archaeology* 33, 47–48.

Mays, S. 2010. *The Archaeology of Human Bones*. Routledge: Taylor & Francis.

McCloy, A. and Midgley, 2008. *Discovering Roman Britain*. New Holland.

McDonnell, J. G. 1993 'The litharge cake'. In: R. J. C. Smith, *Excavations at County Hall, Colliton Park, Dorchester, Dorset*. Salisbury: Wessex Archaeology, 35.

McGill, S., Sogno, C. and Watts, E. 2010. *From the Tetrarchs to the Theodosians: Later Roman History and Culture 284-450 CE*. Cambridge: Cambridge University Press.

McKinley, J. 2004. Compiling a skeletal inventory: disarticulated and co-mingled remains. In: M. Brickley and J. McKinley (Eds.) *Guidelines to the Standards for Recording Human Remains*. IFA Paper No.7.

McWhirr, A. 1979. Roman tile-kilns in Britain. In: A. McWhirr (Ed.) *Roman brick and tile*, 68–97. Oxford: British Archaeological Reports International Series, 189.

Meaney, A. L. 1964. *Gazetteer of Early Anglo-Saxon Burial Sites*. London: George Allen and Unwin.

Meates, G. 1979. *The Lullingstone Roman Villa Volume: the site*. London: Kent Archaeological Society.

Meates, G. W., 1979. *The Lullingstone Roman Villa, Volume I: The Site*. London: Monograph Series of the Kent Archaeological Society.

Meddens, F. and Draper, G. 2014. Out on a limb: insights into Grange, a small member of the Cinque Ports confederation. *Archaeologia Cantiana* 135, 1–32.

Meddens, F., Sabel, K., White, M., Mackley, R., Akeroyd, A., Canti, M., Linford, P., Payne, A., Walsh, N., Williams, D. and Wilson, P. 2002-2003. The excavation of a medieval ceramic production site and tile kiln at Weald view, Noak Hill, Essex. *Medieval Ceramics* 26/27, 3–43.

Megaw, R. and Megaw, V. 1989. *Celtic Art: From its beginnings to the Book of Kells*. London: Thames and Hudson.

Mernick P. and Algar, D. 2001. Jettons or Casting Counters. In P. Saunders (Ed.) *Salisbury and South Wiltshire Museum Medieval Catalogue*, Part 3, 213–60. Salisbury and South Wiltshire Museum: Over Wallop.

Middleton, A., La Niece, S., Ambers, J., Hook, D., Hobbs, R. and Seddon, G. 2007. *An elusive stone: the use of variscite as a semi-precious stone*. London: British Museum Technical Research Bulletin 1.

Millett, M. 1990. *The Romanization of Roman Britain*. Cambridge: Cambridge University Press.

Millett, M. 2007. Roman Kent. In: J. Williams (Ed.) *The Archaeology of Kent to AD800*, 135–186. Woodbridge: Boydell and Kent County Council.

Mills, J. M. 1993. Lead-lined wooden coffins. In: D. E. Farwell and T. I. Molleson. *Excavations at Poundbury 1966–80. Volume 2: The Cemeteries*, 127–32. Dorset: Natural History & Archaeological Society Monograph Series.

Mills, N. 2000. *Celtic and Roman Artefacts*. Witham, Greenlight.

Milner, G. R. 1992. *Determination of Skeletal Age and Sex: A Manual Prepared for the Dickson Mounds Reburial Team*. Dickson Mounds Museum Unpublished Report.

Mitchiner, M. and Skinner, A. 1984. English Tokens *c.* 1200 to 1425. *The British Numismatic Journal* 53 (1983), 29–77.

Mitchiner, M. and Skinner, A. 1985. English Tokens *c.* 1425 to 1672. *The British Numismatic Journal* 54, 86–163.

190   *Bibliography*

Monaghan, J. 1987. *Upchurch and Thameside Roman pottery: ceramic typology for northern Kent, first to third centuries A.D.* Oxford: British Archaeological Reports 173.

Moore, S. 2005. *Spoons 1650–2000.* Shire Album 211. Shire Publications Ltd.

Moore, T. 2011. Detribalizing the late prehistoric past: concepts of tribes in Iron Age and Roman Studies. *Journal of Social Archaeology* 11(3), 334–360.

Moore, P.D., Webb, J.A. and Collinson, M.E. 1991. *Pollen Analysis.* 2nd Edition, Blackwell, Oxford.

Moorhead, T. S. N. 2006. Roman Bronze coinage in Sub-Roman and early Anglo-Saxon England. In: B. Cook and G. Williams (Eds.) *Coinage and History in the North Sea World c500–1250,* 99–109. Leiden: Brill.

Moorhead, T. S. N. and Walton, P. 2014. Coinage at the end of Roman Britain. In: F.K. Haarer with R. Collins, K. Fitzpatrick-Matthews, S. Moorhead, D. Petts and P. Walton (eds). *AD410: The History and Archaeology of Late Roman and Post-Roman Britain,* 99–116. London: Society for the Promotion of Roman Studies.

Morris, E. L. 2007. Making magic: later prehistoric and early Roman salt production in the Lincolnshire fenland. In C. Haselgrove and T. Moore (Eds.) *The Later Iron Age in Britain and beyond,* 430–443. Oxford: Oxbow Books.

Morris, E. L. 2012. Briquetage. In: T. Allen, M. Donnelly, A. Hardy, C. Hayden and K. Powell. *A Road through the Past: Archaeological discoveries on the A2 Pepperhill to Cobham road-scheme in Kent,* 228–245. Oxford: Oxford Archaeology Monograph No.16.

Morris, J. and Jervis, B. 2011. 'What's so Special? A Reinterpretation of Anglo-Saxon 'Special Deposits'. *Medieval Archaeology* 55, 66–81.

Morris, R. 1989. *Churches in the Landscape.* London: Phoenix.

Mortimer, C. 1996. *Assessment of Non-Ferrous Metalworking Debris from Elms Farm, Heybridge, Essex.* Ancient Monuments Laboratory Report 67/96. London: English Heritage.

Mudd, A. 1994. The Excavation of a Later Bronze Age Site at Coldharbour Road, Gravesend, *Archaeologia Cantiana 114,* 363–410.

Myres, J. N. L. 1977. *A corpus of Anglo-Saxon pottery.* Cambridge: Cambridge University Press.

Nayling, N. and McGrail, S. 2004. *The Barland's Farm Romano-Celtic Boat.* London: CBA Research Report 138.

Neal, E. and Cheeseman, C. 1996. *Badgers.* London: T. & A.D. Poyser.

Neef, R., Cappers, R.T.J, Bekker, R.M. 2012. *Digital Atlas of Economic Plants in Archaeology.* Groningen Archaeological Studies Volume 17. Netherland: Barkhuis.

NIAB. 2004. *Seed Identification Handbook: Agriculture, Horticulture and Weeds* (2nd ed). Cambridge: NIAB.

Noddle, B. 1980. The animal bones. In: P. Wade Martin. Excavations at North Elmham Park 1967–72. *East Anglian Archaeology 9 (2),* 375–412.

Noël Hume, I. 1969. *A Guide to Artifacts of Colonial America.* Philadelphia: University of Pennsylvania Press.

O'Connor, T. P. 1983. Aspects of site environment and economy at Caerleon Fortress Baths, Gwent. In: B. Proudfoot (Ed.) *Site, Environment and Economy,* 105–13. Oxford: British Archaeological Reports International Series 173.

O'Connor, T. P. 1987. Why bother looking at archaeological wild mammal assemblages? *Circaea* 4 (no. 2), 107–14.

O'Connor, T.P. 1991. *Bones from 46–54 Fishergate.* The Archaeology of York. The animal bones, 15(4). York Archaeological Trust.

Orton, C., Tyers, P. and Vince, A. 1993. *Pottery in Archaeology,* Cambridge: Cambridge University Press.

O'Sullivan, A. and O'Neill. B. 2019. An experimental archaeological reconstruction of a roundhouse from early medieval Ireland. *Laureshamensia* 2, 74–82.

Ottaway, P. and Rogers, N. 2002. *Craft. Industry and Everyday Life: Finds from Medieval York.* The Archaeology of York, The Small Finds 17/15, York: Council for British Archaeology.

Paddock, J. 1998. Military equipment. In: N. Holbrook (Ed.) *Cirencester: the Roman town defences,* 305–307. Cirencester: Cirencester Excavations V.

Parfitt, K. 2000. A Roman occupation site at Dickson's Corner, Worth. *Archaeologia Cantiana* 120, 107–48.

Patterson, A. 2009. *Fashion and armour in Renaissance Europe: proud looks and brave attire,* London: V & A Publishing.

Payne, G. 1909. Researches and discoveries in Kent, 1905–1907. *Archaeologia Cantiana* 28, LXXXVII-XCVII.

Payne, S. 1985. Morphological distinctions between the mandibular teeth of young sheep, *Ovis*, and goats, *Capra*. *Journal of Archaeological Science 12*, 139–147.

Payne, S. and Bull, G. 1988. Components of variation in measurements of pig bones and teeth, and the use of measurements to distinguish wild from domestic pig remains. *Archaeozoologia 2*, 27–66.

Pearce, J. and Vince, A. 1988. *A dated type-series of London medieval pottery Part 4: Surrey Whitewares.* London: London and Middlesex Archaeology Society Special Paper 10.

Pearce, J. E., Vince, A. G., White, R. and Cunningham, C. 1982. A dated type-series of London medieval pottery Part One: Mill Green ware. *Transactions of the London and Middlesex Archaeology Society 33*, 266–98.

Pearce, J., 2013. *Contextual Archaeology of Burial Practice. Case studies from Roman Britain.* Oxford: Archaeopress.

Pearce, J., Vince, A. G. and Jenner, A. 1985. *A dated type-series of London medieval pottery Part Two: London-type ware.* London and Middlesex Archaeology Society, Special Paper No. 6.

Pelling, R. 2008. Charred and waterlogged plant remains. In: A.M. Booth. Binghman and S. Lawrence (Eds.) *The Roman Roadside Settlement at Westhawk Farm, Ashford, Kent: Excavations 1998-9*, 349–357.Oxford: Oxford Archaeology Monograph.

Perrin, J. R. 1999. *Roman Pottery from Excavations at and near to the Roman Small Town of Durobrivae, Water Newton, Cambridgeshire, 1956–58.* Journal of Roman Pottery Studies Volume 8. Oxford: Study Group for Romano-British Pottery.

Pesch. A. 2007. *Die Goldbrakteaten der Völkerwanderungszeit – Thema und Variation.* Ergänzungsbände zum Reallexikon der Germanischen Altertumskunde Band 36. Berlin-New York: Walter de Gruyter.

Pesch, A. 2004. Formularfamilien kontinentaler Goldbrakteaten. In: M. Lodewijckx. *Bruc ealles well. Archaeological essays concerning the peoples of north-west Europe in the first millennium, AD*157–80. Acta Archaeologica Lovaniensa, Monographiae 15. Leuven: Leuven University Press.

Phenice, T. 1969. A Newly Developed Visula Method of Sexing in the Os Pubis. *American Journal of Physical Anthropology 30*, 297–301.

Philp, B. (nd). *The Excavation of the Roman Cemetery at Keston.* KAR Articles.

Philp, B. 1973. *Excavations in West Kent 1960-1970: the discovery and excavation of Prehistoric, Roman, Saxon and Medieval sites, mainly in the Bromley area and in the Darent Valley.* Second Research Report in the Kent Series. West Kent Border Archaeological Group.

Philp, B. 2005. *The Excavation of the Roman Fort at Reculver, Kent.* Dover: Tenth Report in the Kent Monograph Series.

Philpott, R. 1991. *Burial practices in Roman Britain: a survey of grave treatment and furnishing, A.D. 43–410.* Oxford: British Archaeological Reports British Series 219.

Piggott, S. 1971. Firedogs in Iron Age Britain and beyond. In: J. Boardman *et al.* (Eds.) *The European Community in Later Prehistory: Studies in Honour of C.F.C Hawkes*, 243–270. London: Routledge and Keegan Paul.

Pollard, R. J. 1987. The other Roman pottery. In: G. W. Meates (Ed.) *The Roman Villa at Lullingstone, Kent, Volume II: The Wall paintings and Finds*, 164–305. Maidstone: Kent Archaeological Society.

Pollard, R. J. 1988. *The Roman Pottery of Kent.* Monograph Series of the Kent Archaeological Society 5. Maidstone: Kent Archaeological Society.

Ponting, M. 2009. Roman silver coinage: mints, metallurgy and production. In: A. Bowman and A. Wilson (Eds.) *Quantifying the Roman Economy: Methods and Problems*, 269–280. Oxford: Oxford University Press.

Poole, C. 2011. Chapter 6: Ceramic Building Material and Fired Clay. In E. Biddulph, R. Seager Smith and J. Schuster. *Settling the Ebbsfleet Valley: High Speed 1 Excavations at Springhead and Northfleet, Kent, The Late Iron Age, Roman, Saxon and Medieval Landscape – Volume 2. Late Iron Age to Roman Finds Reports*, 313–350. Oxford: Oxford Wessex Archaeology.

Pooley, A. 2007. *An Archaeological Watching Brief on Land at Grange Farm, Gillingha m, Kent.* PCA Unpublished report.

Puttock, S. 2002. *The Ritual Significance of Personal Ornament in Roman Britain.* Oxford: British Archaeological Reports British Series 327.

Rackham, D. J. 1995. Appendix: skeletal evidence of medieval horses from London sites. In: J. Clark (Ed.) *The medieval horse and its equipment c1150-1450*, 169–174. Medieval finds from excavations in London 5. London: HMSO.

Read, B. A. 1988. *History beneath our feet.* Chippenham: Merlin Books.

Reece, R. 1991. *Roman Coins from 140 Sites*. Cirencester: Cotswolds Studies 4.

Reece, R. 1995. Site-finds in Roman Britain. *Britannia* 26, 179–206.

Reille, M. 1992. *Pollen et Spores D'europe Et D'afrique Du Nord*. Marseille: Laboratoire de Botanique historique et Palynologie.

Richards, M., Hedges, R., Molleson, T. and Vogel, J. 1998. Stable isotope analysis reveals variations in human diet at the Poundbury Camp Cemetery Sites. *Journal of Archaeological Science* 25, 1247–1252.

Riddler, I. 2003. A lesser material. The working of roe deer antler in England during the Anglo-Saxon period. In: I. Riddler (Ed.) *Materials of Manufacture. The choice of materials in the working of bone and antler in northern and central Europe during the first millennium AD*, 41–48. Oxford: British Archaeological Reports International Series 1193–Archaeopress.

Riddler, I. 2009. Fishing Implements and Medieval Fishing Practices in East Kent. In: G. Draper and F. Meddens. *The Sea and the Marsh: The Medieval Cinque Port of New Romney*, 100–4. Pre-Construct Archaeology Monograph 10.

Rielly, K, 2005. The animal remains. In: B. Yule. *A prestigious Roman building complex on the Southwark waterfront, Excavations at Winchester Palace, London, 1983–90*, 158–167. London: MoLAS Monograph 23.

Rielly, K, 2010. Appendix 2: The animal bone. In: A. Mackinder. A Romano-British site at Swanscombe, 21–24. Kent: Museum of London Archaeology. www.kentarchaeology.ac/archrep/swanscombe01.pdf.

Rielly, K. In: prep a. The animal bones. In: A. Haslam. *Excavations at Stone Castle nr Gravesend*. Kent: Pre-Construct Archaeology.

Rielly, K. In: prep b. The animal bone. In: N. Hawkins. Excavations at Drapers' Gardens. London: Pre-Construct Archaeology Monograph Series.

Rippon, S. 2017. Marshlands and other wetlands. In: M. Hyer and D. Hooke (Ed.) *Water and Environment in the Anglo-Saxon World*, 89–106. Liverpool: Liverpool University Press.

Rippon, S., Smart, C. and Pears, B. 2015. *The Fields of Britannia: Continuity and Change in the Late Roman and Early Medieval Landscape*. Oxford: Oxford University Press.

Rivet, A. and Smith, C. 1979. *The Place Names of Roman Britain*. London: Batsford.

Roberts, C. and Manchester, K. 1995. *The Archaeology of Disease*. Ithaca, New York: Cornell University Press.

Roberts, C. and Connell, B. 2004. Guidance on recording palaeopathology. In: Brickley & J McKinley (Eds.) *Guidelines to the Standards for Recording Human Remains IFA Paper No.7* M.

Robertson, A. 2000. *An Inventory of Romano-British Coin Hoards*. London: Royal Numismatic Society Publication 20.

Robinson, M., Fulford, N. and Tootell, K. 2006. The macroscopic plant remains. In: M. Fulford, A. Clark and H. Eckardt (Eds.) *Life and Labour in Late Roman Silchester*, 206–220. London: Britannia Monograph Series 22.

Rogers, A. 2011. *Late Roman Towns in Britain: rethinking change and decline*. Cambridge: Cambridge University Press.

Ruxer, M.S. and Kubczak, J. 1972. *Greek necklaces of the Hellenistic and Roman ages* [in Polish and English], Państwowe Wydawnictwo Naukowe. Oddział w Poznaniu. Warsaw: Poznań.

Saggau, H. 1981. *Bordesholm: Der Urnenfriedhof am Brautberg bei Bordesholm*. Neumünster: Wachholtz.

Sas, K. and Thoen, H. 2002. *Schone Schijn/Brilliance et Prestige. Romaine juweelkunst in West Europa/La joillerie romaine en Europe occidentale*. Leuven.

Saunders, S.R. 1989. Non-metric skeletal variation. In: M.Y. Iscan and K.A.R. Kennedy (Eds.) *Reconstruction of Life from the skeleton*, 95–108. New York: Alan R. Liss, Inc.

Schmid, E, 1972. *Atlas of animal bones for prehistorians, archaeologists and Quaternary geologists* London: Elsevier.

Schoch, W., Heller, I., Schweingruber, F. H. and Kienast, F. 2004. *Wood anatomy of central European Species*. Online version: www.woodanatomy.ch.

Seddon, G. 2008. An Assessment of an Archaeological Excavation on Land at Grange Farm, Gillingham, Kent. PCA Unpublished Report.

Semple, S. 2013. *Perceptions of the Prehistoric in Anglo-Saxon England: Religion, Ritual, and Rulership in the Landscape. Medieval History and Archaeology*. Oxford: Oxford University Press.

Shaffrey, R. 2011. The Worked Stone. In: Biddulph *et al. Settling the Ebbsfleet Valley. High Speed Excavations at Springhead and Northfleet, Kent – The Late Iron Age, Roman, Saxon and Medieval Landscape. Volume 2: Late Iron Age and Roman Finds Reports*. 363–377.

Sharpe, J. 2006a. *Roman Owls at Gatehampton Roman Villa*. South Oxfordshire Archaeology Group. http://www.soagarch.org.uk/vromanowls.html.

Sharpe, J. 2006b. Gatehampton Roman Villa, Goring. *South Midlands Archaeology* 36, 50–5.

Sharpe, R. 2001. The late antique passion of St. Alban. In: M. Henig and P. Lindley (Eds.) *Alban and St Albans; Roman and Medieval Architecture, Art and Archaeology*, 30–37. Leeds: BAA Conference Transactions XXIV.

Shepherd J. 2008. Luxury Colourless Glass Vessels in Flavian London. In: J.Clark, J. Cotton, J. Hall, R. Sherris and H. Swain. *Londinium and Beyond: essays on Roman London and its hinterland for Harvey Sheldon*, 239–250. CBA res. Rep. 156.

Shepherd, R. 1993 *Ancient Mining*. London, Elsevier.

Shepherd, W. 1972. *Flint. Its Origins, Properties and Uses*. London: Faber and Faber.

Sidebotham, S. E., Barnard, H., Pintozzi, L. and Tomber, R. 2005. The enigma of Kab Marfu'a: precious gems in Egypt's Eastern Desert. *Minerva* 16, 24–6.

Simonds, J. B. 1854. *The age of the ox, sheep and pig*. London: W.S. Orr.

Smith, A., Allen, M., Brindle, T. and Fulford, M. 2016. *The Rural Settlement of Roman Britain*. London: Britannia Monograph 29.

Smith, T. P. and Betts, I. 2006. *Building material, fired clay and wall plaster from Thurnham Roman Villa, Kent*. Channel Tunnel Rail Link, London and Continental Railways, Oxford Wessex Joint Venture. CTRL Specialist Report Series.

Smith, V. 2011. Kent's twentieth century military and civil defences, Part 2: Medway. *Archaeologia Cantiana* 131, 159–196.

Smith, W. and Davis, A. 2006. The charred plant remains from Thurnham Roman Villa, Kent (ARC THM 98). CTRL specialist report series, CTRL specialist report series, ADS 2006. Available [online] from: http://archaeologydataservice.ac.uk/[accessed 11/09/2012].

Sparey Green, C. 1993. *Excavations at Poundbury 1966–80: The cemeteries*. Dorset Natural History and Archaeological Society, 1993

Sparks, J. and Soper, T. 1970. *Owls Their Natural and Unnatural History*. New York: Newton Abbot David & Charles.

Spencer, B. 1998. *Pilgrim Souvenirs and Secular Badges*. Medieval finds from excavations in London: 7. Chippenham and Eastbourne: Boydell Press.

Spencer, B. 1990. *Salisbury & Wiltshire Museum Medieval Catalogue Part 2: Pilgrim Souvenirs & Secular Badges*. Over Wallop: Salisbury & Wiltshire Museum.

Spillett, P. J. Stebbing, W. P. D. and Dunning, G. C. 1942. A Pottery Kiln Site at Tyler Hill, Near Canterbury. *Archaeologia Cantiana Vol. 55*.

Stace, C. 1997. *New Flora of the British Isles*. Cambridge: Cambridge University Press.

Stancliffe, C. 1999. The British church and the mission of Augustine. In: R. Gameson (Ed.) *St Augustine and the Conversion of England*, 107–151. Stroud: Sutton.

Starley, D. 1993. *The Assessment of Roman and Later Slag and Other Metalworking Debris from Winchester, Brooks*, 197–8. Ancient Monuments Laboratory Report 81/93. London: English Heritage.

Steane, J. M. and Foreman, M. 1991. The archaeology of medieval fishing tackle. In: G. L. Good, R. H. Jones and M. W. Ponsford (Eds.) *Waterfront Archaeology*, 88–101. London: CBA Research Report 74.

Stevens, C. 2006. *The charred plant remains from North of Saltwood Tunnel, Saltwood, Kent*. CTRL specialist report series, CTRL specialist report series, ADS 2006. http://archaeologydataservice.ac.uk/[accessed 11/09/2012].

Strid, L, 2012. Digital Specialist Report 15: The Animal Bone. In: E. Biddulph, S. Foreman, E. Stafford, D. Stansbie and R. Nicholson. *London Gateway: Iron Age and Roman Salt Making in the Thames Estuary, Excavations at Stanford Wharf Nature Reserve*. Essex: Oxford Archaeology Monograph 18.

Sullivan, J. 2012. *Russian Cloth Seals in Britain: A Guide to Identification, Usage and Anglo-Russian Trade in the 18th and 19th Centuries*. Oxford: Oxbow Books.

Swanton, M. 1973. *The spearheads of the Anglo-Saxon settlements*. London: Royal Archaeological Institute.

Swanton, M. J. 1974. *A Corpus of Pagan Anglo-Saxon Spear-Types*. British Archaeological Reports 7. Oxford: British Archaeological Reports.

Swift, E. 2003. Late Roman beads and necklaces. *Journal of Roman Archaeology* 16, 336–349.

Swift, E. 2000 *Regionality in Dress Accessories in the late Roman West*. Montagnac, Monographies Instrumentum 11.

Swift, E. 2010. Identifying migrant communities: a contextual analysis of late Roman grave assemblages. *Britannia* 41, 237–282.

Swift, E. 2012. Object biography, reuse and recycling in the late to post-Roman transition period and beyond: rings made from Romano-British bracelets. *Britannia* 43, 167–215.

Sykes, N. 2007. Animal bones. In: D. Miles, S. Palmer, A. Smith and G. P. Jones (Eds.) *Iron Age and Roman Settlement in the Upper Thames Valley: Excavations at Claydon Pike and Other Sites within the Cotswold Water Park*, 53–5, 84–5, 151–3. Thames Valley Landscapes Monograph 26. Oxford: Oxford Archaeology.

Symonds, R. and Tomber, R. 1991. Late Roman London: an assessment of the ceramic evidence from the City of London. *Transactions of the London and Middlesex Archaeological Society* 42, 59–99.

Taylor, A. 1993. A Roman Lead Coffin with Pipeclay Figurines from Arrington, Cambridgeshire. *Britannia* 24, 191–225.

Taylor, J. 2001. Rural society in Roman Britain. In: S. James and M. Millett (Eds.) *Britons and Romans: advancing an archaeological agenda*, 46–59. London: Council for British Archaeology Research Report 125.

Taylor, J. 2013. Encountering Romanitas: characterising the role of agricultural communities in Roman Britain. *Britannia* 44, 171–190.

Taylor, M. 1981. *Wood in Archaeology*. Shire Archaeology 17. Aylesbury: Shire Publications Ltd.

Theuws, F. 2009. Grave goods, ethnicity and the rhetoric of burial rites in Late Antique Northern Gaul. In: T. Derks and N. Roymnas (Eds.) *Ethnic Contructs in Antiquity: the role of power and tradition*, 283–320. Amsterdam: Amsterdam University Press.

Thomas, J. 1999. *Understanding the Neolithic: a revised second edition of rethinking the Neolithic*. London: Routledge.

Toller, H. 1977. *Roman Lead Coffins and Ossuaria in Britain*. Oxford: British Archaeological Reports 38.

Tomber, R. and Dore, J. N. 1998). *The National Roman Fabric Reference Collection: a Handbook*. MoLAS Monograph No. 2. London: Museum of London Archaeology Service.

Toynbee, J. M. 1954. The Lead Sarcophagus. In R. Jessup. Excavation of a Roman Barrow at Holborough, Snodland, 34–46. *Archaeologia Cantiana* vol. 68.

Trotter, M. 1970. Estimation of stature from intact long limb bones. In: T. D. Stewart (Ed.) *Personal Identification in Mass Disasters*. Washington, D.C: National Museum of Natural History.

Trotter, M. and Gleser, G. C. 1958. A re-evaluation of stature estimation based on measurements of stature taken during life and of long bones after death. *American Journal of Physical Anthropology* 16, 79–123.

Tyers, P. 1996. *Roman Pottery in Britain*. London: B T Batsford Ltd.

Tylecote, R. F. 1986. Litharge from a second century pit (Site DG, Pit21) in Frenchgate, Doncaster. In: P. C. Buckland and J. R. Magilton. *The Archaeology of Doncaster. 1. The Roman civil settlement*. Oxford: British Archaeological Reports 196.

Tyrrell, A. 2000. Skeletal non-metric traits and the assessment of inter- and intra-population diversity: past problems and future potential. In: M.Cox and S. Mays (Eds.) *Human Osteology in Archaeology and Forensic Science*. London: Greenwich Medical Media.

Ubelaker, J. E. 1989. *Human Skeletal Remains 2nd Edition*. Washington D.C: Taraxacum Press.

Van der Veen, M., Livarda, A., Hill, A. 2008. New plant foods in Roman Britain – dispersal and social access. *Environmental Archaeology* 13(1), 11–36.

Vaggi, M. 2008 *Evidence of Silver Recycling in a Roman Manor House in Grange Farm*, University of London, unpublished MSc Dissertation Thesis.

Von Becker, C. 1980. *Untersuchungen an Skelettresten von Haus- und Wildschweinen aus Haithabu*. Neumunster: Karl Wachholtz Verlag.

Wacher, J. 1975. *The Towns of Roman Britain*. London: Batsford.

Wagner, A. and Ypey, J., 2011. *Das Gräberfeld auf dem Donderberg bei Rhenen: Katalog*. Leiden: Sidestone Press.

Walker, D. 2012. *Disease in London, 1st-19th centuries: An illustrated guide to diagnosis*. MoLA Monograph 56. London: Museum of London.

Walker, H. 1990. Pottery from a possible late medieval kiln dump at 77 High Road, Rayleigh. *Essex Archaeology and History* 21 (3rd Series), 92–102.

Wallace, L. 2018. Community and the creation of provincial identities: a reinterpretation of the Romano-British aisled building at North Wanborough. *Archaeological Journal* 175, 231–254.

Walton, P. 2011. *Rethinking Roman Britain: An applied numismatic analysis of the coins recorded by the Portable Antiquities Scheme*. Unpublished University College London PhD Thesis.

Ward Perkins, J. B. 1940. *London Museum Medieval Catalogue*. London Museum Catalogues 7.

Welch, M. 2007. Anglo-Saxon Kent. In: J. Williams (Ed.) *The Archaeology of Kent to AD800*. Woodbridge Boydell and Kent County Council, 189–248.

Welton, A. 2018. *The Spear in Early Anglo-Saxon England: a social and technological study*. Unpublished Thesis PhD. Gainesville, Fl: University of Florida.

West, B. A. 1982. Spur development: recognising caponised fowl in archaeological material. In B. Wilson, C. Grigson and S. Payne (Eds.) *Ageing and Sexing Animal Bones from Archaeological Sites*, 255–61. Oxford: British Archaeological Reports Series 109.

West, B. and Milne, G. 1993. Owls in the Basilica. *London Archaeologist 7 (2)*, 31–36.

White, R. 1988. *Roman and Celtic objects from Anglo-Saxon graves: A catalogue and an interpretation of their use*. Oxford: British Archaeological Reports British Series 191.

Whitehead, R. 2003. *Buckles 1250–1800*. Witham: Greenlight Publishing.

Whittington, G. 1993. Palynological investigations at two Bronze Age burial sites in Fife. *Proceedings of the Society of Antiquities of Scotland* 123, 211–213.

Wilkinson, P. 2009. *An Archaeological Investigation of the Roman Aisled Stone Building at Hog Brook, Deerton Street, Faversham, Kent, 2004–5*. Faversham: Kent Archaeological Field School.

Williams, H. 1997. Ancient landscapes and the dead: the reuse of prehistoric and Roman monuments as early Anglo-Saxon burial sites. *Medieval Archaeology* 41, 1–32.

Williams, H. 1998. Monuments and the past in Early Anglo-Saxon. *World Archaeology*, 30 (1), 90–108.

Williams, R. J. and Zeepvat, R. J. 1994. Bancroft: a Late Bronze Age/Iron Age Settlement, Roman Villa and Temple Mausoleum. *Buckinghamshire Archaeological Society* 7, Volume 1.

Wilmott, T. 1991. *Excavations in the Middle Walbrook Valley*. London: London and Middlesex Archaeological Society Special Paper 13.

Wilthew, P. 1986. *Examination of Technological Material from Tiddington, Warwickshire*. Ancient Monuments Laboratory Report 4750. London: English Heritage.

Winder, J. 2011. Oyster Shells from Archaeological Sites: A Brief Guide to Basic Processing Online at: http://oystersetcetera.files.wordpress.com/2011 /03/ oystershellmethodsmanualversion11.pdf.

Wise, P. 2011. An unusual brooch and the problem of provenance in the study of Anglo-Saxons Colchester. *Essex Archaeology Society and History* 2 (4th series), 254–6.

Wollman, V. 1996. *Mineritul metalifer, extragerea sării şi carierele de piatră în Dacia Romana*. Cluj: Ministry of Culture.

Wood, I. 2009. Germanus, Alban and Auxerre. *Bulletin du centre d'études médiévales d'Auxerre/BUCEMA* 13, 123–29.

Worrell, S. and Pearce, J. 2014. *Finds Reported under the Portable Antiquities*. Cambridge: Cambridge University Press.

Wright, D. 2019. Crafters of kingship: smiths, elite power and gender in early medieval Europe. *Medieval Archaeology* 63, 271–297.

Yates, D. 2001. Bronze Age Agricultural Intensification in the Thames Valley and Estuary. In: J. Brück (Ed.) *Bronze Age Landscapes: tradition and transformation*, 65–82. Exeter: Oxbow Books.

Yates, D. T. 2006. *Land, Power and Prestige: Bronze Age Field Systems in Southern England*. Oxford: Oxbow.

Young, C. J. 1977. *The Roman Pottery of the Oxford Region*. Oxford: British Archaeological Reports Series 43.

Young, R. and Humphrey, J. 1999. Flint Use in England after the Bronze Age: time for a re-evaluation? *Proceedings of the Prehistoric Society* 65, 231–242.

Yule, B. 1990. The 'dark earth' and late Roman London. *Antiquity* 64, 620–8

Zeiler, J. T. 1988. Age determination based on epiphyseal fusion in post-cranial bones and tooth wear in otters (*Lutra lutra*). *Journal of Archaeological Science* 15, 555 – 561.

Zohary, D. and Hopf, M. 2000. *Domestication of plants in the Old World: the origin and spread of cultivated plants in West Asia, Europe and the Nile Valley* (3rd edn). Oxford: Clarendon.

Index

Page numbers in *italics* denote illustrations.